# Beyond Venice

## Glass in Venetian Style, 1500–1750

JUTTA-ANNETTE PAGE

*with contributions by*

IGNASI DOMÉNECH

ALEXANDRA GABA-VAN DONGEN

REINO LIEFKES

MARIE-LAURE DE ROCHEBRUNE

HUGH WILLMOTT

The Corning Museum of Glass, Corning, New York

*Distributed by Hudson Hills Press, New York and Manchester*

Editor: *Richard W. Price*
Photographic Supervisor: *Nicholas L. Williams*
Design and Typography: *Jacolyn S. Saunders*
Proofreader: *Joan M. Romano*

Reference Librarian: *Gail P. Bardhan*
Rights and Reproductions: *Jill Thomas-Clark,*
    *Brandy L. Harold*
Researcher: *Mary B. Chervenak*

Prepress: *Graphic Solutions, Painted Post, New York*
Printing: *Upstate Litho, Rochester, New York*

Standard Book Number: 0-87290-157-2
Library of Congress Control Number: 2003116008

DISTRIBUTED BY HUDSON HILLS PRESS LLC
74-2 Union Street
Manchester, Vermont 05254

Founding Publisher: *Paul Anbinder*
Executive Director: *Leslie van Breen*
Creative Director: *Randall Perkins*

Distributed in the United States, its territories and possessions,
and Canada through National Book Network

Distributed in the United Kingdom, Eire, and Europe
through Windsor Books International

*Map of Europe from Abraham Ortelius (1527–1598),*
Theatrum Orbis Terrarium, *Antwerp: Coppenium*
*Diesth, 1570. The James Ford Bell Library, University*
*of Minnesota, Minneapolis.*

# Contents

# Preface

This book is a collection of essays—an introduction and six regional studies—that explores the production and consumption of Venetian and Venetian-style glassware between the 16th and mid-18th centuries. Its publication was planned to coincide with an exhibition, titled "Beyond Venice," presented at The Corning Museum of Glass from May 20 to October 17, 2004.

All over Renaissance Europe, possession of Venetian glass was regarded as a sign of wealth and sophistication. Consumers in distant countries imported Venetian glass, recruited Venetian glassmakers to establish and supervise factories, and encouraged local craftsmen to imitate their products. Consequently, glass in the Venetian style is a large subject, and the present volume does not pretend to be comprehensive. It begins with a survey of Venetian glass, which became pre-eminent in the second half of the 15th century. The authors then describe glass made in the Venetian style in five regions: Austria, Spain, France, the Low Countries, and England. As readers will discover, the attribution of an object to one region or another is sometimes contentious, and many questions remain open.

The book and the exhibition were developed by Dr. Jutta-Annette Page, who was curator of European glass at The Corning Museum of Glass until she assumed her present position at The Toledo Museum of Art in September 2003. Following Dr. Page's departure, members of the Corning Museum staff completed the task of readying the text and illustrations for publication. Richard W. Price, head of the Publications Department, edited the text and prepared the index. Nicholas L. Williams, Photographic Department manager, assisted by Andrew M. Fortune, supplied photographs of objects in the Corning Museum's collection. Mr. Williams also supervised the scanning and color correction of all of the illustrations that appear in the book. Jacolyn S. Saunders, publications specialist, created the design and prepared the layout. Gail P. Bardhan, reference librarian, combed the sources cited in the bibliography to answer editorial questions and to ensure that information was presented consistently. Other members of the reference and interlibrary loan staffs at the Museum's Juliette K. and Leonard S. Rakow Research Library provided information and secured loans for titles that were not in the Corning collection. Loans of photographs from other institutions were obtained by Jill Thomas-Clark, rights and reproductions manager; Brandy L. Harold, assistant registrar; and Mary B. Chervenak. Ms. Chervenak also researched picture and bibliographic information.

David Whitehouse
Executive Director
The Corning Museum of Glass
Corning, New York

# Foreword

For more than 200 years, beginning in the mid-15th century, Venetian glass captivated Europe. The careful selection and development of raw materials, technical virtuosity, and a flair for designs that combined refinement with opulence led to the creation of an unprecedented array of luxurious glassware for use and display.

Before Jutta-Annette Page and her co-authors lead us across Renaissance Europe, familiarizing us with glass made by Venetians and some of their imitators, it may be useful to consider the qualities that set Venetian glass apart from other European glassware.

Any list of the characteristics of mid-15th-century and later Venetian glass would include at least some of the following: the glass itself, gilding and enameling, the extensive use of molds, the inclusion of canes and cane slices to decorate objects, diamond-point engraving, and the ability to assemble objects from multiple components.

The first of these characteristics is the glass. Glassmakers in northern Italy and adjacent regions were already producing colorless glass in the 13th century (*Phönix aus Sand und Asche* 1988, pp. 189 and 200–201, nos. 160 and 178, etc.). But it was not until the 15th century that one particular decolorized glass, Venetian *cristallo*, began to attract

Fig. 1

*The Behaim Beaker, showing (a) the archangel Michael, (b) Saint Catherine of Alexandria, and (c) coat of arms, colorless, blown, gilded, enameled. Italy, Venice, about 1495. H. 10.7 cm. The Corning Museum of Glass, Corning, New York (84.3.24, Houghton Endowment purchase).*

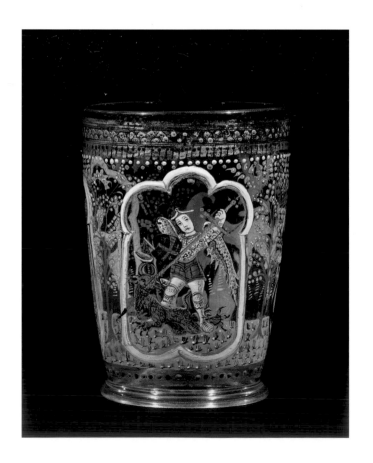

attention all over Europe. *Cristallo* was developed by carefully selecting and preparing the raw materials, quartzite pebbles from the Ticino River and plant ash from the Levant. Despite these precautions, *cristallo* is not always colorless (it may have a grayish or straw-colored tint), and, especially in the 15th century, it was somewhat bubbly. The making of *cristallo* was inspired by the translucence and purity of rock crystal, but few would have mistaken the one for the other. In the hands of master glassblowers, *cristallo* could be transformed into objects of breathtaking grace and fragility.

*Cristallo* was not the only material pioneered by Venetian glassmakers. *Calcedonio* imitated the variegated semiprecious stone chalcedony, and Antonio Neri, who published the first book-length account of glassmaking in 1612, included numer-

ous recipes for glasses that range from opaque white to aventurine and "opal."

The Behaim Beaker (Fig. 1) is a fine example of Venetian *cristallo*, and it demonstrates how glass from Venice commanded attention abroad. The beaker bears a coat of arms and two panels, each of which contains a figure. The coat of arms belongs to the Behaim family of Nuremberg. One panel depicts the archangel Michael killing a dragon; the other shows Saint Catherine of Alexandria. The unusual combination of Michael and Catherine requires an explanation. It is thought that the beaker was made for the wedding, on July 7, 1495, of a Nuremberg patrician, Michael Behaim, and Katerina Lochnerin, the daughter of a rich merchant whose firm controlled trade between Nuremberg and Venice.

If this explanation is correct, the Behaim Beaker is an outstanding illustration of fine Venetian glassware custom-made for export to Germany. It also demonstrates two of the features of Venetian glass that attracted widespread attention: the excellence of *cristallo* and the brilliance of the gilded and enameled ornament. Decorators in Venice had experimented with enamel, occasionally accompanied by gilding, between the late 13th and mid-

14th centuries, and Venetian documents of 1280–1346 mention "painters of beakers." (It is worth noting that the beakers in question, the so-called Aldrevandin group, may have been made in more than one place, since two of the painters mentioned in the Venetian sources came from Nafplio in Greece and Zadar in Croatia [Carboni 1998; Krueger 2002].) These early examples of enameled glass give little hint of the wealth of gilding and enameling applied to Venetian glasses from the mid-15th century, when decorators began to produce objects that were richly ornamented with Renaissance motifs, coats of arms, and figural scenes. The Behaim Beaker appears to be the earliest Venetian gilded and enameled glass that can be dated

FIG. 2

*Tazza with lion-mask stem, colorless with grayish tinge, blown, mold-blown, gilded. Italy, Venice, or Low Countries, about 1560. H. 16.7 cm. The Corning Museum of Glass, Corning, New York (58.3.180).*

precisely. Other apparently datable objects include a dish, a footed plate, and two tazzas decorated with the arms of Louis XII of France and Anne of Brittany (see pp. 144–145, Figs. 1–4), presumably made on the occasion of their marriage in 1499.

The third characteristic of mid-15th-century and later Venetian glass is the use of molds on the grandest scale since Roman times. Venetian glassmakers employed dip molds for decorating the parison with simple, repetitive patterns before it was expanded to its final size and shape; small molds for pressing and stamping applied motifs, such as the masks or lions' heads that appear on Venetian and Venetian-style objects (see, for example, p. 121, **4**); and full-size molds, made in two parts, that were used to form and decorate an object in one operation (see pp. 306–307, **6**) (Gudenrath 1991, p. 234). Sometimes, two or more molds were used in making a single complex piece. The central part of the stem of the tazza in Figure 2, consisting of two lions' heads separated by clusters of dots, was blown in a full-size, two-part mold. (A tazza with a very similar shape, in The British Museum, London, has a gilded and enameled coat of arms that suggests it was made for the marriage of Gilles Happaert of Antwerp in 1559 [pp. 252–253, **1**; see also Tait 1991, p. 163, no. 207].)

The use of canes and slices of canes constitutes the fourth characteristic of Venetian glass. Apart from a limited number of eighth- and ninth-century objects with *reticella* canes (*Phönix aus Sand und Asche* 1988, pp. 69–76, nos. 12–23), medieval glassworkers in Europe did not produce vessels decorated with canes. The technique of making multicolored canes was rediscovered in Venice in the second half of the 15th century, when glassmakers picked up slices of canes, very similar to the canes used by beadmakers, on the parison and formed small millefiori vessels (Gudenrath 1991, p. 235). Later, they made abundant use of opaque white canes to produce *vetro a filigrana*: *cristallo* vessels decorated with patterns of white stripes, sometimes accompanied by blue or red elements. Despite its great variety, most *vetro a filigrana* may be divided into three broad categories: *vetro a fili* (glass with threads), in which white canes were picked

FIG. 3

*Dragon-stem goblet, colorless with pinkish tinge, red, blue, blown, pattern-molded, applied, tooled. Italy, Venice, or in the Venetian style, 17th century. H. 26.2 cm. The Corning Museum of Glass, Corning, New York (51.3.118).*

up on the parison and formed into a pattern of individual stripes; *vetro a retorti* (glass with twisted threads), in which the canes were twisted into a cable of two or more plies; and *vetro a reticello* (glass with a small network), in which the glassworker used canes to produce a mesh- or netlike pattern (*ibid.*, pp. 238–240). The body of the dragon in Figure 3 is formed from a cane of colorless glass with a red twist.

FIG. 4

*Plate, colorless, blown, diamond-point engraved. Italy, Venice, about 1558. D. 23.9 cm. The*
*Corning Museum of Glass, Corning, New York (83.3.51, Houghton Endowment purchase).*

Diamond-point engraving was another feature of Venetian glassworking. It was widely adopted in Renaissance Europe, to the extent that engraved glasses were produced in all the regions described in this book. Figure 4 shows a *cristallo* plate with diamond-point engraving. The plate is decorated with the arms of two aristocratic families: the Orsini and the Medici. This combination strongly suggests that the plate was made for the marriage of Paolo Orsini, duke of Bracciano, and Isabella de' Medici, which took place in 1558.

Finally, Venetian glassworkers mastered the technique of assembling vessels from parts that had been made separately, often fusing one part to another with thin wafers of molten glass (Gudenrath 1991, pp. 230–233). If we count these wafers as separate parts, the tazza in Figure 2 is made up of 14 different elements and the dragon-stem goblet in Figure 3 contains 24 elements, including 10 in the dragon itself.

All of the characteristic features of Venetian glass were imitated elsewhere in Europe as glassmakers strove to produce luxury glassware *à la façon de Venise*.

David Whitehouse
Corning, New York
November 2003

# Beyond Venice

Glass in Venetian Style, 1500–1750

# Introduction

*Jutta-Annette Page*

"Fortuna vitrea est; tum cum splendet frangitur"
(Fortune is like glass; when it shines, it shatters).

— Publilius Syrus, *Sententiae* 189

Glass in Venetian style originated with the enigmatic vessels made on the island of Murano, near Venice, in the 15th century. By that time, Venice had become one of Europe's wealthiest and most powerful cities, with an extensive overseas trade empire. Venetian culture was so marked by material opulence that laws regulating expenditures on luxuries were adopted and enforced, but with only nominal success. Elegant and fragile glass vessels, made by expert glassmakers in a manner befitting the fashionable lifestyle, were quickly in demand both in Venice and abroad.

Italy was not culturally homogeneous. Renaissance glass was created in different forms. In Florence, for instance, some glass vessels were known as "bicchieri fiorentini" (Florentine beakers), while in Milan they were called "bocali da Milan" (jugs [or mugs] from Milan) (Barovier Mentasti 1982, p. 53; Theuerkauff-Liederwald 1994, p. 25). Venetian glassmakers adapted their production to include these specific Italian types and other forms that were popular north of the Alps, thus catering to new markets. Unfortunately, no such beakers can be identified today. Glass vessels called "inghestere todesche" (German *inghisteras*) were probably German flasks known as the *Kuttrolf* or *Angster* (Dreier 1989, p. 21). They featured necks that were divided into two or more tubes, and they produced a gurgling sound when they were emptied.

Italian artists were in demand all over Europe. The demand seems to have been greatest in France, especially at the court. Francis I, for example, owned works by Leonardo (who worked at his court) and Raphael (Burke 1992, p. 10). The French courts were also the most fervent early consumers of Venetian glass, and they were the first to import Venetian glassmakers (see pp. 143 and 146).

Likewise, the courts of the Hapsburgs, Europe's most powerful family in the 16th century, acquired large amounts of fashionable Venetian glass. They

*Detail from* Allegory of Sight (Venus and Cupid in a Picture Gallery), *by Jan Bruegel the Younger (Fig. 6).*

3

were motivated by the sense of power that attached to the Italian Renaissance, by the ideal of human dignity, and by the high purpose of art. Archduke Ferdinand II of Austria embodied the ideal of the Renaissance prince by giving impetus to Venetian-style glass production in Austria and by creating his own workshop at the royal court in Innsbruck, which was staffed with Venetian craftsmen and supplied with Venetian raw materials (see p. 42).

The Iberian Peninsula was also firmly in Roman Catholic Hapsburg hands during this period. Glassmaking in Spain had strong Muslim traditions and production centers ranging from court glasshouses to local workshops. These workshops made glass with various degrees of fidelity to original Venetian styles and techniques by processes of appropriation and adaptation (see p. 85). Meanwhile, the Protestant Northern Netherlands, with its pronounced anti-papal sentiments, soon resented Italian cultural dominance. This resentment extended to glassmaking, and it was expressed in the patronage of glass production that would surpass Italian prototypes. Italophilia was thus matched by an international movement of Italophobia that was evident from England to Poland. Anti-Italian proverbs were in circulation, such as "Inglese italianato è diavolo incarnato" (The Italianized Englishman is the devil incarnate), which was modified in German to "Tedesco italianato . . ." (Burke 1992, p. 13).

Although the Renaissance arrived slowly in England, a country on the periphery of educated Europe, Venetian glass quickly took hold of the social elite and was treasured more than precious metal vessels (see pp. 271–272). It was said that Englishmen "corrupt their natural manners" in order "to italianate the course of their newe ledde life" (Rankins 1586, p. 3). In an unpublished manuscript written about 1540, Richard Moryson argued that English law should adopt the form of Roman law while preserving its own spirit. It would be as easy to do this, Moryson maintained, as "for an English tailor to make of an Italian velvet an English gown" (Starkey 1992, p. 159). Indeed, glassmakers working in Venetian style in England soon developed their own formal vocabulary and fash-

ioned their English ale glass in *cristallo*. The advent of the production of exquisite lead glass in the late 17th century allowed England to break into Venetian markets with a vengeance, but it was forced, almost immediately, to share these markets with a powerful Continental competitor: Bohemian chalk glass, which also closely resembled rock crystal.

The creative and prestigious image of Venetian glass rests on the ascent of *cristallo* in the 15th century, which allowed the Renaissance masters to blow highly sophisticated and fragile objects of a new transparent glass formula. This technological achievement has been viewed as "a glorious revival" of ancient colorless glass, which was praised by Pliny the Elder for its resemblance to rock crystal (Syson and Thornton 2001, p. 186). Educated Renaissance patrons who were familiar with Pliny's writings may have made that connection, but Venetians hardly sought their ancestry in ancient Rome. Instead, they placed great emphasis on creating a historical identity that would set them apart from other Italians and from other nations. The mythical date for the foundation of Venice—March 25, 421—was also thought to be the month and day of the Annunciation and of Christ's Crucifixion. This was significant, as the Venetians saw it, in giving a unique spiritual flavor to their city.

The early luxury glass industry was heavily dependent on the Islamic east for technological inspiration and for its most important raw material: soda of the highest quality. This soda came from the coastal regions of the Levant, and it was used exclusively from the 1280s onward. Most of the silica was extracted from quartzite pebbles that had been gathered from the Ticino River in northern Italy, and manganese, used as a decolorizer, was primarily imported from Germany.

By the 14th century, thanks to its powerful fleet, Venice had become Europe's pre-eminent trading nation. Its glassmakers were praised abroad for their imitation of pearls and precious stones, and for their colored glass decorated with fine enameling. Thinly blown beakers made by the masters Aldrevandin, Ba(r)tolameus, and Petrus are rare examples of this early (pre-*cristallo*) production. A beaker "signed" by Magister Ba(r)tolameus, however, is the first discovered example of the Aldrevandin group with decoration that looks specifically Italian rather than generically European. Fragments of this object were excavated from a cesspit in Stralsund, Germany, in 1991 (Krueger 1998). Its enameled decoration has been shown to have been inspired by the carved square pillars from Acre in the Piazza San Marco. These pillars, richly carved by Syrian artists, were believed to have been brought home in triumph by Lorenzo Tiepolo from the Genoese stronghold of Acre in 1258. The Venetian craftsman had chosen a famous motif from his immediate surroundings, one that was easily recognizable as a "souvenir" from Venice. This colorless glass, called *vitrum blanchum*, was still a far cry from the famous Venetian *cristallo* that emerged in the 15th century.

The development of the technology for purifying soda from imported ashes, as well as the discovery of a stabilizing agent, seems to have occurred around the year 1450 (Jacoby 1993). The glass often had a grayish or straw-colored tinge. The venerable 15th-century Venetian glassmaker Angelo Barovier (d. 1460) has traditionally been credited with the invention of *cristallo* (Dreier 1989, p. 22), and while this attribution is probably incorrect, it is evident that Barovier was at the forefront of this technology. In 1455, he and his son Marino were permitted by the local authorities to leave Venice and to set up a glass furnace for making *cristallo* at the Milanese court of Duke Francesco Sforza (Zecchin 1987, v. 1, p. 238). Angelo Barovier's presence in Milan may have impressed the Italian sculptor Antonio Pietro di Averlino, called "Il Filarete," who also enjoyed Francesco's patronage at that time. He wished to explore the potential of glass in flat wall tiles for the imaginary city of Sforzinda, as described in his *Treatise on Architecture* (1465). Through these tiles, Antonio imagined, one would see sculpted figures, animals, and various other things. A much less fanciful and more practical treatise is a Florentine recipe book dated 1460, which seems to be the earliest document referring to these new glassmaking processes (Milanesi 1864, p. 111).

Although Angelo Barovier was the most prominent Venetian glassmaker during this period (at the time of his death, he was credited with being the city's best maker of *cristallo* vases), he had no monopoly to make *cristallo*. In 1457, he and the owners of two other Muranese furnaces, Jacopo d'Anzolo and Niccolo Mozetto, were granted permission by the Venetian government to keep their furnaces in operation for the production of *cristallo* during the annual glassmaking recess, the *cavata*. This recess, which lasted from August 5 to January 7, was necessary to repair and restock the workshops.

During the time when *cristallo* was being developed, the glass industry had long been settled on the island of Murano. This community of glassmakers emerged as an indirect result of the decree of November 8, 1291, that banned the operation of glasshouses in Venice because of the fear of devastating fires. The relocation of the glass workshops to Murano was not part of this decree, but the industry was tightly monitored by the government through updates of the *Mariegola*, the statutes of the glassmakers' guild. Glassmakers who understood the new technology and had exclusive access to raw materials and foreign markets were assets that Venice zealously guarded. Uncontrolled emigration of glassmakers posed a threat to the financial well-being of the community. Financially strapped glassmakers were often forced to find other work during the long glassmaking recess. In some cases, these economic pressures (or greed) drove them to seek more lucrative permanent employment as glassmakers outside Venice and the Terraferma, the neighboring mainland. For centuries, the Venetian government, the Signoria, severely punished this practice with high fines and galleon service. But on occasion, it was lenient and allowed a glassblower to return without sanctions.

Angelo Barovier and other well-known Venetian glass masters often received lucrative invitations from foreign courts. Negotiations concerning the loan of highly specialized craftsmen were not unusual. For instance, in 1568, Francesco I de' Medici's negotiators arranged a contract that permitted the master armorer Matteo Piatti and his entire atelier to leave Milan and to work in Florence. Piatti was to bring with him at least eight co-workers of his choice for a period of at least seven years

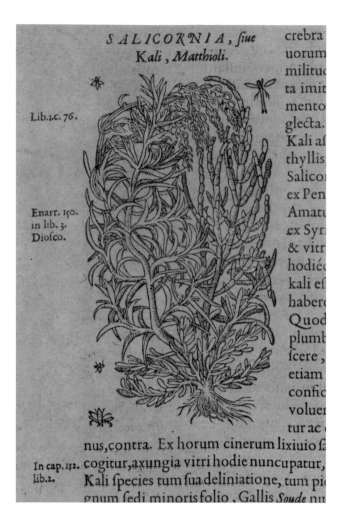

**FIG. 1**

*"Salicornia." Detail from Daléchamps 1586–1587, p. 1378. Division of Rare and Manuscript Collections, Cornell University Library.*

(Pyhrr and Godoy 1999, p. 23, n. 43). The Venetian government recognized the diplomatic and financial potential of such contracts, and it sometimes granted selected glassmakers permission to leave, provided that the engagement was limited and did not endanger the city's economic interests. This practice continued well into the 16th century, when several glassmakers were permitted to work at the Hapsburg court in Innsbruck (see pp. 42–43 and 45).

The technological development of *cristallo* was deeply rooted in alchemical experimentation. Turning salt and sand into what appeared to be rock crystal was interpreted as belonging to the same science that was thought to have the possibility of turning base metal into gold. Angelo Barovier is called "magistri Angeli ab alchymisis cristallis" in a record of payment to his son Marino in 1460 (Zecchin 1987, v. 1, p. 229). Less than a century later, the Sienese metalworker Vannoccio Biringuccio still thought of *cristallo* as "born from the speculation of good alchemistic savants, through whose efforts it imitates the metals on one hand and the transparency and splendor of gems on the other" (Biringuccio 1990, p. 126). Antonio Neri also equates glass with gold in the introduction to his treatise *L'arte vetraria*: "It hath fusion in the fire, and permanencie in it, likewise as the perfect and shining metall of gold." He also advises practitioners to "know the stones that may be transmuted, from those that may not be transmuted into glass" (Merrett 1662, chap. 2). The language is alchemical, and in the preface to the first edition, Neri dedicates his treatise to Antonio de' Medici on account of the nobleman's devotion to alchemical studies (Neri 1612).

The key ingredient for the production of *cristallo* is a plant of the genus *salicornia*, a succulent plant of rather humble appearance, with small, scalelike leaves and jointed nodes (Fig. 1). Its flowers, in the form of rosettes with a central stamen, are tucked into the stem, and they turn into red berries with snaillike seeds. Information about this plant can be found in 16th-century "herbaria," which are actually early pharmaceutical compendiums. The most widely read of these herbals was the *Compendium de plantis omnibus* of Pietro Andrea Mattioli (1501–1577), first published in 1571.[1] Later herbaria improved on Mattioli's drawings. The plant in question for making glass is referred to by many names, including glasswort in English and *alumen catinum* in Latin.

*Salicornia* is found in salt marshes everywhere, but the best varieties for making glass were grown in the warm climate around the Mediterranean, especially in the Levant and along the Spanish coast of Alicante. The plants were harvested at the end of the summer, dried, and slowly burned in covered pits. The resulting hardened lumps or cakes were sold for the manufacture both of perfectly colorless glass and of high-quality soap to whiten linen. Neri indicates that the Spanish *kali* contained more salt than its Levantine equivalent (which is called *rochetta*), but it produced a bluer glass that was not as attractive as the colorless glass (Merrett 1662, chap. 4).

Glasshouses working in Venetian style encountered considerable difficulties and incurred great expense in attempting to procure the necessary quantities of this high-quality *kali* from Spain, and this prompted them to try growing imported plants in saline ground north of the Alps. In the mid-16th century, a desperate experiment in the Austrian Alps failed miserably (see p. 34) because the variety of plant employed could not adapt to the climate. The limited availability of this highly desirable raw material (whether from the Levant or from Alicante) certainly added to the mystique of Venetian glass.

A recurring theme in Venetian glass history is the purported property of *cristallo* of breaking spontaneously whenever it came into contact with poison (see p. 222). This myth may have had its roots in the glass itself. The key ingredient in glassmaking, *alumen catinum*, was also used for its diuretic effects and as an abortive medicine, but in greater quantities it could be deadly. In his *Pseudodoxia epidemica* of 1646, Sir Thomas Browne (1605–1682) says: "That Glass is poyson, according unto common conceit, I know not how to grant. Not only from the innocency of its ingredients, that is, fine Sand, and the ashes of Glass-wort or Fearn, which in themselves are harmless and useful. . . . The conceit is surely grounded upon the visible mischief of Glass grosly or coursly powdered, for that indeed is mortally noxious, and effectually used by some to destroy Mice and Rats. . . . Whereupon there ensues fearful symptoms, not much unlike those which attend the action of poyson" (Browne 1672, bk. 2, chap. 5). The notion of the expulsion of the serpent, as represented in images of Saint John the Baptist, may have been based on a very practical application, in that the caustic smell of burning *salicornia* plants was known to drive away serpents (Gerard 1633, p. 536), and *alumen catinum* was sprinkled around the house to rid it of vermin.

The quest of the early Venetian glassmakers for a material to imitate precious stones was not limited to rock crystal. Glass resembling agate was mentioned in the duke of Berry's 1416 inventory, which lists "une aiguiere de voirre tainte en maniere d'agathe" (a ewer of glass colored in the fashion of agate) (Schmidt 1922, p. 82). *Calcedonio*, a mixture of colored glass that resembles the hardstone chalcedony, a form of banded agate (Fig. 2), was also produced in the workshop of Angelo Barovier. He is said to have been inspired by Paolo dalla Pergola, minister of S. Giovanni Elemosinario on Rialto and the first teacher of philosophy in Venice (Dreier

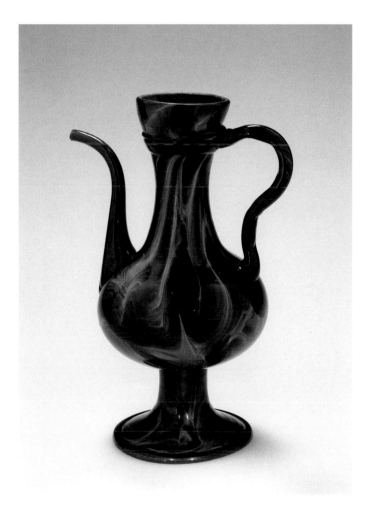

Fig. 2

*Calcedonio ewer, multicolored, blown, applied. Venice, about 1500–1525. H. 29.9 cm. The Corning Museum of Glass, Corning, New York (2001.3.56, gift of Robert and Deborah Truitt).*

1989, p. 22). The first mention of *calcedonio* occurs in a contract regarding the maintenance of a furnace. It was drawn up between Taddeo Barovier and Salvador Visentin shortly after Angelo's death (*Hockemeyer Collection* 1998, p. 73). This glass continued to be made in other Venetian glasshouses, such as that of Jacopo d'Anzolo at the Sign of the Cock, which in 1475 supplied the Florentine Filippo Strozzi with 11 *calcedonio* vessels of various forms (Spallanzani 1978, p. 165, doc. 23).

This exceptional glass was difficult to make and therefore very costly (Theuerkauff-Liederwald 1994, p. 31). Glasshouses working in Venetian style took on this challenge, although *calcedonio* was never part of their main production. In 1609, Antonio Neri made *calcedonio* at the Antwerp glasshouse of Filippo Gridolphi (see p. 229). Glass that resembled agate remained especially popular in France, where Bernard Perrot created vessels that were widely acclaimed (see p. 162), including translucent opaque white vessels with banded decoration (see pp. 188–189, **14**).

The opaque white glass called *lattimo* had been part of Venetian glassmaking since the 15th century. It is a milky glass that is also known as *porcellana contrafacta* because it imitates Chinese porcelain, a material valued as highly as precious stone (Whitehouse 1972, pp. 77–78). Giovanni Maria Obizzo, who is known to have worked from 1488 to 1525, specialized in decorating *lattimo* glasses, which were expensive acquisitions. An order for 42 "goti di lattimo cum figure," enameled *lattimo* goblets with figural decoration by Rado da Zuppa, was filled in 1511 by Giovanni di Giorgio Ballarin, with each vessel priced at one ducat.[2]

Most of the Venetian decorating techniques were developed between 1455 and 1534. Colored vessels with gilding and enameling became fashionable in the second half of the 15th century. *Cristallo* could be colored with a host of mineral additives, such as cobalt for blue, manganese for purple and black, and copper for red. The resulting vessels provided a perfect background for brightly colored religious and mythological scenes, floral and heraldic designs, grotesques, and stylized portrait busts. While the shapes of the glasses were still deeply rooted in the formal vocabulary of Gothic metal vessels, their decorations were *au courant* because they derived from contemporaneous engravings and woodcuts.[3] Whether colorless or colored, they were associated with precious stones, as is evident in the names of such glasses (Dreier 1989, pp. 5–11).

Like furniture that incorporated a family's coat of arms, glass that was specially ordered with such personalized decoration both confirmed and conferred honor (Syson and Thornton 2001, p. 30). However, a coat of arms on a glass is not a firm indication of patronage or ownership, since the object could have been ordered by the holder of the coat of arms either for his or her own use or as a gift for someone else. Glass vessels bearing joint coats of arms are usually considered to commemorate weddings (Fig. 3). Large sets of dishes, such as those with the royal arms of Louis XII of France and Anne of Brittany (see pp. 144–145, Figs. 1–4) or those with the arms of the Fugger family in Augsburg (see pp. 80–81, **10**), were intended to be elegant table settings. More difficult to interpret is a large engraved plate with the monogram of Gaston, duke of Orléans (see pp. 180–184, **10**). Here, the implicit (and, no doubt, political) message of the plate's elaborate decoration acquired another layer of meaning, depending on whether it was commissioned by the duke to convey a carefully shrouded political message to someone else, or whether this was a special gift intended for him.

In the case of many art objects, the patron sent a model or a drawing to the artist. With glass objects, the drawing more frequently served to convey dimensions and proportions. A sample glass, purchased on another occasion, could serve the same function. Communication between artisans and patrons was often heated, and complaints lodged by patrons who were dissatisfied with delivered glassware abound in period documents. For example, in 1496, Isabella d'Este, who had sent drawings of her own design and three-dimensional models to glassmakers in Venice, complained about the large feet on the glasses that she received in return. She also wanted to see the gold rim end precisely at the edge of the bowl.

Fig. 3

*Goblet with the arms of Liechtenberg, colorless with pinkish brown tinge,*
*blown, gilded, enameled. Bohemia, 1500–1530. H. 23.5 cm. The J. Paul*
*Getty Museum, Los Angeles (84.DK.537).*

Members of the Renaissance elite demanded complex shapes and decorations befitting their "magnificence" and "politesse." As "objects of virtue," glass vessels needed to be decorated or designed with sufficient artistry. Despite their considerable virtuosity and innovative techniques, Venetian glassworkers were "considered lacking in artistic invention—*poveri d'invencione*—requiring designs by others to work from" (Syson and Thornton 2001, pp. 183–184). Designs were often supplied by outsiders, either patrons themselves or artists in their employ, and conveyed to the glassmakers. For instance, in a letter dated February 5, 1549, Pietro Camaiani, the Medici ambassador to Venice, confirmed to Pier Riccio, *maggiordomo* of the cathedral in Florence, that he had ordered glassware from Muranese workshops for Cosimo I de' Medici and that he had shown drawings supplied by Riccio for the design of the decorative motifs to the island's master glassblowers.[4]

During the 16th century, designs by famous artists became increasingly important to convey the elevated artistic aspirations of an affluent clientele. The painter Giovanni da Udine, a student in Raphael's workshop, was in demand for his glass designs *all'antica*. Not only private patrons but also

well-known Muranese glassmakers, such as the owners of the glasshouse at the Sign of the Mermaid and the master Domenico Ballarin, desired drawings by this artist (Syson and Thornton 2001, p. 199). Unfortunately, none of his designs has survived. Extant drawings for glass by Jacopo Ligozzi, Jacques Callot, and Giulio Romano also attest this demand for complex designs in glass (Heikamp 1986). Marcantonio Raimondo published a series of engravings after paintings by Raphael, and these engravings were a source for glass painters. They were used, for example, in creating a set of large, complex cold-painted plates (Dreier 1994, pp. 149–162). A *lattimo* bowl made by the Miotti glasshouse in Venice, now in the Kunstsammlungen der Veste Coburg, is enameled with a portrait of

Saint Cecilia after Raphael, taken from an engraving by Gianfrancesco Penni and Perino del Varga (Stefaniak 1991, p. 363).

Glass decorated with references to famous poets and fashionable poetry could also enhance an owner's magnificence. The 1496 inventory of the Venetian glasshouse operated by Maria Barovier and her brother Giovanni lists a milk glass bowl with a portrait of Dante (Levi 1895, pp. 19–20). An early 16th-century goblet, owned for centuries by an Austrian noble family, is decorated with bands painted with poems (see pp. 64–65, **1**). One of these includes the words "AMORVOL [*sic*] FEDE" (Love requires faith), a motto that was regarded in Humanist circles to be of ancient Latin origin (*un ditto antico*) (Syson and Thornton 2001, p. 53).

Motifs and shapes derived from classical antiquity were increasingly preferred by the end of the 15th century. Venetian glass in *all'antica* style, molded with figural bands and decorations in relief, was made to emulate the much-admired ancient Roman Arretine ware. The sculptor Pietro Aretino, not least because of the resemblance in name, was delighted that his designs for glass compared favorably with this ancient red terra-cotta ware (Syson and Thornton 2001, p. 199). These sculptural decorations were surpassed by so-called grotesque decorations derived from newly discovered Roman wall paintings excavated in the palace of Nero known as the Domus Aurea. These paintings caused a sensation, and they were widely copied, as in the *Codex Escurialensis* (about 1490). Grotesques were described as "monsters misconceived through some freak of nature or whim and caprice of the artisans, who make these things without any rule, attaching to the thinnest thread a weight it could not support, to a horse legs formed as leaves, and to a man the legs of a crane, and numberless follies and flights of fancy" (Vasari 1568, chap. 27).

A satirical engraving comments on the exaggerated use of these out-of-control ornaments. It depicts a seller of grotesques that have assumed a life of their own (Fig. 4). Venetian glassmakers accepted the challenge posed by such fashionable and fantastic designs by pushing the possibilities

Fig. 5

*Goblet with serpent stem, colorless, blue, blown, tooled. Venice, 17th century. H. 25.3 cm. The British Museum, London (S.491, bequest of Felix Slade, Esq., F.S.A.).*

of their very ductile material, producing ever more complex and sculptural grotesque glass objects. Their foreign customers delighted in this type of glassware. Glasses with stems made in the shape of snakes and dragons found their way into the collector's cabinets of the European nobility (Fig. 5). Archduke Ferdinand II of Austria dedicated an entire cabinet in his *Kunstkammer* (collector's chamber) to glass (see p. 21), and the works of many a Dutch painter portrayed such creations as symbols

of wealth. In *Allegory of Sight (Venus and Cupid in a Picture Gallery)*, by Jan Bruegel the Younger (1601–1678), grotesque glass objects, including a dragon-stem goblet and a vessel with a stem in the shape of a merman, are found among other precious vessels on a table in the background (Fig. 6).[5]

Flasks in the form of shells and bunches of grapes, shapes that had been made in antiquity, were fitted with multiple spouts, tubes, and disks that challenged and amused their users (Fig. 7). In 1629, Duke August the Younger of Braunschweig-Lüneburg received a shipment of two trick glasses

Fig. 6

*Jan Bruegel the Younger (1601–1678),* Allegory
of Sight (Venus and Cupid in a Picture Gallery),
*about 1660. Oil on copper, H. 58.1 cm, W. 89.7 cm.
Philadelphia Museum of Art (J#656, John G. Johnson
Collection).*

that would function properly only when the hand
was held in a particular position. The glasses puz-
zled the duke to the extent that he requested instructions, but by the time they arrived, he had
solved the problem himself (Gobiet 1984, p. 531).
Such complex glasses were bought, not only to

amuse discerning adults, but also to entertain the
young and the sick. A trick glass that was made for
the youths at Duke August's court had two twisted
serpent's heads that were connected to two separate compartments for red and white wine (*ibid.*,
p. 661). This design was intended to confuse the

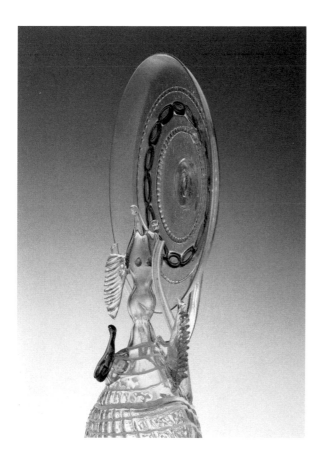

FIG. 7
*Wine taster (with detail showing side view), colorless, yellow, blue, blown, applied. Possibly the Netherlands or Spain, late 17th century. H. 28.6 cm. Royal Ontario Museum, Toronto (907.5.29).*

dy the boredom of a bedridden person (Gobiet 1984, p. 808). Another glass that was appreciated as a delightful novelty, even by those with elevated tastes, was a covered vessel with an internal knop, decorated with naïve marine creatures (see p. 49, Fig. 18). A very similar object, which was once owned by Archduke Ferdinand II at Ambras Castle (*Strasser Collection* 2002, p. 84, no. 39), may have been used for mixing water with wine, as was customary in Italy.

Fragile Venetian glass tableware, packed in straw and transported long distances by ship, by cart, or on foot, did not always arrive intact. At some courts, the major-domo was in charge of making sure that glass was expertly packed. When, in 1591, a shipment of glassware was to be readied at the Medici court for transport accompanying Transylvania's Prince Zsigmond Báthory, the major-domo, Benedetto Fedini, knew where to turn. The shipment was to be prepared by the gold- and silversmith Jacob Bylivelt and carefully wrapped using a packaging technique similar to one that had previously been employed to send items to the duke of Saxony, Christian I of Wettin.[7] Several decades later, in 1636, the Augsburg patrician and gentleman dealer Philipp Hainhofer sent a cabinet of majolica and glass to Duke August the Younger, including the first packing instructions for this fragile material (Gobiet 1984, p. 825).

The fragility of Venetian glass, which became worthless when broken, made it a symbol of fleeting wealth and, in a broader context, of the transitory nature of human life. Regardless of their artistic merits, the Roman Catholic Church frowned on the use of glass chalices during its services (see pp. 166–167, 1). Recently recovered church registers from 16th-century Portugal demonstrate that glass was permitted only for cruets and for ewers that were used in rinsing silver vessels. The precious liquid dispensed during the religious ceremonies could not be entrusted to such a fragile material as glass.

Emperor Frederick III is supposed to have intentionally dropped a glass vessel that was presented to him by the Signoria during a state visit in 1468 because he regarded it as of little value (Syson

drinkers about which of the two kinds of wine they were about to drink. These glasses may have been similar in principle to the *Doppleten* (doubles), which were mentioned by the German lawyer and writer Johann Fischart (1546–1590). Such vessels were meant to be separated by the drinkers (Heikamp 1986, p. 26). The difficulties of handling a trick glass with labyrinthine passages were noted by Fischart in 1575 (*ibid.*, p. 295, n. 12).

Illness was an occasion for gift-giving at Renaissance courts. Fine glass offered as an amusement for the sick is documented by a shipment of Venetian-style glass from the Medici glasshouse to Spain. Curzio di Lorenzo da Picchena, the Medici court secretary, had sent three crates of glassware to the ailing King Philip III in Madrid.[6] Glass fish bowls suspended from the ceiling were thought to reme-

FIG. 8
*Andrea del Sarto (1486–1530), portrait of Domenico di Jacopo Becuccio, called "Becuccio Bicchieraio," 1520–1530. Oil on panel, H. 86 cm, W. 67 cm. National Gallery of Scotland, Edinburgh (NG 2297).*

and Thornton 2001, p. 183). Such glasses were usually accorded the highest value and the greatest care, both by individual owners (see p. 290, Fig. 21) and by entire communities (see pp. 257–259, **3**). Nevertheless, they were sometimes deliberately broken during celebrations. A rare account of the wedding banquet given for the prince of Mantua in May 1593 notes that all of the invited gentlemen broke their glasses after drinking, in celebration of this new alliance and "per segno di grande allegrezza" (as a sign of great joy).[8]

The Netherlands had a particularly complex relationship with Venetian luxury glass. To acquire

gentlemanly status and noble appearance through the ownership and conspicuous display of wealth was considered, especially in the Protestant north, as immoral. Netherlandish art of the 16th and 17th centuries made frequent use of luxury glassware and imported wine as symbols of dissipation.

Throughout the history of Venetian and Venetian-style glass, likenesses of artists and workshop owners are exceedingly rare. The earliest known image of an Italian glassmaker is by Andrea del Sarto (1486–1530) (Fig. 8). He painted the glassmaker Domenico di Jacopo Becuccio, known as "Becuccio Bicchieraio," with two glass objects, a handled mug and a shallow, mold-blown bowl with blue trails near the rim. These most likely exemplified the glassware made in his workshop in Gambassi, a town situated between Florence and Volterra in the Valdelsa. According to Del Sarto's biographer, Giorgio Vasari, Becuccio commissioned Del Sarto, his very close friend, to paint an altarpiece for the church of Becuccio's hometown of Gambassi (now in the Palazzo Pitti, Florence).[9] It is fair to assume that the importance of the artist, not the subject, has preserved the portrait for posterity. The memorial brass plaque with a rather stylized likeness of the Italian glassmaker Jacopo Verzelini in England (see p. 279, Fig. 9) is another rare personal document of a 16th-century glasshouse owner. An engraved portrait of the cloth merchant and accomplished Leiden glass engraver Willem Jacobsz. van Heemskerk (1613–1692) (see p. 269, **9a**) appeared in the wake of 17th-century Humanism in the Netherlands. A printed portrait depicting the Dutch glasshouse owner, inventor, and guardsman Hendrick Heuck (d. 1678) is framed by *façon de Venise* glassware (below) and an assortment of arms (above). It foreshadows the proliferation in the 18th century of handbills and advertisements announcing fashionable shops and their wares (Fig. 9).

Mid-16th-century Venetian and foreign documents signal a period of noticeable instability in Venice's glassmaking industry, and this may have contributed to the emigration of glassmakers. On December 17, 1544, the Florentine envoy Donato Bardi da Vernio reported to Pier Riccio, then canon of the cathedral in Florence, on various items ordered from Venice for the Medici court in Florence. His mission was to procure a rosary for Riccio, glass vases for Duchess Eleonora of Toledo, and other items. A delay in the production of the vases for Eleonora was caused by an explosion of the last pair of these vases executed in the glassworks. This explosion was witnessed by Bardi and Ercole Gonzaga during a visit to the workshop. The letter culminates in comments on the lack of material and trained craftsmen for glassblowing in Venice, "ancorchè s'abbi carestia et di bel vetro et di buoni maestri, perchè questo mestiero è andato molto in

declinatione" (There is a shortage of fine glass and good maestros because the craft has declined considerably).[10]

During this period, the governing body of Venice, known as the Council of Ten, took steps to encourage and protect its industry. Vincenzo d'Angelo of the glassworks at the Sign of the Cock, who had decorated mirrors with diamond-point engraving since 1534, received a privilege on the basis of a strict survey of presented examples. By 1549, others were also working in the "intaglio in vetro" (intaglio glass cutting) technique, as it was called, and his request for a renewal of his privilege was denied (Zecchin 1987, v. 3, p. 66).

Another *Mariegola* ruling of 1549 controlled the production of filigree glass, a Venetian decorative

FIG. 9

*G. Wingendorp, portrait of Hendrick Heuck (d. 1678), about 1672–1676. Engraving, H. 15.3 cm, W. 11.5 cm. Rijksmuseum, Amsterdam (RP-P-1918-1753).*

technique that was fashionable in Europe for 200 years. The state decreed that all glassmakers were to produce glass stems and feet of *redesello* and *retortoli* instead of bubbles for roundels and other plain work. The lacelike appearance of the patterns might suggest that they were inspired by needlework of that period. In lace making, however, the word *reticella* first appeared in 1592, long after the invention of filigree glass. It is shown on the title page of Cesare Vecellio's *Corona delle nobili et virtuose donne*, where it was used for all patterns worked over a grid or netlike structure (Levey 1983, p. 7).

In an inventory of 1527, Francesco Zeno is mentioned as the inventor of *vetro a retortoli* (Hetteš 1960, p. 23). About that same time, Philippo and Bernardo Catanei of the glasshouse at the Sign of the Mermaid requested a privilege to make glass with threads (*vetro a fili*), with twists (*vetro a retorti*), and with a fine network (*vetro a reticello*), and a decade later, they were awarded a privilege that lasted for 40 years (Hess and Husband 1997, p. 8).

Filigree glass had come to represent the quintessential Venetian glass, and by 1549 its production was an important enough source of income for the state to warrant the decree concerning its exclusive production. Consequently, a Misser Liberal Testagrossa, owner of the Testa d'Oro furnace, was penalized for making goblets with feet and stems "plain and not *redesello*."

The Council of Ten also reconfirmed an earlier rule. Glassmakers who were intent on leaving Venice were threatened with a fine of 400 lire, four years of service on a galleon, confiscation of personal property, and restrictions for their relatives. Master glassblowers were not permitted to hire foreigners, that is, sons of non-Venetians (Frothingham 1956, p. 35). The training of foreigners had led to an early form of industrial espionage, a means by which several foreign rulers attempted to secure this desirable technology.

The earliest reference to Venetian craftsmen traveling to England also dates from 1549. Eight Muranese are said to have established a furnace in London at that time (see p. 278). In that same year, Jean de Lame, a merchant from Cremona who was living in Antwerp, was granted the sole right to produce glass in Venetian style in that city (see p. 228).

Negotiations with Venetian glassmakers were often held in secret. For example, when the Medici ambassador Cosimo Bartoli started this lengthy process in August 1567, the grand duke's name as client could not be mentioned (Heikamp 1986, p. 46). The envoy related that the desired glassblower should be a "persona queta et posata et non dozzinale" (calm, level-headed, and not rough) (*ibid.*, p. 47). By this time, experience had shown that Italian glassmakers employed abroad were often difficult workers who did not easily adjust to their new environment. Numerous reports of objectionable behavior can be found in period sources from nearly all of the countries under discussion. The Florentine envoy was therefore well advised to mention an agreeable character as one of the important qualities a glassworker should have.

This image was connected with Altarist as well as Venetian glassworkers. The glassmaking center at Altare, in the marquisate of Montferrat (in modern Piedmont), dates back to at least 1282, and it became a great rival of Venetian production (Zecchin 1965, p. 20). In stark contrast to those working in the Venetian Lagoon, the Altarists were encouraged to work abroad. This has been primarily attributed to the less favorable location of the town, which did not provide it with ready access to markets, and the glass community was in danger of overproduction (Dreier 1989, p. 17). In the 16th century, glass production in Genoa undermined that of Altare and may have accelerated the emigration of Altarist glassmakers (Mendera 2002, p. 267). Altarists were much in demand abroad, and many northern European centers producing glass in Venetian style were staffed with these craftsmen from Liguria.

However, in the late 16th century, it became more difficult to hire Altarist glassmakers than their Venetian counterparts. For instance, on July 8, 1593, Guidobono Guidoboni responded, on behalf of the duke of Mantua, Vincenzo I Gonzaga, to a request from Grand Duke Ferdinand I de' Medici that a group of glassworkers from Altare be permitted employment at the Medici glassworks in

Pisa. Guidoboni explained that this was an extremely rare privilege, since Duke Vincenzo was highly protective of the glassworkers' art.[11]

Pisa was the site of a second Medici glassworks. It had just opened in 1592, probably in the courtyard of the Palazzo Vitelli, during the reign of Ferdinand I, Francesco's brother. Of this factory's production, only a small cup with the Medici coat of arms has been identified (Ciappi and others 1995, pl. XXVI.2). The first glassblower employed at Pisa came from Altare (he was known as Valenza dall'Altare), but he stayed for less than a year. By 1594, Niccolo Sisti, head of the Pisa glasshouse, had hired a new glassblower from Murano, Luigi della Luna, who was also one of the best local masters (Heikamp 1986, pp. 74–75).

Another group of Altarist glassmakers, who had been staying in Mantua, refused to continue on their way to Florence to begin work at the Medici glasshouse without an official contract from Cosimo II de' Medici. Despite the mediation of Catherine de Médicis, they were not persuaded to change their mind. In short order, the grand duke dismissed the glassworkers and sent them back "on the road by which they came."[12] In the meantime, Cosimo had apparently been successful in hiring glassworkers from Venice. Catherine, in a follow-up letter, stated that she approved of Cosimo's decision to employ glassworkers from "Mur.o [Murano], who are as technically advanced as the glassworkers from Altare, but are less demanding in the stipulations of their work contracts."[13] This was quite a turn from the earlier Venetian mind-set of restrictive emigration, one that foreshadowed the gradual loss of Venetian supremacy in the European glass trade during the 17th and 18th centuries.

In the 1670s, new glass formulas were introduced in England and Bohemia. These formulas radically changed the glass trade in northern Europe, crushing established markets for both Italian *cristallo* and glass made in Venetian style. Bohemian potash-lime glass, which is also known as chalk glass (or *Weissglas* in German), was cheaper and more brilliant than *cristallo*, and it could be deeply cut like rock crystal. Wheel engraving was perfect for this far-from-flawless material, since small impurities could easily be incorporated into the elaborate surface designs. Before the end of the 17th century, chalk glass had set a new standard for glass in German-speaking countries (see p. 59), France (see p. 162), Spain, and Scandinavia.

A second, and nearly simultaneous, development of great importance was the introduction of a glass formula with a high (20–30 percent) content of lead oxide. This new glass, perfected by the English entrepreneur George Ravenscroft, was highly refractive, softer than both soda-lime and chalk glass, and nearly flawless. It resulted in widespread changes in the English glass industry (see p. 297), which supplied local markets, as well as the Continent, with a diverse range of products from the early 18th century onward. Glasses made *à la façon d'Anglais* (see p. 162) and *à la façon de Bohème* demonstrate the impact of these new styles. The remaining market for *cristallo* was satisfied by the glasshouses making *façon de Venise* glass in France, the Low Countries, Tyrol, and other areas.

The Venetian reaction was defensive and conservative. The use of potash, and of cullet that contained potash, continued to be prohibited in the production of Venetian glass. Muranese craftsmen translated the exuberance of Baroque forms into elaborate composite vessels and lighting devices with an abundance of colorful floral decorations. The famous diplomatic gift of glass objects from the Signoria to Frederick III of Denmark, which was sent to Copenhagen in 1709, included a sampling of the glassmakers' bravura. It is remarkable to note that, only two years later, Giovanni Sola, who until then had been smuggling Bohemian glass into Venice, was granted a privilege to import Bohemian raw glass to improve the local production (Gasparetto 1975, p. 9).

But Venetian glass continued to have its supporters. The Bohemian bishop Jan Rudolf Hrabe Spork (1696–1759) assembled a cabinet of curiosities in Prague during the 18th century. It contained a flute glass and a Venetian table fountain (*Cabinets of Arts and Curiosities* 1995, p. 8). And about 1775, the Italian poet Gasparo Gozzi (1713–1786) published a work titled *Del vetro* (Of glass), a paean to the magnificence of *cristallo* (Gozzi 1775).

# Venetian Glass in Austria

## *Jutta-Annette Page*

In April 1628, the Augsburg patrician Philipp Hainhofer (1578–1647), a well-connected art dealer and connoisseur, traveled to Innsbruck in Tyrol to deliver a *Kunstkabinet* (collector's cabinet) to the Hapsburg Archduke Leopold V (r. 1619–1633). The Hapsburgs were among the Renaissance's most prominent collectors, and Leopold had inherited one of the earliest and most extensive cabinets of curiosities, the *Kunst- und Wunderkammer*, at nearby Ambras Castle. This celebrated collection had been much enlarged and arranged in new displays by Archduke Ferdinand II of Austria (r. Tyrol 1563–1595). Ferdinand had been passionate about Venetian glass and glassmaking, and he included an entire cabinet of glassware in his extensive *Kunstkammer* (collector's chamber). Like the rest of the collection, it consisted of a mixture of heirlooms, gifts, acquisitions, and exchanges with other collectors. Leopold, who was more interested in music and the performing arts, maintained Ambras Castle largely unchanged (Fig. 1). As a favor to his cultured and wealthy guest, Leopold made arrangements for Hainhofer to tour the castle.

Hainhofer visited Ambras with the eyes of an expert. His travel notes supply only the cursory descriptions commonly found in period documents, so it is difficult to distinguish between references to *cristallo* vessels and rock crystal objects. The *Kunstkammer* consisted of a long hall with two walls of windows and two rows of cabinets back to back along its center. The interior of each cabinet was decorated in a different color. Hainhofer plainly says that the 11th cabinet displayed glasses of various sizes, both engraved and not engraved ("geschnitten und ungeschnitten"), against a black interior (Doering 1901, p. 84). This cabinet may have contained the small polygonal beaker that is said to have been blown by Archduke Ferdinand himself at the Innsbruck court glasshouse in 1583 (Fig. 2), one of the most telling attestations of the archduke's passion for glass (Schmidt 1912, p. 119).

A glass musical instrument was housed with other instruments in the 16th cabinet, suggesting that it could be played and that it was not just a curiosity made of glass. Such objects often served a dual purpose as drinking vessel and musical instrument, a function that was enhanced by metal attachments. Hainhofer himself had supplied a glass bagpipe to one of his clients (Gobiet 1984, p. 758). A rare extant object of this kind is a Venetian glass trumpet that was diamond-point engraved by Georg Schwanhardt with the arms of three promi-

*Detail from an enameled* Stangenglas *with the arms of Georg Willer (Fig. 28).*

FIG. 1

*First-known view of Ambras Castle, from Zeiller 1648.*
*Kunsthistorisches Museum, Vienna (Bibl. B 33.783).*

nent patrician families of Nuremberg. Made about 1634, this trumpet has a silver mouthpiece (*Strasser Collection* 2002, pp. 215–218).

Hainhofer was slightly more eloquent about a collection of elaborate crystal objects that was housed in the 19th cabinet, calling them "treffliche schöne Cristalline geschürr, auf mancherlaÿ art. Darunter wie Vögel, mit ausgespanten flüglen, alle in gold gefasset, thails mit edlen stainen vnd perlen gezieret . . ." (very beautiful crystalline dishes of many different kinds. Among them are birds with spread wings, all mounted in gold, some decorated with precious stones and pearls . . . ) (Doering 1901, p. 87). Two rock crystal vessels from Ambras Castle that fit this description had been made by the prolific 16th-century Saracchi workshop in Milan (Habsburg 1997, p. 105, no. 130). Today, they are in the collection of the Kunsthistorisches Mu-

seum in Vienna. Hainhofer's appreciation of these objects reflects a general preference for items of rock crystal over those made of glass because of their higher value and scarcity.

Continuing on his tour of the castle, Hainhofer noticed a small paneled chamber with credenzas and chests adjacent to a large hall. One of these was filled with beautiful crystal glasses that served as the archduke's table glasses ("Ihrer Durchlaucht mundgläser") (Doering 1901, p. 41, fols. 257 and 258). It is not clear whether these vessels were made of rock crystal or glass, since buffets stocked with silver plate and rock crystal vessels seem to have been in everyday use at some courts (Bencard 2000, p. 234).

Many glasses employed at the Innsbruck court during the reign of Archduke Ferdinand had been made there or at the glasshouse in the nearby town of Hall. The German historian and traveler Martin Zeiller (1589–1661), who visited Hall in the early 17th century, remarked that much beautiful glassware, as well as windowpanes, was made there (Zeiller 1649, p. 140). When Archduke Leo-

FIG. 2

*Polygonal beaker, colorless, blown, tooled; gilded metal mount embellished
with enamel, rubies, and pearls. Said to have been blown by Archduke
Ferdinand II at the Innsbruck court glasshouse in 1583. H. 20.2 cm.
Kunsthistorisches Museum, Vienna (KK 3302).*

pold married Claudia de' Medici in Innsbruck in April 1626, their Italian guest Francesco Folchi had wanted only to see the official mint, which had been in operation continuously since 1451, and the salt pans in Hall (Archivio di Stato di Firenze, *Mediceo del Principato*, v. 2953, fol. u.p.). Hainhofer does not mention the large, once famous Venetian-style glasshouse in Hall. By the 1620s, luxury glass-making in Tyrol, which had flourished a generation earlier, had declined to the point that it was no longer an attraction for visitors.

The production of luxury glass in Venetian style in the Hapsburg-ruled Austrian lands had reached its pinnacle during the lifetime of Archduke Ferdinand II, the second son of Ferdinand I (1503–1564), who reigned as king from 1526 and as emperor from 1556. He was raised at the imperial courts in Innsbruck and (later) Prague, and he continued to live there after his morganatic marriage in 1557 to Philippine Welser (1527–1580), the daughter of the wealthy Augsburg patrician Bartholomeus Welser, which barred him from succession to the throne.[1] While Ferdinand was living in Prague, his interest in glass was not directed exclusively toward Venice and its fashionable products, since he is known to have acquired colorful enameled glassware from Bohemia. In 1561, he purchased many elaborately enameled drinking vessels from the glassworks of Sigmund Berka von Dubá in Falkenau, Bohemia (Klannte 1938, p. 598). This

glassworks had been founded in 1530 by the German Paul Schürer, and his family continued to produce high-quality potash glass. Much later, their products included glass in Venetian style, which was introduced in Bohemia through Austria and the Netherlands (Hejdová 1995, p. 35).

Ferdinand became archduke of Tyrol upon his father's death in 1564, and he settled his family in the newly renovated Ambras Castle. Throughout his life, he spent lavishly—often beyond his means—on works of art and luxury goods. One of the more extravagant ventures was his own workshop for making glass in Venetian style at his court in Innsbruck. The personal patronage of such an expensive craft was still deeply rooted in the 15th-century doctrine of "magnificence." Large expenditures on objects (and their production) were justified by their splendor and scarcity (Dacosta Kaufmann 1994, p. 140), and Renaissance princes were encouraged to hone their skills in a luxury craft for their personal edification.

It was only fitting, therefore, that a member of the Hapsburg family, the most powerful European dynasty in the 16th century, would satisfy his interest in glass with more than the design and purchase of desirable Venetian products. Tyrol was a promising location for the production and distribution of glass in Venetian style, and it would benefit (and suffer) from the close attention of the sovereign.

## VENETIAN GLASS TRADE THROUGH TYROL

The foundations for the success of a luxury glassmaking industry in Tyrol were the continued fashion for Venetian glass, its often restricted availability there and in the adjacent German countries north of the Alps, and its comparatively high price. In the 16th century, most Venetian glass was transported by sea to western and northern Germany via Antwerp, which was also under Hapsburg rule. Glass consignments to Austria, southern Germany, and the eastern part of the Holy Roman Empire

were sent via two major trade routes that traversed Tyrol. Most of them went by cart or on foot, but some also took advantage of navigable rivers.

Members of the imperial court in Prague were able to negotiate their orders of Venetian glass through the imperial envoy to Venice, Veit von Dornsberg. Ferdinand repeatedly contacted von Dornsberg to acquire many types of drinking glasses. These were often made according to his own designs and specifications.

Affluent 16th-century consumers in the German-speaking states, including Tyrol, depended on the services of large German merchant houses, especially those in Augsburg and Nuremberg. These houses were represented in the Fondaco dei Tedeschi, the German trade center in Venice. It had been established in 1222–1225 by the Council of Ten, the governing body of Venice, to control and financially benefit from the lucrative trade with the German states (Stromer 1978, p. 1). For centuries, the members of the Fondaco alone negotiated the trade routes through Tyrol with the local sovereigns and counts, and they also procured final payments (Backmann 1997, pp. 181–182). Among their many other privileges, the members of the Fondaco paid taxes lower than those of many other nations with trade centers in Venice, such as England and the Netherlands.

A tariff of 1572 lists glassware from Venice as one of the luxury export articles traded by representatives of the Fondaco. In turn, one of the goods imported from Germany that was used by the Venetian glass industry was *zaffera*, a mineral mixture produced from cobalt ore and used as a blue colorant for glass (Simonsfeld 1887, v. 2, pp. 197–198). Beginning in the 15th century, *vetri groppolosi* and *picchieri gruppolosi* (blown glass beakers with prunts), as well as mirrors and large numbers of eyeglasses, were shipped by crate from Nuremberg to Rome via Venice (Esch 2002, pp. 130 and 133). There is no archeological evidence of glass production in Nuremberg, although the glass painter Augustin Hirschvogel (1503–1553) once attempted, unsuccessfully, to establish a factory for making glass in Venetian style (Friedrich 1885, pp. 10–18).

Wealthy German merchant families with close trade connections to Venice could be expected to own luxurious glass vessels. Many 16th-century Venetian-style glasses decorated with the arms of Nuremberg and Augsburg families have been identified. One of the earliest datable Venetian glasses commissioned by a prominent Nuremberg family is the so-called Behaim Beaker, which was probably ordered in Venice for the marriage of Michael Behaim and Katerina Lochnerin in 1495 (see pp. ii and iii, Fig. 1).

Travel through the Alps was slow, risky, and expensive, and access to roads was not reliable. Two main roads connected Venice and the Tyrolean trade centers: a lower road via the Brenner Pass and an upper road via Reschenscheideck. The choice of route was determined by local authorities and not by the shipper, and fees and taxes tended to fluctuate according to road conditions (Müller 1901, p. 333). Because of poor road conditions, a journey from Innsbruck to Venice would require a minimum of six days.

Little is known about the distribution of Venetian glass in private homes in Tyrol. In the 16th century, window glass and probably also glass lamps were about as common in modest southern German and Tyrolean households (such as those of artisans) as they were in comparable households in Venice. But even in Venice, *cristallo* vessels were exceptional (Palumbo-Fossati 1984, pp. 123–124). Venetian glass was a desirable luxury, but only small amounts of it were owned by the less affluent, such as the low-level employees at the customs stations and the owners of local transportation services. For instance, the customs clerks at Toblach on the Lueg skimmed a few glasses from shipments of Venetian vessel glass and windowpanes in return for letting these commodities pass as low-tariff goods (Heimer 1959, p. 79).

Travelers were often attacked. Especially between 1599 and 1604, bandits roamed the border between southern Tyrol and Lombardy (Bücking 1968, p. 66). In addition, the political relationship between the imperial house of Hapsburg and the Venetian republic was often strained (Egg 1962, p. 17).[2] In the summer of 1633, Hainhofer informed his German patron Duke August the Younger that there was a serious shortage of Venetian glasses in Augsburg because the passage to Tyrol and Bavaria was blocked (Gobiet 1984, p. 594, no. 1127). The probable cause of this situation was a devastating outbreak of the plague, which had reduced the Venetian population to 100,000 by 1630. Four years later, it was ravaging Tyrol.

The trade route through the Puster Valley in Tyrol, which was traversed by many Venetians on their way to Flanders and France, had an especially bad reputation. At least since the 14th century, the road and the inns situated along it were regarded as both abominable and exceedingly expensive (Simonsfeld 1887, v. 2, pp. 55 and 96). Nevertheless, aristocrats residing in the Puster Valley enjoyed the use of fine Venetian glassware, as is attested by a painted frieze that still decorates the interior walls of a house in Bruneck that was owned in the 1520s by the burgher Veit Sell (Egg 1962, pl. VI, fig. 11). This frieze depicts a *Humpen* and other glass forms, along with the names of their owners below and their mottoes above. The last of these devices showed the arms of the Rattenberg painter Ulrich Springenklee and the date 1526. The aristocrats named include Mohr zu Ainned, Rost, Jöchl, Kern, Wolkenstein, and Künigl.[3] Since the Peasant Wars were still being fought in Tyrol in 1526, these noblemen met at a private house that was not open to the local public and common travelers.

In the socially elevated gathering in Bruneck, two of the guests, Jochum Kraus and the Freiherr von Wolkenstein, used a trumpet-shaped goblet with enameled or gilded decoration that was typical of Venetian production. The family of another guest, the count of Künigl at Ehrenburg Castle, owned an extraordinary and sophisticated Venetian goblet that is dated to the end of the 15th century. It is decorated with a love poem written on intertwined enameled bands, and it was most likely intended for a betrothal or marriage (**1**). In Tyrol, marriages were frequently occasions on which to purchase commemorative glasses decorated with coats of arms. For example, a footed beaker with the arms of Christoph Haller and Anna Imhof is dated to about 1530, the year of their wedding.[4]

Venetian glassware was also popular with Austrian clerics. In 1477, the monastery of Saint Peter in Salzburg acquired glasses that were gilded on both the interior and the exterior, as well as a Venetian glass with a gilded foot (Egg 1962, p. 15). Venetian glass vessels with shallow bowls were often gilded and diamond-point engraved on both the inside and the outside. On a footed bowl that was formerly in the collection of Ferdinand II at Ambras Castle and probably made in Venice, the interior of the bowl is decorated only in the center,

while the majority of the ornamentation appears on the exterior (Fig. 3).

Since the 14th century, Salzburg had derived much of its wealth from its close commercial ties to Venice. Salzburg merchants traded Venetian vessel glass to the north, and colored windowpanes were exported from Germany via Salzburg to Venice (Tarcsay 1999, p. 13). In 1480, Emperor Frederick III permitted Salzburg to trade Venetian goods freely along the Danube (Simonsfeld 1887, v. 2, pp. 55–56). This is the same emperor who, during a state visit, ostentatiously dropped an elaborate Venetian glass given to him by the Council of Ten, signifying his low regard for his hosts' impermanent and intrinsically worthless gift (Klesse and Reineking 1973, p. 13).

An excavation in Salzburg unearthed the cesspit of an inn that was in operation before 1605. It yielded the remnants of 66 wineglasses with lion-mask stems and other fragments of Venetian or Venetian-style glass. In every case, the mold-blown pattern consisted of two opposing lions' heads connected by garlands of raised dots (Wintersteiger 1991, pp. 382–383, no. 497). Innkeepers were often among the wealthiest citizens of a town (Bücking 1968, pp. 152–153). The Venetian aristocrat Marin Sanudo (1466–1536), for example, is known to have held shares in the Campana inn in Venice, which provided him with a sizable income (Labalme and White 1999, p. 62, n. 56). In Tyrol, innkeepers had to prove an honest way of life and a certain amount of wealth before they could be sworn in to the profession (Potthof and Kossenhaschen 1933, p. 101). For such businesses, a large number of luxury glass wares would not have been out of reach financially. The glasses found at the excavated Salzburg inn were probably Venetian, but at that time they could also have been made locally, in Hall or Innsbruck.

Drinking habits in the north were deeply rooted in German traditions despite strong Italian influences that derived from a lively trade and cultural exchange. In the southern part of Austria, most people were bilingual, and even in the north many spoke Italian. Throughout most of the 16th century, Italy also exerted considerable influence on the architecture, dress, and customs of socially conscious Austrians. Innsbruck, for example, had porticoes like those found in Italian cities (Doering 1901, p. 35).

Much of our knowledge of life in Tyrol during the late 16th and early 17th centuries is provided by the treatise *Grewel der Verwüstung menschlichen Geschlechts* (Troublesome causes for the ruination of humankind), published in Ingolstadt in 1610. It was written by Dr. Hippolytus Guarinoni (1571–1654), a physician, theologian, and amateur architect in Hall. Like other doctors and pharmacists of his time—such as the Italian pharmacist Zoan Francisco Catanio, who founded the glassworks in Laibach (modern Ljubljana in Slovenia; see p. 29)—Guarinoni had a vested interest in the manufactory in Hall, which made glassware for medical and pharmaceutical uses (Heimer 1959, p. 64). In 1630,

he offered to bail out the city's once famous but then dilapidated glassworks (*ibid.*, p. 119).

Guarinoni approved of the healthier Italian lifestyle, with its increased consumption of bread and fruit, as well as the custom of diluting wine with water (Bücking 1968, p. 54). Germans had an unsavory reputation stemming from their excessive eating and drinking habits, provoking the Italian epithet "porco tedesco, inebriato" (drunken German pig). In Tyrol, wine was a common beverage in wealthier households, and breakfast habitually included a glass of wine.[5]

In German tradition, it reflected badly on a host if he failed to keep his guests' beakers full at all times. Guests, in turn, were sometimes forced with threats to empty their glasses (Bücking 1968, pp. 148–149). In fact, the degree of inebriation was the measure of the social success of a celebratory feast.

Fig. 3

*Footed bowl, colorless, blown, diamond-point engraved, gilded. Probably Venice, second half of the 16th century. H. 19.4 cm. Kunsthistorisches Museum, Vienna (KK 3367).*

According to a Venetian envoy, the Germans viewed drunkenness as a virtue. They believed that only a villain would refuse to drink for fear of losing his guard to alcohol and exposing his mean character and intentions (Hirn 1885–1888, v. 1, p. 486).

Drinking also played an important symbolic role in the sealing of contracts (Arnould 1990). The historic Petronell welcome glass, dated to 1490, is probably the most significant testament to this custom in Austria. This large Venetian footed beaker with enameling and gilding was twice used to confirm reciprocal loyalty between the counts of Petronell Castle and their sovereigns. The glass was probably a gift from the invading Hungarian king Matthias Corvinus to the count of Petronell, Johannes von Kranichberg, in 1487, and it was used to renew the hereditary rights of the owners of Petronell by Emperor Matthias and Empress Anna in 1613 (*Strasser Collection* 2002, pp. 17–21). Similarly, a goblet engraved with the names of three generations of the counts Fuchs von Fuchsenstein from southern Tyrol attests to its employment on two (unspecified) occasions, in 1674 and 1716 (*ibid.*, pp. 30–32).

Guilds and civic associations (the so-called *Stubengesellschaften*) also counted delicate glassware among their treasures. Christoph Oeri, a goldsmith from Zurich, engraved a *Stangenglas* that was probably made in the Hall glasshouse about 1580, and he dedicated it to the local carpenters' guild in the name of several members and their families from Zurich (Keller 1999, fig. 22).[6] This glass, which is diamond-point engraved with lily-shaped flowers and twisted bands, a typical decoration for this workshop, has reserved fields for additional embellishment. Keller (*ibid.*, p. 34) notes that guild glasses were as valuable as guild silver in Switzerland. The glass trade from the Hall glasshouse to Switzerland has also been documented by Heimer (1959, p. 95).

A Venetian beaker densely inscribed with dates, as well as the names and mottoes of members of such an association (including an attorney and a surgeon), has a silver mount with Vienna mint marks (**2**).

A rare welcome glass, probably from Hall, has a funnel-shaped bowl with pronounced vertical ribs,

applied horizontal trails, a ribbed and gilded knop between mereses, and an applied foot. Above the ribs near the rim, it is diamond-point engraved with names dating from 1599 to 1605 (Winkler 1985, p. 56, no. 100).[7] Another diamond-point engraved *Stangenglas* with a pair of initials commemorates an event that took place on January 1, 1602 (*Strasser Collection* 2002, p. 30, no. 5, and ill. p. 31). Its engraved metal foot is not a replacement, but it was probably intended to preserve the original glass foot. A comparable glass (without mount) is in the collection of The Corning Museum of Glass (**3**).

Hainhofer's extensive notes attest to the importance of a drink in facilitating payments and negotiations with both clients and artists (Böttiger 1909, p. 4). Since the 15th century, the basis for a commission had usually been a drawing (*disegno*) signed by the craftsman and sometimes also by a witness (Schmidt-Arcangeli 1997, p. 57, n. 41). Although Hainhofer's health required him to abstain from alcoholic beverages, he conceded to a drink in contract situations (Böttiger 1909, p. 4). It can be assumed that many of the representational glasses in the offices of the German merchant houses were used for this purpose. A large gilded Venetian goblet with cover, two other large covered Venetian glasses, and filigree goblets were in the Breslau offices of the Fugger company, the largest merchant house in Augsburg, in 1546.[8]

It is against this social backdrop that one must view the drinking customs in the so-called Bacchus Grotto, installed by Ferdinand and Philippine Welser at Ambras Castle.[9] In 1567, the couple decreed that "wegen erzaigung guetter freuntschafft guetwilligkeit und gesellschaft" (for the demonstration of good friendship, benevolence, and companionship), a Venetian barrel-shaped glass was to be emptied by the gentlemen and a ship-shaped glass by the ladies in one draft. Two such vessels from Ambras Castle are now in the collection of the Museum für Angewandte Kunst in Vienna (A KHM 310, A KHM 318). An account of the visit by Prince Karl Friedrich of Cleves to Ambras Castle illustrates these Bacchic rites (Primisser 1972, pp. 37–39). The guests were strapped into a mechanical metal chair, and they remained there until they had successfully emptied their glasses.[10] Following the "Bacchic initiation rites," the participants signed the guest book, which is divided into a section for gentlemen, headed by Archduke Ferdinand, and one for ladies, headed by Philippine Welser.[11] Philippine could certainly hold her own at these festivities, as is documented in this *Trinkbuch* (drinking book). One of the largest glasses attributed to

Hall, a *Passglas* (H. 35 cm), has traditionally been associated with her, although there is no documented evidence to substantiate this claim (*Strasser Collection* 2002, pp. 29–30, no. 4, and ill. p. 31). These drinking glasses from Ambras Castle (some of which still exist) may have been Venetian, but the drinking customs were wholly Germanic.

## THE LAIBACH GLASSHOUSE, 1526–ABOUT 1634

During the reign of Ferdinand I, Archduke Ferdinand's father, the earliest important center for the production of glass in Venetian style emerged in Laibach, capital of the province of Krain (Carniola), located on the eastern border of the Hapsburg empire. In 1526, the newly crowned king awarded a 20-year privilege to Andrej Dolenik and the Italian pharmacist Zoan Francisco Catanio, who may have been related to a glass painter associated with the Serena glasshouse in Murano (Kos 1994, p. 93). They were financially supported by two wealthy patricians of Laibach, Veit Khisl and Hans Weilhamer. From 1527 to 1547, the glasshouse employed 14 glassmakers, probably from Altare (Schmidt 1912, p. 118). Khisl already owned a glassworks in Kaltenbrunn (now Fuzine), near Laibach, where he employed 15 Venetians. The Kaltenbrunn glasshouse was rented to Christoff Pruner. Upon Khisl's death in 1547, his son Hans continued the Laibach business, and he also took over the Kaltenbrunn factory when Pruner died shortly after making his will in 1563. On February 21, 1572, Hans Khisl turned his privilege into a monopoly, which he successfully defended until his death in 1591. His successor, Paul Ciriani, continued production at least until 1634 (Kos 1994, p. 96).

The document settling Pruner's estate includes an inventory of the local glasshouse, which provides invaluable insights into this early production of Venetian-style glass. The list confirms a range of vessels catering to both local tastes and export

markets. Among these are such common Venetian forms as gilded goblets and enameled bowls ("khelichlen mit goldt" and "gemallte schissl"), a drinking barrel in filigree glass ("ein glas wie ein fasl mit weisser arbeit"), and glass with foreign designations, including Hungarian and French goblets ("ungareschi" and "francossini khelich") (Kos 1994, p. 94). It has been suggested that the use of placenames indirectly (and rather loosely) indicates typical production centers (Mendera 2002, p. 278). However, extant examples of these foreign and apparently fashionable shapes are unknown in glass or any other material.

A cobalt blue diamond-point engraved plate in the collection of Rudolf von Strasser, dated to the last phase of the Laibach glasshouse's production, has been tentatively attributed to that factory because of its documented ownership by a Slovenian family (*Strasser Collection* 2002, pp. 50–52, no. 16, and ill. p. 50). Excavations in Ljubljana and its environs have unearthed fragments of Venetian-style luxury glass (including lion-mask stems and millefiori wall fragments). None of these has been firmly attributed to the Laibach or Kaltenbrunn glasshouse, and many of these finds may well be Venetian imports (Kos 1994, p. 95). However, the richest findspots were the sites of a former inn and a glassware shop, and scientific analysis of a large sampling indicates that the glasses recovered here were most likely produced in Laibach because they contain at least two different sources of alkaline compounds (Kos and Šmit 2003).

The commercial distribution network of the Laibach glasshouse included the Venetian trade routes to the eastern, German-speaking countries and the western and northern parts of the former Hungarian empire, which had come under the rule of King Ferdinand I following the sack of Buda by the Ottoman Sultan Suleiman the Magnificent in 1526. The shrewd owners of the Laibach glassworks enjoyed imperial guarantees that shielded them from market infringement by competing operations, which could be established only with the king's blessing.

## VIENNA, 1552–1566

The production of Venetian-style glass in Vienna got off to a bumpy start. The first such glasshouse was founded in 1486 outside the city's walls by Nicolas Walch, who was probably of Venetian descent. He was protected by King Matthias Corvinus, the Hungarian usurper, who was a connoisseur of Venetian glass. The factory was intended to produce glassware that was competitive in quality and price with Venetian products (Tarcsay 1999, p. 8). How long the glassworks was in operation is not clear, but it could not have survived the Turkish siege of Vienna in 1529. The Viennese glasshouse of the Venetian Niclas Pitti, founded in 1530, was equally short-lived, and for more than 20 years no glassmaking in Venetian style is recorded here.

On April 26, 1552, King Ferdinand I granted a 20-year privilege to Dominicus Wiener for the establishment of a glassworks near the Danube. It was in operation for only a short time, but it caused seven years of quibbling between the glasshouse in Hall (discussed below), which had been established in 1534, and the Vienna glassworks about stealing skilled workers and technical know-how, price fixing, and market shares. The dispute abruptly ended with the death of Wiener's successor, Georg Ehn, in 1566 (Heimer 1959, p. 77).

Wiener's glasshouse employed two prominent glass painters from Nuremberg: Albrecht Glockenthon and Augustin Hirschvogel (1503–1553), who settled in Vienna in 1544. In 1553, Glockenthon decorated two silver-mounted *Humpen* with four coats of arms that had been commissioned by Ferdinand I. Hirschvogel was the son of one of Nuremberg's leading glass painters, Veit Hirschvogel.

The younger Hirschvogel, who is best known as an accomplished cartographer (Tarcsay 1999, p. 9), was also one of the 16th century's most versatile artists. In 1531, he had become affiliated with a Venetian-style glasshouse in Nuremberg that was owned by Hanns Nickel and Oswald Reinhard. Three years later, he went to Venice, supposedly to train as a potter in the famous ceramic workshops located on Murano (Friedrich 1885, p. 66; Zecchin 1987, v. 1, p. 215). From August 1536 to about 1540, he was active in Laibach. Hirschvogel is known to have painted two *Magalel* (*maigel* glasses) with the coat of arms of the Bürgerspital (an elaborate building in which care was provided for the infirm and the poor) in Vienna (Tarcsay 1999, p. 9).

In 1559, Wiener's privilege was assumed by the merchant Georg Ehn, who ran the glasshouse jointly with three Italians: Bernhard de Negro, Franz Benigno, and Raphael Jecchiero. Working conditions were more favorable economically in the Viennese glassworks than in Tyrol. The potash used in Vienna came from the nearby marshy Neusiedlersee, which reduced costs considerably. The furnace in Vienna was substantially more efficient in wood consumption than its counterpart in Hall, and its owners were thus granted a privilege by the king. Unfortunately, no additional information about the nature of this furnace's construction is known (Tarcsay 1999, p. 9). But the savings were impressive. While the glassworks in Hall required 12,000 cords of wood to melt 500–570 centners (25–28.5 metric tons) of crushed quartz-rich pebbles, the Viennese consumed only 250 cords for the same amount (Zedinek 1928, p. 105).

Despite these advantages, the Viennese consortium soon dissolved over disputes, and Ehn became the sole proprietor in 1562. The factory had 11 glassmakers, two of whom were maestros dedicated to the production of "christallin" glass. By 1563, the glasshouse made colored as well as colorless glass, and it seems to have favored blue glass (Tarcsay 1999, pp. 10–11). Later that year, the glassworks burned down, and Ehn rebuilt the business in a new location outside the city walls. The glasses he made there were comparable in shape to Venetian wares, but their color was inferior, possibly because the glassmakers were still experimenting with the new furnace.

Following Ehn's death in 1566, his wife continued to operate the Viennese glasshouse with her second husband, Tobias Weiss, but it failed after only a few years (Zedinek 1927, p. 246).

# THE GLASSHOUSE IN HALL, 1534–1540

The idea of founding a Tyrolean factory to make glass in Venetian style was first conceived by the Augsburg entrepreneur and patrician Wolfgang Vittl (1495–1540) at a time when no competitive glasshouse was operating in Vienna. Vittl had made his fortune by investing in the region's lucrative silver and mercury mines. The industries of mining and glassmaking were very well suited to the forest-rich mountain ranges of central Europe, since they both required wood for fuel (Klannte 1938, p. 580).

A Venetian-type glasshouse was unprecedented in Tyrol, and it was a risky business. King Ferdinand I, who ultimately controlled the allocation of resources in this region, protected the profitable local mining and salt-producing industries (Heimer 1959, p. 14, n. 2). Vittl knew of the successful Venetian-style glasshouses in Antwerp and Laibach, and he boldly petitioned the king for a 20-year monopoly to make "beautiful white glasses, as they are also made in Murano near Venice" (*ibid.*, p. 12). The place he selected for his factory was safely outside Hall (Fig. 4, far right) and strategically located at the confluence of the Inn River and a small creek, the Weissenbach. Lumber was floated from upstream forests down to Hall, and the river was navigable at the factory site.

Because such a glasshouse promised local tax revenue and prestige, as well as easier access to luxury glass at lower prices, the king endorsed the project. In 1534, he instructed the magistrates in Innsbruck to grant Vittl a privilege to operate the glassworks for 15 to 20 years. However, free wood and charcoal for his "fireworks" were limited to the support of only one furnace, a restriction intended to prevent conflicts with the needs of the mines and the mint (Schönherr 1900, p. 407).

While Vittl had successfully procured the fuel supplies, his negotiations with the Council of Ten in Venice for their prized soda ash and craftsmen failed. The Venetian republic apparently was not inclined to supply a competitor, especially one positioned along an important trade route for Venetian glass to the north. Vittl settled for second best: on June 2, 1534, he was permitted to obtain soda ash and other ingredients from Alicante in Spain via the harbor of Genoa. The craftsmen were indeed hired from Italy, but they were probably Venetian émigrés from the glass center of Altare, near Genoa, in the duchy of Montferrat (Zedinek 1928, p. 99). The guild statutes of Altare, unlike those of Venice, encouraged glassmakers to leave the area during the period from Saint Martin's Day to Saint John's Day (November 11–June 24), and thus to work abroad. These foreigners received tax-free status in Tyrol, but in times of need they could be drafted for military service (Heimer 1959, p. 13). Genoa, which was always eager to make inroads into the Venetian market, had been used by German merchants as an alternative port since at least the 15th century. The city offered more liberal trade conditions, fewer duties, and access to cargo ships with much larger capacity than the galleons of the

FIG. 4

*View of Hall, from* Schwazer Bergbuch,
*1556. Library of the Tiroler Landesmuseum
Ferdinandeum, Innsbruck (Codex FB 4312).*

Venetians, which were built to navigate the shallow waters of the lagoon (Simonsfeld 1887, v. 2, p. 44). It is uncertain whether glass in Venetian style was produced in Genoa. Fragmentary vessels found at the San Silvestro monastery in Genoa have not been analyzed, and they may have been made in Venice or elsewhere in Italy (Mendera 2002, p. 268).

For Vittl, who set out in a commercial environment that had never supported a factory for making luxury glasses, much of the assistance for his enterprise came from his own compatriots, the Augsburg-based merchant community (Heimer 1959, p. 5). That city's large merchant houses had a network of branch offices, some permanent and some temporary, all over the territory they served. These were generally headed either by Augsburg natives loyal to the house or by relatives. For the crucial position of *Faktor* (agent), Vittl hired the young Sebastian Höchstetter (1511–1569). The

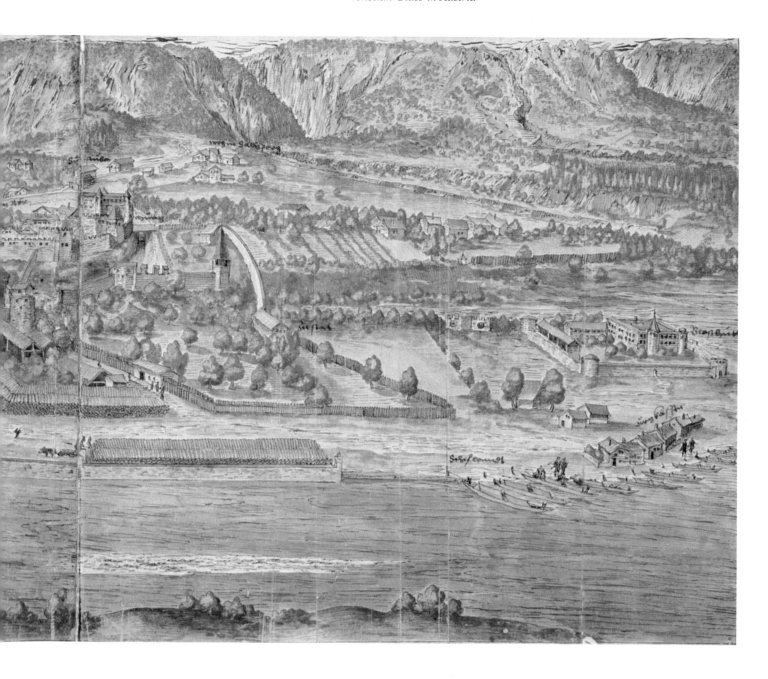

Höchstetters, the third most influential merchant family from Augsburg after the Fuggers and the Welsers, had invested heavily in the mining industry in Tyrol (*ibid.*, p. 8). They also served as bankers to the imperial court in Prague, to which they continued to provide loans, and Sebastian managed the family business in Schwaz at that time.

Sebastian Höchstetter's principal role at the glassworks was that of financier. Glasshouses are characterized by large start-up costs and slow financial growth, and Höchstetter's powerful connections in German finance and commerce were an essential asset. Thanks to his intervention, Vittl received financial support from Anton Fugger, owner of the largest merchant house in Augsburg, who had once before broken an impasse in the importation of Venetian glass in Tyrol. In 1537, Fugger's considerable commercial influence helped to expedite a large shipment of window glass from Venice to the manager of the imperial Hapsburg mine in Rattenberg on the Inn (Egg 1962, p. 15).

Despite Höchstetter's excellent connections, the glassworks struggled against outside pressures, and the supply of raw materials posed constant problems. On at least one occasion, the owners of the Laibach glasshouse, Veit Khisl and Hans Weilhamer, brazenly confiscated a shipment of soda ash that had been sent from Spain to Hall. High-quality imported soda ash, which was the key to Venetian-style glass production, continued to be the raw material that was most difficult to obtain. Ever in search of cost-cutting solutions, Vittl experimented with growing salicornia plants locally on saline soil, probably taking advantage of the close proximity of the salt works. Unfortunately, the results were not commercially viable, and the financial situation of the Hall glasshouse deteriorated (Egg 1962, p. 23). This situation was not helped by the fact that Vittl

seems to have diverted wood, which was allocated by the authorities to fuel the glassworks, in order to support his more lucrative mining enterprises (Zedinek 1928, p. 100). When Vittl died in the spring of 1540, he was heavily indebted to Sebastian Höchstetter and other creditors.

Many of Vittl's customers in Hall belonged to southern German and Tyrolean society, and a number of glasses are attributed to his short-lived glasshouse. The glass, which is thicker than that of the Venetian products, has a smoky color, many minute bubbles, and sand impurities. A large funnel-shaped goblet is enameled on the foot with the arms of Matthäus Lang (1468–1540), an Augsburg native who, since 1519, had served as archbishop of Salzburg and, as a cardinal, had lived in Rome.[12] A goblet of similar form, bearing the arms of the von Puchheim and Dürr families, is also attributed to this period in Hall because of a family connection with Lang (*Strasser Collection* 2002, p. 29). Other glasses thought to have been made in Hall at this time include a pair of covered vessels and a beaker cold-painted with the arms of the bishopric of Freising and the Pfalzgrafen bei Rhein, members of the Bavarian house of Wittelsbach. They were probably made at Vittl's glasshouse as part of a larger set for Philipp, bishop of Freising from 1499 to 1541. One of the covered vessels is in The J. Paul Getty Museum, Los Angeles (Fig. 5), and the other is in the collection of Mrs. H. C. Newgas, London. The beaker is housed in the Musée de l'Oeuvre

FIG. 5
*Covered vessel decorated with the arms of the bishopric of Freising and the Pfalzgrafen bei Rhein, members of the Bavarian house of Wittelsbach, colorless with purplish gray tinge, blown, applied, gilded, cold-painted. Probably Tyrol, Hall, about 1536–1540. OH. 19 cm, D. (max.) 8.5 cm. The J. Paul Getty Museum, Los Angeles (84.DK.548.1-.2).*

FIG. 6
*Plate with coat of arms of Duke Ernst of Bavaria, colorless with grayish tinge, blown, applied, cold-painted. Probably Tyrol, Hall, possibly decorated by Paul Dax, 1536. D. 43.2 cm. Bayerisches Nationalmuseum, Munich (GL 551).*

Notre-Dame, Strasbourg (Hess and Husband 1997, pp. 142–146, no. 36).

Glass ewers were especially desirable in cities north of the Alps during the 16th century (Dexel 1983, p. 89). According to a documented order, bowls with matching ewers were the Hall factory's costliest products (Egg 1962, p. 37; Hess and Hus-

band 1997, pp. 142–146, no. 36). A spectacular royal gift from Ferdinand I to Duke Ernst of Bavaria consists of a cold-painted plate with the duke's coat of arms (Fig. 6), datable to 1536, and a pair of matching ewers (Fig. 7).[13] The decoration is attributed to Paul Dax (about 1503–1561), an artist who had become a specialist in glass painting

**FIG. 7**

*One of a pair of matching ewers, colorless, blown, applied, cold-painted. Tyrol, Hall, 1536. H. 33.6 cm. Bayerisches Nationalmuseum, Munich (GL 517). Detail shows Pera breastfeeding her father, Cimon, from a story told by the Roman historian Festus.*

**FIG. 8**

*Paul Dax (about 1503–1561), self-portrait, about 1530. Oil on wood, H. 50.8 cm, W. 37 cm. Tiroler Landesmuseum Ferdinandeum, Innsbruck (Gem. 93).*

while he worked for Vittl in Hall (Fig. 8).[14] He may have been taught this art by an expert from Augsburg (Zedinek 1928, p. 100). Dax, a devout Roman Catholic, was also a soldier, cartographer, and painter of flags and murals. He continued his career as a court painter in Innsbruck.

A more common example of tableware made in Hall during this period is a goblet with a mold-blown and gilded knop (4).

## HALL AND INNSBRUCK, 1540–1590

Following Vittl's death, ownership of the Hall glasshouse was transferred to Sebastian Höchstetter by the decree of Ferdinand I. In his initial petition for the reinstatement of the old rights and privileges, filed in 1542, Höchstetter affirmed the commitment of his entire personal wealth to the glassworks and his "dedication to art" (Heimer 1959, p. 39). With this statement, he signaled to his royal patron that the support of his glasshouse should be viewed as art sponsorship, not as sup-

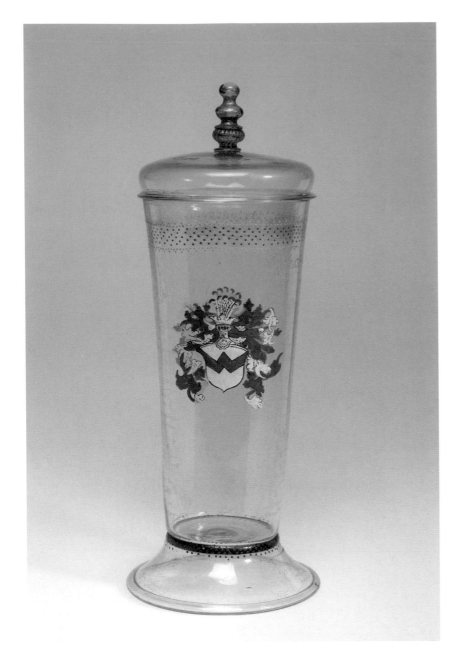

port for an industrial enterprise. Höchstetter's sentiment emphasizes the Renaissance view of Venetian glass production as an art form, positioning it, in a broader sense, as a form of the skill or mastery that is called *ars* in Latin, *technē* in Greek, and *Kunst* in German (Dacosta Kaufmann 1994, p. 141). This statement also echoes the praise of the art of glassmaking in Biringuccio's *De la Pirotechnia* (1540), a recent publication that cannot have escaped Höchstetter's attention. Biringuccio, a Sienese metalworker, was the most verbal advocate of Venetian glassware, noting that "in glass, art surpasses nature"

(Biringuccio 1990, p. 127). Höchstetter's statement may also have implied that his glasshouse was in a different league from the local mining and salt industries, which were so high on the king's list of priorities. In reality, Hall would produce mostly window glass for profit and make vessels as prestige objects (Egg 1962, p. 36). In the last third of the 16th century, the glasshouse made several million windowpanes, but its vessel glass also became commercially successful (Schönherr 1900, pp. 421–422). Two fine examples that are attributed to this early period are a covered welcome glass with the

FIG. 10

*Flute glass, colorless with pur-plish gray tinge, blown, mold-blown, applied, gilded. Probably Tyrol, Hall, about 1550–1560. H. 38.3 cm, D. 16.2 cm. The J. Paul Getty Museum, Los Angeles (84.DK.545).*

arms of the von Trapp family and signed by Arch-duke Ferdinand (Fig. 9) and an elegant flute glass (Fig. 10).

Under Höchstetter's ownership, the formerly ailing glasshouse prospered. Between 1550 and 1554, its buildings were renovated and expanded by several stories. Stone walls with four observation towers now surrounded the compound (Fig. 11). The original single furnace must have been rather large. It has been suggested that it probably had 10 glory holes and 20 workers (Egg 1962, p. 31). Among these workers were nine makers of win-dow glass and only one blower for the production of drinking glasses. By comparison, the number of openings in a Venetian glass furnace was limited, at first, to three, and later to four (Zecchin 1987, v. 1, p. 11). Höchstetter employed a total of about 70 workers (Heimer 1959, p. 68). At the height of its production, the glasshouse exported 1,200 crates with three million windowpanes to custom-ers in the north (Bücking 1968, p. 60). When the Vienna glasshouse collapsed following Ehn's death in 1566, Höchstetter was able to absorb its market shares as well (Zedinek 1928, p. 103).

FIG. 11

*Renovations at Hall glasshouse under ownership of Sebastian Höchstetter, as shown in detail from Schwazer Bergbuch, 1556 (see Fig. 4).*

In appreciation of Höchstetter's continued success at Hall, Ferdinand I bestowed on him the noble honors of count of Scheibenegg in 1551 (Heimer 1959, p. 52). Although Höchstetter's family had held noble status in Augsburg since the reign of Maximilian I (1486–1519), this renewed appointment was based on Höchstetter's professional success as a financial negotiator and political agent for the court. In France, it was customary to lure new glasshouse owners with the title of *gentilhomme*. Glasshouse owners in the Hapsburg empire could also be granted this hereditary honor, but it was not tied to their profession (Hejdová 1995, p. 33).[15]

The year 1552 marked a turning point in the career of Sebastian Höchstetter. In addition to the ambitious expansion of his glasshouse, he had rebuilt his residence. That project had barely been completed when, in June, regular glass production came to a temporary standstill with the arrival in Tyrol of troops led by the Protestant Maurice of

Saxony, who had pursued Charles V and his extensive entourage. The Holy Roman emperor had progressed to Innsbruck by this time, and 50 members of his entourage were accommodated on Höchstetter's property in Hall. On August 8, 1552, his guests included the former elector Johann Frederick I (1503–1554), the deposed leader of the Protestant Schmalkaldic League who was forced to follow Charles,[16] and the 80-year-old painter Lucas Cranach the Elder (1472–1553), a Roman Catholic who supported the elector and sympathized with the Protestant cause.[17] At the time of the royal visit, the glasshouse was closed because of the foreign threat, and the glassworkers had been pressed into service as soldiers.

The fact that such illustrious guests, even in a state of emergency, should be hosted at a glasshouse may seem surprising. However, Höchstetter was an agent of the court in Prague, and thus his house was at the emperor's disposal. An imperial source describes Höchstetter's glasshouse as a *Lusthaus*, a summer residence or pleasure house that had been built with his own finances and dedicated to the delicate and artistic craft of Venetian glass (Heimer 1959, p. 53). The island of Murano was also used as a summer retreat by Venetian patricians during the *cavata*, the period when the glassworks were closed. Even Germans acquired summer retreats on Murano. For example, the Ott family, patricians from Augsburg who traded at the Fondaco dei Tedeschi, acquired a house on Murano in 1593 (Backmann 1997, p. 187). The Otts served as liaison for the Fugger family to sell copper and lead from mines in Tyrol. In return, they received connections in high finance, and they participated in transactions between the Fuggers and Archduke Ferdinand II (*ibid.*, p. 184).

Höchstetter, who had served as head agent for two important mines in Schwaz even while he was rebuilding his glasshouse, now resigned that former position, fully intending to focus on his business in Hall. However, on July 30, 1552, King Ferdinand I called on him as financial negotiator for the court in Prague. Höchstetter's glasshouse venture did not appear to benefit from his connections at court. Because of his frequent travel and business obligations as a courtier, he was compelled to hire a manager for his factory (Heimer 1959, p. 49).

At the glasshouse, the procurement of raw materials continued to be a struggle. Höchstetter repeatedly tried to persuade the Venetian Council of Ten to sell him Levantine soda ash directly, but his efforts failed. He then attempted to bypass the uncooperative Venetians by purchasing the soda ash directly from Syria and transporting it to Hall with the aid of merchants from Cleves via Genoa (Heimer 1959, p. 33, n. 3, and p. 34). This solution also proved to be unreliable and uneconomical. In the end, Höchstetter continued to purchase soda ash from Spain, imported by the Prethoria firm in Genoa. Archival sources list the suppliers as Ale-

sandiero in Galicia and Alcandara in Extremadura. The annual cost of 4,550 guldens was still astronomical in comparison to about 152 guldens for quartz sand from the Valsertal in Bavaria. Arsenic, another purifier, and manganese came from Augsburg in Germany. The cost of the arsenic was 36 guldens (Egg 1962, p. 32). In addition, Höchstetter still had to compete for wood with the other local industries (Heimer 1959, p. 39).

The Hapsburg courts continued to support the Hall glasshouse with orders. The glasses were of desirable quality and expertly decorated, mostly with diamond-point engraving and painting with gold and with red and green lacquer. One of the most accomplished decorators was the glass painter Sebastian Schell, who worked at the glasshouse until 1554 (Zedinek 1928, p. 115). In 1555, Ferdinand I considered glassware from Hall to be comparable to that made in Venice (*ibid.*, p. 101). Three years later, Archduke Ferdinand ordered from Prague a variety of covered drinking glasses that continued to be popular with the German clientele (Egg 1962, p. 37). The more unusual objects on Ferdinand's list were the "*Schwimmerle*," possibly small glass balls with internal floaters, such as a swan documented by Philipp Hainhofer, and the "*Spritzglasl*," an early form of humidifier. No example of these objects is known to exist. Hainhofer's description of a metal "*Spritzapfel*" (squirting apple) indicates a hollow object filled with water (a funnel was provided) and two openings, one at the stem and the other at the blossom. By blowing into one hole, water squirted out of the other (Gobiet 1984, p. 400). Hainhofer's correspondence refers to similar glass wares, attesting their popularity well into the 17th century.

It was a struggle for Höchstetter to consistently deliver glass that measured up to the archduke's exacting standards. In 1566, the Hall glassmaker Samuel Höhenberger was lured to a Viennese glasshouse with the promise of higher pay, although he still owed Sebastian Höchstetter six years of work. Höchstetter claimed to have trained Höhenberger and other German glassblowers at great expense. It was a common practice for wealthy German patrons to send experts in various professions to Italy for specialized training (Jonkanski 1993; Martin 1993). Höchstetter's German glassmakers must have received their training from Italian glassmakers at his expense. He protected his investment, as was customary, by binding these craftsmen with long contracts. Nevertheless, he could not always prevent them from moving on.

In order to remain competitive, Höchstetter petitioned Archduke Ferdinand in 1566 to prohibit any imports of glass from Venice to Austria. His request was firmly denied with the explanation that the Hall glasshouse was not producing goods comparable in quality to Venetian imports, and thus glasses made in Venice would continue to be brought into Tyrol to satisfy the demand for these luxury wares. At the same time, however, the imperial government protected Höchstetter's interests by refusing to allow the establishment of a competitive glasshouse in Bolzano (Heimer 1959, p. 74).

In 1567, the archduke visited the Hall glassworks, and he still did not approve of its current work. The glass post horns he had commissioned for hunting events did not turn out to his liking. Höchstetter countered that his furnace was not suited for "subtle work" because he was limited to one furnace for his entire production (window glass and tableware); moreover, he had to depend on his German workers, whose skills he still considered to be inferior to those of the Venetian masters (Heimer 1959, p. 57).

Archduke Ferdinand, who was dissatisfied with the glass made in Hall, repeatedly turned to Venice to acquire tableware for use at his new residence. These orders included some glasses of his own design. In December 1570, Ferdinand sent to Venice a large order for glass and windowpanes that had been requested by his sisters Magdalena and Helena for the convent at Hall. This order was probably executed by the Venetian glassmaker Pietro d'Orso. The archduke specified that the 44 smaller glasses he had requested should be undecorated, perfectly transparent, and only as thick as a knife's edge (Egg 1962, pp. 43–44). Thin glasses specifically for drinking water were also requested by the Florentine ambassador Orazio della Rena as a gift to Queen Margarete von Hapsburg of Austria, wife of Philip III. These water glasses had become very popular with Spanish women at the court in Madrid (Biblioteca Nazionale Centrale, Florence, MS Magl. Cl. XXXV, cod. 796, c. 48 r.).

## THE COURT GLASSHOUSE IN INNSBRUCK, 1570–1591

At that time, Ferdinand set out to create a private Venetian glasshouse in Innsbruck (Fig. 12). It was erected in the pheasant garden (*Fasanengarten*) according to plans provided by the court architect and technological input from the glasshouse in Hall. (The pheasant garden is shown on the far left, along the river, in the engraved view.) Ferdinand's desire was probably fueled by continuing difficulties with Venetian glass orders, as well as the inadequacies of the glass production in Hall. It was certainly also driven by his own ambition to exert his princely magnificence. His determination may have been inspired by the Medici's successful establishment of a Venetian court glasshouse in Flor-

ence, which was perhaps reported to him by the imperial ambassador along with periodic updates on the status of his glass orders in Venice. In addition, the dynastic connections between Tyrol and Florence were close.[18]

Archduke Ferdinand's venture was much less traumatic for the Venetian glassmakers involved because it was never commercially viable, and therefore it was not a threat to the Venetian industry. Echoing the Medici's request, the ambassador conveyed that the proposed glassmakers should be honorable people and have "am wenigsten 'fantasey'" (the least crazy ideas) (Egg 1962, p. 46).[19] At first, the imperial envoy Veit von Dornsberg had hoped to interest the well-known glassmaker Pietro d'Orso. When that effort failed, he finally arranged for the Altarist glassmaker Antonio Montano to gain access to Muranese workshops by posing as a merchant. Montano arrived in Innsbruck with samples of Venetian glass, soda ash, and an assistant, but he subsequently failed to demonstrate the desired quality of craftsmanship, although he lingered as a glassblower in Hall until about 1590. The glasshouse in the garden of Ferdinand's castle, for which he had engaged the Innsbruck court architect and experts from Hall, required better glassworkers.

The Venetian ambassador was called in for renewed negotiations (Egg 1962, pp. 67–68). He now made it clear that the loan of glassworkers was strictly temporary, and that their work would satisfy only the needs of the court. The furnace itself was an ongoing concern because it had to be rebuilt before each use. In any event, the Innsbruck court glasshouse was in operation for more than 20 years, from 1570 to 1591. The use of soda ash and some tools, such as the molds, had to be negotiated with the Venetian government. Archduke Ferdinand's contract with the glassmakers stipulated, in addition to salary, free room and board. In the later years of the glasshouse's production, the agreement changed. Glassworkers were not paid for their work; instead, they were allowed to make glass wares on their own time and to sell them for their own profit. These workers were not protected by a guild, as they had been at home in Venice. Even "commercial" glassblowers in the Hapsburg empire were not organized in guilds until Emperor Rudolf II granted the Old Town painters' guild, which included the glassblowers, a privilege in 1594–1596 (Šroněk 1997, p. 364).

The first Venetian who came to work at the new glasshouse in Innsbruck was Salvatore Savonetti

FIG. 12

*View of Innsbruck, from Zeiller 1649.*

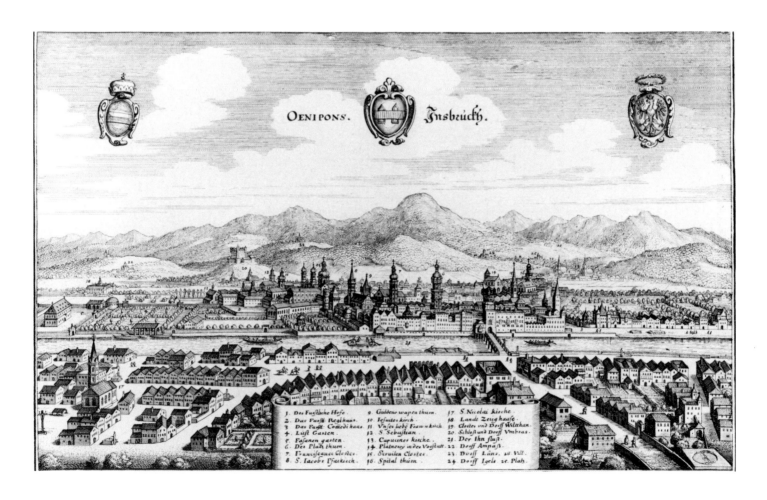

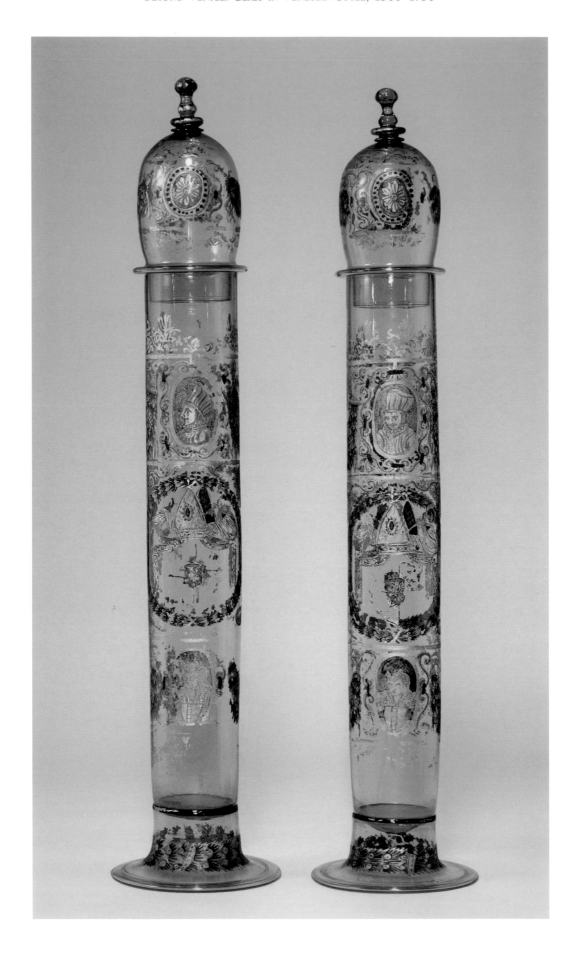

(or Savoneto, 1544–1592), the second son of Bastian or Sebastiano Savonetti (1515–1581) (Zecchin 1987, v. 1, p. 222). He worked in Innsbruck from 1573 to 1575, and again in 1578 together with his father. Another Venetian glassworker, Andrea Tudin, arrived in 1575 and remained until 1583 (Egg 1962, p. 50). Bastian and Salvatore Savonetti were members of a prominent Venetian glassmaking family that owned the Leon Bianco (White Lion) glasshouse (Zecchin 1987, v. 1, p. 193). They brought with them Venetian plant ash, quartz from Ticino,

manganese oxide from Piedmont, and bronze molds in the shape of pine cones.

In Innsbruck, the production of Venetian forms was limited by Ferdinand's taste, and the glassmakers received their assignments directly from this one patron. They first produced special glass panes to protect the reliefs in the court church, then turned to the manufacture of mostly drinking glasses. These vessels were thinly blown and frequently decorated with diamond-point engraving, considerable gilding, and colorful painting. Ferdinand shared the Venetian penchant for lavishly gilding tables bedecked for feasts. In Venice, this could extend from tableware to richly gilded food, a custom that since 1514 had been regulated by sumptuary laws and the *Magistrato alle Pompe* (magistrate for ceremonies) (Labalme and White 1999, p. 62). Cold-painted gilding was generally found on knops, handles, and twisted bands. The gold paint was often sold and mixed in a clamshell. One such shell, with remains of gold paint still adhering to its interior surface, was found during excavations of the late 16th-century cesspit at an inn in Salzburg (mentioned above).[20] The cold painting was usually executed in red, green, and gold, a very Germanic look.

The largest drinking glasses that were presumably made at the court glasshouse are a group of tall covered *Stangengläser* with cold-painted polychrome and gilded decoration. A matching pair are decorated with garlands and profile portraits *all'antica* (Fig. 13), one is embellished with figures in period costumes (Fig. 14), and another has laurel wreaths (Fig. 15). A glass in the shape of a boot, with spur and warrior heads *all'antica*, has also survived. It was probably once used at Ambras Castle on occasions of social drinking (**5**).

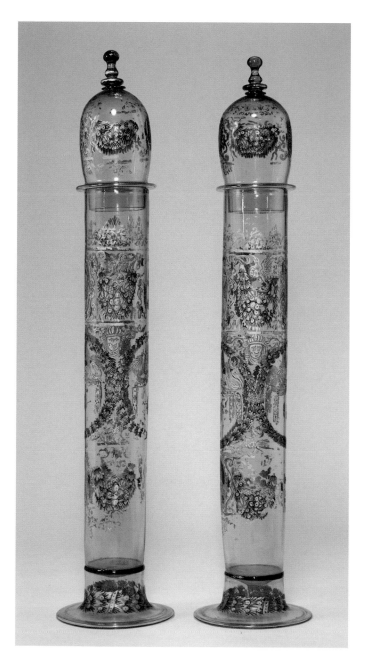

FIG. 13

*Pair of* Stangengläser *decorated with garlands, profile portraits* all'antica, *and the arms of the Breslau archbishop Andreas Jerin, colorless with grayish and purplish tinge, blown, cold-painted, gilded. Probably Tyrol, Innsbruck, court glasshouse, about 1570–1591. H. (taller) 55.9 cm. Bayerisches Nationalmuseum, Munich (G 93, G 94).*

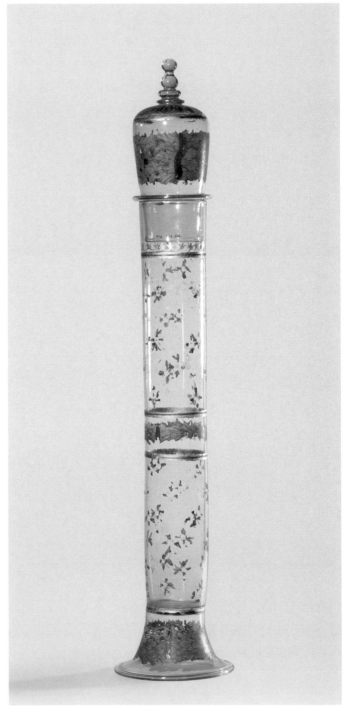

The painters, and probably also the diamond-point engravers, were very likely German artisans working at the court (Egg 1962, p. 55). Ferdinand II employed about 50 painters, each with a specific duty. They included history, portrait, animal, landscape, and decorative painters (Hirn 1885–1888, p. 376). Their sources were often found in the collection of prints and books owned by the archduke, although this is not corroborated for glass.

Glass examples from this period include the so-called *Vasenpokal*, elaborately decorated covered goblets (Fig. 16) (Egg 1962, p. 54). One such covered goblet with diamond-point engraved decoration and painted medallions, including a profile bust of a warrior *all'antica*, is in the collection of Rudolf von Strasser (*Strasser Collection* 2002, p. 33, no. 8, and ill. p. 34). It is attributed to the court glasshouse, and so it is datable to about 1570–1591. Such decorations could also be diamond-point engraved on simpler beakers, such as a covered glass from Hall that is datable to the same period (Fig. 17). At the end of the 16th century, the *Vasenpokal* was fashionable for drinking wine (**6**). A still life by Georg Flegel, datable to about 1610, illustrates such a vessel filled with white wine (Theuerkauff-Liederwald 1994, p. 254, fig. 41).

An unusual object from the archduke's collection is a standing cup and cover, with an internal knop, enameled with marine life, including fish, crabs, and toads. Two other vessels of this kind are known. One is in The British Museum (Fig. 18) (Tait 1979, color pl. 10, no. 34), and the other, in

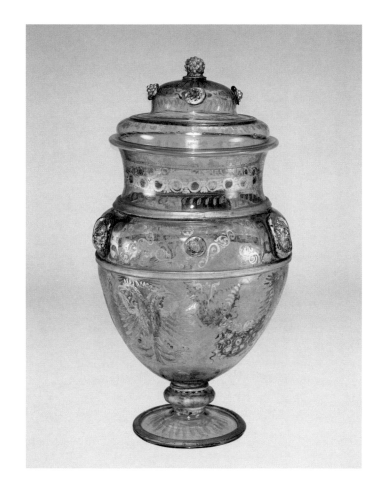

FIG. 16

*Vasenpokal (covered goblet), colorless with greenish tinge, blown, applied, tooled. Probably Tyrol, Innsbruck, court glasshouse, about 1570–1591. OH. 34.8 cm. Bayerisches Nationalmuseum, Munich (GL 516).*

the Strasser Collection, is tentatively attributed to Tyrol (*Strasser Collection* 2002, p. 84, no. 39) because of its distinct grayish tinge, which is typical for Tyrolean glassworks. The marine life, applied to the interior of the vessel, may have been a simple illusion that was intended to delight the user. But in Tyrol, fish had acquired a more specific meaning. As reported by Philipp Hainhofer, the Ducal Cloister in Hall housed a treasured relic: a piece of the two fishes with which Christ had fed 5,000 men in a remote area near the town of Bethsaida (Doering 1901, p. 65; Luke 9:10, 12).

A tall tazza with a composite lion stem (Fig. 19) was probably made in Innsbruck rather than in Venice, as has been suggested for a similar ves-

FIG. 14

*Stangenglas decorated with figures in period costumes, colorless, blown, cold-painted, gilded, decoration possibly slightly fired on. Probably Tyrol, Innsbruck, court glasshouse, about 1570–1591. H. 83.5 cm. Bayerisches Nationalmuseum, Munich (G 656).*

FIG. 15

*Stangenglas decorated with laurel wreaths, colorless, blown, cold-painted, gilded. Possibly Tyrol, Hall, 1580–1590. H. 36.5 cm. Tiroler Landesmuseum Ferdinandeum, Innsbruck (GL 84).*

FIG. 17
*Covered beaker, colorless, blown, applied, diamond-point engraved with
warrior portraits* all'antica. *Tyrol, Hall, about 1580. H. 24.3 cm.
Kunsthistorisches Museum, Vienna (KK 3295).*

**FIG. 18**
*Standing cup and cover, colorless, blown, mold-blown, applied filigree and opaque
white trails, gilded, enameled. Possibly Tyrol or Venice, about 1580. H. 21.4 cm.
The British Museum, London (1855, 12-1, 151). Formerly in the Bernal Collection.*

sel in the Veste Coburg (Theuerkauff-Liederwald 1994, pp. 251–252, no. 228). Few thinly blown large vessels with elaborate diamond-point engraving and cold-painted decoration have survived. A large bowl, possibly for serving fruit, is a typical example of the fragile condition of such pieces (Fig.

FIG. 19
*Tazza, colorless with grayish tinge, blown, pattern-molded, diamond-point engraved. Tyrol, probably Innsbruck, about 1570–1590. H. 14.9 cm, D. (rim) 16.4 cm, (foot) 7.4 cm. The Corning Museum of Glass, Corning, New York (79.3.323, bequest of Jerome Strauss).*

20). Its engraved arches are paralleled on a tall vessel known as the "*Passglas*" of Philippine Welser (*Strasser Collection* 2002, pp. 29–30, no. 4).

When the Venetian envoy was asked to renegotiate the return of Salvatore Savonetti and his father in 1578, a lampworker who could make gilded glass chains ("vergulten glösern ketten") was added to the request. Glass chains were desirable objects of personal ornament, as well as collectibles. The woodcut depicting a glazier in Jost Amman's *Handwerkerbüchlein* of 1568 is believed to illustrate such chains (Fig. 21). An inventory of a *Kunstschrank* (collector's cabinet) assembled by Hainhofer attests to their continued popularity in the 17th century.

FIG. 20

*Bowl, possibly for serving fruit, colorless with grayish brown tinge, blown, diamond-point engraved, cold-painted. Tyrol, Innsbruck, court glasshouse, 1570–1591. H. 16 cm, D. (max.) 40.4 cm. The J. Paul Getty Museum, Los Angeles (84.DK.653).*

FIG. 21

*Jost Amman (about 1539–1591), "Glasschneider," Handwerkerbüchlein, 1568.*

### Der Glaſſer.

Ein Glaſſer war ich lange jar/
Gut Trinckgläſer hab ich fürwar/
Beyde zu Bier vnd auch zu Wein/
Auch Venediſch glaßſcheiben rein/
In die Kirchen/ vnd ſchönen Sal/
Auch rautengläſer allzumal/
Wer der bedarff/ thu hie einfern/
Der ſol von mir gefürdert wern.

           G iij       Der

He included three "colorful and gilded glass chains made in France, which women wear around their neck" (Gobiet 1984, p. 849). By this time, France had become well known for its lampworked objects, and Hainhofer obtained the most fashionable goods, wherever they were available, to meet the demand of his clients. The same collector's cabinet also contained "a fired crystal ear ornament, set in gold, which was made by the Venetian Luca Trono," as well as two more "crystal" ear pendants on chains and a small black necklace (*ibid.*, p. 850).

The 1596 inventory of Ferdinand II also mentions a small black glass chain ("ain glesernes schwarz clains kettl"), and several such chains can be found in the collection from Ambras Castle

51

FIG. 22
*Black glass chain from Ambras Castle. Possibly Tyrol, Innsbruck, court glasshouse, about 1578 or about 1590–1591. L. 83.5 cm. Kunsthistorisches Museum, Vienna (KK 3012).*

(Figs. 22 and 23; for a colorless, gilded glass chain, see **7**). Black jewelry was very popular with upper-class women, and especially with Hapsburg women, in the 16th century. The most popular black stone was jet, and the Iberian court imported great quantities from Bohemia through the Hapsburg court in Austria. Some of the existing chains may have been made by the Venetian lampworker at the Innsbruck court or by another Italian lampworker (probably from Altare), who had been lent by the count of Zimbern at Ferdinand's request in December 1590. He was to stay at the glassworks

for only three weeks, but he remained in Innsbruck for three months (Zedinek 1928, p. 112).

Whether the lampworkers teamed with glassblowers in Venice or in Innsbruck to produce table and other decorative glassware has not yet been investigated, but such collaboration is documented

Fɪɢ. 23
*Black glass chain from Ambras Castle. Possibly Tyrol, Innsbruck, court glasshouse, about 1578 or about 1590–1591. L. 80.5 cm. Kunsthistorisches Museum, Vienna (KK 3015).*

for Florence. The Medici court provided a climate of boundless technological creativity. Here, lampworking was the specialty of Niccolo di Vincenzo Landi, a Lucchese who was also one of the leading glassblowers at the Florentine glasshouse. He was a good friend of Antonio Neri, who admired him as a "maestro di cristalli a lume di lucerna" (master of *cristallo* [made] at the lamp) (Neri 1612, p. 67). His famous lampworked creations included devotional objects such as the crucifixes that were sent to Christina of Lotharingia and the duchess of Alba. A covered lion-stem goblet from Ambras Castle that

contains a lampworked Crucifixion scene may have been a product of Landi's workshop, or it may have been made in Innsbruck (*Lehman Collection* 1993, p. 232, fig. F). It is decorated with lampworked flowers and small figures that are applied to the foot, bowl, and lid. The delicate pendants with putti

(Fig. 24), once owned by Ferdinand, resemble the figurines on the goblet.

In Pratolino, where he worked from September to mid-October 1591, Landi created numerous butterflies, crickets, spiders, *moschoni doré* (gilded flies), sea horses, scorpions, roses, rosettes, feathers, the Medici coat of arms, and a host of other objects. A marvelous glass scorpion from the collections at Ambras Castle survives (**8**), and scorpi-

ons are documented by Hainhofer, who also lists glass feathers (some as writing quills), fruit forming a face, and buttons in his shipments (Gobiet 1984, pp. 840 and 849). Most of these came from Venice, but Hainhofer also sent a shipment of Florentine glass flowers and feathers to his client Duke August the Younger in July 1627, to be distributed as gifts to the women attending an upcoming baptism (*ibid.*, p. 485).

Lampworked jewelry (Fig. 25), buttons (Fig. 26), and other ornaments of clothing were undoubtedly worn, despite their obvious fragility. Hainhofer imported Florentine lampworked feathers, flowers, and fruit to decorate the hats and hair of the ladies at the Brunswick court (Gobiet 1984, p. 484). Glass jewelry and imitation stones are known to have adorned the costumes created for the elaborate pageants and performances that were staged during official celebrations during the Renaissance. For instance, at the pageant of the Muses performed for the marriage of Duke Cosimo I de' Medici and Eleonora of Toledo in 1539, the character of Euterpe wore a necklace of greenish yellow glass (Rousseau 1990, p. 419). These fragile and intrinsically worthless glass creations were ideal to convey the rich effects that the designers and artists of such events desired.

**FIG. 24**

*Pendants with putti. Possibly Tyrol, Innsbruck, court glasshouse, about 1578 or about 1590–1591. H. (tallest) 9.0 cm. Kunsthistorisches Museum, Vienna (KK 2798, KK 2801, KK 2877).*

FIG. 25

*Earring pendants, lampworked. Possibly Tyrol, Innsbruck, court glasshouse, about 1578 or about 1590–1591. H. 3.5 cm. Kunsthistorisches Museum, Vienna (KK 2852).*

FIG. 26

*Buttons. Possibly Tyrol, Innsbruck, court glasshouse, about 1578 or about 1590–1591. D. 2.3 cm. Kunsthistorisches Museum, Vienna (KK 2898, KK 2883, KK 2905, KK 2912, KK 2925).*

# CHRYSOSTOMUS HÖCHSTETTER, 1569–1599

While the court glasshouse was being developed, the operation in Hall was directed by Sebastian Höchstetter's brother, Dr. Chrysostomus Höchstetter (1523–1599), who was an attorney and one of Archduke Ferdinand's advisers. His older brother, Walter, remained a silent partner. Chrysostomus inherited the thankless and nearly impossible task of recovering the large sums that Sebastian had lent to the Crown, which were now essential to operate the glasshouse (Zedinek 1928, p. 104). Hall also provided the technical expertise to maintain the Innsbruck facility whenever the archduke requested it. Since the furnace was operated only when the Venetian glassblowers were present, it had to be restored—and often rebuilt—before they arrived.

During Chrysostomus's tenure, window glass continued to be the primary product at Hall, but fine drinking glasses were still made there as well. A well-known *Stangenglas* with the coat of arms of Christoph von Madrutz (1512–1578), prince-bishop of Trent and cardinal since 1543, was probably made in Hall at that time.[21] The glasses made at the Hall factory may have been decorated in Innsbruck (*Glas des 16. bis 19. Jahrhunderts* 1992, p. 13). A glass engraved with a mythical bird (Fig. 27), a footed beaker (**9**), and a more simply engraved *Stangenglas* (**3**) were probably produced during this period.

A glass of similar form, with the arms of the noted Augsburg bookseller Georg Willer (1514/1515–1593/1594), is dated 1581 (Fig. 28). Aside from the enameled coat of arms, this unusual drinking glass is decorated with pale green leafy decoration, often attributed to Venice and Spain, as well as with colorful finches (Rückert 1982, pp. 88–90, no. 150). Rückert has convincingly argued for a Hall or Innsbruck provenance for this *Stangenglas*, noting that the color scheme of its leaves may be related to that of Spanish vessels from Barcelona. However, the shape of the decoration on the latter more closely resembles Spanish-Moorish ornamentation on ceramics and differs from that found on vessels also ornamented with finches (*ibid.*, p. 88). In ad-

dition, Rückert noted the close similarity of the coloring on the Willer *Stangenglas* and that on pieces from a large set of tableware enameled with the arms of the Fugger family, which are in the collections of several European museums (**10**).

The economic circumstances in Hall did not improve when Archduke Ferdinand finally closed the Innsbruck court glasshouse in 1591. His beloved wife, Philippine Welser, had died in 1580, and two years later, Ferdinand entered into a political marriage with the devout Anna Catarina Gonzaga of Mantua (1566–1621). A covered gob-

Fig. 27
Stangenglas, *colorless with grayish tinge, blown, diamond-point engraved. Southern Germany or Austria, about 1600. H. 27.9 cm. The Corning Museum of Glass, Corning, New York (73.3.449, gift of Jerome Strauss). Formerly in the Strauss Collection (S1959).*

let commemorating their wedding is painted with gold, as well as red and green lacquer. It prominently displays the couple's joint coat of arms, and it dates to the last decade of the glasshouse's activity (Kunsthistorisches Museum, Vienna, 3363). The glasshouse was presumably abandoned because of a more demure lifestyle at court.

**FIG. 28**
*Enameled* Stangenglas *with the arms of Georg Willer, colorless with smoky tinge, blown, applied, enameled, gilded. Probably Tyrol, Hall or Innsbruck, about 1581. H. 25 cm. Bayerisches Nationalmuseum, Munich (62/55).*

With Ferdinand's death in 1595, Tyrol lost its great sponsor of glass production. By that time, Hall needed protection, not only from Venetian competition in the south, but also from the booming Bohemian potash glass production in the north. Since the 1570s, Hall had complained that the Bohemian glass industry was encroaching on its territory, but by the time that Chrysostomus Höchstetter died in 1599, the situation was nearly desperate. Hans Kripp, who signed up as the new owner of the Hall glassworks, received some regulatory protection from Archduke Maximilian. He was given the exclusive right to collect all broken Venetian and Hall glass for cullet. This was an im-

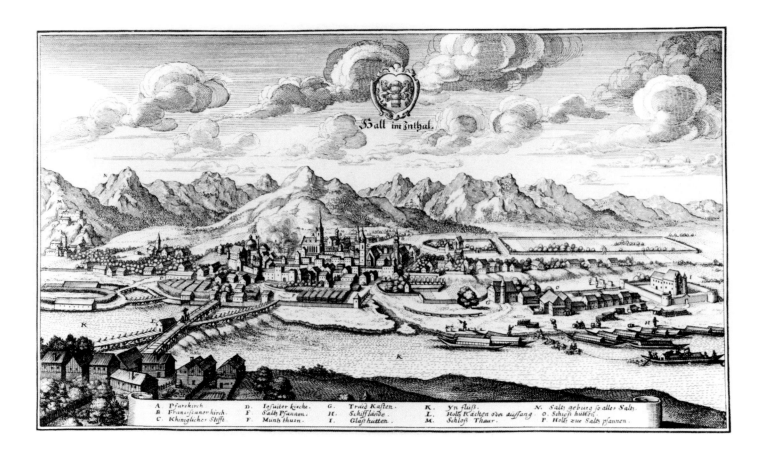

FIG. 29
*View of Hall, from Zeiller 1649.*

portant privilege, since Spanish soda ash was becoming ever more difficult to obtain (Heimer 1959, p. 116). When Kripp's lease expired in 1615, Dr. Hieronymus Höchstetter (d. 1635), one of Chrysos-

tomus Höchstetter's sons, half-heartedly assumed control. He repeatedly tried to sell the financially troubled business (prospective buyers included the abovementioned Dr. Guarinoni and Archduke Maximilian), but it closed permanently in 1636 (Fig. 29). In the 1920s, remnants of the furnace were still visible in the foundation of a large house that was built on the site (Zedinek 1928, pl. 86).

## AUSTRIAN GLASS PRODUCTION IN THE 17TH CENTURY

The Thirty Years' War (1618–1648) certainly curbed the production and the market for fragile luxury wares north of the Alps. Nevertheless, Bohemian glass production flourished and exerted pressure on the traditional markets in the north that were held by the Venetians, Austrians, and Germans. In Bohemia, glasshouses working in the Venetian style negotiated the importation of soda ash

via Genoa, but when Bohemian colorless potash glass, which used chalk as a stabilizer, was invented by 1590, this was no longer necessary (Pause 1996, p. 113). By the end of the 16th century, more than 50 Bohemian glassworks were documented, and about half that many in Moravia and Silesia (Kybalová 1997, p. 382). To these countries, as in Austria, Venetian expatriates brought their glassmaking knowledge and traditional tools. In the Tambach glasshouse in Thuringia, an inventory list signed by Antoni Feretello on June 23, 1639, noted a brass mold in the shape of a lion's head (Stieda 1915–1916, p. 41). But even the numerous lion-mask stems found on goblets dating from the first half of the 16th century cannot be automatically associated with the lion of Saint Mark (Weiss 1974, pp. 96–97). For the Hapsburg court, the lion mask had a special meaning. The emperor, as governor of Bohemia, bore that country's heraldic symbol, the lion (Pyhrr and Godoy 1999, p. 206). An olive green covered goblet with a lion-mask stem, a German inscription, and the date 1625, formerly in the Royal Saxon-Anhalt collection at Dessau Castle, was probably made in Saxony of potash glass by a Venetian glassblower who formerly worked at the Innsbruck court (**11**).

Despite increased production of glass in Venetian style in the late 16th and early 17th centuries, many among the European elite still desired Venetian originals, and their quality is attested in their prices. In 1583, Wilhelm IV, margrave of Hesse-Cassel in Germany, paid 13 florins for a chest of windowpanes from Venice, compared with just six florins for a chest from Bohemia (Heimer 1959, p. 96). In the same year, a glasshouse in Cassel that made glass in Venetian style (including filigree glass) began production. It was operated by Italians who had been trained in Venice, and it used Spanish soda ash for the batch (*ibid.*). A Viennese customs tariff of 1626 still stipulated eight crowns for a common Venetian drinking glass, compared with just two crowns for a common drinking glass made in Bohemia (Tarcsay 1999, p. 14).

There were some additional short-lived attempts in Austria to establish factories for the manufacture of glass in Venetian style during the 17th century. In 1624, Ferdinand II revised the import laws for glass, which until that time had been mostly exempt from taxation. Venetian glass, as the most valuable import, was assigned the highest tax (Tarcsay 1999, p. 13).

One of Hieronymus Höchstetter's employees, Gilg Schreier, founded his own glasshouse in Kramsach, near Brixlegg, before 1627 (Egg 1962, pp. 91

and 97). Some of this factory's glasses continued to be made during the Thirty Years' War (Rückert 1982, pp. 91–92, nos. 158 and 159). About 1633, another glasshouse was founded. It was located in Neuburg on the Danube and operated by Venetian glassworkers (*ibid.*, p. 80). A Viennese glasshouse was established by Bernardo Marinetti under the protection of Leopold I in 1676, but it collapsed three years later under economic pressure from Bohemia's luxury glass production (Zedinek 1927, p. 256).

Reichenau had one of Austria's oldest glasshouses for everyday wares. Glass had been made in this area since the late medieval period under the counts of Landau von den Starhemberg (Hampl 1951). In the 16th century, three glasshouses overseen by independent glassmakers and one managed by a serf named Shälly were in operation on the count's properties. One of these factories was burned down by Bohemian troops in 1620, and its owner re-erected it to make glass in Venetian style. Four engraved illustrations of the rebuilt factory were published in the *Topographia Windhagiana* in 1656 (Fig. 30). In addition to the usual facilities of a glass factory, such as the furnace house, the mill for grinding quartz pebbles, and buildings for the grinding and polishing of vessels, it included a tin foundry and a glass painting studio. The furnace was oval in form, and this later became known as the "Bohemian type." An adjustable metal rack below the base of the furnace allowed for the regulation of airflow (Tarcsay 2003, p. 74). Some of the raw material was recycled glass in Venetian style, delivered from a Viennese supplier in 1610 (*idem* 1999, p. 12).

In 1997, one of Reichenau's glasshouses, which had been in operation between 1601 and 1686, was excavated, and the results are forthcoming. Finds from the site show that the production included mostly windowpanes, small bottles, and *Humpen*. Fragments of table glass in Venetian style attest to the production of wineglasses with twisted colored stems, complex filigree glass, and goblets with applied colored prunts (Tarcsay 1998, p. 33). Colorless glasses with baluster stems and blue raspberry prunts have been excavated only in the Nether-

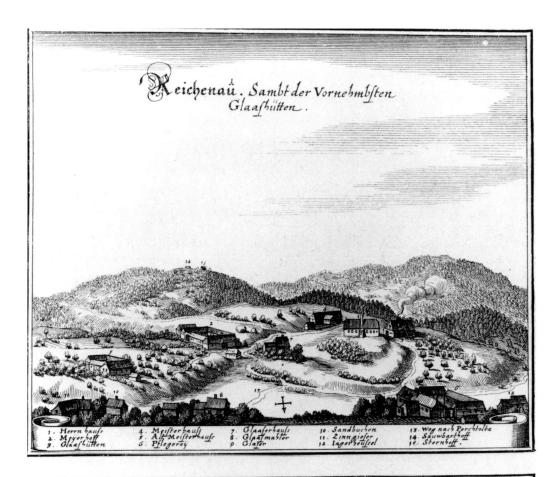

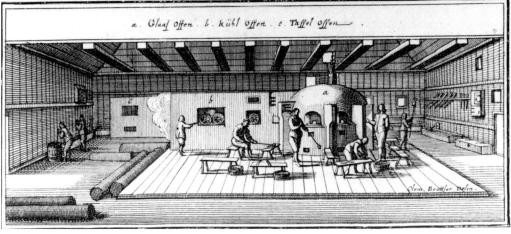

lands. In Reichenau, an earthenware stamp used to produce such prunts was also unearthed (*idem* 2003, p. 76, fig. 9). Chemical analysis showed that all of the finds sampled were made of the same chalk-potash-silica formula (*idem* 2001, pp. 129–130). In the 1650s, the production of the Reichenau glasshouse far exceeded that of other workshops. Its constant need for cost-efficient fuel was satisfied by its feudal owners for more than 30

FIG. 30
*Engraved views of the Reichenau glassworks from* Topographia Windhagiana, *1656.*

years, but production was then halted by a lack of sufficient raw materials and skilled workers, as well as economic pressures from a changing market (Knittler 1994, pp. 145–146).

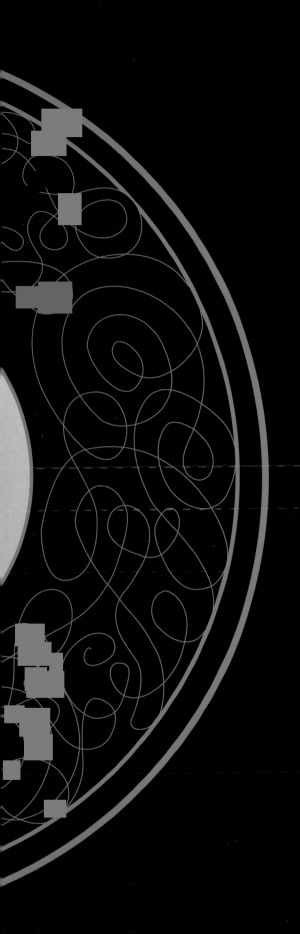

Venetian Glass in Austria

# *Objects*

## 1

### *Enameled Goblet*

*H. 13.8 cm*

VENICE, FIRST HALF OF THE 16TH CENTURY.
TIROLER LANDESMUSEUM FERDINANDEUM,
INNSBRUCK (GL 101). FORMERLY IN THE
COLLECTION OF COUNT LEOPOLD KÜNIGL,
EHRENBURG CASTLE, NEAR BRUNECK.

COLORLESS. BLOWN, MOLD-BLOWN,
ENAMELED.

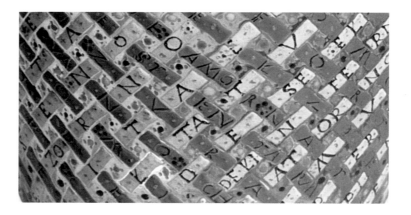

This goblet, which has a bucket-shaped bowl and a fire-polished rim, is applied to a pedestal foot that is embellished overall with gold leaf. The foot consists of a short stem and a solid, annular knop, followed by a tall, trumpet-shaped base with pronounced mold-blown ribs and a foot-ring that is folded under. A band of gold leaf below the rim is scratch-engraved with a stylized wreath that is framed on either side by three engraved lines. Four vertical ropelike bands divide the wreath into equal parts. Above the wreath, near the rim, is a row of dots in white enamel. The wreath is inscribed "ME DISPREZIA," possibly a later addition. The wall of the vessel below the wreath is densely decorated with entwined bands in white and blue enamel, which are inscribed with two verses of a love poem in block capitals. These letters are in black enamel on the white bands, and in gold with black outlines on the blue bands. Small, stylized florets with central dots in yellow, red, and green enamel decorate the spaces reserved by the bands. The stem, knop, and foot are cold-painted in gold with a scale pattern. The inscription on the white bands is:

NON DUBITAR SORELLA MAI PODISE
   FAR TORTO ALO TUO
VOLTO TANTO ADORNO. SI NEL MIO
   COR MILE COR TELI AVESE
E TURMENTADO FOSE NOTE E ZORNO
   MIA VITA E FACULTA
TUTA PER DE SE EL FOCO DEL INFFRNO
   AVESE A TORNO,

NO, NON MUTERIA PERRO MIA OPINIONE
   E TESER TE
SEMPRE SERVO E TUO PREXONE
   AMORVOL FEDE.

On the blue bands, the inscription reads:

AMOR ME ACEXO DE TUA GRAN BELEZA
   FORTUNA OGNOR DA TE ME
TIEN LUNTANO ALNASER EL ZIEL ME
   PRIVO
DE RICHEZE NATURA BRUTO MACRIATO
   EST(E)R
NO GIO CHIO AMO MORTE E QUELA
   PER FAR CH'OGNI
DE SEGNO MIO SIA VANO CHUSI ANZU-
   RATO DESTENTARME
FORTE AMOR NATURA EL CIEL FORTUNA
   O MORTE.

COMMENT: The goblet, which probably had a matching cover, is listed in a 1725 inventory of the counts Künigl, and it was donated to the Tiroler Landesmuseum Ferdinandeum by Count Leopold Künigl in 1825. It was attributed by Egg (1962, p. 16, and pl. II, fig. 3) to about 1500. The rounded bowl of the goblet, which is placed atop a rather Gothic-style mold-blown foot, would point to a slightly later date, about 1500–1525. The unidentified verses appear to derive from two Renaissance poems, the second of which may indicate a Spanish provenance, considering such non-Venetian words as "anzurato" and "destentarme." Derivations of the formulaic inscription "AMOR VOL FEDE" (Love requires faith), found in the first poem, frequent-

ly appear on Renaissance objects that are associated with weddings. A green glass wedding goblet in The British Museum is enameled with the inscription "AMOR VOL FEE" (Tait 1991, p. 36, no. 22). A 15th-century silver ring from Italy is inscribed "AMOR VOL FE" (*Franks Collection* 1912, pp. 157–158, no. 986).

The goblet's expertly executed decoration was certainly the work of a Venetian master. As early as the 15th century, enameled figural glasses were considerably more expensive than those that were decorated with simple gilding. A dispute between glassmakers in 1474 noted that gilded beakers cost 4 1/2 scudi, while one decorated with two figures was priced at nine scudi. Glasses with complex narrative scenes could cost as much as 40 soldi (McCray 1999, p. 103). This goblet, with its elaborately painted inscription, was probably a special commission by a patron with literary aspirations.

BIBLIOGRAPHY: Egg 1962, p. 16, and pl. II, fig. 3; *Lehman Collection* 1993, p. 31, fig. 7.1.

## 2

### Covered Beaker

*OH. 27.5 cm, (beaker) 19 cm,*
*(cover) 10 cm; D. (rim) 12.3 cm*

POSSIBLY VENICE, ABOUT 1540–1545.
THE CORNING MUSEUM OF GLASS,
CORNING, NEW YORK (50.3.1).
FORMERLY IN THE COLLECTIONS OF
MAX ROSENHEIM, LONDON; MENSING,
AMSTERDAM; A. VECHT, AMSTERDAM;
HENRY BROWN, TRING, ENGLAND; AND
STEUBEN GLASS INC., CORNING, NEW
YORK.

COLORLESS. BLOWN, APPLIED, DIAMOND-
POINT ENGRAVED.

The beaker has a truncated conical
body. Its original applied base is now
missing, and the object is mounted in
a gadrooned silver replacement foot.
The mount is held in position by acan-
thus lappets. The foot shows a horizontal surface, and it must have been a
tacked-on low pedestal. A large, jagged
cavity remains in the base where the
pontil was removed. The low, domed
cover has a projecting flange. The top
is pulled out in an ogee, and the finial
consists of a depressed knop followed
by two mereses and a ball knop on top.
   Both the beaker and the cover have
many diamond-point engraved inscriptions. The cover is inscribed as follows,
from top to bottom:

15M97 / Wan got will / Hieronimus Fürner
1586 / Christof Pruckner
Michael Curtius / 1706
15 ♥ 82; A M H / Werner(?) Coburg R. /
   Abraham Schollius / Gregorius Günther
15 V 91 / BMG
H. Deam [or Beam]
GMAH / [. . .] / 15 H 97 / Gott halft mir /
   allain aus nott [God alone relieved me
   from misery]
Georg [. . .] / Hans Phleger, Paull Garben-
   prüger
[. . .] 1651, Theodorus Källius(?) Martbach-
   ensis Wurtembergius
Indies Meliosa A 1861
Hannes Krablaus Aichensis Bonestangiam /
   indignus in sui memoriam hac subscripsit
   amici / tia ergo S.T.P M. MDLXXXVI

[1586]. Memento [Hannes Krablaus
   Aichensis of the beanstalk, the unworthy,
   signed this in the memory of friendship]
15 BGBM 88 / Lanrat Krafft / Ratherr
   Möller / 15 * 90 / 15 M 91
GJAAO. / Wolf Gunninger / [. . .]
Johann D[. . .] / 1665 / Exponentia veritus /
   Eucharius Kufig(?) / 1591 / 23 Jhary /
   Wan Gott hilff / 16[. . .] 17
15 M 78 / T W / Isaac Scholl / Hannes
   Hamel / Die Zeit [. . .] 1617 / Sebastian
   Kramerhueber / Joh. [. . .] Schulz(?)

On the edge of the rim is inscribed
"F. Meinradus Helmberger [. . .] / Con
DVCentIam von 10 February / J. Virgily
[. . .]."

The beaker shows the following inscriptions, in no particular order:

MDLXXXI [1581?] / Anfangs bedenckss Endt
   [Consider the end at the beginning] /
   [. . .] / 15 L 78 / DDS / Han. Brabner /
   1576 / kain Glücke [No luck] [. . .] / Gert
   Felshofer / 1575 / DCF / B. Ernpreysser /
   1575 / Georg Schröter / Franz G[. . .] /
   15 a 74 / VSW / Wilh. Köneboder [. . .] /
   1673 / 15 m 76 / Got hat es geben [God
   has given] / Georg Setzenstollen / Tileman Mair Chirurg / ord. / 74 / EMDM /
   Jorg(?) Bieng / 1575 / EPV / W. [. . .] /
   1587 [. . .] / T1576 / [. . .] / 15 B 78 /
   JBG / [. . .] / 15 M 79 / Fridericus Meltelius / Imperialis Notarius / Juris P. Candi-
   datus / PJJZ / Hanns Adamas Lobner /
   Jörg Spiller /1580
Wolff Christoph Liedermair / [. . .] zu Pern-
   haim / 1657 / 15M74 / ich [. . .] Gott /
   [. . .] / 15 S 76 / Vgi. Gattermair / 1576 /
   DSSB / Franz Baumgarten / B Heftner /
   1578 / [. . .] / ABMH / Mi. Pruggner /
   1579 / [. . .]
1574 / Verzig macht gefarlighkait [Forty(?)
   is dangerous] / 15*75 / [. . .] Franz Kierb-
   man / 1576 / WSB / Hanns Handl /
   1576 / NBM / 1576 / [. . .] / 1578 / Jacob
   [. . .] / 1579 / BLM / Franz [. . .] / Sebastian Winckler / 1579 / [. . .] / 1581 / [. . .]
15 A 80 / BJA / [. . .] / 15 M 75 / Primius
   Wangler(?) / 15M 75 / Eri. Perglman /
   15 A 76 / got [. . .] / Jo. Rothaus / 1576 /
   WSV / Jacob Kruger / 1579 / Georg
   Ege[. . .]hofer / 1579 / WLB / B Egger /
   1580 / [. . .] / 1612 / [. . .]
1574 / DBM / Wolff Elner / 15 A 75 / D.
   herz begnad / andre fur [. . .] / 15 R75 /
   JAN / Jo. Turgg / 15 D 76 / Ut deo placet
   [As God wishes] / Von Ebenperger / 1578

1574 / Gott gibt gnad [God has mercy] /
   Landfrid Gobenkirch / [. . .] / 15 ∕♥75 /
   [. . .] / [. . .] / 15 R 76 / NAOPD / 1578 /
   [. . .] / Maur.? Schwarz / 1578 / DMT /
   Wilh. Krugler / Georg Han 1630 / 1579.
   Rudolph Opp / 1580 / H Gartman

COMMENT: The beaker has a fitted
case of turned fruitwood, which is dated 1545 in black ink on the outside
wall. The inscriptions date mainly to
the 1570s and 1600s. On the cover,
the earliest inscription appears to be
dated 1578, and the latest—the only
18th-century date—is 1706. In addition, there is one 19th-century signature, "Indies Meliosa A[nno] 1861."
The beaker may have been that of a
southern German confraternity, as
the place names Martbach (Marbach
on the Neckar?) in Württemberg and
Aichen (Bavaria) seem to indicate. The
professions added by some of the in-
scribers designate well-educated burghers. The surgeon Tileman Mair, the
district magistrate Krafft, the town
councilor Möller, and the imperial no-
tary and candidate of law Fridericus
Meltelius all proudly recorded their
professions.
   Long- and shortwave fluorescence
shows that both the beaker and the
cover glow homogeneously a very dull
yellow color. It can be concluded that
the two pieces were manufactured con-
temporaneously. The stamped silversmith's mark atop the flat lip of the foot
is a "man in the moon" facing right, followed by the letter "A," and the whole
is framed in a double lozenge (Rosenberg 1928, p. 435). This stamp, applied
in Vienna in 1806 or 1807, was used on
older silverware of medium size, which
was taxable .

BIBLIOGRAPHY: *Exhibition of Early
German Art* 1906, p. 173, no. 24, pl.
LXII; *Rosenheim Collection* 1923, lot
322; *European Glass* 1938, lot 135, ill.
opp. p. 45; Charleston 1980, pp. 90–
91, no. 37; Charleston 1990, pp. 90–91,
no. 37.

# 3

## Stangenglas

*H. 21.7 cm, D. (rim) 7.4 cm, (foot) 10.6 cm*

PROBABLY TYROL, HALL, ABOUT 1570–1599. THE CORNING MUSEUM OF GLASS, CORNING, NEW YORK (72.3.35, GIFT OF JEROME STRAUSS). FORMERLY IN THE STRAUSS COLLECTION (S1921).

COLORLESS WITH GRAYISH GREEN TINGE. BLOWN, DIAMOND-POINT ENGRAVED.

This cylindrical vessel has a straight-sided bowl with a fire-polished rim and an applied trumpet-shaped foot with a rim that is folded under. In the center of the slightly convex base is a small circular pontil mark. The wall is diamond-point engraved with a stylized border of alternating palmettes and foliage, followed by two cordlike bands framed by double lines. The central part of the body is divided vertically into two oval fields framed by ornamental panels. These panels consist of a heart-shaped symmetrical pattern of foliate scrolls forming central palmettes. Below this section are two more cordlike bands and a foliate border extending into stylized bell-shaped flowers.

The glass has many pin-size bubbles and small sand inclusions. It is likely that the plain bands and panels were originally decorated with paint, which has since been rubbed off. A few tiny flakes of gold leaf remain in the scratched lines.

COMMENT: The floral border near the rim is similar to that on a *Stangenglas* in the Museum für Angewandte Kunst, Vienna (GL 2199) (Egg 1962, p. 84, no. 1, and pl. XXVIII, fig. 63), and a *Stangenhumpen* in the Tiroler Landesmuseum Ferdinandeum, Innsbruck (GL 283) (*ibid.*, pp. 84–85, no. 6, and pl. XXVIII, fig. 65). The heart-shaped panel decoration is similar to that on a goblet with a lion-mask stem in the Kunstsammlungen der Veste Coburg (HA 29) (Theuerkauff-Liederwald 1994, pp. 247–248, no. 224, color pl. p. 305) and a tall *Stangenglas* with a metal-mounted foot, added later, which is dated January 1, 1604 (*Strasser Collection* 2002, p. 30, no. 5). Here, the scrolls are divided vertically by a reserved narrow field framed by double lines. This object also has stylistic similarities with the guild glass donated by the Zurich goldsmith Christoph Oeri (see p. 28 and p. 308, n. 6).

## 4

*Goblet* (Kelchglas)

*H. 17.1 cm, D. 10.6 cm*

PROBABLY TYROL, HALL, ABOUT 1540–1569. THE CORNING MUSEUM OF GLASS, CORNING, NEW YORK (56.3.193).

COLORLESS WITH GRAYISH TINGE. BLOWN, MOLD-BLOWN, GILDED.

This elegant goblet has a flaring, trumpet-shaped bowl that is joined by a merese to a hollow, depressed spherical knop with a mold-blown design of raised lozenges within raised hexagonal compartments. The depressions of the lozenges show traces of applied gold leaf that fractured when the parison was inflated in the mold. The knop is connected by a second merese to a tall pedestal foot of concave profile with a rim that is folded under. There is a roughly triangular pontil mark beneath the apex of the foot.

The glass has minute bubbles and inclusions.

COMMENT: This type of goblet was apparently produced in great quantities during the 16th century (Theuerkauff-Liederwald 1994, pp. 207–208). The glasses frequently show traces of gilding on the mold-blown knop, and they come in a variety of sizes, ranging from about 17 to 35 centimeters. This is the smallest of these goblets. The size of the foot, in proportion to the bowl and knop, can also vary considerably. Some of these goblets have bowls with additional optic-molded and pattern-molded decoration. Such vessels have been tentatively attributed to Venice (for an example in Frankfurt, see Bauer 1980, p. 62, no. 112), France, Austria, the Southern Netherlands, and other centers that produced glass in Venetian style. Gasparetto suggested glasshouses in France, such as Saint-Germain-en-Laye and Poitou, as the possible makers of a goblet in the Victoria and Albert Museum,

London (Gasparetto 1958, no. 109). He thus confirmed the assessment of Honey (1946, p. 68, fig. 35A), who, in turn, had revised Buckley's first attribution to Venice (Buckley, W. 1939, p. 251, no. 174, and pl. 39), but he dated it to the 17th century. In discussing a parallel in the Musée des Arts Décoratifs in Paris, Bellanger (1988, p. 469) added this goblet to the corpus of 16th-century French glasses. A provenance in the Southern Netherlands was preferred by Chambon for a glass in the Musée Curtius, Liège (Chambon 1955, p. 315, nos. 44 and 45, and pl. XIV). Archeological finds from a house near Saint Vitus Cathedral in Prague may indicate a Bohemian provenance for these objects (Hetteš 1963, pp. 43–44).

Examples for which an Austrian origin was proposed are a medium-size *Trichterpokal* (funnel-shaped goblet) in the Museum für Angewandte Kunst, Vienna (GL 659/1869, H. 21 cm) because it comes from the monastery of Saint Peter in Salzburg (Egg 1962, p. 41, no. 5, and pl. VIII, fig. 15), and a goblet at the *Stubengesellschaft* in Hall (*ibid.*, p. 40, no. 1, and pl. VI, fig. 12), a society of local dignitaries, of which Sebastian Höchstetter was a member (*ibid.*, p. 38). These goblets may have been two of the *Kelchgläser* made by the glasshouse that he owned (Heimer 1959, p. 61). All of these vessels probably once had a cover, like the glass in the Tiroler Landesmuseum Ferdinandeum, Innsbruck (Egg 1962, p. 42, no. 13, and pl. X, fig. 20). Theuerkauff-Liederwald (1994, pp. 207–208, no. 185) argued for the Hall glasshouse as a probable provenance for the tall goblet in the Kunstsammlungen der Veste Coburg (HA 4, H. 27.3 cm), since its closest parallels in proportion, glass quality, and mold pattern are the two vessels that originated in Tyrol. Furthermore, a very large, fragmented goblet (H. 35 cm) with a ribbed bowl that was diamond-point engraved in the 17th century with the names and dates of the counts Fuchs von Fuchsenstein of southern Tyrol is also attributed to Hall

(*Strasser Collection* 2002, pp. 30–32, no. 6).

For the small and well-preserved Corning goblet, Perrot proposed a French provenance and suggested a date in the early 16th century (Perrot 1958, pp. 46–47, no. 26). The knop of this vessel is proportionally large and well molded in comparison with that of the object discussed by Theuerkauff-Liederwald, but the glass has the numerous tiny bubbles, occasional sand impurities, and distinct grayish tinge that are associated with products from Hall. In terms of glass quality, the molding of the knop, and proportion, it compares best with a slightly taller glass in the Lehman Collection at The Metropolitan Museum of Art, New York (1975.1.1157, H. 23.9 cm), which is believed to have originated at the Stift Heiligenkreuz in Vienna (*Lehman Collection* 1993, pp.127–128, no. 45). An unpublished glass that is now on the London art market is nearly identical in size and quality to the Corning goblet.

BIBLIOGRAPHY: Perrot 1958, pp. 46–47, no. 26; *CMG Guide* 1974, p. 39, no. 41; *Islam and the Medieval West* [1975], no. G 28.

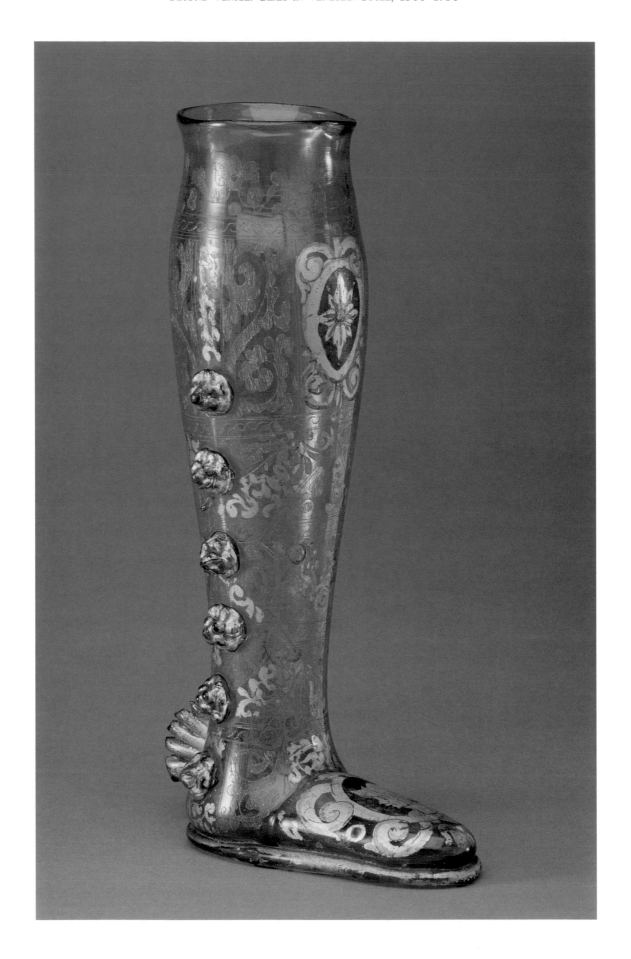

## 5

*Laced Glass Boot* alla
romana antiqua

*H. 19.6 cm*

TYROL, INNSBRUCK, COURT GLASSHOUSE,
1570–1591. KUNSTHISTORISCHES MUSEUM,
VIENNA (KK 3386). FORMERLY IN THE
COLLECTIONS OF ARCHDUKE FERDINAND,
AMBRAS CASTLE.

COLORLESS. BLOWN, APPLIED, DIAMOND-
POINT ENGRAVED, COLD-PAINTED, GILDED.

The glass boot consists of a tall cylindrical body that increases in diameter to the slightly splayed, uneven, and fire-polished rim. The tip of the boot was applied to one side of the base. A thick applied trail around the base represents the sole, and an applied blob of glass, flattened and sheared vertically into five ridges, represents the spur on the boot's heel. Six high-relief raspberry prunts were applied vertically along the right side of the boot. The calf of the boot is divided vertically into five zones that are densely decorated with diamond-point engraving. Each zone is separated by horizontal lines framing a stylized cord. The heel section is divided, with double vertical lines, into rectangular fields that are decorated with floral scrolls. A crisscross pattern of stylized straps with scroll decoration dominates the next three zones. The fifth zone is divided into vertical fields embellished with large S-shaped scrolls.

Near the rim is a wide band of stylized floral decoration. The glass is also painted with floral ornaments and emblems in red and green lacquer, and in gold. The tip of the boot is decorated with a gilded portrait medallion in profile, facing left, framed by large scrolls. It depicts a warrior wearing a burgonet *alla romana antiqua* (in ancient Roman style), with an upturned neck plate, visor, and plume. The front panel of the fifth zone is decorated with an oval gilded medallion displaying a gold starburst on a green-lacquered field. The crisscrossed straps are ornamented in gold with stylized floral scrolls. Gold paint also enhances the sole, the prunts, and the spur of the boot.

COMMENT: The boot from Ambras Castle is a typical example of such vessels, which were part of the repertoire of skilled late 16th-century Venetian glassmakers (Theuerkauff-Liederwald 1994, pp. 192–193, no. 174). Most of the extant vessels are boots for the right foot. These tall glasses were always made from two gathers, one for the blowing of the calf of the boot,

and the other for forming the toe. The second gather, which was applied to a small area near the base, melted the wall of the vessel and allowed the glassmaker to inflate and shape the tip of the boot. Numerous examples with filigree decoration, which show inflated stripes encased in colorless glass, attest to this technique.

**5** does not have the thin "ankle strap" that was commonly applied to such vessels, which appear to resemble riding boots. Instead, the laced straps on the vessel recall the footwear of ancient Roman soldiers. Archduke Ferdinand, a passionate collector of armor, favored parade armor made *alla romana antiqua*, a term that was first used in Filippo Orsoni's 1554 album of armor designs (Pyhrr and Godoy 1999, pp. 105–110, no. 15). An elaborate 16th-century parade helmet of the kind worn by the warrior illustrated on the boot, made in Milan, was formerly in the collections at Ambras Castle (*ibid.*, pp. 204–209, no. 39). This boot, which was probably made to order by the Venetian glassmakers working in the court glasshouse, reflects the specific interests of the archduke. It is the earliest datable Renaissance vessel of its kind (Theuerkauff-Liederwald 1994, p. 193).

BIBLIOGRAPHY: Schlosser 1951, p. 27, fig. 16; Egg 1962, p. 65, no. 45, and pl. XXIV, fig. 53.

# 6

## Vasenpokal

*OH. 31.9 cm, D. (base) 8.5 cm, (rim) 10.4 cm*

TYROL, PROBABLY INNSBRUCK, COURT GLASSHOUSE, ABOUT 1570–1591. THE CORNING MUSEUM OF GLASS, CORNING, NEW YORK (68.3.21).

COLORLESS WITH GRAYISH TINGE. BLOWN, APPLIED, DIAMOND-POINT ENGRAVED, GILDED.

The egg-shaped body of this waisted vessel merges into a concave neck with a flaring, fire-polished rim. The composite stem consists of a small blob of glass that connects the body to a merese and a knop, followed by a hollow lion-mask stem and another thin merese, which attaches the vessel to the shallow foot with an upfolded footring. The rounded, bell-shaped lid has a hollow, folded lip, the vertical edge of which tapers slightly to accommodate the curve of the vessel's rim. On the rounded shoulder of the lid is an applied, milled trail, and three raspberry prunts decorate the domed top of the lid. The tall finial consists of a thin merese, a short stem, a molded and ribbed knop, another merese, and a cone-shaped knop ending in a ball.

The vessel is covered with diamond-point engraving. A band of hatched drops encircles the top of the foot. The lower part of the body is decorated with a broad band that is divided vertically into four ornamental fields. These fields are filled with a heart-shaped symmetrical pattern consisting of foliate scrolls that form central palmettes. Narrow vertical bands with short horizontal hatchings separate the fields, which are framed above and below by a cordlike horizontal border and a row of vertical ovals that is repeated above the milled trail. The neck is ornamented with another horizontal band consisting of a stylized cord, followed by a foliate band that extends alternately into palmettes and bell-shaped blossoms. The shoulder of the lid is engraved with concentric bands of elongated, hatched ovals.

COMMENT: A similarly shaped and engraved vessel, which also has traces of cold painting, is in the Kunstsammlungen der Veste Coburg (HA 170) (Egg 1962, p. 60, no. 14, and pl. XVII, fig. 35; Theuerkauff-Liederwald 1994, pp. 240–243). This object had two scroll handles, each of which was applied, with a scalloped blob surmounted by a raspberry prunt, to the shoulder of the vessel. One of the handles, as well as an associated lid, is missing. An example from Ambras Castle, now in the Kunsthistorisches Museum, Vienna (KK 3370), has additional green, red, and gold painted decoration between the diamond-point engraved bands and in the (slightly larger) reserved fields on the body (Egg 1962, pp. 58–59, no. 7, and pl. XIV, fig. 27). A goblet in the Wallace Collection, London (III E 179) also has scroll handles, but its stem includes a knop (*ibid.*, p. 59, no. 11, and pl. XVI, fig. 33). It is similar to an example in the Museo Vetrario, Venice (*ibid.*, p. 59, no. 9, and pl. XV, fig. 30).

This type of object resembles the so-called *Birngläser mit Deckeln* (pear-shaped glasses with covers), which were cited in an order of 1558 (Egg 1962, p. 37). The mold of the lion-mask stem is similar to those found in Salzburg (Wintersteiger 1991, pp. 382–383, no. 497). The lion-mask stem, a generic Venetian glassmaking device, may have found special favor at the Hapsburg court because Ferdinand II, as governor of Bohemia, bore its heraldic symbol, the lion. The association of the lion with Hercules and his mythical qualities of strength and invincibility becomes evident in an engraved portrait of the archduke by Terzio, published in 1569, which depicts him with the lion-mask helmet and the knotty club (Pyhrr and Godoy 1999, p. 206).

BIBLIOGRAPHY: *CMG Guide* 1974, p. 42, no. 45; *Hikari no shouchu* 1992, p. 22, no. 31.

## 7

### Glass Chain with Pendant

*L. 69.0 cm*

POSSIBLY TYROL, INNSBRUCK, ABOUT 1578
OR 1590. KUNSTHISTORISCHES MUSEUM,
VIENNA (KK 3040). FORMERLY IN THE
COLLECTIONS OF ARCHDUKE FERDINAND,
AMBRAS CASTLE.

COLORLESS. LAMPWORKED, GOLD-PAINTED.

This chain was assembled from a
large number of nearly identical and
slightly oval loops of colorless glass that
were painted in gold. Each link consists
of a thin, twisted rod that was repeatedly wrapped around a mandrel and
fused to form a solid ring. These "jump
rings" were then resoftened and cut
open, linked together, and fused shut
again. The necklace was constructed of
two pairs of chains that were doubled
up to form, on either side, four strands
of equal length that are linked together
at the front. A lampworked pendant
medallion was attached, with colorless
glass links, to the center of the chain.
It was built up with fused, concentric
circles of twisted glass rods. An imitation glass pearl is set into the center of
the medallion, which is quartered by
four undulating ribbed glass ribbons
that extend from the pearl. The edge
of the medallion is embellished with a
wavy trail of opaque white glass.

COMMENT: The chain imitates heavy
ornamental chains made of gold wire,
which were popular in the 16th century.
These precious metal chains were not
only valuable because of their gold content, but they were also socially significant gifts. In 1518, a man who was to be
knighted in Venice was ceremoniously
awarded a gold chain and spurs as symbols of his new position (Labalme and
White 1999, p. 68). Contemporaneous
portraits, such as Lucas Cranach's portrait of Sybille of Cleves, in the Schlossmuseum, Weimar, depict ladies of the
German court wearing such heavy
chains around the neck and shoulders.

In replicating precious gold chains,
the lampworker closely followed the
jeweler's technique of forming and assembling jewelry from gold wire, using
glass rods to provide the appearance of
a metal original. Glass pearls, such as
the one mounted in the center of the
medallion in 7, were part of the 16th-

century lampworker's standard repertoire for the production of *gioie false*
(false jewels), which were used in large
quantities to embellish elegant clothing.
The wardrobe accounts of England's
Elizabeth I from 1566 note that 520
*faux* pearls were purchased for the
queen at one penny apiece to trim
partlets and ruffs (*Princely Magnificence*
1980, p. 66, no. 57).

Aside from the lampworked jewelry
from Ambras Castle, glass chains securely datable to the 16th and early 17th
centuries are rare. A chain consisting of
12 loops, which may have been made
in the Netherlands about 1550–1650,
was found at Kasteel van Ijsselmonde
(Rotterdam) (Chambon 1961, p. 43, fig.
7.32; Henkes 1974, p. 21; Terlinden and
Crossley 1981, p. 195; Henkes 1994, p.
318, no. 65.8).

## 8

### *Black Scorpion Pendant*

*H. 9.0 cm, W. 2.4 cm*

POSSIBLY TYROL, INNSBRUCK, COURT GLASSHOUSE, ABOUT 1590–1591. KUNSTHISTORISCHES MUSEUM, VIENNA (KK 2788). FORMERLY IN THE COLLECTIONS OF ARCHDUKE FERDINAND, AMBRAS CASTLE.

OPAQUE BLACK. LAMPWORKED.

The scorpion has a solid, flat, ovoid body, with a triangular indentation on one side that indicates the head. At the opposite end, the body is drawn out into a tail that curves upward and terminates in a globular stinger with two short points. It has eight applied, segmented legs that point forward, as well as a pair of pincers and claws.

COMMENT: The scorpion may have been made at the court glasshouse by one of the Italian lampworkers recruited by Archduke Ferdinand in 1578 and 1590. Lampworked scorpions were among the popular novelty items that were curiosities and gifts to wealthy patrons in the 16th and 17th centuries (see p. 54). The scorpion is best known as an astrological symbol, but during the Renaissance, it was imbued with complex symbolic meanings that can be elucidated only by their context At Ambras Castle, the scorpion appears as part of the zodiac on the ceiling of the dining room. Here, the archduke was following his father, Ferdinand I, who commissioned the zodiac to be

painted on the ceiling of the summer palace in Prague (Simons 1997, p. 88, n. 38).

The scorpion appears on a late 16th-century Venetian covered glass dish in the Lehman Collection at The Metropolitan Museum of Art (1975.1.1214a, b; *Lehman Collection* 1993, pp. 92–93, no. 28). Two opposing scorpions are diamond-point engraved on the cover. The decoration's meaning is ambiguous. The double image of the scorpion may refer to its symbolic representation of destruction and death, as well as the triumph of life over death (Hall 1979, p. 301). In that respect, the scorpion as a table ornament can assume similar negative associations as the crayfish, which often appears in depictions of the Last Supper (Rigaux 1990, p. 224).

On a majolica plate (Victoria and Albert Museum, London, C.2127-1910) of about 1515 from Cafaggiolo, the well-known Renaissance pottery center near Florence, the scorpion assumes another meaning.[22] This object is decorated with a woman holding a shield with an emblematic scorpion that

8A

*Portrait of Elisabetta Gonzaga of Mantua, attributed to Raffaello Sanzio (Raphael) or Francesco Bonsignori, about 1500–1502. Wood, H. 52.9 cm, W. 37.4 cm. Galleria degli Uffizi, Florence (1890), no. 1441.*

probably represents the allegorical figure of Philosophy dressed as Artemis. In Greek mythology, Apollo arranged for the scorpion to attack Orion so that he would not pursue Apollo's sister, Artemis, the virgin huntress. Orion attacked the scorpion, but he was unable to kill it. Artemis was later tricked into shooting an arrow at Orion, and she killed him. She then placed him in the sky as a constellation, eternally pursued by the scorpion (Graves 1960, p. 152).

It is in a similar sense that a rare example of a scorpion worn as jewelry (of unidentifiable material) has to be seen. In a portrait that is identified on the reverse of the panel as Elisabetta Gonzaga of Mantua (1472–1526), datable to about 1500–1502, and attributed to both Raphael and Francesco Bonsignori (Meyer zu Capellen 2001, p. 314, X-13), the duchess of Urbino wears a small scorpion that is attached to a thin band at the center of her forehead (**8a**). Elisabetta was considered to be a virtuous woman of high moral principles who was also highly cultured and versed in Humanist thought. This scorpion ornament probably referred to her intellectual prowess and unfaltering morals. In Renaissance art, the scorpion frequently appears as an attribute of the personified Logic (Dialectic), one of the liberal arts. For example, in Sandro Botticelli's mural *Lorenzo Tornabuoni and the Liberal Arts Personified*, dated 1486, formerly at the Villa Lemmi and now in the Musée du Louvre, Logic holds a black scorpion in her left hand (Bulard 1935, pl. X).

The sculptural lampworked scorpion from Ambras Castle may well have retained some of the symbolic meanings of the 15th century, while it attracted attention as an artful creation that imitated nature in glass.

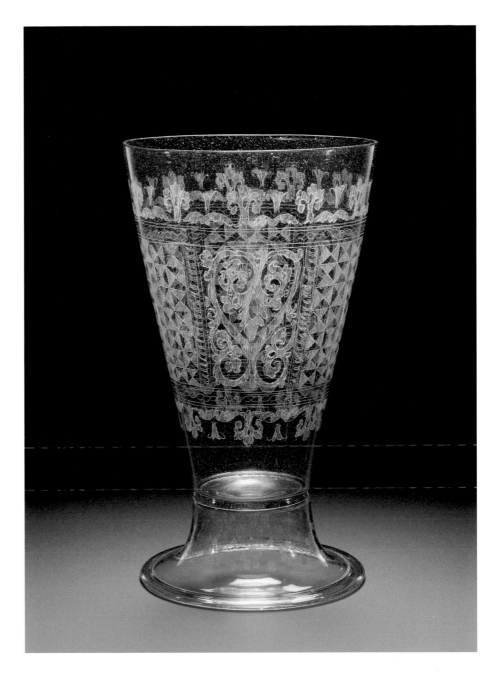

*9*

*Footed Beaker*

H. 24.2 cm

PROBABLY TYROL, HALL, ABOUT 1570–
1590. THE CORNING MUSEUM OF
GLASS, CORNING, NEW YORK (79.3.329,
BEQUEST OF JEROME STRAUSS). FORMERLY
IN THE COLLECTIONS OF MR. STRAUSS
(S2307) AND WALTER F. SMITH (773).

COLORLESS WITH GRAYISH TINGE. BLOWN,
DIAMOND-POINT ENGRAVED.

The straight-sided conical bowl of
this vessel is engraved with a border
of formal foliage at the top and bottom.
The zone between these borders is divided into six panels. Three fields of
crosshatched diamonds alternate with
three fields decorated with formal foliate scrolls. The trumpet-shaped foot,
which has a folded rim, is engraved
with a stylized floral band. The foot has
a rough pontil mark beneath the base,
and its upper side is inscribed "13" in
white paint.

COMMENT: The two-dimensional
rendering of the raised diamonds on
this beaker may have been inspired by
mold-blown Venetian vessels showing
this distinct pattern in relief. An
umbo vase in The J. Paul Getty Museum, Los
Angeles, is decorated in this fashion
(Hess and Husband 1997, p. 138, no.
35). Similar patterns were also painted
on buildings in Tyrol, including the
lower facades of Ambras Castle. The
vessel shape is represented by examples
from the castle collection, such as a covered *Humpen* with cold-painted floral
decoration (Egg 1962, p. 63, no. 30,
and pl. XX, fig. 45) and a similar vessel with the cold-painted coat of arms
of Ferdinand and Philippine Welser
(Kunsthistorisches Museum, Vienna,
KK 3385).

BIBLIOGRAPHY: *Heye Collection* 1957,
lot 766.

## 10

### Armorial Table Setting of the Fugger Family

*Bowl: H. 12 cm, D. 22 cm; plate: D. 21.5 cm; ewer: H. 27 cm*

TYROL, PROBABLY HALL OR INNSBRUCK, ABOUT 1570–1580. FUGGER MUSEUM, BABENHAUSEN, GERMANY (283-1961, 291-1961).

COLORLESS WITH GREENISH GRAY TINGE. BLOWN, APPLIED, GILDED, ENAMELED.

The bowl is shallow, with an up-turned wall and a fire-polished rim. It was applied to a hollow, flattened knop on a flared pedestal foot with an up-folded rim. The center of the bowl is enameled with a large coat of arms of the Fugger family. The shield displaying the arms is framed on the left by leafy decoration in blue and gold enamel, which is mirrored on the right in white and black. Wavy bands in blue and black undulate around each side. The shield is outlined in green and red enamel. It displays, on the field, the quartered Fugger coat of arms, which

is surmounted by a pair of helmets with panaches, shown full-face. Fields I and IV are partitioned vertically into blue and white fields, with a fleur-de-lis in transposed colors in each field, framed by a gold and pale blue line respectively. Field II has a white field with a crowned black maiden with long golden hair, walking left, holding a bishop's miter in her right hand, and wearing a long, flowing coat edged with ermine. Field III displays three white hunting horns pointing right, *en suite* vertically on a red field. The helmet dexter is displayed on a blue mantle and crowned

by a pair of buffalo horns and a partitioned blue and white fleur-de-lis. The helmet sinister is shown against a black mantle and surmounted by a bust of the black female maiden wearing a white and gold bishop's miter.

The plate has a shallow center and a slightly upturned rim with an edge that is folded under. A thick circular trail underneath the base serves as a foot-ring. The rim is decorated near the edge with a band of gold leaf that is scratch-engraved with two rows of scales and ornamented with blue enameled dots; it is framed by a row of small opaque

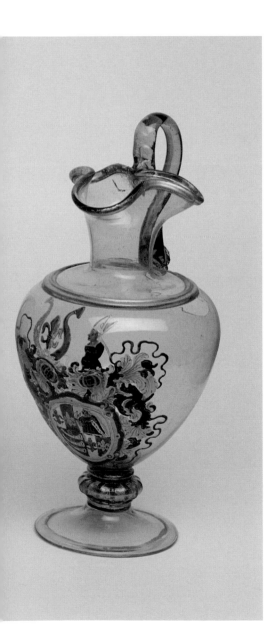

white dots. The plate is emblazoned in the center with the same Fugger arms.

The ewer has an ovoid body with a short, waisted neck and a flaring trefoil rim with an edge that is folded under. The body was applied to a short stem, consisting of a ribbed, mold-blown knop between two mereses, and a flaring pedestal foot with an upfolded rim. A thick ribbed trail encircles the shoulder of the vessel. The S-shaped handle was applied to the folded edge of the rim, drawn up, and dropped onto the shoulder on top of the applied trail. Gold paint was applied to the knopped stem, the trail, and the rim. The same Fugger family coat of arms that is shown on the other two objects decorates the front of the ewer's body, opposite the handle.

The glass has minute bubbles, and the ewer is fractured where the handle attaches to the body.

COMMENT: The enameled decoration on these three objects is rather crude, and in the case of the plate and others from the same set, it extends beyond the center of the object onto the rim. These objects belong to a large table service, and a number of its pieces have survived in European public collections. The Fugger Museum has the largest group of these objects—four plates, four shallow bowls, and four footed bowls—and they were first mentioned by Rainer Rückert in his discussion of an identical

plate in the collection of the Bayerisches Nationalmuseum, Munich (Rückert 1982, pp. 87–88, no. 149, fig. 39, color pl. VI). He also compiled a comprehensive list of additional plates from the set, which are owned by the Württembergisches Landesmuseum Stuttgart, the Kunstsammlungen der Veste Coburg (Theuerkauff-Liederwald 1994, p. 143, no. 106), and the Museum für Angewandte Kunst, Vienna (Schlosser 1951, pl. 48). Other pieces from the service are in the Victoria and Albert Museum, London (Buckley 1926, p. 51, no. 28, and pl. 28); a bowl is in the Museo Lazaro, Madrid; a plate is in the Musée du Louvre, Paris (OA 1105) (Sauzay 1882, F 142); and another plate was formerly in the Spitzer Collection (*Spitzer Collection* 1891, pp. 93–94, no. 23).

The original owner of this service has not been identified. The coat of arms is rather generic for the Fugger family, and it was used by both the Raymund Fugger and Anton Fugger branches of the family from 1535 on (Theuerkauff-Liederwald 1994, p. 143). Ruckert (1982, pp. 87–88, no. 149, fig. 39, color pl. VI) first attributed the plate in the Bayerisches Nationalmuseum to the glasshouse in Hall or Tyrol on the basis of its physical similarity to a *Stangenglas* in the same collection that is dated 1581 and is believed to have been made in Tyrol (*ibid.*, p. 88, no. 150, and pl. 39, color pl. VI).

## 11

### *Covered Goblet*

### H. 29.1 cm

PROBABLY SAXONY, DATED 1625. THE
CORNING MUSEUM OF GLASS, CORNING,
NEW YORK (79.3.304, GIFT OF THE RUTH
BRYAN STRAUSS MEMORIAL FOUNDATION).
FORMERLY IN THE COLLECTIONS OF JEROME
STRAUSS (S1362); FREDERIC NEUBURG,
LEITMERITZ; AND THE ANHALT FAMILY OF
DESSAU CASTLE, SAXONY.

OLIVE GREEN. BLOWN, DIAMOND-POINT
ENGRAVED.

The tall conical bowl is diamond-
point engraved with a formal scroll
border above a narrow band that is
inscribed "GOT . IST . MEIN . TROST .
1625." Below this is a band divided
into four panels, two with palmettes
and two with formal daisies. The decoration also includes a band above spiral
decoration and a formal scrollwork border. There are disks above and below
the hollow inverted baluster stem. The
thin, spreading foot has a rough pontil
mark. On the underside of the foot are
a painted red crown and "50."

The shallow cover has a trailed rim
and a tapered edge. It is decorated
with three concentric diamond-point
engraved bands. The delicate finial
consists of a ball knop above a thin
baluster, with two swelling knops at

the base. The inside of the cover has a
rough pontil mark in the center.

COMMENT: The Venetian master Ludovico Savonetti, who was related to
the glassworkers Salvatore and Bastian
or Sebastiano Savonetti (see pp. 43
and 45), first worked for Archduke
Ferdinand at the court glasshouse in
Innsbruck. In 1579, he was employed
in Vienna. Later that year, he moved on
to open a Venetian-style glasshouse in
Dessau (Egg 1962, p. 47). The covered
goblet, which may have been made at
the Dessau glasshouse, is made of potash glass.

BIBLIOGRAPHY: *Hikari no shouchu*
1992, p. 24, no. 34.

# Spanish *Façon de Venise* Glass

## Ignasi Doménech

During the 16th and 17th centuries, Muranese glassmaking techniques spread to glassworks on the Iberian Peninsula. Catalonia and Castile were the two principal regions that produced *façon de Venise* glass. In the south, however, a number of glasshouses appropriated some elements from the Muranese tradition to develop their own types of glass while retaining techniques based on their Islamic roots. By the time of the Renaissance, most of southern Spain had been living under Islamic rule for 800 years, and this had resulted in a sophisticated material culture. That culture was directly associated with the glassworks of the eastern Mediterranean, where, in the Middle Ages, the most exquisite glass wares were produced (*Glass of the Sultans* 2001, p. 203).

Catalonia was Spain's foremost interpreter of Muranese glassmaking innovations. Important holdings of Catalan glass from that period have been preserved, and they permit a more comprehensive study than the less numerous surviving wares produced in Castile or Andalusia. In those regions, glass wares were of inferior quality and made for everyday use. In other areas, such as Valencia and Majorca, glass production was limited. At present, we are unable to link specific pieces to particular glassworks. However, the island of Majorca and the ancient kingdom of Valencia formed a political unit with Catalonia, which was governed by the king of Catalonia and Aragon. In other artistic spheres, such as architecture, painting, and sculpture, local expressions were clearly linked by many common elements, and this could well have happened in the art of glassmaking as well.

## CATALAN GLASS

Catalan glass of the 16th and 17th centuries was based on an outstanding tradition of late medi-

*Detail from an oil painting by Juan van der Hamen, 1622 (Fig. 7).*

eval manufacture that continued into the Renaissance. Few examples of the earlier glass have survived (Figs. 1 and 2), but a wide range of glass types used for domestic, liturgical, and pharmaceutical purposes was produced until the 19th century

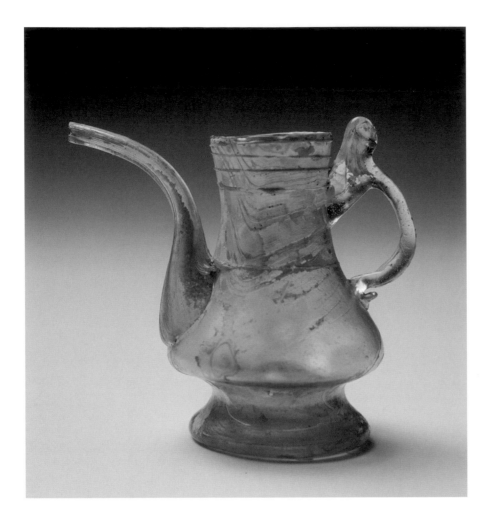

FIG. 1
*Jug, colorless, opaque white, blown, lattimo trails. Spain, Catalonia, mid- to late 15th century. H. 6.5 cm. Museu del Cau Ferrat, Sitges (Barcelona) (31.201).*

(Carreras and Doménech 1994, p. 74). From the 14th century on, vessel types described as *damasquina* (Damascene) or *alexandrina* (Alexandrian) were frequently mentioned in inventories, and they document the widespread presence of Eastern glass in the Catalan region. The king of Catalonia and Aragon had opened a consulate in Alexandria in 1262, in Beirut in 1340, and in Damascus in 1379 to control trade routes that provided the monied classes with luxury objects, including highly prized Islamic enameled glass.

The Eastern glass wares sold by Catalan merchants were in great demand, and they brought high-quality designs and techniques to Catalan glassmaking. References to Damascene glass gradually disappeared in early 15th-century inventories, and they were replaced by *contrafets de Damasc* (reproductions of Damascene glass). This designation clearly referred to local imitations of earlier designs that no longer reached Europe following the appro-

priation of Egypt and Syria by the nomad ruler Timur, who is also known as Timur Lenk and Tamerlane (1336?–1405). The short supply of Eastern glass prompted the cities of Venice and Barcelona to increase their own production of luxury glass. These objects replaced the most popular styles of ornamental glass that had been manufactured since the 13th century. The influx of Muranese designs and techniques had a strong impact on Catalan glassmaking, bringing an end to local medieval traditions (Doménech 1999, p. 490). Catalonia was thus fully aware of the increasing taste for Venetian glass throughout Europe—a taste that fostered the development of a new Renaissance aesthetic.

What was the role of Muranese glassmakers in the development of Catalan glassmaking? These artisans began to arrive in Spain during the second half of the 16th century, but most of the literature on this subject dates from the following century. One study recorded only a single Venetian glass-

FIG. 2
*Goblet, colorless with brownish tinge, blown, applied, enameled, gilded. Probably Spain, Catalonia, early 16th century. H. 18.8 cm, D. 12 cm. The Corning Museum of Glass, Corning, New York (63.3.37).*

maker who was working in Barcelona in 1580, and the locations of other Italians employed in Spain at that time have not yet been identified.[1] Some were probably based in Castile (Rodríguez García 1986, p. 299), having been attracted to the region by the presence of the Spanish court (Frothingham 1956, p. 36). The best-known example is Domenico Barovier, a member of a renowned Muranese glassmaking family, who was recorded in Spain from the time he worked in Palma de Mallorca about 1600 until his death at the Escorial in 1608 (Rodríguez García 1990).

Muranese *cristallo* glasses of harmonious proportions and refined ornamentation were indispensable table wares in Catalonia, and in aristocratic and cultured circles they became collectors' items as well as new symbols of prestige. The skill of Italian glassmakers in creating and decorating colorless glass forms elevated their works to the status of art, and they were as highly regarded as vessels made with costly gemstones and metals. The popularity of this glass led Catalan glassworkers to adapt Venetian designs and techniques. This was not a simple case of imitation, but rather a new interpretation that was rooted in existing local techniques and glassmaking traditions. The Catalan version of the phenomenon known as *façon de Venise* played an important role in European glassmaking at that time. While the Muranese glassworks clearly had a technical and formal influence on Catalan production, the glass produced in Catalonia had unique characteristics of its own.

## The Prestige of Catalan Glass

The extensive list of laudatory reports by chroniclers, travelers, and scholars indicates the fame achieved by local glass wares, which were considered to be on a par with their Venetian counterparts. As early as 1491, Jerónimo Paulo noted, in a letter to Paolo Pamphili, how economically competitive Spanish glassware had become in national and foreign markets, adding that glass from Barcelona adorned the tables of the Roman court. In his *Chorographia* of 1569, the Portuguese geographer Gaspar Barreiros wrote that "excellent glass wares are being made in Barcelona, of almost the same quality as those produced in Venice" (Gudiol Ricart 1936, pp. 40 and 46). But it was Tirso de Molina (1584–1648) who offered what is perhaps the most enthusiastic review of Barcelona glass. In *El bandolero* (The bandit), published in 1635, he stated:

> The Catalan nation competes with all others in Spain in the precision and skill of its crafts, such as its exquisite glass wares that rival those of Venice, although as the latter are foreign, they are held in higher esteem. In spite of this, they are both equal in their subtlety, although their peculiar differences and complexity of form mean that they cannot be confused with Venetian wares. [Production was not restricted to glass vessels, but also included imitations of gemstones.] Proof of this is shown in Barcelona's practice of bestowing its glass jewels upon ladies throughout the land. They adorn hands, throats and necks, garments, oratories, and chambers, and thus the imitation of all things by the inventive industry of glass enhances the value of metals but does not cause us to yearn for their qualities, as the crystalline beauty of glass can make gold seem paltry (Molina 1902, p. 42).

Robert de Nola, who served as cook to King Ferdinand I of Naples (r. 1458–1494), made another interesting observation in his *Libre de coch*. This cookbook, published in Barcelona in 1520, presents a curious comparison between glass and silver (Mestre Robert 1996, p. 55). It says that Catalan gentlemen preferred to drink wine from glass goblets rather than from vessels made of precious metals because glass made with samphire was so pure that it contained no poisons. These accounts embraced the popular legend that glass would break if it came into contact with poisoned drinks. (See also p. 222.)

In his "Historia natural de Cataluña," written about 1600, the Jesuit priest Pere Gil emphasized the quality of Catalan glass wares made with marsh samphire (*Salicornia* sp.) gathered on the coast of Roussillon or with highly prized barilla (*Salsola soda* or *Kali hispanica*) from the coast of Valencia. Gil also described another type of Catalan glass that he said was superior to that made with barilla. It was produced with tartar, the sediment left by wine in barrels, to which a small amount of bloodstone from Genoa was added (Gil unpub., fol. 36).

Catalan glass was widely collected by aristocrats, who displayed it in their private apartments alongside the most refined works in precious metals and gemstones, and assemblages of medieval objects made of rare and exquisite materials. A large number of inventories attests the high esteem in which these fragile objects were held (Doménech 2001). The most detailed of these accounts was the one sent by Ferdinand the Catholic in Barcelona to his wife, Isabel, in Alcalá de Henares (Gudiol Ricart 1936, pp. 142–154). This inventory was compiled by the queen's chambermaid, Violante de Albión, in May 1503. Her extensive descriptions of these objects offer valuable insights into the decorative forms and techniques of Catalan enameled glass. The 273 pieces of glassware described here were added to the collection kept by the queen at the Alcázar de Segovia. Years later, she donated this collection to the Royal Chapel of Granada. The Venetian ambassador to the court of the Holy Roman Emperor Charles V (r. 1516–1556), Andrea Navagero, was able to see these objects in the sacristy of the chapel in 1526, displayed alongside other collectors' pieces. There is no doubt that some of the wares listed in the inventory of 1503 were produced by Catalan glassworks. The purple and blue colors of the glass, as well as the enameled decoration, remind us of similar objects that have survived to the present day. We can thus associate a magnificent vessel from the collection of Barcelona's Museu de les Arts Decoratives with a number of descriptions in the inventory. One reads, "Another jug . . . the neck bears Moorish lettering, and the body is decorated with white-enamel flowers that look like dewdrops." An earlier reference also describes a vessel with "Moorish lettering," which refers to vessels with pseudo-Arabic script (**1**).

Catalan glass wares, like Venetian and Flemish glass, continued to form part of the collections of the Spanish monarchy, as can be seen in the inventories of Charles V and his son Philip II (r. 1556–1598). One inventory, made at the Palacio del Pardo in 1564, informs us that the holdings included more than 100 pieces of Catalan glass and an even longer list of Venetian glasses (Sánchez Cantón 1934, p. 73). The Catalan objects consisted mainly of tazzas, some of which were gilded and engraved, and there were also some pieces of ice glass. These were clearly ornamental works designed exclusively for display, like the collection of Venetian glass that Philip II had set out on walnut shelves in the garden of the Madrid palace, where he went "to delight in looking at the glass and take his leisure" (Porreño 1639, fol. 25). The inventory of this monarch's household goods also states that a jasper table placed under the vault of the palace displayed three dozen pieces of glass from Barcelona. Literary sources make a clear distinction between the glass objects purchased and stored as collectors' items and those acquired as objects for everyday use in the palace. For example, the *Cuentas de la difunta reina Ana* (Accounts of the late Queen Ana), published in 1589, notes this sum, which was paid to the secretary of the Catalan viceroy: "843 reals for a box consisting of 300 glass pieces of different styles that were purchased in Barcelona for the use of their highnesses" (Bassegoda y Amigó 1925, p. 381).

The Hapsburg dynasty's love of Venetian-style glass is demonstrated in a document from Florence. It relates the gift of three boxes of Florentine glass by Giuliano de' Medici Castellina, the Florentine ambassador in Spain, to King Philip III on his deathbed in March 1621. The ambassador reports that his gift pleased the king greatly:

> I sent the king some of the best by way of Doña Leonor [Pimentel], and I have heard from her and others that the king greatly appreciated them and has received no better amusement during his illness. He examined these drinking glasses one by one, tried them out, now and again distributing some of them to his children as he thought best, then he had the rest carefully stored away. I will give away the remaining glasses as seems appropri-ate, since this is truly one of the most curious and esteemed presents that we can bestow (Medici 1621).

The descriptions of glasses in the inventories vary from the 15th to 16th centuries. Initially, many glass objects were prized for the intricacy of their settings and inlaid stones, but in time, luxury glasses were recorded more frequently. These wares were also valued for their sophisticated forms and for the beauty of the materials used. This change reminds us of the technical and aesthetic perfection of Catalan glass, which explains why it was much sought after by collectors and why it was so highly praised in published accounts. The fact that only a small number of glasses from this period have survived makes it difficult to supply irrefutable proof of these qualities, even though they are widely documented in the literature. One of those surviving objects is a goblet from the former Prats Collection, now in the collection of the Instituto Amatller de Arte Hispánico in Barcelona. It is possible to date this goblet because it was found inside the walls of a 15th-century building in Barcelona (Carreras and Doménech 1994, p. 74). A few additional pieces can also be identified as having been produced during the 1400s. They help us to understand the technical and aesthetic development of glassmaking that took place during the following century.

## The Barcelona Guild and Catalan Glassmaking

The Barcelona glassmakers' guild was founded in 1456. Archival sources indicate that this organization had a complex structure and wielded considerable economic power in the city. The first glassmaker in Catalonia was documented in 1189, when the monks of Poblet gave permission to a certain "Guillem, a glassmaker" to pick nettles in order to make glass (the ash from this plant was used as a flux). In 1324, the government *consellers* (ministers) in Barcelona decided to ban the establishment of glassworks within the city, worrying that the large number of workshops and their massive consumption of firewood presented a constant threat of fires (Capmany i de Montpalau 1779–1792, p. 135). Six years later, however, pressure from the glassmakers prompted the king to permit the construction of another glassworks, and in 1345, glassworkers ignored the ban, which the ministers were forced to revoke shortly thereafter. Antonio de Lalaing, chronicler of Archduke Philip the Handsome (1478–1506), noted that glass workshops continued to be built outside the city walls for many years. Reporting on his visit to Barcelona in January 1502, Lalaing praised the glass produced there, and he added that he and the archduke had seen the work of glassmakers outside the city as well (García Mercadal 1952, p. 502).

The glassmakers' guild was set up in association with the esparto (grass) weavers. The glassmakers manufactured bottles, and the weavers made protective coverings for them. Bernardino of Siena (d. 1444, canonized 1450) was the subject of great popular devotion at the time, and the guild adopted him as its patron saint. The guild's leading role in the commercial life of the city is underscored by its relocation from its original chapel, in the church of the monastery of the Friars Minor, to the chapel of the Holy Guardian Angel in Barcelona Cathedral. A key event was the commissioning of Jaume Huguet, the city's most famous painter at the time, to execute the reredos in the chapel. He completed the work in 1480, in collaboration with Rafael Vergós, and it is now in the Barcelona Cathedral Museum. The guild was dissolved in 1595 following disputes between the two trades, and the glassmakers retained the highly prized cathedral chapel. A great deal of literature about this organization survives, and it provides considerable information about the various manufacturing methods used, the training of the master glassworkers, and their often strained relations both internally and with the city's governing bodies. Legal proceedings stemming from the erection of a glasshouse and the vigorous defense of rights to sell and decorate glass offer evidence of a bustling trade with significant turnover.

The Ninou Fair⁷ offers a glimpse of the interaction between the glassmakers and civic authorities in Barcelona. This fair, which was first documented in 1434 but probably originated earlier (Gudiol Ricart 1936, p. 37), afforded the city an opportunity to display its manufacturing capabilities. On New Year's Day, the glassworkers exhibited their wares at the fair, which was visited, with great solemnity, by government officials, accompanied by the sound of trumpets and drums. In 1588, when the glassmakers reduced their displays because they did not wish to incur major losses due to frequent breakages, they were reprimanded by the municipal government, and in 1610, despite the suspension of the guild, the *consellers* vehemently demanded that all glass sellers take part in the fair (*ibid.*, pp. 51–52). In 1646, the glassmakers asked to be exempted from this obligation, thus revealing the disparity between their interests and those of the city. The pomp and ceremony surrounding the opening of the fair, the goods on display there, and the fair's impact on the city's prosperity are described by Tirso de Molina (Molina 1902). Although the setting for this text is the time of James II of Aragon (r. 1291–1327), there can be no doubt that the writer wished to present an account of what had become the most splendid civic spectacle of 16th-century Barcelona.

Glass production in Catalonia was not the exclusive domain of its capital, Barcelona. There are records listing a wide range of glassworks throughout the region, dating from the 14th to 17th centuries. The towns of Palau del Vidre (Roussillon), Vic, Vallromanes, Montcada, Corbera, and Mataró all manufactured glass. The particular importance of Mataró is evidenced by the fact that the cardinal-infante Ferdinand of Austria traveled by sea from Barcelona to Mataró in 1632 to see the magnificent glass wares being made there. Moreover, on October 19 and November 2, 1630, orders from the Madrid court had been received in Mataró for glass items similar to those that had been purchased in the town four years earlier by the duke of Cardona and other courtiers (Giménez i Blasco 2001, p. 184).

*Enameled Glass*

Enameled glassware produced in Catalonia between the 15th and early 17th centuries was dis-

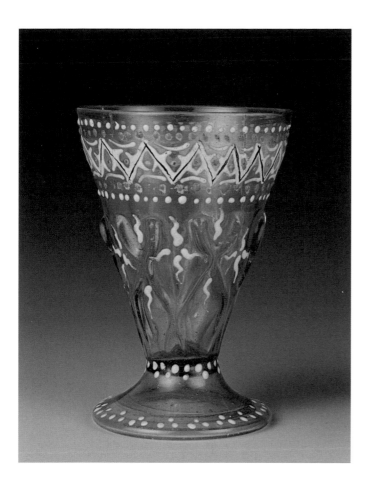

FIG. 3
*Footed beaker, colorless, blown, applied, enameled,*
*gilded. Spain, Catalonia, about 1500. H. 14.5 cm,*
*D. 10 cm. Museu de les Arts Decoratives de Barcelona*
*(23.293, bequest of Emili Cabot).*

tinguished by its originality and beauty. Very few examples survive today (Carreras 2001, p. 145). This glassware, which was based on Islamic prototypes, is frequently mentioned in Catalan documents from the mid-14th century onward, and the fact that no reference is made to its Damascene origins might suggest that it was made in Catalonia.

Production of Catalan enameled glass reached its peak during the 16th century, and it ceased soon after 1650. The oldest surviving examples date from the end of the 15th century. These objects are characterized by a fairly consistent combination of elements. Particularly striking is the *horror vacui* seen in the arrangement of the enameled motifs, with green and white as the predominant colors

and, to a lesser extent, yellow and blue. The earliest of these glasses have formal and aesthetic associations with vessels described in the inventory made by Violante de Albión in 1503, mentioned above (see p. 88). Their forms and decoration reveal Gothic and Islamic elements, as well as the influence of the Venetian Renaissance. The footed beaker in Barcelona's Museu de les Arts Decoratives (Fig. 3) has a conical bowl and a flared base, with lozenges in relief, and enameled and gilded decoration that points to its 14th-century origin and Venetian typology. A handled vessel with pseudo-Arabic script from the same museum (**1**) is ornamented with a variety of elements that are also found in Catalan Gothic painting. White and yellow enamel predominates, with several elements in green. Throughout the 16th century, this color scheme was reversed, with green being the chief color. The surfaces are often covered with stylized plant elements, such as serrated leaves, palm leaves, or small lilies of the valley with intertwined stems, and with white flakes, droplets, or pearls. Human figures and animals are less frequently shown, although there are some interesting glasses depicting dogs and birds (Figs. 4–6) and, in a few cases, people and animals on the same object (**2**). The figures are presented in a naïve style, and there is no suggestion of space and depth. The decoration was adapted to fit the shape of the object.

Typologically speaking, some surviving Venetian Renaissance enameled pieces parallel the *façon de Venise* glassware that was made in Catalonia. These include the *salvillas* (dessert trays or stands) (Fig. 4 and **2**) and the sumptuous covered goblets or jars (Fig. 6). Some *pitxells* (small ewers), baluster vessels, and small lamps can be dated by the clothing worn by the figures that appear on some of the pieces. For example, the garments of the couple depicted on the *salvilla* in Barcelona's Museu de les Arts Decoratives (**2**) allow us to date this object to about 1550–1570. Later examples, following the practice with the entire repertoire of luxury glassware produced in Catalonia, have thicker walls and are less concerned with form. This can be seen in a small lamp from the Cabot Collection that is now displayed in the Barcelona museum. It shows

FIG. 4
Salvilla (*dessert tray or stand*),
*colorless with grayish tinge,
blown, applied, enameled. Spain,
Catalonia, probably Barcelona,
about 1560–1600. OH. 7 cm,
D. (rim) 22.6 cm. The Corning
Museum of Glass, Corning, New
York (68.3.1).*

FIG. 5
*Bucket (aspersory), colorless
with grayish tinge, blown,
applied, enameled. Spain,
Catalonia, probably Barcelona,
about 1560–1600. H. 6.5 cm,
D. 13.7 cm. Museu de les Arts
Decoratives de Barcelona (23.286,
bequest of Emili Cabot).*

Fig. 6

*Covered goblet, colorless, blown, enameled. Spain, Catalonia, second half of the 16th century. H. 25 cm, D. 9.5 cm. Museu de les Arts Decoratives de Barcelona (23.290, bequest of Emili Cabot).*

the name of the individual who commissioned the piece and the year "1638."

That large quantities of this glassware were produced is attested in Pere Gil's manuscript (Gil unpub., p. 12). The author presents an extensive description of the various types of glass produced, their components, and their exportation to Castile, the Americas, France, and Italy. The Italian importation of Catalan glass can be seen in the work of the Italian engraver Giovanni Maggi. His *Bichierografia*, compiled in 1604 and dedicated to Cardinal del Monte, Caravaggio's patron and the principal agent of the Medici in Rome, illustrates glassware that includes Catalan pieces made during the 16th century (Rodriguez García 1990, p. 131). These objects were once part of one of the most important art collections in Italy (*idem* 1989).

### Colorless Glass

In addition to the elaborately enameled pieces discussed above, Catalan glassmakers produced elegant colorless glassware with extremely thin walls that reflects a Venetian sensibility. Some of these objects are shown in the paintings of Juan Bautista de Espinosa and Juan van der Hamen (Fig. 7).

The colorless glassware of Catalonia is renowned for the high quality of the materials employed in its manufacture. Its amber tinge, which resulted from the method used to decolorize the glass, is often helpful in distinguishing Catalan glass from objects produced elsewhere in Europe (Figs. 8 and 9). Gil's manuscript provides a detailed description of various glass recipes. Utilitarian glassware in Catalonia was made either with glasswort (barilla) or with tartar. Barilla, mainly from Alicante, had been exported for centuries throughout Europe for the making of glass. This salt-marsh plant was burned, and the ashes were added to the batch as a flux. Marsh samphire, another plant used as a fluxing agent, afforded even better results. The Venetians

**FIG. 7**
*Juan van der Hamen (1596–1631), still life with sweetmeats and glass vessels, 1622. Oil on canvas, H. 52 cm, W. 88 cm. Museo Nacional del Prado, Madrid (1.164).*

Fig. 8

*Drinking tazza, colorless with yellowish tinge, blown, molded, gilded. Probably Spain, 17th century. H. 16 cm. The Corning Museum of Glass, Corning, New York (79.3.489, bequest of Jerome Strauss).*

Fig. 9

*Wineglass, colorless with yellowish tinge, opaque white, blown. Spain, Catalonia, 17th century. H. 14.1 cm. The Corning Museum of Glass, Corning, New York (66.3.58, gift of Jerome Strauss).*

acquired it from the Syrian coast to produce their *cristallo*, and some Catalan documents indicate that it was imported from the coasts of Roussillon (Giralt i Raventós 1957, p. 57). Chalcedony (*calcedonia*) or bloodstone (*pedra sanguina*) was added to these ingredients as a decolorizer.

These recipes were used to create a wide variety of designs that, while inspired by utilitarian typologies, were highly prized as decorative objects because of their sophistication and fragility. Their forms can also be found in ceramic and silver wares. The largest and most important component of this glassware consists of goblets and dessert stands with a conventional three-part structure (bowl, stem, and base) and a boundless variety of forms. For example, fluted and cylindrical goblet bowls with colored trails could be stretched horizontally at the rim or made excessively wide (3). A number of these goblets have undulating profiles and ear-shaped loop handles on the lower part of the bowl (Fig. 10). The *salvilla*, which derived from the Italian *alzata*, was used as a stand for displaying food or objects on the table (Fig. 11). It is somewhat bigger than its Italian prototype, and it has a slightly concave or flat bowl with a rim that is occasionally reinforced.

The stems of such objects are particularly noteworthy. The most elaborate examples have solid sections alternating with spherical or pear-shaped hollow, molded knops decorated in relief with lions' heads or human masks (4). Complex stems decorated with prunts attached by small cabochons, nonfaceted droplets of glass made in an

open mold, required great technical expertise (**5**). Some goblets have cylindrical blown stems with an annular knop at the point where they join the bowl and another near the base. These objects usually have fluted bases and, occasionally, everted rims to reinforce them.

A variation of this form is the compote with a larger, more closed bowl, which could be covered by a tight-fitting lid, just like the stylized molded bottle. This object featured a complex stem and was set on a base.

Examples of refined Catalan glassware of the 16th century include delicate bowls with handles (Fig. 12), cruet sets, lion-shaped ewers (Fig. 13 and **6**), glasses and oil lamps (Fig. 14) with cane decoration in relief, mold-blown flasks, and trick glass-

**FIG. 10**

*Goblets, colorless, opaque white, blown,* lattimo *trails. Spain, Catalonia, mid- to late 16th century or early 17th century. Left: H. 17.5 cm, D. 10 cm. Museu de les Arts Decoratives de Barcelona (23.680, 23.384, 23.380).*

**FIG. 11**

*Footed stands (salvillas), colorless, blown. Spain, Catalonia, mid- to late 16th century or early to mid-17th century. Left: H. 16 cm, D. 22 cm. Museu de les Arts Decoratives de Barcelona (38.306, 5.069, 23.571).*

**FIG. 12**

*Three bowls with handles, colorless, blown. Spain, Catalonia, mid- to late 16th century or early to mid-17th century. Left: H. 10.5 cm, D. 6 cm. Museu de les Arts Decoratives de Barcelona (23.462; 23.463, 23.647, bequest of Emili Cabot).*

es shaped like pineapples or in ornate forms that make them extremely challenging to use (Fig. 15 and **7**). Most of these objects continued to be manufactured until the first half of the 17th century. A thorough review of the inventories and other notarial sources from the Episcopal Archive in Vic and the Historic Protocol and Municipal History Archives in Barcelona presents an extensive list of terms pertaining to glasses that have not survived. It is not always easy to associate these terms with the types of glass that are known to us, but they do emphasize the amazing diversity and richness of Catalan glassmaking between the Renaissance and the early Baroque period.

These glass objects were blown and decorated with great skill, and they reflect a splendid repertoire of techniques. Although they were mainly transparent and colorless, they were also produced in green, blue, white, and purple glass, or in a combination of colored and colorless glass (**4**). No matter how small the object, its components were always perfectly assembled. Plain surfaces were

**FIG. 13**
*Ewer in the shape of a lion, blue, mold-blown, applied, tooled. Spain, Catalonia, second half
of the 16th century or first half of the 17th century? H. 23 cm, (without base) 16.5 cm.
Museu de les Arts Decoratives de Barcelona (4.972, Plandiura Collection).*

Fig. 14

*Oil lamp and goblet, colorless with yellowish tinge, opaque white, blown, gilded, lattimo trails. Spain, Catalonia, mid- to late 16th century or early to mid-17th century. Right: H. 14.3 cm, D. 11.5 cm. Museu de les Arts Decoratives de Barcelona (4.970, 23.652).*

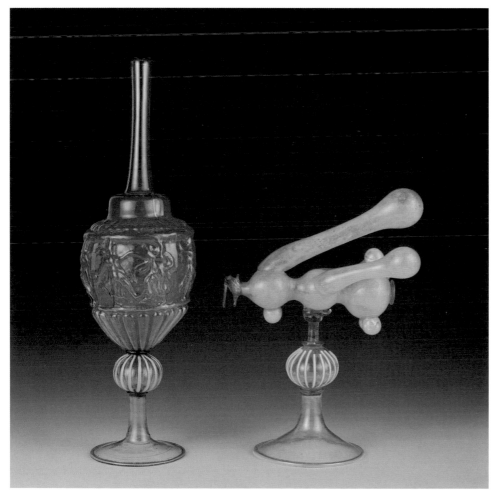

Fig. 15

*Decanter and trick glass, colorless, opaque white, blown, lattimo trails. Spain, Catalonia, mid- to late 16th century or early to mid-17th century. Left: H. 35 cm, D. 11.5 cm. Museu de les Arts Decoratives de Barcelona (4.974, bequest of Emili Cabot; 23.373).*

combined with mold-blown ones, or with surfaces that were partly decorated and expanded during the blowing process. Lozenges, ribs, trails, and concentric ribs and prunts are among the motifs that decorated these objects.

Ice glass (*helado o escarchado*) is another technique that was used to produce glass at the furnace. The parison was quickly immersed in water, and the thermal shock caused crackling on the surface of the glass. The piece was then reheated so that it could be worked while retaining its frosted appearance (Fig. 16). By adding ground glass to the sides

of an object while it was being shaped, a similarly rough surface could be achieved.

Another Venetian technique that was widely used in Catalonia involved the application of *lattimo* (opaque white glass) canes and trails that were not fully incorporated into the walls of the finished

**FIG. 16**

*Goblet, colorless, blown, applied, ice glass technique. Spain, Catalonia, mid- to late 16th century or early to mid-17th century. H. 16.2 cm, D. 21 cm. Museu de les Arts Decoratives de Barcelona (23.306).*

FIG. 17

*Wineglass, colorless with yellowish tinge, blown, applied. Spain, Catalonia, 17th century. H. 18 cm, D. 11 cm. Museu del Cau Ferrat, Sitges (Barcelona) (31.213).*

FIG. 18

*Goblet, colorless with yellowish tinge, blown, applied, tooled. Spain, Catalonia, 17th century. H. 13.5 cm, D. (rim) 9.7 cm, (foot) 7.8 cm. The Corning Museum of Glass, Corning, New York (79.3.1031, bequest of Jerome Strauss).*

vessel and did not attain the regular pattern of Muranese filigree ornament. Venetian glass wares employed *lattimo* in the forming process, whereas Catalan *façon de Venise* glass applied it to the surface either as vertical or spiral trails smoothed into the glass (Fig. 10) or, more often, as canes in high relief (Fig. 14). In addition to this unique style of applying stripes, the Catalans sometimes decorated their glasses with tiny multicolored dots in the style of Venetian millefiori (**8**). The application of prunts in the shape of a raspberry, or a mask (**5**, left) is also reminiscent of the Muranese repertoire. Some of these ornaments were applied to gilded surfaces, and vertical trails or knops decorated with gold were also added to the bowl and stem (**5**, center). Many surviving pieces have plain surfaces with

no decoration, but they are equally compelling because of the regularity of their profiles and the thinness of their walls (Figs. 17 and 18).

Diamond-point engraving subtly enriched the bowls and feet of some of the most refined glass wares (**9**). Because of the extreme thinness of the walls of the glass, the engraving had to be executed with the greatest of care. Plant and abstract motifs were the most common themes. This technique was also closely linked to Muranese practices, and in both cases, the results achieved were so good that it is often difficult to determine the provenance of the pieces. A large goblet, engraved in 1586 and dedicated to Prince Giovanni Andrea Doria (d. 1606), is one of the most spectacular objects of its kind from this period (**10**).

## Popularization of Glassware during the 18th Century

During the 18th century, there was a growing trend in Catalonia toward the local production of glassware, which resulted in forms that were markedly different from those produced on the rest of the Iberian Peninsula and elsewhere on the Continent. Forms that had been produced during the preceding two centuries were popularized. This aesthetic change mirrored far-reaching transformations in Catalan society.

The taste for Renaissance-style glass that emulated Venetian models had begun in the second half of the 17th century, when Catalan glassworks started to disregard the demands for transparency, thin-sided vessels, and sophisticated balusters. This tendency was strengthened in the following decades with the establishment and development of new typologies that still managed to retain elements of earlier forms.

The accession to the throne of Louis XIV's grandson, who ruled as Philip V, brought great changes to Spain. Among them was the creation of a French-style centralized state and of a court organized like that at Versailles. Part of the Catalan nobility emigrated to the capital, and the manufacturers of luxury glass objects in Catalonia thereby lost many of their regular customers.

The construction of the royal glassworks at La Granja was followed, in the mid-1700s, by laws that prevented the sale, near the court and over a wide area of Castile, of glassware that had originated in other regions. Catalan craftsmen responded by devoting themselves to the production of glass for the inland market.

FIG. 19

Càntir, *colorless with yellowish tinge, opaque white, transparent blue, blown, applied, tooled. Spain, Catalonia, 18th century. OH. 27.5 cm. The Corning Museum of Glass, Corning, New York (50.3.35).*

FIG. 20

Càntir, *greenish, blown, applied, ice glass technique. Spain, Catalonia, 18th century. H. 24 cm. Museu del Cau Ferrat, Sitges (Barcelona) (31.058).*

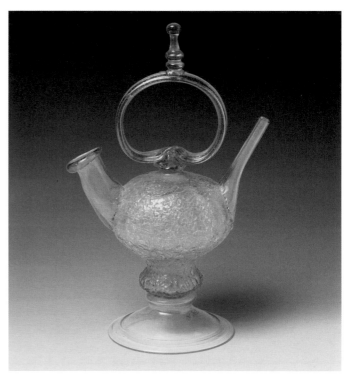

After 1714, when the War of Succession ended in Catalonia, the economy of Spain took a dramatic upward turn, partly because of the exportation of wine, brandy, and textiles to the American colonies. The new Bourbon dynasty allowed this trade to continue, and it brought considerable wealth to small craftsmen, farmers, and traders.

A new market for Catalan glassware, consisting of those who had been unable to afford glass objects purchased by the nobility, was formed. These new customers demanded locally made glass that was more baroque in style and less tied to glass-making trends elsewhere (**11**). While it lacked refinement, the hot-worked decoration on this glass was nevertheless highly effective. Pinched trails, elongated or embossed prunts, crests, stylized cockerels, and other ornaments were made either exclusively of colorless glass or by combining colorless, traditional white, and blue glass (**12** and Fig. 19). The glasses created in this manner showed technical virtuosity but a more whimsical and folk-art style. As a result, the glassmakers lost the prominence they had enjoyed as leading manufacturers of luxury glass during the 16th and 17th centuries.

Goblets and *salvillas*, which had previously been extremely intricate, were now made with simple, repetitive motifs and little additional ornamentation. At this time, when regional designs were at the height of their popularity, Catalan glassmakers produced wares with a clearly popular appeal. Perfumed water sprinklers (*almorratxas*) (**13**) and *càntirs* (drinking vessels shaped like a closed jug, with a ring handle at the center and two spouts) (Figs. 19 and 20) were in great demand, as were *porrones* (drinking vessels with an elongated spout) (Figs. 21 and 22).

The *almorratxa*, a rose water bottle, was one of the most important examples of the Catalan glassmaker's art. It was of Islamic origin, as is evidenced by the fact that its name is the same in Arabic. This object had a bulbous body and vertical spouts, and it was made with and without a base (**13**). (In the latter case, it was held in the hand, especially during processions.) There are frequent references to the *almorratxa* in 14th-century inventories, but the earliest surviving examples date from two centuries

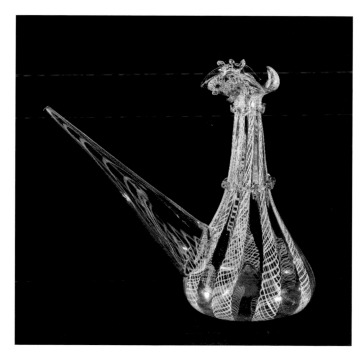

FIG. 21
Porrón, *colorless, opaque white, blown, applied, tooled. Spain, Catalonia, 18th century. H. 26 cm. Museu del Cau Ferrat, Sitges (Barcelona) (31.006).*

FIG. 22
Porrón, *colorless, opaque white, blown. Spain, Catalonia, late 17th–early 18th century. H. 27.2 cm. The Corning Museum of Glass, Corning, New York (79.3.481, bequest of Jerome Strauss).*

later. Because the decoration of these objects was often complex, they were used only for special occasions or for display During the 18th century, the *almorratxa* became a symbol of popular culture, and it was used in folk dances such as those that can still be seen at festivals in coastal Catalan villages.

Some scholars believe that changes in 18th-century Catalan glassmaking marked a true crisis or a decline in production (Frothingham 1963, p. 48). Close inspection of documents in municipal, parochial, and notarial archives, however, demonstrates just the opposite. In the 1700s, the number of glasshouses in Catalonia was larger than during the preceding two centuries. Instead of a decline, this period was characterized by a change in the use of the formative and decorative resources of *façon de Venise*.

Nevertheless, most of the earlier techniques continued to be employed. Among them was the making of frosted glass, as is exemplified by a *càntir* in the Museu del Cau Ferrat in Sitges (Fig. 20) (Carreras and Doménech 2003, p. 107). However, the most widely used decorative technique throughout the 18th century was the application of *latticino* trails. Catalan makers of glassware in the Venetian style did not apply these trails with the skill of their Muranese counterparts, who created impressive filigree effects. In Catalonia, white trails were added to glass in the same manner as in previous centuries. They were applied, toward the end of the manufacturing process, in a spiral or by combing them into irregular designs.

Another surviving technique with important links to *façon de Venise* was the application of blue glass decorations that were in marked contrast to colorless glass surfaces and the white of *latticino*. A widely used technique was the pinching or molding of glass into various zoomorphic, floral, and abstract shapes, adding to the irregularity of forms that were often far removed from the Muranese output. This glass was used in religious, folkloric, and domestic contexts.

## CASTILIAN GLASS

The provinces of Castile—Toledo, Madrid, Cuenca, and Guadalajara—were very important centers of glassmaking. Both the Catholic kings and the Castilian nobility were avid consumers and collectors. Glass for the monarchy was purchased in Venice, especially during the reign of Philip II (1556–1598). Collections of glass and other decorative objects were widespread among Castilian aristocrats, who wanted to maintain an ostentatious lifestyle. They usually purchased their glass from manufacturers in such places as Murano, Flanders, and Catalonia, and this compelled local glassmakers to meet the challenges of harsh competition. The vessels fashioned by Castilian glassmakers displayed a clear Venetian influence, either through the reinterpretation of techniques and forms or through the presence of Venetian masters working in Castile.

Flanders was a major source of glassworkers who were eventually employed in Castile. During the reign of Charles V and under the patronage of his sister Mary of Hungary, governor of the Netherlands, various privileges were granted to Flemish glassmakers for the production of Venetian-style glass. These privileges continued to be awarded during the reign of Philip II. Among the glassmakers from Flanders who were brought to Spain to produce wares for the court was Dieudonné Lambotte, who left his hometown of Namur and moved with his family to Madrid in 1679. One year later, Lambotte, who enjoyed the patronage of the Flemish governor, the duke of Villahermosa, opened a glassworks in San Martín de Valdeiglesias, near Cadalso (Frothingham 1963, p. 63). When he died three years later, his glasshouse was operated by the Italian Giacomo Bartoletti, and Antonio de Ovando was appointed as supervisor.

Even before Lambotte's arrival, however, there was a glassworks producing *façon de Venise* wares at San Martín de Valdeiglesias. This is documented in *"El tratado de la fábrica de vidrio" de Juan Danís y "El modo de hacer vidrieras" de Francisco Herranz* ("Treatise on the glass factory" by Juan Danís and "Ways of producing stained glass" by Francisco Herranz), written in Segovia in 1676 (Nieto Alcaide 1967). Both of these men had a furnace in Valdemaqueda, and they worked on a project to complete stained glass windows for Segovia Cathedral that had been interrupted during the 1500s. In a chapter titled "Vidrio cristal, como se hace" (Colorless glass and how it is made), Danís wrote, "This is the glass they make in France, Flanders, and other parts, and today in San Martín." This treatise is an interesting Spanish contribution to the glassmaking literature of Europe. It was written with a markedly educational slant. The authors intended to inform master glaziers about the techniques required to produce stained glass windows, ranging from formulating and melting the batch to the execution of leaded work. Danís supplied extremely valuable information regarding glassmaking tools, materials, and processes. On several occasions, this author also revealed his knowledge of *L'Arte vetraria*, published by the Florentine priest Antonio Neri in 1612.

Although an extensive list of Castilian glassworks (including Arbeteta, Vindel, Villanueva de Alcorón, Valdemaqueda, El Quexigal, and Medina del Campo) is reported in the literature, it is impossible to attribute the works they produced to any particular factory. Cadalso de los Vidrios in Madrid (formerly in the province of Toledo) and Recuenco in Guadalajara were the foremost of these glassmaking centers, based on the quality and variety of their wares. Both were ideally located near large forested areas, which they utilized to fuel their furnaces.

The factory at Cadalso was in operation as early as the beginning of the 15th century, when the archpriest of Talavera reported that glass wares made there were "commonplace throughout the kingdom" (Frothingham 1963, p. 68). Between 1478 and 1480, two glassworks from this town paid an annual rent to the Guisando Monastery. At the beginning of the 16th century, Lucio Marineo

Sículo wrote that glass "is also made in many places in Castile, but Cadalso has the advantage over all of them because it supplies the entire kingdom." Sículo considered the works made in Cadalso to be the finest on the Iberian Peninsula aside from those produced in Catalonia (*idem* 1956, p. 5). There is a considerable amount of information about these glassworks during the 16th and 17th centuries, when they had reached the peak of their success and manufactured an important group of glasses that deserves to be the subject of further in-depth study.

As Sículo indicated, the glass made in Cadalso was almost always inferior to that from Catalonia. However, during the 16th and 17th centuries, the wares from Cadalso showed a clear Venetian influence, which included a tendency to decolorize glass batches and a preference for decorative techniques such as ice glass and the application of blue trails, occasionally in a chain pattern similar to that made on Murano. In the 17th century, the glassmakers of Cadalso employed *lattimo* to fashion elements such as handles, lips, prunts, and applied trails.

A wide range of forms, including lobed shapes and unorthodox proportions that were not part of Muranese production, was created by the glasshouses of Cadalso. The surviving examples also lack enameled and engraved decoration, which was a common feature of Venetian-influenced wares (Doménech 1997, p. 22). Among the forms of glass made in Cadalso were two-handled jugs with mold-blown ribs, applied trails of blue glass or of the same color as the base glass, and wide, frequently lobed rims (Fig. 23); *salvillas* decorated with blue trails and chains; glasses with crimped rims (Fig. 24); and vessels that occasionally contained a bulbous prunt (usually transparent blue, and sometimes figural) applied to the base of the bowl (**14**). Despite the glassmakers' efforts to decolorize the batches, however, nearly all of these pieces have a yellowish or greenish tinge, and by the end of the 16th century, the glass had become thicker and marked by an increasing number of imperfections.

The output of the glassworks at San Martín de Valdeiglesias, which was active mainly in the 17th

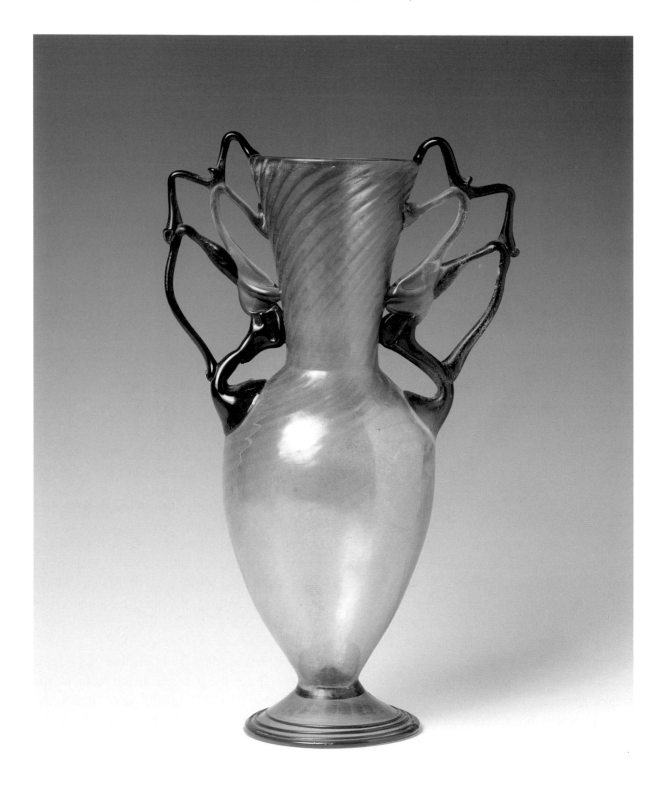

FIG. 23
*Jug with handles, yellowish, blue, blown, applied. Spain, Castile, Recuenco,*
*late 16th–early 17th century. H. 22 cm. Museu del Cau Ferrat, Sitges*
*(Barcelona) (31.069).*

century, is thought to have been similar to that of Cadalso, so much so that some of the wares traditionally attributed to the latter may have been produced by the former. For this reason, it seems appropriate to use the generic term "Cadalso-type wares" to describe all of this glass.

Despite attempts to restore these glassworks to their former glory during the reign of Charles II (1665–1700) and the official patronage of Spanish glassware by the monarchy in the 18th century, the industry was in crisis, and the situation was to worsen throughout the 1700s. At mid-century, there were two glasshouses in Cadalso, but their inability to compete with foreign imports and with glass produced at the Real Manufactura de Vidrios y Cristales of La Granja accelerated their decline. An extensive memoir published in the late 18th century by Eugenio Larruga described the increasingly poor quality of Cadalso's work, noting that "its glassware is no longer famed throughout Castile for its purity and diversity" (Larruga y Boneta 1995, p. 222). At that time, these glassworks were producing sizable vessels that served a principally dec-

orative function. These vessels featured a tall stem, an often crimped rim, and prunts in the form of stylized cockerels or spheres inside the bowl (**14**).

The glasshouses at Recuenco and in the towns near Guadalajara created less refined glassware. Attributions are difficult, but we know that glassworks had been established there as early as the 16th century. Forests in that area provided fuel for the operation of the furnaces. In the inventories and price lists, the glass produced here was characterized as utilitarian, as is indicated in a royal warrant issued in Madrid toward the end of the reign of Charles II. That warrant fixed the prices at which these objects were to be sold (Frothingham 1963, p. 69). Recuenco was also an important producer of flat glass, which it supplied in large quantities to the Escorial Monastery throughout the sec-

FIG. 24

*Bowl with handles, colorless, transparent blue, blown, applied. Spain, Castile, Cadalso, late 16th–early 17th century. H. 6.5 cm, D. 13.8 cm. Museu del Cau Ferrat, Sitges (Barcelona) (31.012).*

FIG. 25

*Vase, colorless with yellowish tinge, blown, applied. Spain, Castile, Recuenco, late 17th century. H. 23.3 cm, D. (rim) 11 cm, (foot) 9.6 cm. The Corning Museum of Glass, Corning, New York (79.3.1125).*

ond half of the 16th century. At that time, the town was awarded important commissions for pharmaceutical bottles and glassware to be supplied to the monastery. This type of work continued until the 18th century, when the town supplied the royal household with stills and flasks made in its furnaces (Sánchez Moreno 1997, p. 250).

"Recuenco-type glass" was marked by colors deeper than those made at Cadalso. The glass frequently contained bubbles and had a yellowish (Figs. 25 and 26) or greenish (**15**) tinge. Its high soda content produced unstable wares that gradually lost their brilliance and transparency due to crizzling. The forms of these glasses were highly original, and they offered a wide-ranging typology that was somewhat removed from the fashions dictated by the great European glassmaking centers

in Venice, Bohemia, and France. The round-bellied jugs with large, funnel-shaped spouts and small handles recall the formal structure of the lamps used in mosques. There was often a lack of proportion between the components. The handles of these objects were decorated with pinched trails that extended vertically in elaborate crested shapes. Like other Castilian glass wares, these vessels had no engraved or enameled decoration.

At the end of the 17th century, Castilian glassworks suffered a period of steady decline. The monarchs and aristocrats began to acquire decorative glass wares from France and central Europe. The poor quality of Castile-made glass ensured that the court of the new French dynasty, the Bourbons, was very unlikely to purchase it. Philip V (r. 1700–1746), that dynasty's first Spanish king, had been

FIG. 26
*Vase with flower, colorless with yellowish tinge, blown, applied. Spain, Castile, Recuenco, late 17th century. H. 26.4 cm, D. (rim) 10.9 cm, (foot) 11.6 cm. The Corning Museum of Glass, Corning, New York (60.3.29).*

educated at Versailles, and he initiated the establishment of a royal glassworks, the Real Fábrica de Vidrio y Cristal, on the model of the royal glasshouse that his grandfather, Louis XIV, had founded in France. Philip's glassworks was situated near the Real Sitio de La Granja de San Ildefonso. Bohemian crystal, which was the glassware of choice when the factory began production about 1750, formed the core of its output. Nevertheless, for a short time, it also created jugs and beakers decorated with *lattimo* and pink filigree ornament that were inspired by Venetian glass.

## ANDALUSIAN GLASS

The blown glass of Andalusia in southern Spain differed considerably from most Castilian and Catalan pieces produced at that time. In their forms and decorative elements, they displayed a clear Islamic influence. These objects were generally made for everyday use, and many of their features were the result of close ties to ceramics factories. For the most part, the exacting disciplines of Venetian-style glassmaking did not extend to Andalusia, which continued to manufacture traditional forms of glass wares into the 18th century. These wares are known to have been produced in the areas of Granada and Almería, although some data indicate that glassworks were located in other parts of the region.

Some of the most outstanding southern Spanish glassware was produced at the factory in Castril de la Peña. The surviving Andalusian glasses that show clear connections with Venetian output are thought to have been made here. It is evident that the glassmakers set out to create recipes that would result in highly transparent wares. The forms

FIG. 27

*Mug, colorless with greenish tinge, dark brown overlay, blown, cased, applied. Spain, Andalusia, probably Almería, about 1700–1850. H. 11.9 cm. The Corning Museum of Glass, Corning, New York (79.3.600, gift of The Ruth Bryan Strauss Memorial Foundation).*

FIG. 28

*Four-handled vase, transparent green, blown, applied, tooled. Spain, Andalusia, probably Almería, about 1550–1650. H. 14.9 cm, D. (rim) 7 cm, (body, max.) 11 cm, (foot) 7 cm. The Corning Museum of Glass, Corning, New York (51.3.279).*

of these objects, which were thin-walled and decorated with crimped ornament, are very similar to those of glasses made in Castile. However, they were not enameled, engraved, or decorated with *lattimo* trails. While there is documentary evidence that transparent glass was also produced in Seville during the 16th century, we are unable to attribute any objects to specific glassworks. Seville, which was the leading economic and cultural power in Spain throughout the 1500s, seems to have been an important glassmaking center. When Juan Rodríguez, a native of Cadalso who had honed his craft in Venice and Barcelona, applied to open a glassworks in Seville in 1557, he stated that he knew the *lattimo* technique and was able to make glass wares of all qualities (Frothingham 1963, p. 53). The customary presence of colorless glass objects in the paintings of the Seville School during this period would lead us to suppose that some of them were produced in Seville, although there was a flourishing trade in Venetian, Flemish, and Catalan glass in

that city during the 16th and 17th centuries (Frothingham 1963, p. 57).

Other glass manufacturing centers in the province of Granada were Puebla de Don Fadrique, where a glassworks was documented in 1620 (*Macaya Collection* 1935, p. 66), and Pinar de la Vidriería. Both of these factories were located in the vicinity of Castril. Although historians have linked the wares produced by these glasshouses with those made in Castril, we cannot identify with certainty any of the objects manufactured in these areas between the 16th and 18th centuries. This is not the case, however, with many of the glass wares produced in María, Almería. Glassmaking there dates back to Muslim times, and its glassworks created

mainly deep-colored, thick-sided glass that was both very popular and far removed from the Venetian style (Fig. 27). Its distinguishing features include Baroque forms and intense colors (yellow, amber, green, violet, and blue) that were deliberately made because glassmakers had difficulty decolorizing the glass. Technically, these wares were quite rudimentary in form and naïve in style. The same shapes continued throughout the 17th and 18th centuries, and many of them persisted into the 19th century. A wide variety of drinking glass forms was produced here. Some of these forms showed interesting similarities to Islamic mosque lamps, with globular bodies, flared bases, and a profusion of tiny handles (Fig. 28 and **16**).

## GLASSWARE FROM VALENCIA AND MAJORCA

Glassmaking in Majorca and Catalonia seems to have been closely similar. In 1347, the Barcelona glassmaker Guillem Barceló was granted permission to erect a glassworks in Palma. This followed the repeal, by Peter IV the Ceremonious, of a law, dating from 1330, that prohibited the establishment of glassworks on the island because of the resulting deforestation (Sanchis Guarner 1952, p. 2). Toward the end of the Middle Ages, fresh impetus was given to the manufacture of glass in Majorca. Documentary evidence indicates that, during the following two centuries, various glassmaking centers were located on different parts of the island.

Despite the presence of these glasshouses, the mention of Catalan glassware in inventories of the Majorcan nobility demonstrates the high esteem in which these wares were held in the Spanish culture of the Renaissance and Baroque periods. One mid-17th-century inventory details the purchases of glass at the monastery of Lluc, and it frequently notes the provenance of that glass (Mir 1890, p. 214). Glass from Majorca, Barcelona, and Catalonia is listed here, and numerous other examples of glass from these locations are found in 16th-century inventories. There seems to have been no differ-

ence in the forms of Catalan and Majorcan glass. The close links between these glassmaking centers may have resulted from the direct importation of wares or from an assimilation of styles.

The Venetian Domenico Barovier moved to the island in 1600, after the powerful Barcelona guild banned him from producing glass in that city. In May 1605, he requested permission from the governors of Majorca to teach the island's artisans the secrets of glassmaking in the Venetian style (Sanchis Guarner 1952, p. 7; Rodriguez García 1990, p. 65). Barovier's request included his claim that he had been banished from Venice for five years, and he added that the island's authorities would be well advised to make use of his services, since he was offering instruction in his own formulas. As a result, he said, Majorcan glassmakers would be able to produce fine wares and would no longer be required to import them from "Venice or anywhere else." One month later, Barovier repeated his request, but it does not appear to have engendered a satisfactory response. This caused him to leave the island and to offer his services to the court of Philip III (r. 1598–1621). He obtained a privilege from the king to manufacture glass at the Escorial.

The surviving documents, which have been studied only in part, do not allow us to distinguish between contemporaneous Majorcan and Catalan glass. Inventories may show that certain glass objects originated in Majorca, but they do not offer a general picture of the type of wares produced there. Two important examples of 16th-century enameled glass attributed to Majorca are a *salvilla* and a pitcher. The former, from the collection of the Majorcan furniture maker Gaspar Homar, is in the Museu de les Arts Decoratives de Barcelona (23.299) (Gudiol Ricart 1936, fig. 58). The decoration, which covers a large area of the object, shows a circle of figures inside a frieze with a plant motif, characteristic of the ornamental and formal repertoire of Catalan enameled glass wares. The pitcher, from the Macaya Collection (*Macaya Collection* 1935, p. 123), was found in the convent of Santa Clara in Palma. It, too, displays a clear link with surviving examples of enameled glass from Catalonia.

The history of glassmaking in the ancient kingdom of Valencia presents a similar picture. This area, which now spans the provinces of Alicante, Valencia, Castellón, and Murcia, was the focus of glassmaking activity that dates back as far as the Roman period. Documents report the existence of glassworks in Valencia in the second half of the 15th century, and royal warrants and inventories of the 16th and 17th centuries, which include descriptions and prices, indicate that ordinary glass wares must have been produced in the area (Pérez Bueno 1942, p. 89). These inventories present interesting examples of luxury glasses, the origin of which is uncertain. It would be helpful to discover the provenance of the seven glass goblets purchased by Ferdinand the Catholic from a Valencian trader, Andrés Fuster, in 1486, as well as the 200 pieces of enameled glass sold by the same trader some months later (*Macaya Collection* 1935, p. 61). Fuster's status as a trader clearly reveals that he was not a glassmaker, but was instead known as a "reseller." Documents from this period show that, with occasional exceptions such as the one just noted, glassmakers usually sold their products themselves. The pieces sold in 1486 could have been Venetian, Oriental, Catalan, or even Valencian.

It is important to note that one of the most important examples of enameled glass from the Iberian Peninsula, which is now in the collection of the Museu de les Arts Decoratives de Barcelona (Fig. 1), was found in Valencia. However, as in the case of Majorcan glass, we do not have enough reliable information to attribute to Valencia the manufacture of luxury glasses at the beginning of the 16th century. Documents of the 1500s and 1600s refer us to more utilitarian glassware. At that time, Barcelona had a powerful guild of glassmakers, but Valencia, like Palma, lacked such an organization. However, there were other guilds in Valencia then, and this leads us to suppose that the city's glassmakers did not form a guild because they were relatively few in number.

Records show that there were glassworks in the towns of Ollería, Busot, Salinas, Alcira, and Liria, although they appear to have been active at a later date. Documents referring to Ollería mention a glasshouse in the mid-16th century, a time when the town had secured its independence from Játiva (Grau Monpó 2001, p. 203). It seems that glassworks and ceramic factories, which were also very important in this area, became more firmly established and underwent major expansions until the 18th century. A curious document dating from 1672 reports that a community of nuns from the convent of the Barefoot Augustinian Sisters of San José and Santa Ana purchased materials necessary "to build an oven to make glass," and this purchase was documented a year later, when the "oven" was repaired (*ibid.*, p. 204). The fact that this was a cloistered convent permits the construction of the "oven" to take on another dimension. Far from being an anecdotal report, it emphasizes the spread of glassmaking in the town, and the community may have decided to make glass production a means of support because the venture was well received commercially.

In spite of our limited knowledge concerning glass made in Valencia, it is likely to have been a type of ware in everyday use, far removed from styles that were popular internationally. Sumptuous glass wares that were purchased or used in that region were probably produced in Catalonia or Venice.

## Conclusion

The Catalan glass wares of the 16th and 17th centuries demonstrated a highly developed form of the *façon de Venise* style, using high-quality ingredients and great technical expertise. Some of these glasses so closely resembled their Venetian counterparts that they have been ascribed to Muranese manufacture. Often, we must rely on the honey color of the objects or a decorative element such as an annular knop on the stem in order to identify the Spanish glasses. This is especially so with some examples of undecorated colorless glass and engraved wares with intricate stems that are almost identical to works produced in Venice, and it underscores the high quality of Catalan glass.

Just as Catalan glassware is often attributed to Venice, so the glass production of Venice is frequently thought to be the work of Catalan artisans. This is usually the case with typologies that are seldom found in the Venetian repertoire, some 16th-century enameled wares, and pieces that show variable technical skill in manufacturing or decoration.

On the whole, Castilian glassware is not as closely associated with Venetian glass, but there are some examples that show a clear Venetian influence in designs and techniques. Despite that influence, however, Catalan and Castilian craftsmen produced pieces of great originality and made a significant contribution to the development of European glassmaking.

*Translated by Mark Waudby*

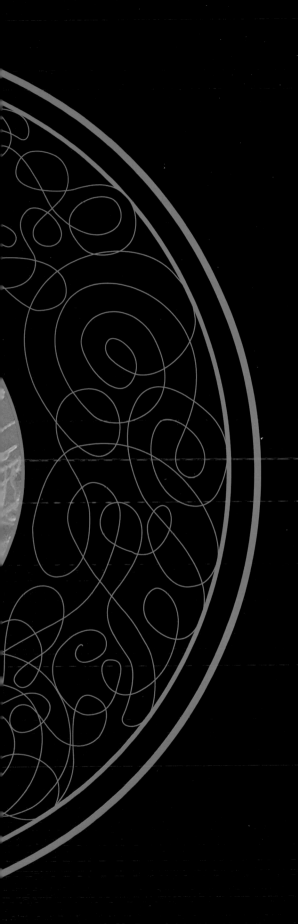

Spanish *Façon de Venise* Glass

# *Objects*

Jutta-Annette Page

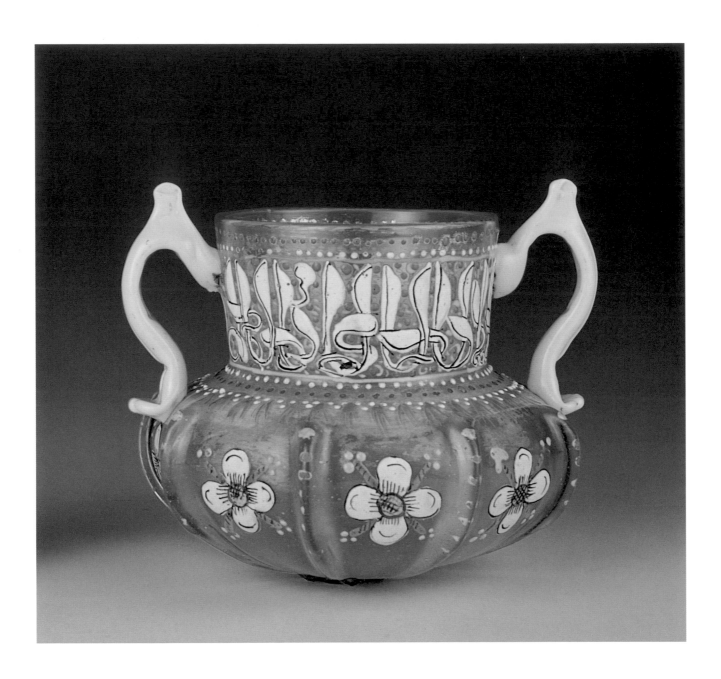

## 1

### *Jar with Handles*
### H. 13.5 cm

Spain, Catalonia, about 1500. Museu de les Arts Decoratives de Barcelona (23.280, bequest of Emili Cabot).

Colorless with yellowish tinge, opaque white. Blown, applied, enameled, gilded.

The bowl has a squat, globular body with eight pronounced mold-blown ribs and a slightly flaring cylindrical neck. Two opposing S-shaped handles in opaque white glass are applied below the rim and to the shoulder of the vessel. The tops of these handles are pincered to form a rounded protrusion. The vessel has a fire-polished rim and a trailed foot-ring.

The ribs on the body are enameled with vertical rows of opaque yellow dots. Between the ribs, the vessel is decorated with large stylized blossoms consisting of four petals in opaque white enamel, alternating with four floral stems in green enamel that terminate in a set of three yellow dots, around a yellow center. Simple cross-hatched lines in black enamel provide visual depth to the center of the blossoms. The shoulder and the rim of the vessel are decorated with a wide band of gold leaf.

The neck is embellished with a calligraphic, pseudo-Arabic inscription in opaque white enamel, enhanced by thin black outlines. Raised dots of pale blue on top of yellow dots fill in the field between the letters. The inscription is framed on either side by thin yellow lines, followed by rows of small white and pale blue dots. On the shoulder is a band of raised pale blue dots, pulled out to form three rays, alternating with groups of three white dots.

COMMENT: The cursive pseudo-Arabic script on this vessel recalls the enameled inscriptions found on 14th-century Islamic glasses (*Glass of the Sultans* 2001, pp. 265–269). Similar blossoms are found on a glass vessel in the shape of a wine keg, dating from about 1500, in the Instituto Amatller de Arte Hispánico, Barcelona (Frothingham 1956, fig. 8). The stylized blossoms resemble the Messianic rose, a symbol of the prophecy of the coming of the Christ Child (Ireland 1962, p. 22, no. 2301). Although this symbol is rendered conventionally with five petals, the decoration on the vessel may combine Christian symbolism with Arabic decoration.

BIBLIOGRAPHY: *Macaya Collection* 1935, p. 65, pl. XVIII; Pérez Bueno 1942, p. 73; Almela y Vives 1954, p. 15; Frothingham 1956, fig. 7; *Mille anni di arte del vetro a Venezia* 1982, p. 110, fig. 127; Doménech 1999, p. 490; Carreras and Doménech 2000, p. 421; Carreras 2001, p. 144, fig. 1.

*Acknowledgment.* I thank Ignasi Doménech for reviewing all of the entries in this section and for supplying additional information and bibliographic sources for some of the objects.

## 2

### Salvilla (Stand) or Serving Dish

*H. 5 cm, D. 22 cm*

SPAIN, CATALONIA, ABOUT 1550–1570. MUSEU DE LES ARTS DECORATIVES DE BARCELONA (23.305).

COLORLESS WITH GRAYISH TINGE. BLOWN, APPLIED, ENAMELED.

This shallow, thinly blown plate is mounted on a flared pedestal foot. The surface of the plate is enameled with a central stylized rosette consisting of triangular shapes in opaque yellow and white enamel. The primary design shows three rectangular arbors in green enamel, separated by stylized branches with rounded leaves in a symmetrical arrangement. A couple in early 16th-century dress are shaking hands under the first arbor. The woman wears a green jacket and apron over a yellow dress, and a green headdress. The man is dressed in a yellow cape over a white doublet and pleated pants, green stockings, and a green cap. The next arbor (clockwise) shows a shepherdess(?) in a green dress, holding a yellow staff. A four-legged animal resembling a goat or sheep, rendered in white, leaps in front of her. The last arbor surrounds a man (probably a hunter) in a green jacket worn over a yellow and white doublet, green pants, and yellow boots. He is playing a large yellow wind instrument. A second four-legged animal seems to be resting in the background. A white bird decorates the space on the left of each arbor. A floral scroll border with stylized yellow drop-shaped blossoms or fruit surrounds the rim.

COMMENT: The leafy floral decoration and the stylized birds and other animals appear on numerous glass vessels from Catalonia. Representations of human figures, however, are exceedingly rare. A pilgrim-shaped flask (*pitxer*) in the Instituto de Valencia de Don Juan in Madrid is decorated with the bust of a right-facing male wearing a tight-fitting cap. Another *pitxer*, in the collection of The Hispanic Society of America, New York, shows a rather crudely rendered couple, in elegant dress with ruffs, holding hands (Gudiol Ricart 1941, no. 54). The center of a plate in the Museu de les Arts Decoratives de Barcelona depicts a musician wearing a long robe and playing a string instrument for a male dancer wearing a doublet and *tonnelets* (pants) (*ibid.*, no. 48). The most unusual object in this group is a footed plate in the Barcelona museum. Its surface is decorated with 12 nude figures arranged in a circle. Some of these figures are holding hands, and two of them are playing wind instruments (*ibid.*, no. 58).

BIBLIOGRAPHY: *Macaya Collection 1935*, p. 49, pl. X; Gudiol Ricart 1941, no. 57; *Mille anni di arte del vetro a Venezia* 1982, p. 110, fig. 129; Carreras 1998; Doménech 1999, p. 491; Carreras 2001, p. 145, fig. 2.

## 3

*Goblet*

*H. 17.8 cm*

SPAIN, CATALONIA, EARLY 17TH CENTURY. THE CORNING MUSEUM OF GLASS, CORNING, NEW YORK (60.3.86); ACQUIRED FROM EDWIN R. LUBIN, NEW YORK.

COLORLESS WITH YELLOWISH TINGE, OPAQUE WHITE. BLOWN, APPLIED.

This goblet has a shallow bowl consisting of a short cylindrical base with a flat bottom and a wide, splayed lip with an upfolded rim. The bowl was applied with a short merese to a thin tubular stem that slightly narrows toward the shallow, domed foot with a fire-polished rim. The filigree decoration on the bowl is made of thin opaque white canes in a vertical arrangement. They increase in width toward the rim and narrow toward the base, but not all of the canes extend fully to the center of the bowl.

COMMENT: Such thinly blown glasses with filigree decoration, which recall the shallow drinking tazzas favored in Italy, are typical of Catalan glass production in Venetian style. Numerous examples survive (Gudiol Ricart 1941, pls. 26 and 81; Doménech 1999, pp. 496–497; Carreras and Doménech 2003, p. 97).

BIBLIOGRAPHY: Charleston 1980, pp. 104–105, pl. 44; *Mille anni di arte del vetro a Venezia* 1982, p. 127; Charleston 1990, pp. 104–105, pl. 44.

# 4

## *Group of Goblets with Lion-Mask Stems*

*H. (tallest) 17 cm*

SPAIN, CATALONIA, MID- TO LATE 16TH CENTURY. MUSEU DE LES ARTS DECORA-TIVES DE BARCELONA (4.971, 23.389, 4.978).

COLORLESS, TRANSPARENT DARK GREEN, BLUE. BLOWN, MOLD-BLOWN, APPLIED, TOOLED.

All three of these composite goblets were constructed in the same manner. The goblet on the left (4.971) has a molded lion-mask knop of colorless glass between a bowl and a pedestal foot of transparent dark green glass. Its funnel-shaped bowl was tooled to form a wide, flaring lip with a thick rim that is folded up. The bowl was applied with a thin merese to a small, solid ball knop, followed by a short stem section and a second merese. The hollow, bulbous lion mask knop was blown in a two-part mold, with oppos-ing lion masks separated by a scroll de-sign and surmounted by a fluted relief pattern. The ribbed decoration beneath the heads was tooled to fashion a short tubular stem, which was applied to a small merese of green glass and a tall pedestal foot with a shallow, slightly domed base and a fire-polished rim.

The goblet in the center (23.389) is made entirely of colorless glass. Its bowl was mold-blown with horizontal ribs, and it has a saucer-shaped lip and an upturned rim that is folded inward. The blue goblet on the right (4.978) has a bucket-shaped bowl that was blown in an optic mold, and a splayed lip with a fire-polished rim.

BIBLIOGRAPHY: Doménech 1999, p. 493; Carreras 2001, p. 147, fig. 4.

# 5

## *Group of Engraved Tazzas*
*Largest: H. 20.9 cm, D. 15.2 cm*

SPAIN, CATALONIA, MID- TO LATE 16TH
CENTURY. MUSEU DE LES ARTS DECORA-
TIVES DE BARCELONA (4.969, 4.975,
23.298). FORMERLY IN THE COLLECTION
OF LLUIS PLANDIURA (4.969, 4.975).

COLORLESS WITH YELLOWISH TINGE,
OPAQUE WHITE. BLOWN, DIAMOND-POINT
ENGRAVED, GILDED, APPLIED, MOLD-BLOWN.

The short-stemmed tazza on the
left (4.969) has a shallow, dish-shaped
bowl with a slightly flaring rim. The
center of the bowl is decorated with
a radiating pattern of short opaque
white cane sections that are encircled
by two bands of white canes. All of the
canes were applied to the outside of
the vessel wall. The sides of the bowl
are diamond-point engraved with a
floral scroll pattern. The bowl was applied with a small merese to a short
stem section resting on an ovoid lion-
mask knop that was tooled at the lower
end to form a short stem. A second
merese connects the stem to a slightly
domed foot with a fire-polished rim.

The tall tazza in the center (4.975)
has a shallow hemispherical bowl that
is crimped into eight tooled lobes. Its
outside wall is embellished with opaque
white canes in an arrangement similar
to that of the tazza on the left. The wall
above is diamond-point engraved with
alternating wide and narrow vertical
bands of stylized floral scrolls fitted to
the outline of the lobes. The bowl was
applied to a complex stem consisting
of a short section between wide, thin
mereses and a small knop above. This
is followed by a central, solid rod,
which is decorated below the merese
with four gilded raspberry prunts applied to small pads of glass. This rod
section is also ornamented with elaborate openwork consisting of four applied trails tooled into a pronounced
L-shape followed by a C-shape. This

rests, in turn, on a hollow, mushroom-
shaped knop decorated with vertical
opaque white stripes. Gilded raspberry
prunts embellish the top of the right
angles and the ends of the trails, terminating on the filigree knop. Another
short and spindle-shaped rod section
between wide mereses is attached to a
domed foot with drop-shaped diamond-
point engraving. The vessel has a fire-
polished foot-ring and a small pontil
mark beneath the base.

The tazza on the right (23.298) has
a bowl that is similar in shape and
decoration to that of the tazza in the
center, but the crimped lobes are more
pronounced and angular. Its lion-mask
stem was made in a manner similar to
those of the goblets in **4**. It consists
of a short stem section between mereses, a mold-blown ovoid knop with
lion masks above a small merese, and
a slightly domed foot that is pushed
up into a narrow cylindrical stem. Diamond-point engraved bands of drop
shapes, encircled by thin lines, decorate
the foot of the vessel.

BIBLIOGRAPHY: *Macaya Collection*
1935, pl. XII opp. p. 52 (23.298);
Gudiol Ricart 1936, figs. 14 (23.298)
and 16A (4.969); Pérez Bueno 1942,
pl. opp. p. 93.

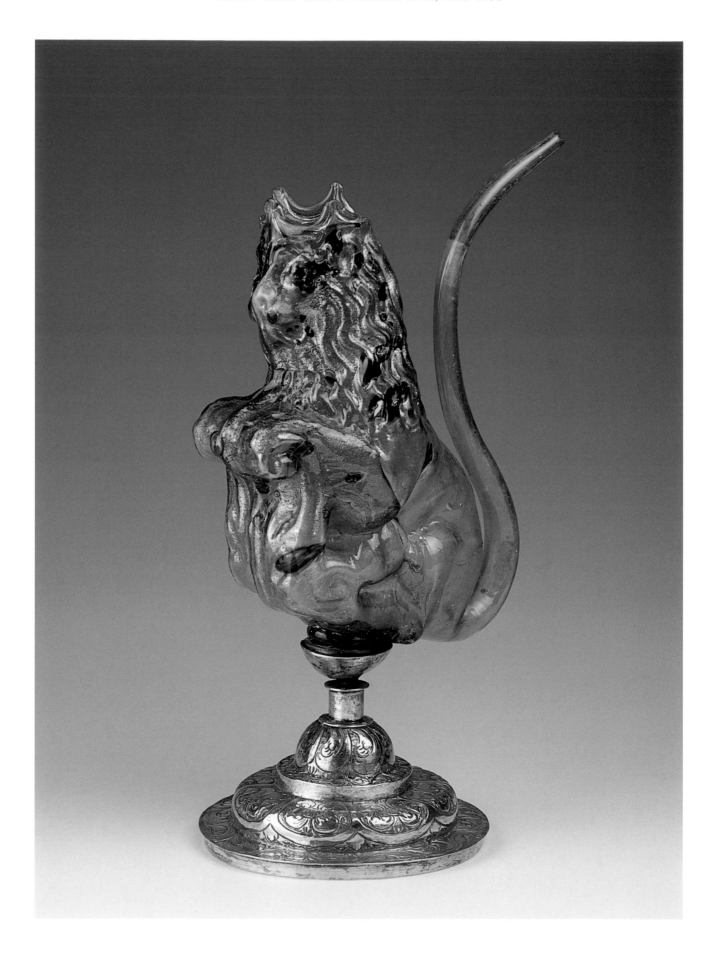

## 6

### *Ewer in the Shape of a Lion*
OH. 26.8 cm

SPAIN, CATALONIA, SECOND HALF OF THE 16TH CENTURY TO FIRST HALF OF THE 17TH CENTURY? MUSEU DE LES ARTS DECORATIVES DE BARCELONA (23.275, BEQUEST OF EMILI CABOT). FORMERLY IN THE COLLECTION OF MIQUEL I BADIA.

COLORLESS WITH GRAYISH TINGE. MOLD-BLOWN, MILLEFIORI APPLICATIONS, GILDED; CHASED SILVER FOOT.

6A

This ewer was blown in a two-part mold in the shape of a crouching lion. Its head is surmounted by a five-pointed crown, and it is holding an S-shaped shield that scrolls outward between the forepaws. The lion's tubular tail curves up in a tapering S and forms the spout of the ewer. The mane is dotted with blue and red flecks, which, along with gold leaf, had been marvered into the parison before it was inserted into the mold. After the vessel was removed from the mold, the top of the lion's head was opened and the crown was formed by tooling an applied trail around the rim into five points.

The glass stem and the base of the ewer were lost and later mounted on a stepped, silver-gilt foot with stylized floral repoussé decoration.

COMMENT: An almost identical lion ewer with red and blue flecks and traces of gilding, also without its original base and most of its tail spout, is in the Hakone Glass Forest, Japan (*Venetian Glass* 1996, p. 110, no. 34, color pl. 53). Several parallels of this vessel, but without the colored decoration, are also known. A similar object in the Museo Arqueológico Nacional, Madrid (13144), has a restored or replaced glass foot that is connected to the body by a metal joint (Pérez Bueno 1942, pl. facing p. 93). An example with its original ribbed foot and traces of gilding is in the Musée National de Céramique at Sèvres, France; it was formerly (until 1885) in the collection of Baron Jean-Charles Davillier (Frothingham 1941, p. 44 and fig. 31). Another piece, with its original mold-blown stem with masks and foot, was in the Emile Gavet Collection (*Gavet Collection* 1897, lot 598, ill.).

Two other variations of this type of ewer are known. A lion with overall *lattimo* decoration in *vetro a fili*, holding a shield of a different design and bordered by a scroll, was formerly in the collection of Ferdinand de Rothschild at Waddesdon Manor, London (Charleston and Archer 1977, pp. 96–99, no.

19). A winged lion with a spiral tail spout, formerly in the Lanna Collection, Prague, is now in the Kulturhistoriska Museet (Museum of Cultural History) in Lund, Sweden (*Sammlung . . . Lanna* 1911, no. 741, ill.; Kjellberg 1953, fig. 13). A similar winged lion ewer is also depicted in the drawings of Giovanni Maggi (**6a**) (Maggi 1977, v. 2, p. 153).

The winged lion ewer appears to represent the lion of Saint Mark, the symbol of Venice, which is found on many of that city's public buildings. For the iconography of the winged lion in Venice, see Pincus 1976, pp. 384–389; and Wolters 1983, pp. 231–236.

The Barcelona ewer showing a lion holding a shield conjures up more general connotations of protection, as expressed by the Greek philosopher Physiologus: "When the lion sleeps in his den, his eyes are watching because they are open" (Treu 1981, p. 6). But the lion as a symbolic guardian can also be found in Venetian architecture, as on the main portal of the Scuola Grande di San Marco (built 1485–1534) (Schmidt-Arcangeli 1997, p. 49, n. 19). Therefore, the presence (or absence) of wings on the lion is not a reliable argument against a Venetian provenance for the ewer.

Charleston argued that Spanish glassblowers had not mastered the elaborate technique of accurately arranging filigree canes, and that the Waddesdon vessel, with its canes neatly combined at the forehead of the lion, must therefore have originated in Venice. On the other hand, the undecorated lion ewers with scroll shields are of Spanish origin (Charleston and Archer 1977, p. 99).

BIBLIOGRAPHY: *Macaya Collection* 1935, pl. XIV; Gudiol Ricart 1941, color pl. 34.

# 7

## *Trick Glass*
### *H. 21.9 cm, W. 27.0 cm*

SPAIN, CATALONIA, EARLY 17TH CENTURY.
THE CORNING MUSEUM OF GLASS,
CORNING, NEW YORK (79.3.280, GIFT
OF THE RUTH BRYAN STRAUSS MEMORIAL
FOUNDATION); ACQUIRED FROM ARTHUR
CHURCHILL LTD. FORMERLY IN THE
COLLECTIONS OF JEROME STRAUSS (S918)
AND R. W. M. WALKER.

COLORLESS WITH YELLOWISH TINGE,
OPAQUE WHITE. BLOWN, FILIGREE
DECORATION.

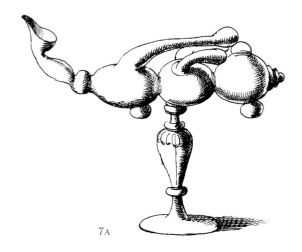

7A

This complex drinking glass is composed of 14 pieces. The conical bowl is tooled to a right angle from the body, which consists of three vertically connected ovoid bubbles. A short applied trail, pulled out to three points, decorates the base of the bowl. An elongated bubble, protruding horizontally away from the bowl, is connected to the top of the first bubble. Two other, slightly shorter vertical protrusions are applied to the sides of the second bubble, and they point in the same direction. A small, round bubble is inflated off the base of the first bulbous compartment, and three others extend from the top and base of the last compartment,

which is closed by a small merese. The whole device is applied, at the base of the second compartment, to a short stem section between two mereses, followed by a hollow spherical knop with vertical stripes in opaque white glass, and another short stem section that rests on a slightly conical foot with a rim that is folded under.

COMMENT: The trick glass from the Museu de les Arts Decoratives de Barcelona (Fig. 15) has a very similar construction, but the drinking funnel has been lost and its applied canes are in greater relief (Carreras 2001, p. 151, fig. 6). Another closely similar object

was illustrated by Giovanni Maggi (Maggi 1977, v. 2, p. 281; see **7a**). A vessel with applied blue decoration resembling a rooster was formerly in the Chopitea Collection (Gudiol Ricart 1941, no. 72). Such vessels were intended to be an amusement for drinking games. As one drinks from this glass, the liquid in the tubes and bulbs suddenly rushes out, dousing the drinker.

BIBLIOGRAPHY: Haynes 1948, pl. 17a; *Glass Drinking Vessels* 1955, p. 60, no. 157; "Important Acquisitions from the Strauss Collection," *JGS*, v. 22, 1980, p. 106, no. 21; Whitehouse 1993, cover.

## 8

### Ewer with Millefiori Decoration

*H. 24.9 cm*

PROBABLY SPAIN, CATALONIA, 16TH CENTURY. THE CORNING MUSEUM OF GLASS, CORNING, NEW YORK (2003.3.70, PURCHASED IN PART WITH FUNDS FROM THE HOUGHTON ENDOWMENT). FORMERLY IN THE COLLECTION OF CHRISTOPHER FISH.

COLORLESS WITH GREENISH TINGE, MULTICOLORED CANE SLICES. MOLD-BLOWN, APPLIED, GILDED, TOOLED.

This ewer has an ovoid body that is optic-molded with pronounced ribs and inclusions that consist of millefiori sections in white, red, blue, and yellow glass, applied over gold leaf. The colored decoration extends only to the shoulder of the vessel, while the gold leaf–embellished ribs continue up the narrow, slightly flaring neck with a counterclockwise twist and terminate in a cup-shaped rim. A colorless trail encircles the neck below the cup. An S-shaped, double-ribbed handle was applied to the shoulder of the flask and to the neck, just below the trailed ring. A pair of protrusions, serving as a thumb-rest, were pincered vertically from the top of the handle upward. The ewer has an applied ribbed spout, which gracefully curves up from the shoulder opposite the handle to the height of the lip. A colorless trail is at the opening of the spout, with a pair of opposing bifurcal protrusions below its lip. The applied pedestal foot is also optic-molded, with densely applied chevron bead–chip inclusions. It was tooled to form a bulging step, then waisted, and finally flared to a base with a wide, upfolded foot-ring.

COMMENT: This is the only known ewer of this shape with millefiori decoration. More common are blue ewers, some with pincered decoration and applied opaque white trails. Examples are found in the Hockemeyer Collection, Bremen (*Hockemeyer Collection* 1998, p. 172, color ill. p. 173, and pp. 277–278, no. 34); the Lehman Collection at The Metropolitan Museum of Art, New York (*Lehman Collection* 1993, no. 39); the Museo Poldi Pezzoli, Milan (*Museo Poldi Pezzoli* 1983, pp. 174–175, no. 55); the Museo Civico, Turin (Mallé 1971, p. 43); and the Museo Vetrario, Venice (Barovier Mentasti 1982, fig. 76). A tall, footed goblet with a bowl similar in profile to that of **1** has nearly identical millefiori cane sections that were marvered into the lower part of the vessel's bowl (Victoria and Albert Museum, London, 10.68.1871). This goblet had been preserved in a convent near Cadalso de los Vidrios in the province of Madrid, Spain (Frothingham 1956, pp. 16–17, and fig. 5).

In all instances, the millefiori pieces are cane sections, not beads or bead chips with holes (Hollister 1981, p. 222). Venetian-made vessels with this decoration are rare. A shallow, slightly lopsided bowl is in the Museum of Art at the Rhode Island School of Design, Providence (73.0.33) (*Selection IV* 1974, p. 30, no. 19). Fragments of a ribbed goblet with similar decoration have been found in an archeological context near Menges, in the vicinity of Ljubljana, Slovenia (Kos 1994, p. 96, fig. 2). A complete goblet that is similar in shape and decoration to the Ljubljana fragments was once in the collections of the Kunstgewerbemuseum, Berlin, but it was lost during World War II (Netzer 2000, p. 155, fig. 19). A footed goblet, a so-called *Scheuer*, which was popular in Germany, was formerly in the same collection (*ibid.*). A lid with optic-molded and millefiori bead decoration was excavated at Orléans (*Archéologie de la ville Orléans* 1987, no. 365, ill. on title p.). A similar piece (MS 3370M) is owned by the University of Pennsylvania Museum of Archaeology & Anthropology, Philadelphia (*The Museum Journal*, v. 4, no. 4, December 1913, p. 140, fig. 121). A covered bowl (G.P. 189) is in the Courtauld Institute Gallery, London (Hollister 1981, p. 224, fig. 1), and a wall fragment that was formerly in the Gréau Collection is now in The Metropolitan Museum of Art (MM 17.194.396) (*Gréau Collection* 1903, v. 2, p. 113, pl. 119, nos. 2 and 5). Two other examples of blown vessels with such decoration are a small ewer and a flask in The British Museum (Tait 1979, p. 104, no. 164, and p. 105, no. 166).

The blue ewer in the Hockemeyer Collection, cited above, is presumably identical to the one that was formerly in the collection of Frédéric Quesnel. In 1876, Quesnel found the object, together with glass beads, during the excavation of an Indian grave containing a female mummy on his property in Ancon, near Lima, Peru, at a depth of about two meters. A glass plate photo of the ewer, with a letter by Quesnel documenting this find, is in the Wilhelm Gretzer ethnographic archive at the Niedersächsisches Landesmuseum Hannover. A publication of this find by Andreas Behrens of the Hannover museum is forthcoming. The ewer was very likely a Spanish import to Peru in the late 16th century.

Because of the wide distribution of these vessels, the presence of Venetian-made cane sections cannot serve as proof that they were made in Venice. Instead, a wider range of production centers—including Spain, where the Islamic style of such ewers would be favored—can be suggested.

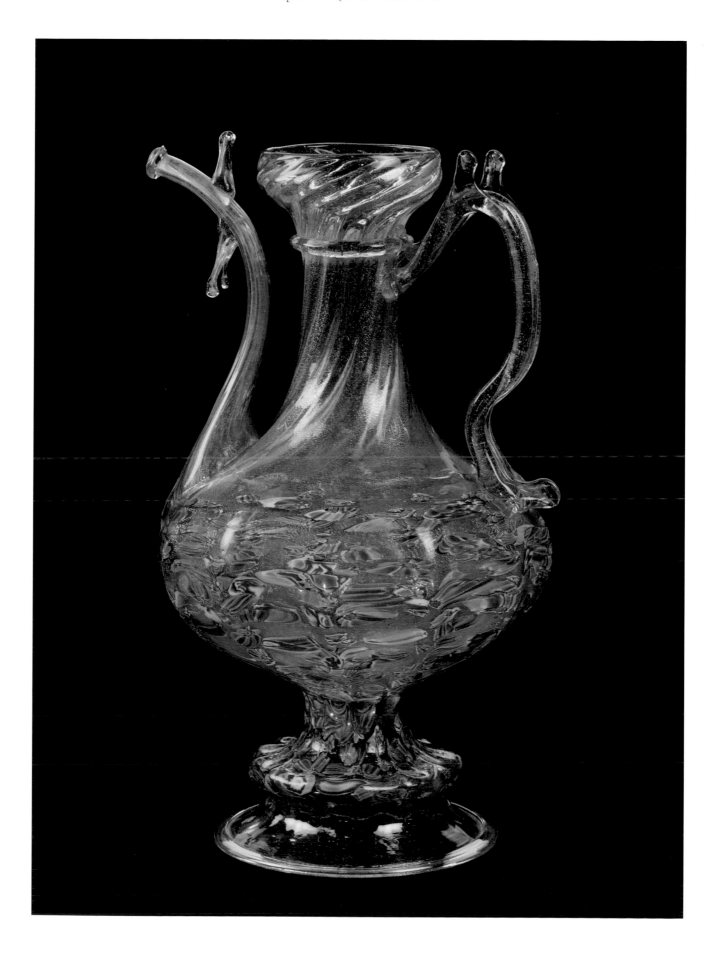

# 9

## *Covered Goblet* (Confitero)

### H. 25.7 cm

PROBABLY SPAIN, CATALONIA, 16TH CENTURY. THE CORNING MUSEUM OF GLASS, CORNING, NEW YORK (79.3.283, BEQUEST OF JEROME STRAUSS). FORMERLY IN THE COLLECTIONS OF MR. STRAUSS (S931) AND R. W. M. WALKER.

TRANSPARENT YELLOWISH, OPAQUE WHITE. BLOWN, DIAMOND-POINT ENGRAVED, MOLDED, GILDED.

The flat foot of this object was drawn into a hollow, tubular stem that was applied with a flattened knop to the flat base of the cylindrical body. A rough pontil mark remains on the lower part of the hollow stem. Three opaque white glass trails divide the bowl horizontally into four zones, with gilded mask prunts applied over the middle trail. There are four small molded and gilded raspberry prunts, two in the upper zones and two in the lower zones. The wall of the vessel is engraved with two formal foliate bands in one of the upper zones, with a band of curved and straight flamelike devices in the zone below it. The two adjoining zones show a band of foliate scrolls above and winged ovals below.

The foot is decorated with diamond-point engraved S-shaped devices alternating with pointed ovals. The flat, circular lid has a flared shoulder and a tapering rim. The center of the lid tapers to a drawn hollow finial topped with a merese, followed by a straight section with a ball knop at the top. The edge of the folded rim, which protrudes slightly, is decorated with an opaque white trail and three raspberry prunts. A rough pontil mark remains under the bottom of the lid. Its diamond-point engraved decoration consists of bands of long, pointed ovals alternating with small ovals.

COMMENT: For an identical glass in the collection of Rudolf von Strasser, Vienna, see Strasser and Spiegl 1989, p. 176, no. 15; and *Strasser Collection* 2002, pp. 56–57, no. 19, and ill. p. 58. A similar glass with green and yellow enameled decoration is in the collection of the Musée de Cluny (Frothingham 1963, p. 38, pl. 8). Another enameled parallel was formerly in the collection of Batsheva Rothschild, Tel Aviv (*Rothschild Collection* 2000, lot 30). For a parallel featuring a bowl with a rounded base, trails, and diamond-point engraving in the collection of Miquel Mateu at Perelada Castle near Figueras, Catalonia, see Gudiol Ricart 1941, no. 15. Other comparable objects are published in *Four Approaches to Glass* 2001, pp. 44–45 (blue glass); and *3000 Jahre Glaskunst* 1981, p. 30, no. 663, F 22 (formerly in the Biemann Collection, Zurich).

This type of vessel has been known in Spain since the 16th century as the *confitero*, a container for sweets. The inventory of household goods belonging to a woman from Majorca mentions such a glass in 1594 (Frothingham 1963, p. 38). The type is also illustrated in two drawings by Giovanni Maggi (Maggi 1977, v. 1, pp. 37 and 39).

## 10

### *The Principe Doria Goblet*

*Goblet: H. 41.1 cm, D. (max.) 17.4 cm; cover: H. 4.4 cm, D. (max.) 14.4 cm*

SPAIN, PROBABLY BARCELONA, DATED 1586, ENGRAVED BY IACOBUS BLANC DE VILASAR (SIGNED). PRIVATE COLLECTION.

COLORLESS WITH GRAYISH TINGE. BLOWN, APPLIED, TOOLED, ENGRAVED.

The ovoid body of this monumental goblet flares slightly toward the fire-polished rim. A stepped pedestal foot was applied to the body with a short stem consisting of three flat mereses. The four steps have rounded edges, and they increase in size toward the base. The edge of the slightly flaring foot-ring is folded under. The matching cover has a wide lip and a high, slightly tapering flange to fit the vessel's opening. Similar to the base, it is tooled into four stepped sections, which decrease in size toward the top. The cover is surmounted by a solid baluster finial consisting of two mereses followed by two short stem sections that alternate with ovoid knops.

The entire surface of the goblet and its cover are densely decorated with diamond-point engraving. The foot is engraved with ornamental and floral patterns. Thin horizontal lines accented by crosshatching emphasize the edges of the steps. The second step is inscribed, in capital letters, with the opening of the Hail Mary: "AVE MARIA GRACIA PLENA DOMINUS TECUM BENEDICTA TU IN MULIERIBUS ET BENEDICTUS FRUCTUS" [Hail, Mary, full of grace, the Lord is with thee; blessed art thou among women, and blessed is the fruit of thy womb, Jesus] (**10a**). The third step above this salutation is signed "IACOBUS BLANC DE VILASAR ME FECIT A · 25 · DE ABRIL ·

10A

10B

10C

10D

10E

10F

1586" [Iacobus Blanc of Vilasar made me on April 25, 1586] (**10b**).

The decoration on the body is arranged in five panels divided by horizontal lines. The first panel, near the bottom, is engraved with a row of flame motifs. This is followed by a figural frieze depicting a young wild boar, a roebuck, an ox, and a fawn, facing left. The third panel shows four large portraits surrounded by scrollwork. Two of these are in three-quarter composition, and they alternate with two others that are in profile, facing left. The first portrait, below the inscription "AN-DREA DORIA," shows a whiskered man in three-quarter profile, wearing a feathered cap and shouldering a halberd (**10c**). The next portrait, proceeding counterclockwise, depicts a soldier in profile, wearing a helmet resembling a *cabasset* (**10d**). The third figure is an

older, bearded man in three-quarter profile; he wears an old-fashioned cap and gown, and he holds a flagpole with a banner that bears a cross (**10e**). The fourth figure is another soldier in profile. Attached to the base of his burgonet is a panache (**10f**). Above the busts is the widest panel of the vessel's body, separated by two vertical bands with floral motifs. On one side, a large scroll cartouche displays the Doria family's coat of arms, an eagle surmounted by a crown (**10g**). It is flanked by two warships above banderoles inscribed "PRINCIPE / DORIA" [Prince Doria]. The panel on the opposite side is engraved with the same large armorial cartouche, flanked by the inscription "REX / MRS (MARIS)" [King of the sea] on banderoles and two warships surrounded by stylized stars (**10h**). Above the coat of arms, below the rim of the

vessel, is a frieze depicting, in profile, the heads of two soldiers on horseback and six others wearing helmets (**10i**). The stepped cover is engraved with ornamental and floral patterns, including stylized bands of crosses atop domes, as well as rows of vertical flame motifs.

COMMENT: Tall lidded goblets with ovoid bodies were prevalent in Venetian and Spanish glass production of the 16th and 17th centuries (Gudiol Ricart 1941, fig. 70). Similar lidded vessels are illustrated in the *Bichierografia* of Giovanni Maggi (Maggi 1977, v. 1, nos. 19 and 31). However, the stepped shape of the foot and lid is more common in Spanish glass *à la façon de Venise*, where it is often additionally embellished with molded and enameled decoration (*Macaya Collection* 1935, p. 63, fig. XVII, and p. 8, fig. XXV.1). This form also ap-

10G

10H

10I

pears in the bowls of goblets (Gudiol Ricart 1941, fig. 27; Frothingham 1963, fig. 21). A number of these glasses have been convincingly attributed to Spain and, more specifically, to a glasshouse in Barcelona (Folch i Torres [1926], ills. III–V). Diamond-point engraving, referred to as "grabadas a punta de diamante," is also common on Spanish luxury glass of the late 16th century (Frothingham 1956, ill. 30; Ainaud de Lasarte [1952], p. 355, ills. 899 and 901). The flame motif, as well as the peculiar scroll decoration surrounding the large busts on the bowl, appears on elegant glass *confiteros* attributed to Barcelona (**9**). These scrolls, unknown in Venetian glass, may derive from Moorish traditions in ceramics. They are found especially on 16th-century plates from İznik, Turkey, and other Islamic ceramics (two dishes from İznik, dated about 1585, are published in *Lagonico Collection* 1991, lots 31 and 32).

The figural decoration on this goblet, however, is unique. The inscribed name, Andrea Doria, most likely refers to Don Giovanni Andrea Doria I (1540–1606), prince of Genoa and Melfi and great-nephew of the famous Genoese statesman and admiral Andrea Doria (1466–1560). In 1586, the date inscribed on the goblet, Giovanni Andrea was serving as general admiral of Spain XI./XII., a title he had been awarded three years earlier. Later, in 1594, he became that nation's royal counselor. The decorative program on the glass goblet celebrates Doria's naval achieve-ments. Although he was not as out-standing as his great-uncle, Giovanni fought successfully with the Spanish in the decisive Battle of Lepanto against the Turks. In this bloody battle for naval supremacy in the Mediterranean, the allied Christian forces of the Holy League, united under the 24-year-old Prince Don Juan of Austria, defeated the Muslim fleet of Sultan Selim II. The Turkish admiral, Ali Pasha, was pitted against the Spanish, commanded by Santa Cruz; the Genoese and Maltese, under Giovanni Andrea Doria; the Venetians, headed by Sebastiano Venier; and the papal fleet, led by Marcantonio Colonna. It is possible that the large profile busts on the goblet depict the four victors at Lepanto. However, their severely stylized rendering does not permit us to make a more specific identification.

Two of the warships engraved on the vessel fly flags with the Christian cross, which are also shown in many period paintings of the Battle of Lepanto.

As noted above, the foot of the goblet is engraved in Latin with the first verses of the Hail Mary, the salutation to the Virgin Mary that is customarily prayed with a rosary. The inscription "Ave Maria Gracia Plena" is also found on a vessel listed in the inventory of the Spanish Queen Isabel's household goods, drawn up in 1503 (Frothing ham 1956, p. 8). However, the inscription on **10** may specifically refer to the Battle of Lepanto. Before this conflict, Pope Pius V had led a Rosary Crusade in western Europe to pray for victory, and the naval officers themselves are said to have prayed the rosary before engaging in battle with the Turks. In gratitude for the victory, the pope declared the first Sunday in October the Feast of the Holy Rosary. The Hail Mary on the goblet, therefore, may be another reference to this historic event, which was celebrated with large triumphal processions in every allied country. The frieze of soldiers on the glass may represent such a procession.

The name of the engraver, Iacobus Blanc de Vilasar, suggests that he or his family had emigrated from France and found work in the glassmaking center of Vilasar on the Catalan coast north of Barcelona. During the second half of the 16th century, the French persecution of the Huguenots forced many craftsmen into exile. It has been suggested that this engraver was a goldsmith from Toulouse who is traceable between 1507 and 1605. His father was the goldsmith Etienne Blanc, who in 1532 sent his son Jacques (Iacobus) to be apprenticed to Jehan Lagarde in Mazères (*Allgemeines Künstler-Lexikon* 1995, p. 373).[3] However, no known documents corroborate his presence in Spain. The occasion for the creation of the glass goblet in the spring of 1586 is also unknown, but the vessel was most likely commissioned as a gift for the wealthy statesman and Spanish ally Giovanni Andrea Doria.

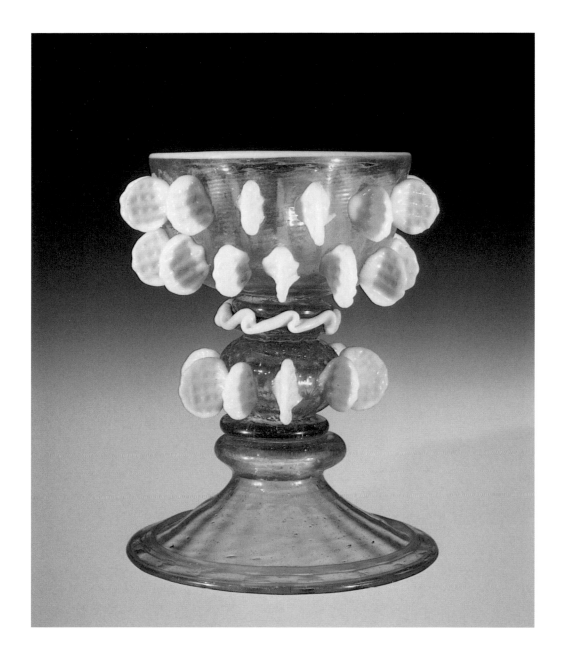

*11*

*Salt Dish*

OH. 11.1 cm, D. (rim) 7.3 cm,
(at crimped wings) 9.5 cm, (foot)
8.7 cm

SPAIN, CATALONIA, 18TH CENTURY. THE
CORNING MUSEUM OF GLASS, CORNING,
NEW YORK (59.3.50); ACQUIRED FROM
LEOPOLD BLUMKA IN 1959.

COLORLESS WITH GREENISH TINGE,
OPAQUE WHITE. PATTERN-MOLDED,
APPLIED, TOOLED.

This vessel consists of a hemispherical bowl that is mold-blown with a
pattern of thin, nearly horizontal stripes;
an elaborate stem that features an optic-
molded hollow knop between two thin
mereses; and an optic-molded pedestal
foot with a tooled, annular knop below
the stem and a wide, upfolded foot-
ring. Two offset rows of opaque white
pincered leaf shapes are applied to the
wall. The knop of the stem is decorated,
at its largest circumference, with another
row of pincered leaf shapes, and an undulating, pincered trail of opaque white
glass decorates the merese below the

bowl. One thin opaque white trail is
applied to the rim of the bowl, and
another appears on the edge of the
foot-ring.

The glass is bubbly.

COMMENT: Similar vessels are illustrated in Frothingham 1941, fig. 77; and
Gudiol Ricart 1941, pls. 93b, d, and
109c.

BIBLIOGRAPHY: Frothingham 1963,
fig. 27B (identified there as a wineglass).

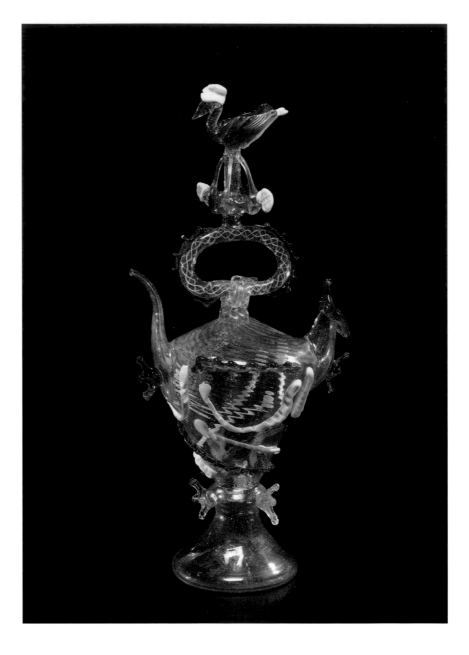

## 12

### Drinking Flask (Càntir)

H. 40.8 cm

SPAIN, CATALONIA, 18TH CENTURY. THE
CORNING MUSEUM OF GLASS, CORNING,
NEW YORK (54.3.143); ACQUIRED FROM
NICOLAS DE KOENIGSBERG, NEW YORK.

COLORLESS, OPAQUE WHITE, TRANSPARENT
BLUE. BLOWN, MOLD-BLOWN, APPLIED,
TOOLED.

This elaborate vessel has a conical body and a domed top. It was blown in an optic mold, and the thin ribs were twisted into a spiral pattern. A slender, pointed drinking spout and a short, broad filling spout were applied near the shoulder on opposite sides of the body. Both spouts have a blue three-pointed pincered trail at their base; in addition, the rim of the filling spout has a thick blue trail that was pincered to a point. The body is decorated with thick trails of looped and pincered white and blue glass. It is mounted on an angular, tooled knop above a hollow conical foot, which has a pushed-up base and a rough pontil mark in the center. A composite handle-finial surmounts the vessel. It consists of an oval ring with internal white spiral decoration, which was mounted with a thick trail of colorless glass across the ring's center and across the base. The base is a short filigree cane section between two pads of colorless glass. The whole is crowned by a stem surrounded by four trailed triangular loops decorated at the base with applied pairs of crimped opaque white and transparent blue pads. Perched on top is a stylized, tooled bird of colorless glass with blue wings and a white tail and crest.

COMMENT: A similar vessel is in the Museu de les Arts Decoratives de Barcelona (*Macaya Collection* 1935, p. 176, no. 155; Buckley, W. 1939, p. 29; Frothingham 1941, pp. 136–137, pl. IV; Gudiol Ricart 1941, p. 117 and pls. 99b and 106 (colorless); Pérez Bueno 1942, pl. opp. p. 84; Honey 1946, p. 145).

BIBLIOGRAPHY: *CMG Guide* 1958, p. 46, no. 44; *CMG Guide* 1965 and 1974, p. 46, no. 50.

## 13

*Rose Water Sprinkler*
(Almorratxa)

*OH. 24.7 cm, D. (max.) 12.7 cm*

SPAIN, CATALONIA, 18TH CENTURY. THE
CORNING MUSEUM OF GLASS, CORNING,
NEW YORK (53.3.41); ACQUIRED FROM
CECIL DAVIS, LONDON, ENGLAND.
FORMERLY IN THE COLLECTION OF MRS.
APPLEWHAITE-ABBOTT.

COLORLESS WITH GREENISH TINGE.
BLOWN, APPLIED, TOOLED.

This sprinkler has a biconical body
with a rounded shoulder, a base that
is constricted to form a short biconical
knop below, and a small and narrow
neck with a thick, flaring rim. The wall
of the body is decorated with white
filigree. The opaque white trails were
tooled in a helicoidal pattern, twisting
clockwise at the bottom, then becoming
horizontal, and twisting again at the
neck. Four vertical spouts were applied
to the shoulder of the vessel at roughly
equal distances from one another. During this process, the filigree decoration
on the body was pulled up into the wall
of the spouts. On the shoulder, between
the spouts, are four thick colorless trails

that were pincered into rows of peaks.
The lower part of the body has thin vertical trails of colorless glass that form a
series of loops. A trail applied around
the center of the hollow knop below
the body was pincered into a wavy
line.

The body was applied to an undecorated hollow foot and a columnar stem
that were tooled from the same bubble.
The cylindrical stem piece is followed
by a biconical knop and a domed foot
with an upfolded rim. The vessel has
a rough pontil mark on the interior of
the stem, near the body.

The glass is very bubbly and slightly
weathered.

COMMENT: A similar vessel, but without the knop in the columnar stem,
is in The Hispanic Society of America,
New York (Frothingham 1963, p. 49
and fig. 31), another example is in the
collection of the Instituto Amatller de
Arte Hispánico, Barcelona (Pérez Bueno
1942, ill. opp. p. 84), and two others
are in the Museu de les Arts Decoratives
de Barcelona (*Macaya Collection* 1935,
p. 182, no. 162, and ill. p. 183). Another
glass of this type, without filigree decoration, is in the Victoria and Albert Museum (Honey 1946, p. 145, pl. 39C).

BIBLIOGRAPHY: *Applewhaite-Abbott
Collection* 1953, pt. 4, no. 654.

## 14

### Footed Bowl with a Bird

H. 20.8 cm, D. 16.5 cm

SPAIN, CASTILLE, CADALSO, 18TH CENTURY.
MUSEU DE LES ARTS DECORATIVES DE
BARCELONA (4.973).

COLORLESS, TRANSPARENT BLUE. BLOWN,
APPLIED, TOOLED.

This vessel has a bucket-shaped bowl with a wide, flaring rim. Linked loops of transparent blue glass were trailed around the bowl near the base, and very thin colorless trails were repeatedly wound around the rim to form a wide ornamental band. The rim was then tooled into irregularly undulating lobes. The bowl is mounted on a bulbous, hollow stem, which is waisted near the middle; its upper part is encircled by a colorless pincered trail. It rests on a slightly domed foot with a folded foot-ring. In the center of the bowl is a stylized bird. A single bubble of transparent blue glass was constricted to form two ovoid forms for the bird's body and the knop beneath it. The bird's S-shaped neck, head, beak, and crimped tail are made of colorless glass and applied.

BIBLIOGRAPHY: Doménech 1999, p. 515.

## 15

### Vase

H. 23.6 cm, D. (rim) 12.2 cm,
(foot) 10.8 cm

SPAIN, CASTILLE, RECUENCO, LATE 17TH
CENTURY. THE CORNING MUSEUM OF
GLASS, CORNING, NEW YORK (59.3.4).

COLORLESS WITH GREENISH-YELLOWISH
TINGE. BLOWN, TOOLED, APPLIED.

This vessel was tooled from one bubble of glass. It has a high, funnel-shaped bowl above a squat inverted baluster and a high trumpet-shaped foot with a rough pontil mark. The irregular, solid annular knop above the foot is made of a thick trail of glass, which fused the opening between the bowl and the base. Two thin, curved handles with pincered trails were applied to the lower part of the bowl and to the baluster.

The glass is very bubbly, with small black impurities and, near the rim, faint amethyst striations.

## 16

### *Vase with Four Handles*
### H. 17.2 cm

Spain, Andalusia, Almería, 17th
century. The Corning Museum
of Glass, Corning, New York
(79.3.880, gift of The Ruth Bryan
Strauss Memorial Foundation).
Formerly in the collection of
Jerome Strauss (S304).

Transparent dark green. Blown,
stamped, applied, tooled.

This vase has a short, bulbous body
with a sloping shoulder and a tall conical neck with a fire-polished rim. It is
densely decorated with trails that end
near the base in a circuit of three-rib
guilloches. Four elaborate hollow handles are attached halfway up the neck
and to the shoulder of the body. They
are crested with pincered ribbons that
were attached to the neck and then
trailed down along the top of the handles. Four stamped clamshells were
applied to the shoulders between them.
The base of the vase has a pincered
foot-ring with a rough pontil mark.

Comment: An even more complex
vase of this type, with four additional
bulbous spouts between the handles,
was formerly in the Cabot Collection,
Barcelona (*Macaya Collection* 1935, pl.
XIX). Other examples are in the Victoria
and Albert Museum, London (Liefkes
1997, p. 59, fig. 67), and the Museu del
Cau Ferrat, Sitges (Barcelona) (Carreras
and Doménech 2003, p. 150, fig. 283).

Bibliography: Pérez Bueno 1942,
pl. opp. p. 85; Haynes 1959, pl. 22g.

# Venetian and *Façon de Venise* Glass in France in the 16th and 17th Centuries

## Marie-Laure de Rochebrune

Historians have abundantly underscored Italian influences on the French Renaissance in such fields as painting, sculpture, architecture, ceramics, and even the art of gardening. On the other hand, they have neglected consideration of another Italian influence: Venetian glass, in particular *cristallo*, for which a lively taste developed among the highest levels of French society. This fascination profoundly altered the nature of French glass production in the 16th and 17th centuries. It originated in court circles, where purchases of glasses blown in Venice were mentioned in early 15th-century documents, notably in the duke of Berry's accounts.[1] None of those early glasses seems to have survived. However, four pieces bearing the coat of arms of Anne of Brittany (1477–1514) may be among the oldest Venetian glasses of French provenance known today. These four objects, which can be dated between 1499 and 1514 (the years of the queen's reign), are a large dish with mount in the Victoria and Albert Museum, London (Fig. 1); a footed plate in The Toledo Museum of Art (Fig. 2); and tazzas in the Musée National de la Renaissance, Ecouen

(Fig. 3), and The Metropolitan Museum of Art, New York (Fig. 4). The tazza in the Metropolitan Museum shows distinct symptoms of crizzling, and it has therefore been suggested that the set could be of French rather than Venetian manufacture (*Lehman Collection* 1993, p. 11).

The court purchased Venetian glass continually. On several occasions, pieces that had been blown in Murano were bought by Francis I (r. 1515–1547) through a Venetian intermediary, Domenico Balbani (Bondois 1936–1937, p. 50). The 1532 inventory of the famous collector Florimond Robertet mentions "400 beautiful glasses in all colors and other Venetian *cristallo* vessels" (Crépin-Leblond 1995, p. 85). The French interest in Venetian glass continued during the reigns of Henry II (r. 1547–1559) and his sons. During the following century, it is attested by the paintings of Jacques Linard (1600–1645),[2] which depict pieces from Murano, and finds of small colored Venetian dishes in excavations at the Cour Napoléon in the Louvre, on the site of two semidetached houses built about 1622 (*Archéologie du Grand Louvre* 2001, p. 75, no. 12; pp. 107–110; and p. 172, fig. 120).

Throughout the 16th and 17th centuries, French sovereigns and other enlightened patrons, such as the dukes of Nevers, encouraged the emigration of

*Detail from* Peasants' Meal, *by Louis or Antoine Le Nain (Fig. 23).*

FIG. 1

*Dish with arms of Louis XII of France and Anne of Brittany, colorless, with blue, red, and white enamels; blown, enameled, gilded. Venice, 1498–1514. D. 42.5 cm. Victoria and Albert Museum, London (C.132-1914). Purchased from the Fitzhenry Collection in 1913; on loan to the museum since 1902.*

FIG. 2

*Footed plate with arms of Louis XII of France and Anne of Brittany, colorless, with blue, red, and white enamels; blown, pattern-molded, enameled, gilded. Venice or France, 1498–1514. D. 24 cm. The Toledo Museum of Art, Toledo, Ohio (1932.1).*

FIG. 3

*Tazza with arms of Louis XII of France and Anne of Brittany, colorless, with blue, red, and white enamels; blown, enameled, gilded. Venice, 1498–1514. H. 21 cm, D. 28.8 cm. Musée National de la Renaissance, Ecouen, France (E.Cl. 1567). Formerly in the collection of the Musée de Cluny, Paris.*

FIG. 4

*Tazza with arms of Louis XII of France and Anne of Brittany, colorless, with blue, red, and white enamels; blown, pattern-molded, enameled, gilded. Venice or France, 1498–1514. H. 22.1 cm, D. (rim) 27.6 cm. The Metropolitan Museum of Art, New York, Robert Lehman Collection (1975.1.1194).*

*Detail of Fig. 1.*

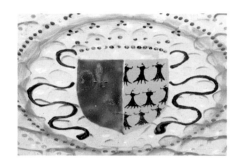

*Detail of Fig. 2.*

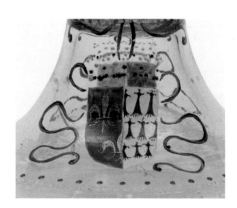

*Detail of Fig. 3.*

*Detail of Fig. 4.*

FIG. 5
*Peeter Jansz Pourbus (1523–1584, attrib.), portrait of Henry II, 1555. Oil on wood, H. 109 cm, W. 77 cm. Musée Crozatier, Le Puy-en-Velay, France (833.20).*

start of the 18th century, its leading position was overtaken by French, Bohemian, and English glass, and in time these wares were even imitated by Venetian glassmakers.

France was not the first nation to develop an appreciation of glass made on the island of Murano.[3] But it does appear to have been the first to persuade Italian glassmakers to relocate to its territory. The Italian Ferro or Ferri is said to have entered the service of René d'Anjou (1409–1480) in Provence in 1443 (Gaynor 1991, p. 73). During the 1500s, thanks to negotiations involving Henry II in Saint-Germain-en-Laye, Ludovico Gonzaga in Nevers, and Henry IV in Paris, Nantes, or Rouen, glassmakers from Italy settled in several French cities. The glass they made there was strongly influenced by Venetian production, and their work was said to be "à la façon de Venise." One of the earliest documented uses of this term in France is found in the privilege received by Teseo Mutio at Saint-Germain-en-Laye in 1551 (*ibid.*).

In France, the patterns and manufacturing processes were seldom disseminated by the Muranese themselves, who were not allowed to leave the lagoon without permission (under the threat of severe punishment; see p. 18), but mostly by glassmakers native to other regions of northern Italy. Among them was Mutio, a Bolognese, who was entrusted with the direction of the Saint-Germain-en-Laye glasshouse by Henry II (Fig. 5). The king granted Mutio a 10-year privilege for the making "en nostre dict royaume . . . verres, mirouers, canons [d'émail] et autres espèces de verreries à la façon de Venise" (in our kingdom . . . glasses, mir-

Italian glassmakers, who were directed to produce vessels similar to Venetian wares. Venetian-style glasses made in France were often represented in still-life paintings, notably in works by Lubin Baugin, the Le Nain brothers (see Fig. 23), and Simon Renard de Saint André (Rochebrune 2002b). In the second half of the 17th century, during the reign of Louis XIV, Muranese glassmakers were also invited to France to manufacture mirrors in the Venetian manner. The most famous of these emigrants was Paolo Massolao. With the help of the French ambassador to Venice, François de Bonzi, Massolao and other Venetians were hired in 1665 to blow glass in the Parisian suburb of Saint-Antoine (Girancourt 1886, pp. 106–107).

The popularity of Venetian glass began to decline in the last quarter of the 17th century. At the rors, enamel cakes, and other specialties of glass-ware in the Venetian style) (Gaynor 1991, p. 73).

Exerting a more significant influence on French glassmaking at that time was the massive exodus of glassmakers from Altare, a small town near Genoa in the duchy of Montferrat. These artisans had per-fectly assimilated Venetian techniques, and the au-thorities at Altare were willing to permit them to make Venetian-style glass abroad, as long as they did not reveal the secrets of their craft. Their work was certainly of very high quality, and for that they were praised in 1597 by Henry IV (r. 1589–1610), who noted that most of the glass used at court had been produced by Altarists working in Lyons and Nevers (Boutillier 1885, p. 17). By the end of the 16th century, glassmakers from Altare were employed in other parts of France, principally in Nantes, Paris, Bordeaux, and cities in Normandy and Poitou.

Despite governmental sanctions, a few Vene-tians secretly settled in France during the 16th cen-tury. There is documentary evidence that Mutio, in Saint-Germain-en-Laye, did not hesitate to seek support for Venetian workers in his glasshouse.[4] In 1572, the Venetian Fabiano Salviati was employed in Poitou, where he was protected by the count of Lude, governor of the province (Schuermans 1885, p. 196).

In France, the art of glassmaking had tradition-ally benefited from government support. At the end of the 14th century, Charles VI (r. 1380–1422) showed a considerable interest in glass. On Janu-ary 24, 1399, he granted the glassmakers of the

"lordship of Parc de Mouchamps" in Bas-Poitou their first privileges (Dugast-Matifeux 1861, p. 231; Garnier 1885, p. 66). By his act, the king recog-nized "the nobility of this profession" that was prac-ticed by masters from very old, patrician families, and he exempted them from various taxes (Garnier 1885, p. 66). These privileges, which remained in force until the French Revolution, were renewed on several occasions by Henry II and his sons, and later by Henry IV, Louis XIII, and Louis XIV.[5] Hen-ry IV (Fig. 6) was particularly concerned about the development of glassmaking and other luxury in-dustries. In 1600, he organized the profession of "marchands verriers, maîtres couvreurs de flacons et bouteilles en osier et autres espèces de verres de la ville de Paris" (glass merchants, masters who cover flacons and bottles in wickerwork, and oth-ers specializing in glass in the city of Paris).[6] Three years later, he decided to settle the status of glass-makers, ruling that this occupation did not auto-

Fig. 6

*Ambroise Dubois (1542/3–1614, attrib.), Henry IV as Mars, undated. Oil on canvas, H. 186 cm, W. 135 cm. Musée National du Château de Pau, Pau, France.*

matically grant noble standing to the practitioner; nevertheless, it could be pursued only by members of noble families (Barrelet 1953, p. 73). Indeed, glassmaking was the only activity of this kind that the French nobles were permitted to practice.

Henry IV encouraged the founding of new glasshouses by awarding them enormous privileges. In 1598, he favored the creation of a factory in Rouen by two Italians from the duchy of Mantua, Vincent Buzzone and Thomas Bertoluzzi, and he granted them an exclusive right to manufacture "verre de cristal, verres dorez, esmaux et autres ouvraiges qui se font à Venize" (crystal glasses, gilded and enameled glasses, and other works that they make in Venice) (Le Vaillant de la Fieffe 1971, p. 276). This privilege was transferred in 1605 to a noble glassmaker from Provence, François de Garsonnet, and confirmed on May 4, 1613 (*ibid*., p. 277). In 1619, Garsonnet gave up his rights to the Azémar brothers from Languedoc. Their rights were renewed by the king on several occasions (*ibid*., pp. 279, 280, 285, and 287).

Jean Maréchal, an associate of Henry IV's courtier and *valet de chambre* Pierre de Béringhen, received from the king in 1606 an exclusive right to make and sell Venetian-style glass in and around Paris. Maréchal, whose privilege was confirmed in 1612 by Louis XIII, maintained his glassmaking monopoly until 1650 (it was reconfirmed in that year by the young Louis XIV), causing some of his competitors to close their doors (Bondois 1936–1937, pp. 57, 71, and 72). A similar privilege for the region of Nantes was received from Henry IV by the Altarist Jean Ferro, allowing him to create four glasshouses. One of them, situated in La Fosse, Nantes, was founded in 1598, and it remained active for more than two centuries under the direction of the Sarode family (Barrelet 1953, p. 77). This family also settled in Bordeaux, where it was mentioned in 1605 (Bellanger 1988, p. 145), and in Vendrennes in Bas-Poitou, where a forest glass factory had already existed in the 13th century.

From the last quarter of the 16th century to the end of the 17th century, Nevers was the main French center of production of glass "à la façon de Venise." The art of glassmaking was staunchly supported there by Ludovico Gonzaga (1539–1595), a prince of the House of Mantua and grandson of Isabella d'Este. In 1565, upon his marriage to Henriette of Cleves, he became duke of Nevers (Rochebrune 2002a, p. 369). The duke, who had received an excellent education at the court of Henry II, supported the establishment in Nevers of glassmakers from the duchy of Montferrat, a possession of the Gonzaga family since 1533.[7] Ludovico's eldest son, Charles I (1580–1637), inherited his father's love for the arts and followed his policy of patronage. On several occasions, he renewed the privilege that had been granted to a glasshouse created during his father's reign,[8] and in 1612 he founded a second glassworks in Charleville, part of his principality of Arches (Archives n.d., LXXIII, 281, fol. 23 bis). Among the Altarists mentioned as working in Nevers at the end of the 16th century are the Pontis, the brothers Jacopo and Vincenzo Sarodo (who had been called from Lyons by Ludovico Gonzaga), the Castellanos, the Perrottos (Rose-Villequey 1971, p. 483), and the Borniolos. All of them adopted French names and received letters of naturalization from the king.

Shortly after it was founded, the Nevers glasshouse was awarded a manufacturing monopoly within 20 "lieues" (about 80 kilometers) of the city (Barrelet 1953, p. 75). This factory became so well known that, in 1590, Ludovico Gonzaga sent Jacques de Sarode (Jacopo Sarodo) to create a new glassworks in the duchy of Montferrat.[9] On that occasion, Louis asked his nephew, Vincenzo I Gonzaga (1562–1612), duke of Mantua, to grant the glassmaker a 20-year privilege for the manufacture "des verres polis et clairs, pour servir aux verreries comme on fait ici en France" (of bright and clear glasses for the table from the glasshouses as they are made here in France) (*Mantova e i Gonzaga di Nevers* 1999, p. 24).[10] The quality of the glass blown in Nevers must have been comparable to that of Venetian *cristallo*. At the beginning of the 17th century, the Nevers glasshouse was operated by Horace Ponte (Roumegoux 1991, p. 135). Following a brief interruption after his death, the factory reopened in 1647 under the direction of Jean Castellan, who had formerly lived in Liège. In 1661, Castellan obtained a privilege from Cardinal Mazarin to supply Venetian-style glass to all of the cities located along the Loire and its tributaries. He shared this privilege with his nephew, Bernard Perrot, who became one of the most innovative and prolific glassmakers in France.

The Altarists residing in Nevers were united by many family links. For instance, on February 28, 1601, a contract was signed in Paris for the wedding of François Ponte, a glassmaker from Montferrat, and Marie de Sarode (Archives n.d., XXIII, 219, fols. 128 and 129). Castellan was the husband of Marie Ponte, daughter of a glassmaker. In 1658, their own daughter, Marie, wed another Altarist, Marc de Borniol (Boutillier 1885, pp. 62 and 72). These families were also linked professionally. On March 12, 1601, Jacques de Sarode, who was already working in Paris, formed a partnership in Nevers with his nephew Horace Ponte (Archives n.d., XXIII, 219, fol. 159). The sale of the duchy of Nevers by Duke Charles II to Cardinal Mazarin in 1659, as well as the departure of Bernard Perrot for Orléans in 1662, contributed to the decline of glassmaking in Nevers. However, the city remained a center for the production of glass until 1780, when the factory closed. Although most of the glassworkers resident in Nevers at that time were natives of Liguria, the city retained its nickname "le petit Muran de Venise" (little Murano of Venice) (Thomas Corneille, cited in Honey 1946, p. 137).

France also benefited from the arrival, in the late 16th century, of many glassmakers from Lorraine. Since 1448, when they were granted a favorable charter, workers from this region enjoyed important privileges in their native country (Rose-Villequey 1971, p. 436). However, during the 16th and 17th centuries, Lorraine was the focus of political struggles between the French Crown and the House of Hapsburg.[11] The glassmakers were eventually harassed and expelled by the administration of the duchy in the early 17th century, and they also suffered from tragic conflicts such as the invasion of Lorraine by French troops in the 1630s, during the reign of Louis XIII. Glassmakers native to Lorraine had traditionally specialized in the production of window glass, but they learned the new technique of manufacturing hollow glass in the Venetian style. Thanks to the mobility of these workers, this technique was widely disseminated in France. They also supplied glass wares to the Paris market. For example, a contract of June 24, 1618, committed Claude Thomas, a Lorraine-born glassmaker, to sell "verres de Venise" to the Parisian merchant Judas Deguerre (Archives n.d., XXIII, 256, fol. 410).

Inevitably, the many forest glasshouses in France were also influenced by the influx of Venetian-style glass. These factories originally produced rather impure fern glass, but improvements introduced by Italian glassmakers prompted them to refine their wares, notably in a more careful selection of raw materials. Many of these forest glasshouses were operated by families that had long resided in southern France or Normandy. Some of the owners of these factories, including Garsonnet and Azémar, adopted new Venetian techniques (Bondois 1936–1937, p. 51).

Although these communities of glassmakers were never united by matrimonial alliances, they did enter into a number of commercial agreements. For example, on September 16, 1603, the Sarode brothers, who were working both in Nevers and in Paris, negotiated with the Hennezels, glassmakers native to Lorraine, the manufacture of "12,000 *liens* of window glass" (Archives n.d., XI, 86, fol. 212, rº et vº). (The Altarists never made window glass.) In 1611, Abraham de Hennezel collaborated with Italian glassmakers at the La Nocle glasshouse in the Nevers region, where he was employed (Rose-Villequey 1971, p. 487). Glassmakers from noble Lorraine families were recruited by the Italian glasshouse at Montenotte, near Altare, to make window glass there (Boutillier 1885, p. 139).[12] On September 19, 1626, the Altarist nobleman Jean de Borniol, a native of Montferrat and resident of Nevers, entered the service of Pierre d'Azémar, who had been master of the glasshouse in Rouen since 1619 (*ibid.*, p. 30).

## PRODUCTION

Recent archeological research has helped to sharpen the outlines of Venetian-style glass production in 16th- and 17th-century France. However, there are still many uncertainties about manufacturing sites. In general, the shapes of the objects made in France reflect the Venetian repertoire, including tazzas, dishes, ewers, drinking glasses, and goblets. The techniques used to make and decorate these glasses, such as selecting *cristallo* or colored glass, enameling, and gilding, are also part of the Venetian tradition. However, a thorough examination of Venetian-style glasses made in France during the reigns of the last Valois kings shows both a new spirit and new recipes. This deviation from Venetian prototypes increased in the 17th century.

The small group of enameled and gilded glasses blown "à la façon de Venise" in the mid-16th century are among the oldest known vessels made in France by Italian glassmakers (Gaynor 1991). All of these objects are decorated with religious or secular subjects, and they bear French or Latin inscriptions. The clothing worn by the figures on the glasses, much of which comes from the reign of Henry II (r. 1547–1559), is helpful in dating the vessels. The group of French enameled glasses has been augmented in recent years with pieces published by Suzanne Gaynor (*idem* 1994) and objects that have either appeared on the art market or been found in excavations. Among the forms in this group are goblets (**1** and Fig. 7), footed beakers (Fig. 8), tazzas (**2**), ewers, pilgrim flasks, and all of the usual shapes of Venetian glassware. It seems, however, that the glassmakers who created these objects took great liberties with their Venetian models, producing large-scale pieces that display a clumsiness of construction and a naïveté in the execution of the decoration that one never encounters in glasses made in Venice. In addition, by the 1550s, the presumed date of the French-made glasses, Muranese glassmakers had long since abandoned enameling. Instead, they had adopted new decorative techniques such as diamond-point engraving and filigree ornament.

Among the French enameled glasses, the most remarkable examples are the footed glasses in the form of a chalice with a religious theme. The most famous of these vessels, whose shape is unknown among Venetian glasses, belongs to the Wallace Collection in London. It presents a scene of the Crucifixion accompanied by a snake, evoking John

FIG. 7

*Goblet with portrait of a woman, grayish green, with blue, red, white, black, and orange enamels; blown, enameled, gilded. France, about 1540. H. 14.5 cm. Musée du Louvre, Paris (OA 3111, bequest of Baron Jean-Charles Davillier, 1883). Formerly in the Davillier Collection.*

Fig. 8

*Footed beaker, colorless with grayish tinge, with white, blue, brown, yellow, and red enamels; blown, enameled, gilded. Probably France, 16th century. H. 17 cm. Victoria and Albert Museum, London (C.260-1936).*

the Evangelist (**1**). The Crucifixion also appears in association with the Virgin Mary and John, on a superb object in the Bayerisches Nationalmuseum in Munich (Fig. 9), and on a vessel recently acquired by the Musée du Louvre (**3**). On the Louvre glass, the scene is located under an arch-shaped door, with a representation of the donor, whose name, "Guillerme Pastor," is inscribed in a phylactery in front of a bishop, perhaps the donor's patron saint. The form of this vessel probably derives from contemporaneous silver objects. The three glasses (**1**, Fig. 9, and **3**), blown of light grayish glass, also bear a gilded and engraved stripe punctuated with enameled dots that is quite traditional

in Venetian glassware. The French-made drinking glasses, which more often have a secular iconography and simple geometric decorations, display a great variety of shapes and subjects, as can be seen in examples in The British Museum in London (Fig. 10) and the Musée National de la Renaissance in Ecouen (Fig. 11).

A few well-executed vessels can be closely dated because of the costumes of the enameled figures shown on them. One example is a footed beaker in the Victoria and Albert Museum in London (Fig. 8), and a footed beaker in the Musée National de la Renaissance presents three halberdiers standing on small grassy elevations (**4**). Several glasses are relief-molded in older forms, such as an inscribed vessel in The Corning Museum of Glass (**5**).

While the techniques used in making this group of glasses, such as the use of *cristallo*, gilding, and colored enamels, derive from Muranese practices, the shapes seem to have been adapted by glass-makers in France to suit the preferences of their customers. These vessels, which were principally employed in the drinking of wine, were larger than their Venetian counterparts, and their enameled decoration was both simpler and more symmetrical. The provenance of the group is an open question. Enameled glasses may have been made in Saint-Germain-en-Laye, Poitou, Nevers, or Montpellier.[13] Suzanne Gaynor has noted that the Italian glassmakers to whom these glasses are attributed continued to use enameling for a considerable period of time, since examples of their work dating from the reign of Louis XIII (r. 1610–1643) are known (Gaynor 1991, pp. 58–59; Rochebrune 2002a, p. 373, fig. 5).

Three pieces decorated with the coat of arms of Catherine de Médicis are probably contemporaneous with this group. A footed bowl in the Musée National de la Renaissance was blown of light grayish *cristallo* (Fig. 12). While its slightly heavy form recalls that of some glasses blown in Murano about 1500, it cannot have been made before 1547, when Catherine's husband, Henry II, acceded to the throne, because the tazza bears her arms as queen of France. Some scholars attribute this piece to the glasshouse at Saint-Germain-en-Laye, which was founded by Henry in 1551 and often protected by the queen (Crépin-Leblond 1995, p. 92). This attribution appears to be convincing, since "façon

FIG. 9

*Two views of a goblet depicting the Crucifixion, colorless with grayish tinge, blown, tooled, enameled, gilded. France, 1526–1550(?). H. 17 cm. Bayerisches Nationalmuseum, Munich (60/67). Formerly in the collection of Heinrich Brauser.*

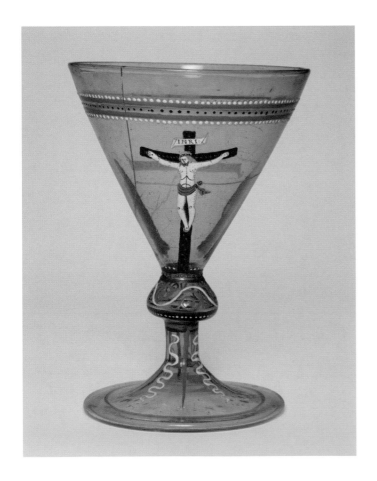
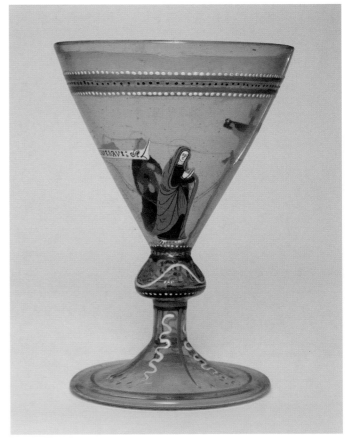

FIG. 10

*Wineglass, colorless, with blue, white, red, yellow, and brown enamels; blown, enameled, gilded. France, 16th century. H. 16.5 cm. The British Museum, London (S.824).*

FIG. 11

*Goblet, colorless with pinkish tinge, with pale blue, white, red, black, gold, and yellow enamels; blown, enameled, gilded. France, 16th century. H. 22.0 cm. Musée National de la Renaissance, Ecouen, France (E.Cl. 10830). Formerly in the collections of Baron Jean-Charles Davillier and the Musée de Cluny, Paris.*

FIG. 12

*Footed bowl with arms of Catherine de Médicis, colorless with grayish tinge, transparent blue, with blue, red, and white enamels; blown, mold-blown, enameled, gilded. France, mid-16th century. H. 15 cm, D. 25.5 cm. Musée National de la Renaissance, Ecouen, France (E.Cl. 14438). Formerly in the collection of the Musée de Cluny, Paris.*

de Saint-Germain-en-Laye" glasses are listed, unfortunately without much precision, in the inventory written after the queen's death in 1589 (Bonnaffé 1874, p. 87, no. 262).

A basin bearing Catherine's arms and rather similar enameled decoration is in a private collection in Amsterdam, and it supports the notion that a full service was executed for the queen (Crépin-Leblond 1995, pp. 91–92). The third piece related to Catherine, recently acquired by the Musée National de la Renaissance, is a small lobed bottle blown of translucent blue glass, enameled, and gilded (6). One of the ribs bears the queen's arms in perfect heraldic accord with the coat of arms on the *cristallo* tazza in the same museum. The rest of the decoration consists of a gilded scale pattern, stripes, milling, and foliage. The very narrow opening is enriched with gold. When this bottle was ac-

quired, Pierre Ennès correctly supposed that it could very well be one of the "huict potz de verre bleu doréz à mettre confitures" (eight containers of gilded blue glass to hold jams) mentioned in the inventory of 1589 (Bonnaffé 1874, p. 87, no. 260; Ennès 1997, no. 8). This fascinating document offers ample evidence of Catherine's taste for glassware. The shape of the bottle is unknown in glass made in Venice or elsewhere in Europe. This suggests that it was probably produced in France, perhaps in the Saint-Germain-en-Laye glasshouse that was especially favored by the queen.

A small group of pale blue pilgrim flasks, usually dated to the mid- or late 16th century, illustrates perfectly how difficult it is to distinguish Venetian-style glass blown in France during the reigns of Henry II and his sons from glass created in Venice. The form of these pale blue flasks is well known

FIG. 13

*Pilgrim flasks, dichroic, opalescent pale blue in reflected light and brownish red in transmitted light (left), opalescent blue in reflected light and reddish in transmitted light (right), blown; silver-gilt mount (enameled and cold-painted, left). Probably France (glass), southern Germany (mounts), about 1550-1600. H. (taller) 47.5 cm. Museum Grünes Gewölbe, Dresden (IV 268, IV 205).*

in Italian majolica. The five finest examples of this type later received metal mounts. Four of these objects are identical in shape, while the fifth has a more slender profile.

The Louvre houses one of these flasks (**7**), which was purchased in 1825 with the famous collection of Chevalier Durand. This piece, which is enriched with gilded birds, flowers, and foliated scrolls, has a partly gilded mount made of metal bands. The mount contains two small enameled plaques from Limoges showing Hercules and Fortune, which may date from the 1550s. In his unpublished catalog of glass at the Louvre, James Barrelet attributed this flask to France because of the Limoges plaques, and to the Saint-Germain-en-Laye glasshouse because the figure of Hercules was traditionally emblematic of the French kings who offered protection to this court factory. A nearly identical example is in the collection of the Victoria and Albert Museum. Another of these flasks, in a private collection in Paris, has the same pewter mount enclosing two enameled plaques from Limoges, but it is not gilded.

The remaining two of these flasks are in the collection of the Grünes Gewölbe in Dresden (Fig. 13). One is fitted with a fine gilded silver mount with a pedestal foot (Menzhausen 1968, p. 80, no. 27, pl. 27). The museum's curators had always attributed this object to glassmakers in Murano, since they had striven to create the appearance of hard or semiprecious stones. The other example has a spindle shape and a sumptuous enameled and gilded silver mount. It is dated to 1574 (*ibid.*).

The origin of these flasks is uncertain. There is no irrefutable argument that allows us to posit a French or Venetian provenance for them, although it seems unlikely that the Saxon court imported French glasses. On the other hand, the importation of Venetian glasses both in France and in Saxony was well established during the 16th century.

A similar group of flasks, blown of dichroic glass, is equipped with simpler mounts. One example, in a lead mount, is in the collections of the Louvre (**8**). Another is in The J. Paul Getty Museum in Los Angeles, and it features an engraved pewter mount that recalls the art of Isaac Briot (Fig. 14) (Hess and Husband 1997, pp. 170–173). While the

FIG. 14

*Pilgrim flask, dichroic (Prussian blue to smoky brown), blown; pewter mounts. Possibly France, 1550–1600. H. 33.5 cm. The J. Paul Getty Museum, Los Angeles (84.DK.519).*

metal mounts of these objects appear to have been made in France, nothing allows us to assert that the glass was manufactured there. The crudest flask of this group, in The Corning Museum of Glass, is decorated in enamel (**9**).

The difficulty of identifying Venetian-style glasses made in France during the second half of the 16th century arises again in the case of the famous tazza of Marthe Mansion de la Pommeraye (Fig. 15), which is in the Musée National de la Renaissance. This object was purchased in 1867 from Benjamin Fillon, who, in turn, had bought it from a Poitiers collector named Marganne (Pelliot 1930, pp. 307 and 311–314). The tazza, which has a

FIG. 15

*Tazza said to show initials of Marthe Mansion de la Pomme-raye, light green, blown, arms of France, emblems, animals, dia-mond-point engraved. Probably France, Poitou, dated 1578. H. 14 cm. Musée National de la Renais-sance, Ecouen, France (E.Cl. 8629). Formerly in the collection of the Musée de Cluny, Paris.*

ribbed knop, was blown of light greenish *cristallo*. Its neat diamond-point engraved decoration consists of the French coat of arms, the initials of its presumed owner, the date "1578," a band of real and mythical hunted animals, and a heart pierced with two arrows. The last of these indicates that the vessel was certainly decorated for a wedding. On the basis of the initials (*A.M.M.D.L.P.*), Fillon attributed the ownership of the tazza to Marthe Mansion de la Pommeraye, wife of the 16th-century Protestant physician Gedeon Picart in Foussay, Bas-Poitou.

The iconography of the object initially suggests that it was made in France by Italian glassmakers. But several scholars, including Robert Charleston, have classified it among a group of 11 diamond-point engraved pieces that are attributed, based on their form, to the famous Venetian glassmaker Jacopo Verzelini and to the French-born engraver Anthony de Lysle (see pp. 278–279). Verzelini succeeded Jean Carré at London's Crutched Friars glasshouse in 1572, and de Lysle is mentioned as a glass and pewter engraver in London in 1583

(Charleston 1984a, pp. 56 and 58 and pl. 12c). Similarities between the Ecouen tazza and pieces attributed to Verzelini and de Lysle, notably in the representation of unicorns and other animals, make the idea of English production enticing. However, it seems strange to suggest that the tazza would have been ordered from England on the occasion of a simple wedding in Poitou when the Salviati glasshouse, protected by the count of Lude, was making Venetian-style glass in that very region at the same time (Pelliot 1930, p. 313). Perhaps an investigation of the object's history prior to its acquisition by Marganne, as well as a reconsideration of the initials (which may have been too quickly identified by Fillon), will shed new light on this mystery.

Historians of French glass have always had difficulty in attributing objects made during the first half of the 17th century. Until recently, this effort relied on oral traditions, on contemporaneous descriptions, on paintings (notably works by the Le Nain brothers, Jacques Linard, and Lubin Baugin), and on a few glasses from French collections that were said to date from the reign of Louis XIII. All of this was far from satisfactory. Furthermore, the state of the collections of Louis XIII at the time of his death is unknown, and there is not a single object that can safely be said to have belonged to him. The inventory of the possessions of his wife, Anne of Austria, written after her death in the Louvre on January 20, 1666, was published in 1930 (Cordey 1930). Unfortunately, it does not mention any French glassware. Instead, it describes only hand-held mirrors, inserted in gold or silver mounts, that were probably made in Venice (*ibid.*, nos. 80 and 81). While the word *cristal* appears several times in this document, it is, of course, a reference to rock crystal. The absence of glassware in this inventory is rather surprising, given the large number of glasses contained in the 1589 inventory of Catherine de Médicis. The only piece that may be said to have belonged to a member of the French royal family in the first half of the 17th century is a remarkable diamond-point engraved plate in the collection of The Corning Museum of Glass (**10**). It bears the monogram of Gaston of Orléans, the brother of Louis XIII, and it was probably created in France by an Italian glassmaker (Rochebrune 2002a, pp. 373–375, fig. 1).

Until recently, ignorance prevailed concerning glass made in France in the first half of the 17th century. In the last few years, however, numerous excavations at Parisian and provincial sites have brought to light hollow-ware pieces that can be securely dated to that period. Recent finds in Paris, Lyons, Nevers, Metz, Epinal, and Châlons include many objects blown "à la façon de Venise" that most scholars attribute to France. While the forms of these objects derive from the Venetian typology, they are unknown in Venetian, Flemish, English, German, and Spanish excavations and paintings. These objects retain the innovations that were introduced in the 16th century. Mold-blown pieces were largely abandoned in favor of glasses that were blown and then decorated. Drinking glasses often featured a stem with a simple, flattened knop that was sometimes ribbed (Fig. 16). Their bowls were

FIG. 16

*Tazza, colorless with brownish tinge, blown, mold-blown, applied, tooled. France, first half of the 17th century. H. 7 cm, D. (rim) 20.5 cm. Musée du Louvre, Paris (MRR 128). Formerly in the collection of Pierre Revoil; acquired in 1828.*

circular or polygonal (Fig. 17), and smooth surfaces were preferred because they permitted the greatest freedom for the decorator, who could select diamond-point engraving, applied trails, enameling, filigree, and teardrops. Some glasses were equipped with balusters, and they sometimes had an amber, light blue, brown, or gray tint (**11** and Fig. 18). The Venetian wineglass inspired considerable variations in the shapes of bowls and baluster stems (**12** and Fig. 19).

A few glasses with balusters in the shape of a lion's head have been found in French exacavations. This type of object was made all over Europe during that time, from Italy and Spain to England and the Low Countries, so it is difficult to determine whether the glasses found in France were made there. Notable examples were uncovered in the Cour Napoléon at the Louvre (Barrera 1990, p. 356, type 16, fig. 12, no. 38) and in Metz (Cabart 1990, p. 226, no. 47, fig. 3). The Cour Napoléon site has also produced high-quality asymmetrical serpent-stem goblets (Fig. 20) (Barrera 1990, p. 357,

**FIG. 17**

*Octagonal drinking glass, colorless, blown, mold-blown, tooled, applied. France, first half of the 17th century. H. 16.2 cm, D. (rim) 15.3 cm, (foot) 8.0 cm. Musée des Arts Décoratifs, Paris (2000.1.1).*

**FIG. 18**

*Tazza, colorless with grayish tinge, blown, mold-blown, tooled, applied. France, first half of the 17th century. H. 12.0 cm, D. (rim) 21 cm. Musée des Arts Décoratifs, Bordeaux, France (7560).*

FIG. 19

*Fluted wineglass, colorless with grayish tinge, blown, mold-blown, tooled, applied. France, first half of the 17th century. H. 19.5 cm, D. (rim) 11 cm. Musée des Arts Décoratifs, Bordeaux, France (78.3.6).*

FIG. 20

*Serpent-stem drinking glass and details of the stem, colorless with pinkish tinge, blown, tooled, applied. France, first half of the 17th century, excavated in the Cour Napoléon. H. 16 cm. Musée du Louvre, Paris (5487-17).*

type 17, fig. 13, nos. 39–41). They are very different, both in appearance and in chemical composition, from their Venetian and Low Countries counterparts, and this suggests that they may have been made in France by Altarists (Velde 2000, p. 16).

Some of these objects are shown in paintings of the same period. For example, a glass like the one in the Wirth Collection (Fig. 21) can be seen in a superb basket of glasses by Sebastian Stosskopf, which was painted by this Strasbourg artist during his stay in Paris (Fig. 22) (Rochebrune 2002b, pp. 38–40), and in several works by the Le Nain brothers, especially in *Peasants' Meal* (Fig. 23).

One of the principal activities of Altarist and Venetian glassmakers working in Nevers and Saint-Germain-en-Laye was the creation of "enamel cakes" for lampworked glass. This technique, executed with tongs by enamelers, had been introduced in France by Italians in the mid-16th century. In 1551, Teseo Mutio's privilege in Saint-Germain-en-Laye

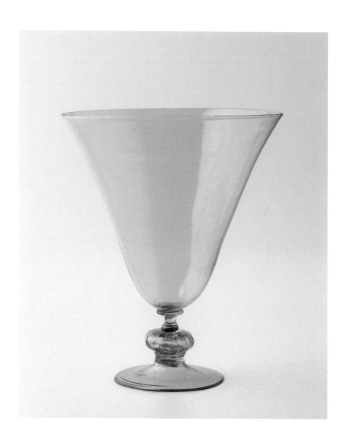

included the production of these cakes (Girancourt 1886, pp. 106–107). One of the first Italian enamelers in France, Thomas Dagu (perhaps a Venetian), is said to have settled in Nevers before 1577 (Broc de Segange 1863, p. 248). By the end of that century, two other enamelers, Jean and Léon Prestereau, were working there. Barthélémy Bourcier, who practiced this technique from 1626 to 1631, was called

**FIG. 21**
*Stemmed drinking glass, colorless with pinkish tinge, blown. France, first half of the 17th century. H. 16 cm, D. 13.2 cm, (foot) 6.6 cm. Collection of Barbara Wirth, Paris (39).*

**FIG. 22**
*Sebastian Stosskopf (1597–1657), Basket with Glasses and Pie, about 1630–1640. Musée de l'Oeuvre Notre-Dame, Strasbourg, France (Mba 1776).*

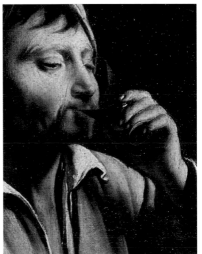

FIG. **23**
*Louis or Antoine Le Nain (about 1600–1648), Peasants' Meal, 1642. Oil on canvas, H. 97 cm, W. 122 cm. Musée du Louvre, Paris (R.F.M.I. 1088).*

"master enameler to the queen mother [Marie de Médicis]" (*ibid.*, p. 64). In 1632, he founded a faience factory (*ibid.*, pp. 64 and 249).

Lampworked objects were often presented as gifts to distinguished visitors to Nevers. For example, in 1622, the city gave Louis XIII "a work in enamel" depicting his victory over Protestants on Ré Island (*ibid.*, p. 249). When he was a child, the king appears to have had several lampworked figures as toys. His physician, Jean Héroard, reports that, on September 13, 1605, his wife offered the young dauphin "small glass dogs and other animals made in Nevers" (Héroard 1989, p. 754). On January 21, 1615, Héroard wrote that the young king played with "ses petits marmosets d'aismal" (his small marmosets of enamel) (*ibid.*, p. 2263).

The production of lampworked glass continued in Nevers until the end of the 18th century, and it spread to other cities, such as Paris and Orléans. It is one of the more unusual variants of Venetian-style glass in France, and it survived after the introduction of new styles from Bohemian and British glassmakers. However, there are no surviving French lampworked pieces that can be securely dated to the 16th or 17th century. All of the examples in public and private French collections were made during the 18th century.

In the last quarter of the 17th century, the art of making glass "à la façon de Venise" began to decline in France. Several reasons may be offered for this change. The introduction of Ravenscroft's lead crystal in the 1670s, and that of chalk glass from Bohemia, led to a change in the public's taste in glass. These thick, brilliant, and transparent glasses were ideal for carving and wheel engraving, two traditional techniques from the repertoire of rock crystal makers that were impracticable on crystalline Venetian glass. The two new glasses were quickly welcomed throughout Europe, and French glassmakers attempted to imitate them before the end of the 17th century. By the early 1700s, they had replaced Venetian-style production.

Ironically, part of the move away from glass made "à la façon de Venise" can be attributed to one of the best Altarists working in France during the reign of Louis XIV (r. 1643–1715). Bernard Perrot

(1619–1709) had been born into a glassmaking family allied by marriage to the Castellanos, who became famous for their glass made both in Liège and in Nevers. In 1648, Perrot settled in Orléans, where he thrived as a glass technician of genius. Having considerably improved the Venetian process of making *lattimo* glass, he applied these advances to the production of glass that imitated porcelain, a response to the sizable importation of Chinese porcelain in France at that time. Perrot, concurrently with Kunckel in Berlin, also experimented with formulas for a translucent ruby glass made with gold (**13** and **14**). Unfortunately, no French gold ruby glass is securely attributed to Perrot (Kerssenbrock-Krosigk 2001, p. 59). He sometimes combined his red glass with Venetian *cristallo* to fashion French forms such as the beautiful cask-shaped ewer that is now in Rouen's Musée de la Céramique. (This shape is also known in metal and ceramics.) Perrot also further developed agate glass, which can be seen in the famous ewer in the collection of the Musée National de la Renaissance (**14**). Finally, Perrot's innovations in the casting of glass revolutionized the manufacturing of window glass, mirrors, and large medallions (**15**). These processes, presented to the French Academy of Sciences in 1687, were approved by the king during the following year. Although the royal glass manufactory at Saint-Gobain deprived Perrot, quite unjustly, of the acclaim that his discoveries should have deserved, his work rendered the Venetian techniques of mirror making obsolete and caused the Muranese to lose their monopoly in the production of this type of glass.

A final reason for the decline of Venetian-style glass in France at the beginning of the 18th century was the developing fashion for "pivette" drinking glasses, blown of very light *verre de fougère* (Fig. 24). These new vessels, which were often represented by such painters as Chardin (notably in his 1728 *The Buffet*, now in the Louvre), were considered to be more suitable than Venetian glass for the drinking of wine. In his *Dictionnaire universel de commerce*, published in Geneva, Switzerland, in 1742, Jacques Savary des Brûlons (1657–1716) noted, "As in regard to glasses, the fine gourmets them-

FIG. 24
*Three wineglasses (verres pivettes), colorless, blown, pattern-molded, tooled.*
*France, early 18th century. H. (tallest) 14 cm. The Corning Museum of*
*Glass, Corning, New York (60.3.16, 58.3.174, 79.3.550).*

selves believe that wine would be finer and more delicious in the simple fern glass, hardly known in France, than in the glass from Venice" (Barrelet 1957, p. 104; Rochebrune 2000, p. 48).

For nearly three centuries, Venetian and *façon de Venise* glass played a very important role in France, especially in drinking and eating habits at court. This glass, which was initially used only in royal and aristocratic circles, eventually entered more modest environments, as can be seen in paintings of that time. Wherever it was found, however, it was sumptuous. The fashion for Venetian glass ended in the late 17th century with the advent of new types of glass discovered in England and Bohemia. The qualities of these new materials, especially those of the English lead glass, captivated the wealthier French public. In more modest homes, the locally made *verre de pivette* gained popularity.

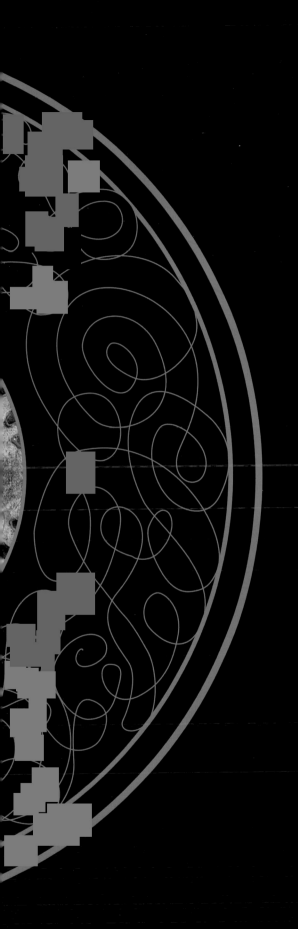

Venetian and *Façon de Venise* Glass
in France in the 16th and 17th Centuries

*Objects*

Jutta-Annette Page

# 1

## Goblet Depicting the Crucifixion

### H. 22.4 cm

FRANCE, 16TH CENTURY. WALLACE
COLLECTION, LONDON (XXVB96).
FORMERLY IN THE COLLECTION OF SIR
RICHARD WALLACE, LONDON, AND
(UNTIL 1868) THE ROUX COLLECTION,
TOURS.

COLORLESS WITH GRAYISH TINGE;
WHITE, RED, BLUE, YELLOW, OLIVE
GREEN, AND BROWN ENAMELS.
BLOWN, ENAMELED, GILDED.

The goblet consists of a bowl with straight, flaring sides and a flat, slightly tapering base that is applied to a straight, hollow stem with a central, trailed-on merese above a large globular knop. A short tubular stem-piece connects it to a trumpet-shaped foot with a folded rim. One pontil mark is located under the foot, and another is in the center of the bowl.

The bowl is decorated with a wide band of gold leaf, framed by thin bands in blue and red enamel and a row of small opaque white dots on either side. The gold band is incised with a motif of triangles enclosing demiflower heads. On the lower third of the bowl, rays in blue and yellow enamel alternate with undulating white lines. The painted decoration on the stem, above the merese and on either side of the knop, consists of vertical lines alternating with red dots on gilded grounds that are bordered by horizontal red and white lines. The merese is emphasized with a pattern of diagonal lines in red, white, and blue enamel. The honeycomb pattern of the knop is outlined in yellow enamel, each field enclosing four-petal florets in white with blue centers.

The front of the large foot is prominently enameled with a scene of the Crucifixion. Above the bearded Christ on the Cross, painted in white enamel with a blue loincloth, are the letters "INRI" (Jesus of Nazareth, King of the Jews). The figure of Christ is flanked by two white scroll bands, inscribed "SINE ME" (Without me) on the left band and "NICHIL" (nothing) on the right one. Two snakes and grotesque ornament fill in the space between the Crucifixion and a bundle ornament, surrounded by foliate scrolls on the back of the foot.

COMMENT: The goblet was initially dated to the 1530s (Schmidt 1912, p. 275). Gaynor (1991, p. 43) proposed a mid-16th-century date based on this object's similarity to a goblet in the Louvre depicting busts with a costume style of the 1540s (Fig. 7). She also noted the representation of the loincloth, as well as the comparison of the knop and the foot with an undecorated fragment excavated at Châlons-sur-Marne in a late 16th-century context that included two coins, a *double tournois* of Francis I (1541–1547), and a *liard* of Henri d'Albret (after 1548).

Snakes often appear near the base of the Cross in scenes of the Crucifixion. They are a reference to the miracle of the bronze serpent (Num. 21:6–9). John's Gospel provides the typological parallel: "As Moses lifted up the serpent in the wilderness, even so must the Son of Man be lifted up" (3:14). Christian imagery on glasses (here, the Crucifixion) does not necessarily imply an ecclesiastical use of the vessels. It has long been established that the church considered glass chalices to be unsuitable for the Eucharist because of their fragility. In France, the 1520 Synod of Tournai explicitly upheld earlier church laws prohibiting the use of glass chalices (Braun 1932, p. 47).

The object was bought at the sale of the Roux Collection by the dealer Nieuwerkercke, and subsequently acquired by Sir Richard Wallace.

BIBLIOGRAPHY: *Roux Collection* 1868, pp. 25–26, no. 128; Gaynor 1991, pp. 43–44.

## 2

### Drinking Tazza

H. 11.8 cm

FRANCE, SECOND HALF OF THE 16TH CENTURY. THE CORNING MUSEUM OF GLASS, CORNING, NEW YORK (65.3.112, GIFT OF JEROME STRAUSS). FORMERLY IN THE STRAUSS COLLECTION (S1616); ACQUIRED FROM DELPLACE IN BRUSSELS.

COLORLESS WITH PALE GREEN TINGE. BLOWN, ENAMELED, GILDED.

This tazza has a hemispherical bowl, a stem with an annular knop, and a trumpet-shaped foot with a hollow edge. The bowl is decorated with an enameled border of white and blue elongated scrolls separated by squares of gold foil inscribed "I(E) ?IS A VO V(S)" (Je suis à vous; I am yours). The band of scrolls is framed by blue and red lines and rows of white dots. Three white and blue four-lobed S-scrolls are painted on the inside of the bowl, and the knop is decorated with a narrow band of scrolls in opaque white enamel.

The enamel decoration on the knop is rough and slightly chipped, probably because this part of the tazza was not heated sufficiently. The gilded decoration has been completely rubbed off, and only a shadow of the lettering is visible.

COMMENT: The tazza was formed from one cylindrically shaped glass bubble by constricting it to form the base of the bowl and then sucking in air through the blowpipe. This forced the end of the bubble to fold inward, closing the bowl at the constriction. The lower part of the bubble was tooled to form the double-walled stem with an annular knop and the foot. Numerous bubbles were trapped in the wall of the stem and foot while it was fused from the two layers of glass. The underside of the base was then attached to a pontil and cracked off the blowpipe at the edge of the bowl. The bowl was tooled further to produce a hemispherical shape, and the rim was fire-polished. After cooling, the bowl and the knop of the stem were decorated with gilding and enamel, and the goblet was heated a second time to fuse the decoration. A second pontil mark, lower inside the stem than the other one, shows that this procedure was employed.[14]

A goblet with a conical bowl in the Bayerisches Nationalmuseum in Munich (Fig. 9) appears to have been made in a similar fashion (Rückert 1982, p. 72, no. 110, fig. VI/VII). Its enameled scene depicts Christ on the Cross, flanked by Mary and Saint John. The decorative inscribed band on the Corning tazza is also very similar to that on a footed beaker in the Victoria and Albert Museum, London (Fig. 8).

BIBLIOGRAPHY: *Glass Drinking Vessels* 1955, pp. 45–46, no. 109; Gaynor 1991, p. 50, fig. 8.

## 3

*Goblet*

H. 18.5 cm, D. (bowl) 13.7 cm,
(foot) 10.5 cm

FRANCE, ABOUT 1550. MUSÉE
DU LOUVRE, PARIS (OA 11191);
ACQUIRED IN PARIS IN 2002.

COLORLESS WITH GRAYISH TINGE.
BLOWN, MOLD-BLOWN,
APPLIED, ENAMELED, GILDED.

The goblet has three parts. The funnel-shaped bowl is applied to a large, bulbous, mold-blown knop with pronounced ribs, and the trumpet-shaped foot has a folded rim. One pontil mark is located beneath the foot, and a second one is in the center of the bowl.

The bowl is decorated, on one side under an arch, with the Crucifixion, surrounded by an inscription in white enamel taken from the Psalms (118:20): "PORTAM IUSTI INTRABV[NT] HANC" (The just shall enter this portal). On the other side are two figures. A saint/bishop, holding a staff surmounted by the cross of Lorraine in his left hand and a book in his right hand, faces a

suppliant kneeling in prayer. The bands separating them bear the inscriptions "O GUILLERME PASTOR" (O Father William) and "BONNE NOBIS SUCCURE" (Come to our aid). Above the figures is a wide ornamental frieze consisting of a band of gold leaf with a scratch-engraved scale pattern that is emphasized by red dots. This band is bordered by two opaque blue lines and rows of white dots. The base of the bowl is decorated with small stylized floral sprays surmounted by three dots, which alternate with small, horizontal S-scrolls.

The large, hollow knop is molded with eight pronounced vertical ribs

accentuated by a blue stripe. The wide spaces between these ribs are outlined with rows of white dots, with a vertical row of red dots in the center. The shoulder of the knop is decorated with alternating vertical stripes in red and white enamel, terminating in a blue band at the base of the bowl. The stem below the knop is tooled to form a small knop that is decorated in blue enamel, and a white band with red dots appears at its greatest circumference.

The top of the foot is enameled with red and white rays that alternate with white serpentine lines. Below this decoration is the inscription "JE SUIS A VOUS" (I am yours), flanked by blue quatrefoil florets whose centers are accented with white rays and red centers.

The goblet has been broken and restored.

COMMENT: The unusually shaped knop was most likely derived from contemporaneous metal forms. The inscription on the foot may indicate that the glass was created on the occasion of an engagement or marriage. It has been suggested that the glass may have been made for someone named after the patron saint Guillaume of Bourges (d. 1209). He served as bishop of that city, and he was a member of the Berruyer family, counts of Nevers. However, the staff surmounted by the cross of Lorraine may point to Guillaume of Fillastre (or Fillâtre) the Younger (1400–1473), bishop of Verdun, Toul, and Tournai. Guillaume served at the court of Philip the Good (1396–1467), duke of Burgundy. He also wrote the history of the Golden Fleece (*Toison d'or*), which he dedicated to his patron. The book held by the figure depicted on the goblet may refer to this literary work.

BIBLIOGRAPHY: *Revue du Louvre*, v. 5, 2002, p. 88, no. 9.

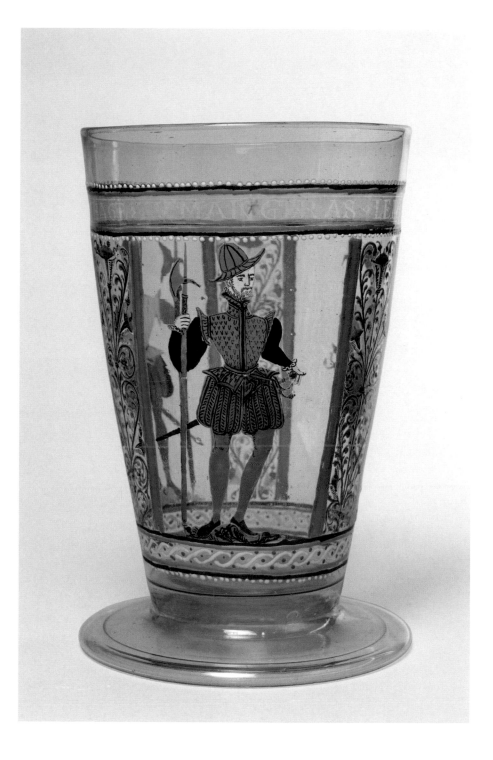

## 4

### Footed Beaker
### with Halberdiers

*H. 17 cm*

FRANCE, MID-16TH CENTURY. MUSÉE NATIONAL DE LA RENAISSANCE, ECOUEN, FRANCE (E.CL. 8627). FORMERLY IN THE COLLECTIONS OF BARON JEAN-CHARLES DAVILLIER AND THE MUSÉE DE CLUNY, PARIS.

COLORLESS WITH GRAYISH TINGE; WHITE, OCHER, LIGHT BLUE, RED, BLACK, AND YELLOWISH BROWN ENAMELS. BLOWN, ENAMELED, GILDED.

This beaker has a tall conical bowl with an uneven, fire-polished edge and a short, applied pedestal foot with a wide flanged rim and a folded edge. Below the rim of the bowl is a band of gold leaf inscribed "EN * LA SEVVR [SUEUR] ? DE TON VISAGE ? TV-MANGERAS ? LEPAYN ?" (By the sweat of your face you will eat bread;

Gen. 3:19). The gold band is bordered by two thin lines of blue and dark red enamel, followed by a row of small opaque white dots. The base of the bowl is ornamented with a corded border in white enamel. It has yellowish brown dots in the spaces within and around the stylized S-shaped band, which is also bordered by pairs of blue

and red lines. A row of white dots emphasizes the lower double line near the foot.

The zone below the two friezes is divided vertically into six elongated, trapezoidal spaces that are alternately decorated with figures and flowers. The floral panels show heart-shaped scrolls in yellowish brown enamel ac-

171

cented in brown, which issue from a central vertical line. The scrolls bear two symmetrical pairs of bell-shaped flowers in white and blue enamel, topped by a single flower. The figural panels are decorated with three halberdiers. These well-dressed foot soldiers are armed with a halberd, a weapon that combines the spear and the battle-ax, held in the right hand, and a sword that is fastened to a belt strap. They wear a morion (helmet) and a doublet with a high collar over a *gilet* (waistcoat) with puffed sleeves and white cuffs, as well as *tonnelets* (padded and slashed breeches) and *bas-de-chausses* (hose) in yellowish brown. The colors of the clothing vary from one figure to another, and the three soldiers strike slightly different poses.

The glass has numerous small bubbles.

COMMENT: The shape of this object is most comparable to that of the beaker shown in Figure 8, with a similar sharp angle at the shoulder of the foot. The carefully rendered foliage recalls that of a goblet in The Toledo Museum of Art. An incorrect letter "S" in the gilded inscription was painted over with an asterisk in brownish yellow and red by the enameler (see *A travers le verre* 1989, p. 296). Gaynor (1991, p. 55), following Fillon 1864, dated this object, on the basis of the costumes, to the 1560s. The beaker's earlier attribution to a glasshouse in Poitou (*L'Art pour tous*, April 15, 1887) can no longer be substantiated. This object and another goblet (Fig. 11) were acquired from the Davillier Collection by the Musée de Cluny. They have since been transferred to the Musée National de la Renaissance, Ecouen. A third goblet from the Davillier Collection was acquired by the Louvre (Fig. 7).

BIBLIOGRAPHY: Fillon 1864, p. 206; *L'Art pour tous*, April 15, 1887, no. 5518; Barrelet 1953, pl. XXXIX-A; *A travers le verre* 1989, p. 296, no. 313; Gaynor 1991, pp. 55–56.

# 5

## Footed Beaker

*H. 14.8 cm*

PROBABLY FRANCE, EARLY 16TH CENTURY. THE CORNING MUSEUM OF GLASS, CORNING, NEW YORK (72.3.52); ACQUIRED FROM A. VECHT, AMSTERDAM, IN 1972.

COLORLESS WITH GRAYISH TINGE. BLOWN, MOLD-BLOWN, PATTERN-MOLDED, ENAMELED.

The lower half of the bowl was blown into a conical dip mold with 12 vertical ribs. "POVRMOSVRLELEOTENÂTRENALDI" (For Monsieur the Lieutenant Trenaldi) is enameled in white between two lines of repeated dots below the rim. Two dogs and a stag, painted in white and dark brown enamel, and a bird in white and blue enamel decorate the zone between the inscription and the ribbing. The applied hollow trumpet-shaped foot has a rim with an upfolded edge. A rough pontil mark remains on the underside of the foot.

BIBLIOGRAPHY: "Recent Important Acquisitions," *JGS*, v. 15, 1973, pp. 190–191, no. 23; Gaynor 1991, p. 53, fig. 12.

## 6

## Bottle with Coat of Arms of Catherine de Médicis

*H. 19.5 cm, D. 12 cm*

FRANCE, GLASSHOUSE OF SAINT-GERMAIN-EN-LAYE, THIRD QUARTER OF THE 16TH CENTURY. MUSÉE NATIONAL DE LA RENAISSANCE, ECOUEN, FRANCE (EC. 282).

TRANSLUCENT DARK BLUE; RED AND WHITE ENAMELS. MOLD-BLOWN, ENAMELED, GILDED.

The cylindrical, slightly ovoid bottle was blown in a mold forming eight vertical flutes. It has a rounded base and a domed shoulder with a short, narrow neck that faintly flares toward the rim. Each convex lobe of the bottle's undulating surface is outlined by wide gilded and inscribed bands, forming rounded arches at the shoulder and near the base. The flutes are decorated with a pattern of gilded and inscribed scales, which are arranged vertically and embellished with red and white dots. These alternate with flutes decorated with inscribed gilded floral scrolls surrounded by a profusion of small white dots. This pattern is also repeated on the shoulder of the vessel. The central flute on either side is embellished with the crested coat of arms of Catherine de Médicis, impaled with that of King Henry II of France, and surmounted by a crown.

COMMENT: This bottle was probably one of 13 blue glass vessels noted in the queen's 1589 inventory that were intended to contain "confitures." These "confitures" could have had a rather liquid consistency, such as the "rob di ribes" (or "robes"), a syrup of black currants, which was thought to have medicinal properties, especially against fevers (Rose 1989, p. 104). A large bowl with a pedestal foot, blown of colorless glass and enameled with the same coat of arms, may have been made in the same workshop (Crépin-Leblond 1995, pp. 89–90).

BIBLIOGRAPHY: Ennès 1997, no. 8.

# 7

## *Pilgrim Flask*
### *H. 32 cm*

FRANCE, 16TH CENTURY. MUSÉE DU
LOUVRE, PARIS (MR 2404). FORMERLY
IN THE COLLECTION OF CHEVALIER
DURAND (UNTIL 1825).

OPAQUE BLUE; OPAQUE WHITE STRIATIONS.
BLOWN, TOOLED, GILDED; GILDED PEWTER
MOUNT WITH TWO ENAMELED COPPER
ROUNDELS.

The flask has a wide, gourd-shaped body with flattened sides and a short, slightly flared neck. It is decorated overall in gold leaf, which is scratch-engraved with stylized floral scrolls, flowers, and exotic birds. A gilded pewter mount, which encloses the glass vessel, consists of two ornamental bands that are fitted to the narrow sides of the body and connect to a wide circular ring below the base and a metal cap enclosing most of the neck. Stylized leaves with serrated edges, cut from sheet metal and fitted to the shape of the body, are soldered to either side of the bands near the shoulders, to the base-ring, and to the neck-ring. Cast and chased dragons are soldered to the side bands at the shoulder. The heads of the two dragons are turned backward, and each forms a loop for the attachment of an ornamental metal chain.

A wide pewter collar encloses most of the neck and caps the rim. The cylindrical metal stopper is topped by a chased fluted dome surmounted by an ogee-shaped finial. A small metal chain, attached to the finial, secures the stopper to the rim mount of the flask.

Two circular Limoges medallions set in profile frames decorate the center of each side of the body. The obverse is enameled with a profile bust of a bearded Hercules facing left on a blue ground. He wears a green laurel wreath and a purple jacket with fashionably slashed sleeves. He is surrounded by the French inscription "HERCVLES IE

SVIS APELE" (My name is Hercules) in painted gold. The reverse medallion is fragmented and depicts a nude Fortune facing left on a black ground; her long golden hair is tied behind her neck. She is seated on an orb floating above stylized blue water, and she holds the ends of a cloth billowing around her. The inscription reads "[FORT]VNE IE" (I [am Fort]une). The medallions are set in profile frames that are connected to the mount by four stylized metal leaves.

COMMENT: The image of Hercules, juxtaposed with that of Fortuna, alludes to an age of fortune and plenty won by the labors of Hercules. Hess and Hus-

band (1997, p. 173) believe that the French enameled medallion set into the mount points to a French origin for the group of mounted flasks that includes 7. The myth of Hercules was very close-ly connected with the official images of French kings, as is attested by contem-poraneous documents, medals, and prints (Scailliérez 2003, p. 41). A nearly identical flask is in the Victoria and Albert Museum, London (5700-1859) (Honey 1946, p. 68). It is also mounted with a Limoges plaque, which depicts Paris as a bearded warrior *all'antica*, facing right. The inscription, "PAR IS S . . . ," is partly lost. The medallion on the opposite side has been lost. The mount is heavily worn, but two suspen-

sion rings remain in the loop formed by the dragons' heads. Such a flask is also represented in the painting *Still Life with Fruit and Venetian Glass* (about 1865) by Blaise-Alexandre Desgoffe (1830–1901), formerly in the Willet Collection and now in the Amsterdam Historical Museum (Vreeken 1998, p. 18, fig. 12). Desgoffe was known to use objects in the Louvre collections as sources for his paintings. The fact that he rendered the medallion with a red rather than blue background may be attributed to artistic license.

BIBLIOGRAPHY: Ennès 1982, pp. 18–19; Bellanger 1988, p. 376; Hess and Husband 1997, p. 173, fig. 45D.

## 8

### *Pilgrim Flask*

H. 24 cm

PROBABLY FRANCE, 16TH CENTURY. MUSÉE DU LOUVRE, PARIS (OA 457-1412, GIFT OF CHARLES SAUVAGEOT, 1856).

DICHROIC (OPAQUE BLUE BY REFLECTED LIGHT, BROWNISH BY TRANSMITTED LIGHT). BLOWN; PEWTER MOUNT.

The flask has a gourd-shaped body with flattened sides and a short, slightly flared neck. A fitted pewter mount en-closes the glass vessel. Two unembel-lished metal bands encircle the body vertically and horizontally; they are joined below the base to a chased pedestal foot and soldered around the shoulder to a circular band enclosing the neck. The bands are joined, on either side of the body, to a cast and pierced relief medallion with a male profile bust *all'antica*. One side depicts a bearded male facing left; he wears ar-mor and is crowned by a laurel wreath. This bust is framed by a stylized laurel wreath. The opposite side shows a bearded male facing right; he wears a Renaissance helmet and armor with a ruff. He is framed by concentric rings of scrolled and beaded decoration.

On either side of the neck, two short bands are mounted with cast protomas of swans, their curved necks serving as loops for a chain with large links. These ornamented bands are attached to a fitting that caps the rim. The flask is closed with a flat pewter stopper that is surmounted by a finial consisting of three rings arranged vertically.

COMMENT: A similar flask is in The J. Paul Getty Museum, Los Angeles (Fig. 14). Its more elaborately decorated pewter mount is attributed to François Briot, a metalworker from Lorraine (Hess and Husband 1997, p. 173).

BIBLIOGRAPHY: Sauzay and Sauvageot 1861, p. 217, no. 924.

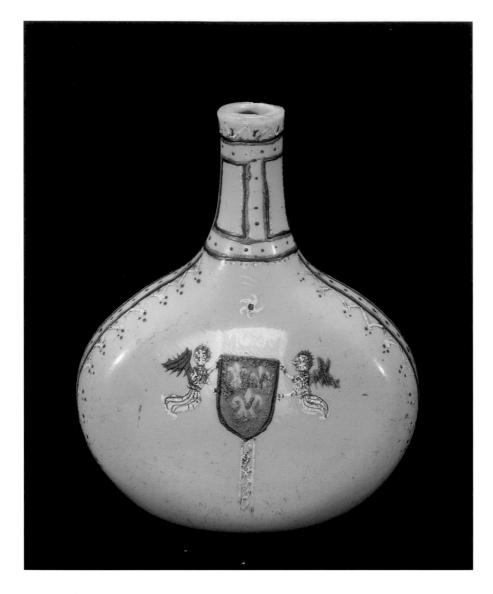

## 9
### *Enameled Flask*
*H. 17.7 cm*

PROBABLY FRANCE, SECOND HALF OF THE 16TH CENTURY. THE CORNING MUSEUM OF GLASS, CORNING, NEW YORK (97.3.30, GIFT OF FRITZ AND JOST KUMMER AND IRENE HÄBERLI-KUMMER IN MEMORY OF SIBYLL KUMMER-ROTHEN-HÄUSLER).

DICHROIC (BLUISH BY REFLECTED LIGHT, BROWNISH BY TRANSMITTED LIGHT). BLOWN, ENAMELED.

The thick-walled flask has a wide, gourd-shaped body and a slightly concave base, which was cracked off from the blowpipe at the rim, leaving a rough, unfinished surface. The object is enameled from the rim to the base along the sides with two parallel red and blue stripes framing a band of gold-leaf squares separated by red dots. The decoration is bordered by a white zig-zag pattern ending in a triangle formed by three red dots. On the neck, red lines form a framework embellished with rows of red dots around vertical fields.

One side of the flask is decorated with two flying angels in white robes flanking a blue shield with three gild-ed fleurs-de-lis surmounted by a gold crown with a central fleur-de-lis that is largely worn away. Above the shield is a stylized sun. The other side of the vessel is decorated with two stylized red dragons flanking a blue shield with a gilded dolphin jumping to the left. This shield was also once surmounted by a crown, now largely lost, and it has a stylized sun above. Beneath each shield is a vertical band, in white enamel with a rope design consisting of S-shaped scrolls, which extends to the base of the flask.

COMMENT: The enameled bands recall the strapwork of the metal mounts on **7** and **8**. The shields with the fleurs-de-lis and the dolphin indicate that the flask may have been made for a dauphin.

BIBLIOGRAPHY: Gaynor 1991, pp. 57–58, no. 18, figs. p. 56; *The Corning Museum of Glass Annual Report 1997*, 1998, p. 19; "Recent Important Acquisitions," *JGS*, v. 40, 1998, p. 145, no. 9.

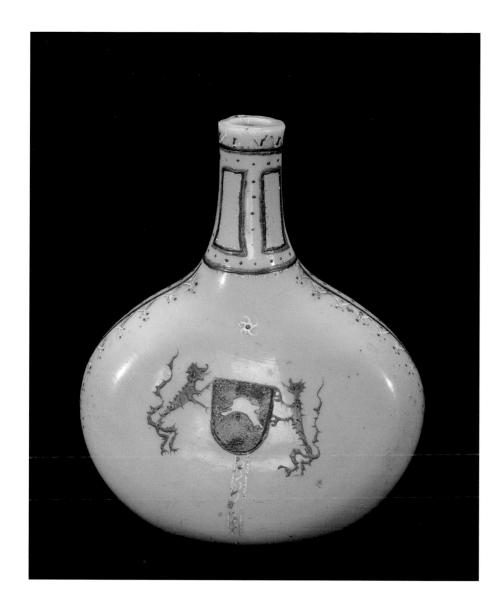

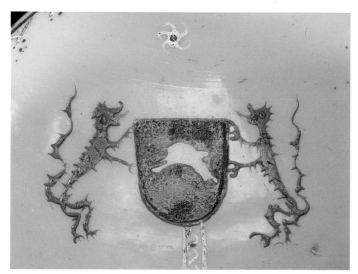

## 10

### *Plate with Monogram of Gaston of Orléans*
*D. 48.4 cm*

FRANCE OR LOW COUNTRIES, ABOUT 1630–1640. THE CORNING MUSEUM OF GLASS, CORNING, NEW YORK (77.3.34, PURCHASED WITH FUNDS FROM THE MUSEUM ENDOWMENT FUND).

COLORLESS WITH GRAYISH TINGE. BLOWN, DIAMOND-POINT ENGRAVED.

The deep center of the plate is slightly convex and surrounded by a straight, nearly vertical wall. The broad, flanged rim is slightly flared, and its edge is folded under. A large circular pontil mark remains beneath the center of the plate.

The center and rim are densely covered with diamond-point engraving, executed from the front by an expert hand. The center is decorated with the interlaced mirror-monogram "GG" under an open crown with fleurs-de-lis, surmounted by the All-Seeing Eye of God among clouds and rays, a well-known Christian symbol. The whole is framed by a floral wreath emerging from two cornucopias that are crossed and tied with ribbons and filled with flowers and fruit. The rim of the plate is engraved with four oval cartouches alternating with four rectangular cartouches, encircled by garlands of foliage. Small stylized insects, such as butterflies, bees, and flies, fill the spaces between the cartouches. The oval cartouches are engraved with emblems, while the centers of the four rectangular cartouches are undecorated.

The emblem in the cartouche directly above the monogram includes an orb surmounted by a cross (**10a**). It is suspended upside down by a thread that is held by a hand emerging from clouds, while a second hand severs the thread with a knife. The frame of this emblem is inscribed, above, with the motto "ABRVMPAM" (I will sever [it]). Next, continuing clockwise, is an obelisk on a pedestal, situated in a stylized grassy landscape under a cloudy sky (**10b**). The obelisk is surmounted by an orb that supports a cross and is entwined by stylized ivy. This frame displays the motto "TE STANTE VIREBO" (When you stand, I flourish).

The emblem below Gaston's monogram is embellished with a palm tree in a stylized grassy landscape with trees, and a house with a spire is visible in the *fatto* (background image) to the right (**10c**). Its frame bears the motto "VERITAS PREMITUR NON OPPRIMI-TUR" (Truth may be oppressed, but not crushed). The last emblem, to the left of the monogram, is engraved with a classical male bust wearing a laurel wreath and a Roman tunic (**10d**). It is mounted on a pedestal with a scroll profile. The *fatto* shows a stylized landscape under a cloudy sky. The emblem's motto is "CONCEDO NULLI" (I yield to no one).

COMMENT: This glass plate was commissioned for (or by) Jean Baptiste Gaston, duke of Orléans (1608–1660), the third son of Henry IV and the younger brother of Louis XIII. Gaston was an avid collector with a keen eye. The four emblems on the plate (**10e–h**) derive from a portfolio of emblems owned by Gaston. This portfolio was published in Utrecht in 1613 by Gabriel Rollenhagen, a German from Magdeburg. It is titled *Selectorum Emblematum Centuria Secunda*, with engraved *picturas* (plates) by Chrispijn van de Passe the Elder. Gaston may have kept the portfolio at the Château de Blois, which housed his significant library. It is now in the collection of the Bibliothèque Nationale in Paris.

Since the early 17th century, an emblem has traditionally consisted of a motto, *pictura*, and epigram. The motto is usually short, with a classical word or quotation, while the epigram is usually composed of two or three distichs, but other verse forms are occasionally employed. It is not known what influence the author of the text had on the choice of the pictorial motifs. Passe may have had a free hand in interpreting the text. However, as has been frequently noted, the three components were received as an incorporated whole.

The selection, modification, and arrangement of the emblems on the plate serve to communicate a message (or messages) to the viewer. The choice of these images from the 100 emblems in Rollenhagen's portfolio no doubt suggests a purpose. On the plate, only the *picturas* and the mottoes are depicted, relating them closely to the two-part

10A

10B

10C

10D

form of the *impresa* (personal badge) (Daly 2000, p. 385). In addition, the *picturas* have been altered, and the *fatti* are largely omitted.

The engraved cartouches are based on the emblems numbered 27, 38, 55, and 68. The central Eye of God (above the crowned monogram) was inspired by a fifth emblem, no. 65. In the original print source of this emblem, the Tetragrammaton is set in a blazing sun surrounded by clouds. On the glass plate, this Christian symbol is omitted, and the benevolent Eye of God radiates on Gaston's crowned monogram.

The most significant change was made in the emblem directly above the monogram. In Rollenhagen's publication, the *pictura* of emblem no. 55 depicts a globe with latitudinal and longitudinal lines, surmounted by a cross

(**10e**). Here, the thread is attached to the cross and suspended against a *fatto* with a pastoral landscape showing Christ preaching to a group of people. The full *subscriptio* (epigram) of the emblem is "*Omnia sunt hominum tenui pendentia filo, / Quod DEUS ABRUMPET cum volet Esto pius*" (All things of men are hanging by a thin thread, which God severs as he wishes; be pious).

Instead of a globe, the glass plate shows a sphere surmounted by a cross, symbolizing kingly power and justice. In addition, the hands holding the thread and the knife emerge from sleeves that terminate in lacy ruffs rather than in long, plain sleeves with folded cuffs, as in the print. More significantly, the orb is suspended upside down, with the cross pointing downward. This symbol may well be charged

with several covert meanings. The most obvious interpretation of the upside-down orb is a negative comment on the regime of Louis XIII and his religious advisers, which is terminated through God's will. The elegant, ruffed sleeves holding the knife and thread may also be a reference to Louis XIV, whose birth in 1638 ended Gaston's hopes of succeeding to the throne.

The *impresa* with the obelisk depicts the monument surmounted by a moon on a sphere (**10f**, Rollenhagen 68). The *fatto* is a vista into a formal garden with a palm tree. The Annunciation is shown on the right, and two figures approach a fountain on the left. The motto is "Te stante virebo" (As long as you stand, I shall flourish). The emblem's full *subscriptio* is "*Auxilÿs suffulta tuis* Te stante virebo, / *Donec eris*

*Omnia sunt hominum tenui pendentia filo,*
*Quod Deus Abrumpet cum volet.Esto pius.*

10E

*Auxilijs suffulta tuis Te stante virebo,*
*Donec eris felix,integra semper ero.*

10F

*Sæpé equidem pressa at nondum oppressa inclyta veri,*
*Diva fuit, dextrâ præside tuta Dei.*

10G

*Numen agro positum, fines ego terminus agri,*
*Concedo nulli, cuiqué suum tribuens*

10H

10E–F

*Emblems from Gabriel Rollenhagen, Emblemata volsinnighe uytbeelsels, Tot Arnhem: Ian Ianszen 1615.*

*felix, integra semper ero*" (As long as you stand, I shall flourish, supported with your help. As long as you are felicitous, I shall always be vigorous).

During this period, educated Frenchmen may have identified this *pictura* and motto with the *impresa* of the cardinal of Lorraine, depicting a pyramid entwined by ivy and topped by a half-moon (Paradin 1583, p. 72). (The image also appears on a *jeton* [token] of Cardinal Charles de Lorraine. See Bie 1634, p. 26, no. VI.) The reference to Lorraine on a plate associated with Gaston of Orléans is hardly coincidental. In 1629, he took refuge there for a short time after declaring himself to be in opposition to Cardinal Richelieu and thus displeasing his brother, Louis XIII. Gaston's ties to Lorraine became even stronger in 1631, when he married Marguerite of Lorraine (1613–1672) in Nancy with the blessing of his mother, Marie de Médicis, and against his brother's wishes. A few days after the ceremony, Gaston retreated to the Spanish Netherlands. On the glass plate, the obelisk is clearly surmounted by an orb with a cross similar to that on the emblem discussed above. This may refer to French rule in Lorraine after Charles IV submitted to Louis XIII following the French invasion of 1632.

In the *pictura* of the emblem with the palm tree (Rollenhagen no. 38), the tree's growth is obstructed by a rectangular wooden board lodged between the trunk and the crown. The image is placed against a *fatto* with a wooded landscape and a lake (**10g**). In the background, one hunter rests on the ground, while another aims a rifle at a flock of birds taking off in the distance. The *subscriptio* reads "*Saepé equidem* pressa *at nondum* oppressa *inclyta* veri / *Diva fuit, dextrá praeside tuta* Dei" (The glorious goddess of truth, truly often pressed, but never suppressed, has been safe under the favorable protection of God). The emblem is an allegory of the triumphant truth. It was once believed that the

palm tree would grow straight and tall despite interference or weights suspended from it. During the Middle Ages, this characteristic made it a symbol of triumph over adversity, inspired by the notion that people are often made stronger by overcoming various hardships. This failure to bend under adversity, coupled with the palm tree's fruitfulness, made it an emblem of the righteous (Ps. 92:12). On the glass plate, this emblem is paired with the one above, the orb to be severed. Combined, these two images emphasize the perseverance of the righteous upon the termination of an unjust regime.

The last of the engraved images derives from an emblem showing the head of Terminus, the Roman god of boundaries, as a youthful 17th-century male. The bust is mounted on a square block (Rollenhagen no. 27). The motto is "Concedo nulli," which is expanded in the emblem's *subscriptio* to "*Numen agro positum, fines ego* terminus *agri,* concedo nulli, *cuiqué suum tríbuens*" (A deity placed in the field, I am Terminus, the boundaries of the field, I yield to no one, and I give to each his own). During this time, this image was best known as the *impresa* of the Humanist Erasmus, personifying knowledge and its self-assertiveness. On the glass plate, the god is depicted as a Roman emperor wearing a tunic with ornamental bands and a laurel wreath. The classical bust is mounted on an elaborate scroll base. It vaguely resembles youthful portraits of Louis XIII on relief-cut gems of this period (Gougeon 2002, pp. 288–289, no. 177b). Again, this image is probably an unfavorable comment on the sovereign. Rollenhagen's Terminus emblem was also used to attack those who disregarded border stones and intruded where they had no right to be (Daly 2000, p. 414). Positioned opposite the *impresa* of Lorraine, the two images on the glass plate may refer directly to the French claim of sovereignty over Lorraine by the detested Cardinal Richelieu in 1632 because the Lothringian Duke Charles IV (r. 1624–1634) sided with

the obstinate Gaston of Orléans. The downward-pointing cross on the orb may well be a caustic comment on the Roman Catholic Church's (or, more specifically, Richelieu's) overwhelming power and negative influence at the French court.

The symbolic significance of the glass plate remains ambiguous, but the four mottoes suggest a decidedly libertarian and rebellious meaning, which must have appealed to the dissentious Gaston. The emblematic references to Lorraine support an attribution of the glass plate to this tumultuous period in the 1630s, when Gaston's personal and political life was most closely linked with this duchy.[15]

BIBLIOGRAPHY: Charleston 1990, pp. 122–123, pl. 53; *CMG Guide* 2001, p. 74; Rochebrune 2002a, pp. 373–375.

## 11

### *Drinking Tazza*
H. 15.7 cm, D. 18.0 cm

PROBABLY SOUTHWESTERN FRANCE, ABOUT 1610–1630. COLLECTION OF KEITH KING, PARIS (K27A); ACQUIRED FROM DRAGESCO AND CRAMOISAN, PARIS. FORMERLY IN THE COLLECTION DE SEVIN, TOULOUSE.

COLORLESS WITH BLUISH GRAY TINGE. MOLD-BLOWN, TOOLED, APPLIED.

The tazza's shallow bowl was formed in a mold with 12 ribs and tooled into an open, undulating shape. It is applied to a hollow stem consisting of a bulbous gourd-shaped knop over an annular knop and an inverted baluster section, with thin mereses beneath the bowl and above the shallow conical foot.

COMMENT: The gourd-shaped knop appears to be a uniquely French device. An early version is seen on two enameled glasses attributed to the mid-16th century; one is in the Musée du Louvre, Paris (Fig. 7), and the other is in the Bayerisches Nationalmuseum, Munich (Fig. 9). Gourd-shaped stems very similar to that of **11** are found on several glasses: *Venetiaans & façon de Venise glas* 1991, pp. 98–99, no. 81 (now in the collection of Keith King, 27c); "Recent Important Acquisitions," *JGS*, v. 40, 1998, p. 145, no. 10 (The British Museum, MLA 1997, 11-4, 1); and two glasses with a similar stem but mold-blown decoration in the Musée des Arts Décoratifs, Bordeaux (Figs. 18 and 19). For a tazza with a similar bowl, see Figure 18.

Several fragmentary examples of this tazza were uncovered in Peyremoutou (Foy, Averous, and Bourrel 1983) in what may have been the site of a pottery and/or glasshouse owned by de Robert. This suggests that this type of glass is indigenous to the Périgord, Languedoc, and Tarn region, and that it was produced to supply a local market.[16]

## 12
### Goblet
*H. 20.9 cm*

SOUTHWESTERN FRANCE, ABOUT 1610–
1630. THE CORNING MUSEUM OF GLASS,
CORNING, NEW YORK (62.3.47).

COLORLESS WITH BLUISH GRAY TINGE.
BLOWN, APPLIED, TOOLED.

The thinly blown gun metal blue glass object has a conical bowl with a faint ring indentation located about two centimeters above the base. The bowl is set on a wide collar over a hollow, pear-shaped stem, followed by a wide merese and a plain conical foot.

COMMENT: This goblet is related to a number of others that feature a similar faint ring indentation. The mark may have identified a particular glasshouse. A vessel identical in form, formerly in the Geyssant Collection, was sold by Ricqles in Paris on June 23,

2000. Two nearly identical goblets are in the collections of the Victoria and Albert Museum, London (8503), and Keith King, Paris (27b). A glass with a stem of similar form but with a fluted bowl is in the Musée des Arts Décoratifs, Paris (22741) (Davis 1972, pl. 90).

Evidence indicating a southern or southwestern French provenance comes from a glasshouse excavated at Peyremoutou, between Castres and Carcassonne, which was operated by the de Robert family (Foy, Averous, and Bourrel 1983). Fragmentary examples recovered there show the characteristic

pear-shaped stem. The de Roberts were a celebrated family of *gentilhommes verriers* who operated the majority of glasshouses in the Tarn region. The name of Jacques de Robert de la Rouquette first appeared in 1683, and he was succeeded by his son Jacques de Robert de Lautier, who became a master glassmaker in 1691. The family manufactured glassware in the area throughout the 17th century.

BIBLIOGRAPHY: "Recent Important Acquisitions," *JGS*, v. 5, 1963, p. 147, no. 32.

## 13

### *Ice Glass Beaker*
*H. 14.2 cm, D. (rim) 10.2 cm*

PROBABLY FRANCE OR SOUTHERN NETH-
ERLANDS, 17TH CENTURY. THE CORNING
MUSEUM OF GLASS, CORNING, NEW
YORK (79.3.441, GIFT OF THE RUTH
BRYAN STRAUSS MEMORIAL FOUNDATION);
ACQUIRED FROM ARTHUR CHURCHILL
LTD. FORMERLY IN THE COLLECTIONS OF
JEROME STRAUSS (S266) AND BARON L.
ROTHSCHILD, LONDON.

COLORLESS CASED IN TRANSPARENT RED.
BLOWN, ICE GLASS TECHNIQUE, TOOLED,
APPLIED.

This beaker has slightly conical walls
that are outsplayed toward the sheared
and fire-polished rim. The walls and
base are decorated with a crackled ice
glass effect in high relief, which retains
a few sharp points. The thickness of
the wall increases noticeably from the
base to the rim. The base, encircled
with a trail of colorless glass, has a
shallow kick and a small, rough pontil
mark. The glass has numerous small
bubbles.

COMMENT: This rare object was decorated by dipping the parison into cold
water. A slightly smaller beaker of similar shape and manufacture is in the
Museum für Angewandte Kunst, Vienna
(Gl. 341). 13 was previously thought
to be an example of gold ruby glass
(Kerssenbrock-von Krosigk 1997, p.
114, no. 439; when that dissertation
was published in 2001 [Kerssenbrock-
Krosigk 2001], this object was not included). A recent X-ray fluorescence
analysis performed by Dr. Philip M.

Fenn could not confirm the presence
of gold. The vessel proved to be made
of potash glass with added amounts of
copper and calcium. Tin was not de-
tected. Potash glasses with a relatively
high calcium content were reported
from excavations at the Cour Carrée
in Paris (Fleury, Brut, and Velde 2002,
p. 107).

BIBLIOGRAPHY: *Glass Drinking Vessels*
1955, p. 59, no. 153; Kerssenbrock-von
Krosigk 1997, p. 114, no. 439.

## 14

*Ewer*

*H. 17.8 cm, D. (foot) 10.6 cm*

FRANCE, ORLÉANS, BERNARD PERROT, SECOND HALF OF THE 17TH CENTURY. MUSÉE NATIONAL DE LA RENAISSANCE, ECOUEN, FRANCE (E.CL. 8626). FORMERLY IN THE COLLECTION OF THE MUSÉE DE CLUNY, PARIS.

TRANSLUCENT WHITE, TRANSLUCENT RED, MARBLEIZED. BLOWN, APPLIED, TOOLED.

The ewer has a conical bowl with a rounded base and horizontal red bands, a tooled spout, and a double lip-wrap around the rim. A hollow blown C-shaped handle is attached, opposite the spout, to the top of the bowl. The handle is applied below the rim, curves upward in a graceful arch, and meets the bowl again just above the base, ending in a small loop. A stem consisting of a hollow quatrefoil knop between two large mereses is followed by an ogee-shaped foot with an upfolded rim. Small specks and trails of red glass decorate the handle, knop, and foot. The ewer has numerous small black inclusions, noticeably in the red areas.

COMMENT: A similar ewer, but with a simple pedestal foot, is in a private French collection (Bénard and Dragesco 1989, p. 112, no. 36, and ill. p. 69). Another example was formerly in the Barrelet Collection (Barrelet 1964, ill. p. 275). The latter has a globular body with a wide cylindrical neck and an ogee-shaped pedestal foot that was applied with a wide merese. Its red marbled decoration was more randomly applied over the entire vessel.

Bernard Perrot was born Bernardo Perrotto in Bormida, near Altare, Italy, in 1619, and he died in Orléans in 1709. He is the most celebrated French glass-maker before the 20th century. He emigrated to France, working first in a Nevers glasshouse and later in Liège. On December 7, 1668, Perrot was granted a privilege by the duke of Orléans to establish his own glasshouse there. He made several important technical discoveries (or rediscoveries), notably translucent red glass, opaque white glass, and particularly the casting and rolling of molten glass for the production of mirrors.

Two of Perrot's many achievements were the sophisticated production of Venetian-style marbled glass with ruby red striations and the reinvention of transparent red window glass, for which he received a royal privilege in 1668 (Kerssenbrock-Krosigk 2001, p. 58). Much of his tableware production consisted of opalescent white glass with random specks or marbling. It was intended to rival porcelain imported from the East, and to have the appearance of agate and other semiprecious stones.

BIBLIOGRAPHY: Bellanger 1988, p. 212.

## 15

*Medallion with Portrait
of Louis XIV*

OH. 35.5 cm, W. 29 cm,
H. (frame) 38.7 cm

FRANCE, ORLÉANS, PROBABLY GLASS-
HOUSE OF BERNARD PERROT, ABOUT
1675–1685. THE CORNING MUSEUM
OF GLASS, CORNING, NEW YORK
(99.3.2).

COLORLESS WITH GRAYISH TINGE, BRASS.
MOLDED, GILDED.

The medallion bears the portrait of
the Sun King, Louis XIV (1638–1715),
in profile facing right. He is wearing a
luxurious curled wig, a cuirass with the
sun emblem on the breastplate, and
a sash loosely draped across his right
shoulder. Traces of gilding remain on
the reverse of the portrait. The edge
of the glass is beveled at the front and
mounted in a thick tubular brass frame
with a turned fitting for the suspension
loop. The frame is original.

The thick glass has numerous bubbles and slight impurities.

COMMENT: The medallion was cast
in a mold based on official gold medals of the king that date to the 1670s,
after he had established his absolute
monarchy. This is one of seven such
medallions known today, and they were
made in three different molds. The first
mold, dated to about 1670, shows a
young king with a thin nose and lightly
marked features. The only surviving
example, with no traces of further
embellishments on the glass, is in the
Musée Historique et Archéologique
de l'Orléanais, Orléans (Bénard and
Dragesco 1989, p. 44). It is set in an
original carved and gilded wood frame.

The second mold, from which **15**
and four other examples were cast,
dates to about 1675–1685. It presents
the portrait of an older king. One of
these medallions is in the Compagnie
de Saint-Gobain, Paris (the bust of the
king was painted on the reverse to look
like patinated bronze), and it is also set
in an original gilded wood frame. Two
more are in private French collections,
and one of them has a gilded and mirrored back. The last example, which is
on the Paris art market, is mounted in
a similar brass frame.

A third mold, made about 1690,
shows a much older king wearing a
lace cravat. The only existing medallion
from that mold is in the Musée du Louvre. The bust of the king was gilded on
the reverse, and the background was
mirrored. The medallion is mounted in
a modern brass frame in period style.

One of Perrot's most important contributions was a secret method of casting glass in a mold to produce relief
figures, busts, medals, inscriptions, and
coats of arms (Frémy 1909, p. 264).
After 10 years of petitioning the French
Academy of Sciences regarding this
remarkable invention, he was finally
granted permission for its manufacture
on September 25, 1688. It has been
suggested that Perrot produced his cast
glass medallions during the decade in
which he was seeking this permit. He
very fittingly may have chosen the effi-
gy of the ruler to win the support of
French officials and influential noblemen.

BIBLIOGRAPHY: *English and Continental Glass* 1995, lot 116; *The Corning
Museum of Glass Annual Report 1999*,
2000, pp. 6–7; "Recent Important Acquisitions," *JGS*, v. 42, 2000, p. 182,
fig. 14; *CMG Guide* 2001, p. 76; Geiselberger 2002, p. 43, fig. 70.

# Longing for Luxury: Some Social Routes of Venetian-Style Glassware in the Netherlands during the 17th Century

*Alexandra Gaba-Van Dongen*

## The Desire for Glass

In the first half of the 17th century, the Dutch poet Simon van Beaumont (1574–1654) wrote a poem that describes the desire of a man to shop for luxury items in Amsterdam. While he wants to spend his money on such things as "Veneetsche glasen" (Venetian glasses), he cannot make up his mind, and he eventually returns home with some ordinary domestic utensils:

Jorden traveled to Amsterdam to go shopping,
With a filled purse and courageous heart,
To buy all sorts of precious things.
He visited all the shops.
He noticed tall silver ewers,
Head cap brooches, gold bracelets,
Large diamonds of many carats;
He studied them carefully in front of the door.

*Detail from* Easy Come, Easy Go,
*by Jan Havicksz Steen (Fig. 12).*

He tried on rings to see if they fit;
He saw velvet, satin, damask,
Turkish carpets, Milanese understockings,
Beautiful porcelain, Venetian glasses,
Mirrors [with frames] of ebony, heavy fireplace
    equipment,
Brass candelabra, large and garish.
He coveted famous paintings
Of the best masters from the old days,
By Lucas van Leyden or by [Jan Gossaert] Mabuse.
After a long trip through many shops,
After careful consideration and investigation,
And after tiring out 20 shop clerks,
Guess what he bought, that sensible Jorden?
Four wooden spoons and six plates for the table
    (Komrij 1986, p. 43).[1]

The poem demonstrates that the desire to own precious objects, displayed by Jorden as a typical wealthy Dutch consumer, included Venetian glassware. It was a very popular commodity among the Dutch middle class at that time. In fact, there seems to have been an insatiable demand for this glass, despite its high cost and the difficulty of obtaining it. This social phenomenon of longing for luxuries seems to have provided the impetus for the continued production of Venetian-style glassware in northern Europe. From the mid-16th century, despite a Venetian ban on emigration, hundreds of Italian glassmakers had relocated to northern cities to work in glasshouses *à la façon de Venise* (in the Venetian style), enticed by promises of wealth and social prestige. During the 16th and 17th centuries, the Venetian influence came to dominate luxury glassmaking in Spain, France, Germany, the Netherlands, England, and Sweden.

It is impossible to determine whether the glass mentioned in the poem is the original imported Venetian *cristallo* or a product of local manufacture. (The same is true of the Turkish carpets, which were being copied in the southern Netherlands in the 16th century. See Ydema 1991, p. 104.) In 1607, the Antwerp glassmaker Filippo Gridolphi found it almost impossible to distinguish Venetian imports from Venetian-style glass made in the southern Netherlands (Tait 1979, p. 8). But for interested buyers, such as Jorden in the poem, provenance was often unimportant as long as the glass had the characteristic appearance, quality, and feel of real Venetian glass. Dutch glassmakers were rather proud of their Venetian-style glass "imitations." The scientist Johannes Isacius Pontanus, writing about the city of Amsterdam in 1614, expressed it as follows: "Furthermore, among the new enterprises and ornaments in town, the glasshouse opposite the Cloveniersdoelen [shooting range] certainly may not be overlooked. It has a number of ovens and workshops in which artists apply themselves to fashioning crystalline glasses of great beauty in innumerable variety and with such marvelous and consummate skill that they are in no way inferior to the Venetians hitherto so widely praised" (Pontanus 1614, p. 273).[2]

This passage refers to the glass workshop operated by Jan Hendrickz. Soop (Roever 1991, p. 157). A later book about Amsterdam, written by Melchior Fokkens in 1663, devoted an entire chapter to the Rozengracht glasshouse, in which a number of glass forms are described:

Glasshouse. It stands near the aforementioned Doolhof at the end of Rozengracht, and it is one of the most important and ingenious projects not just in Amsterdam but in the whole world. Upon entering, one encounters the most astonishing sight in town. There are two ovens where there is usually space for only one. This year, the supervisor or head of this house caused an additional oven to be placed. About 30 men are employed here; these ovens burn night and day; the fire is not allowed to go out. The substance from which glass is made is placed in hollow vessels, from which it is retrieved with long iron tongs; this matter resembles incandescent mud and is shaped and bent into the desired glasses. Each oven has five or six apertures through which the aforesaid matter can be removed. Every imaginable kind of glass is made in this glasshouse. The crystal and fine glassware, which hitherto only Venetians could make, can now be fashioned as skillfully as ever a Venetian could do it. [This glassware is] famous, not only in Amsterdam but further afield too, for nothing but such crystal is made in this glasshouse, which is truly a marvelous device and well worth seeing. Here are made not only plain and simple drinking glasses, to which one is accustomed, but also all manner of decorative and unusual creations such as flutes, bowls, costly covered cups in the style of golden chalices, precious vessels, and small and attractive drinking cups, some of which are plain, while the rims of others are blue or other colors. There are also extremely choice wineglasses, cups, and other old and new pieces, the likes of which have never been seen before, for they are fashioned in accordance with the wishes of the gentlemen and ladies. One passes here through great warehouses filled with thousands of glasses in all shapes and sizes; moreover, there is a shop whose showcases are filled with an abundance of fine crystal. Work goes on night and day, and the fire must burn without cease; it consumes peat and wood to the tune of 150 or 160 guilders every week. With so many workers, this means that the annual expense is very high (Fokkens 1663, pp. 305-306).[3]

The Rozengracht glasshouse, which had been built in 1656, was first owned by Claes Rochuszn Jaquet. Jan Vrouling, a glassmaker from the Southern Netherlands, assumed control of the factory in 1661, when he married the widow of one of Jaquet's grandsons. Apparently the richly decorated glasses, dishes, and pitchers that Vrouling produced competed successfully with the porcelain and silver luxury articles that decorated the houses of wealthy Dutch burghers at that time (Roever 1991, p. 173).

People always express themselves through the way in which they live and interact with objects. Objects represent the complex social relations of a culture, as they carry its values, ideas, and emotions. Until recently, material culture was a rather marginal aspect of social studies, although sociology is of growing interest to students of material culture. Because our material environment is a social product, it always mediates meaning: "The things of the world are incorporated into social interaction and provide an embodiment of social structures reflecting back the nature and form of our social world" (Dant 1999, p. 7).

This essay will explore some of the social aspects of Venetian-style glassware in the Netherlands, based on iconographic, material/archeological, and written sources. The goal is not to uncover the Venetian *roots* of this glassware, but rather to trace some of the social *routes* it traveled beyond Venice.

## COLLECTING NOVELTIES

As early as the 12th century, Venice was asserting itself as an overseas power, and it eventually became the crossroads of East–West trade (Howard 2000). For the role it played in the capture of Tyre in 1110, Venice was rewarded with a third of the city and its hinterlands. This created a "state within a state," in which the inhabitants of the Venetian quarter were subject to Venetian jurisdiction, while the king of Jerusalem ruled the rest of the territory. The Venetian *bailo* (consul) Marsilio Zorzi reported to the doge in 1243 that "in Tyre we have a third of the city, and we have our own complete court, just as the king has his own" (*ibid.*, pp. 30–31). When trading privileges were confirmed for the last time in 1277, Venice had complete parity with the kingdom (Prawer 1973). The conquest of Tyre also gave the Venetians access to the city's well-established luxury glass industry, whose products were praised in the West for their remarkable transparency (Huygens 1986, bk. 13, chap. 3).

In the 15th century, inspired in part by exotic glass gifts they had received in trading with the Near and Middle East, the Venetians advanced the art of fine glassmaking and dominated the world market. Venetian ships laden with glass docked in Flanders, introducing Venetian styles to northern Europe and the Netherlands (Schmidt 1922, p. 65). Thus began an intense interest in Italian luxury goods and fine art objects (Jardine 1996, p. 436). Collecting, which was originally the pursuit only of Italian and French aristocrats, soon became popular among Dutch patricians, too (Muensterberger 1994, p. 209).

During the next several centuries, luxurious novelties were imported from Italy by the Dutch bourgeoisie. They included the fork, brilliant white faience tableware, and *cristallo* drinking vessels. At first, these objects were quite rare and expensive, serving as collector's items that were handed down within a family for generations.

The earliest example of a Dutch room specially created for a collection is in the Hof van Zessen at Rapenburg 28 in Leiden. (Rapenburg was a major canal street that was inhabited by the upper classes.) There, Gilles van Heussen Steffensz (1614–1660), a wealthy man, placed his acquisitions, including costly "marbled [Venetian] goblets," in his

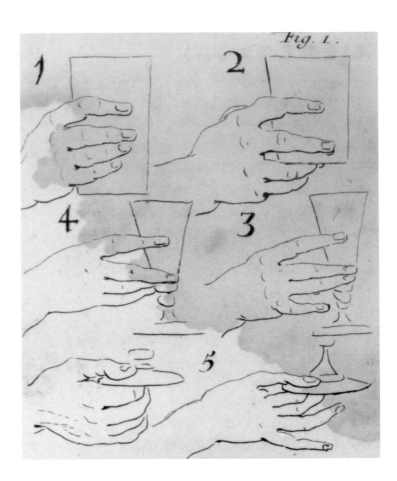

**FIG. 1**

*Engraving showing five ways in which drinking glasses were held around the beginning of the 18th century. From De Lairesse 1707, ill. facing p. 54. Museum Boijmans Van Beuningen, Rotterdam.*

*cabinetkamer* (cabinet room). As recorded in the probate inventory, part of his collection was stored in eight drawers of a tortoiseshell cabinet. Another small cabinet and several small traveling cases and boxes stood on a nearby table (Lunsingh Scheurleer, Fock, and van Dissel 1989, p. 669; Fock 1992, p. 80).

Collecting decorative objects seems to have been a common practice among 17th-century Dutch burghers. It may have been a reflection of the young nation's prosperity and commercial prominence. As wealth increased, there was a new emphasis on comfort and good living: "Together with prosperity and a growing commitment to individual liberties, there appeared a distinct shift in values, and collecting soon became one of the phenomena of change in terms of inner and outer reality. In historical reconstruction, the widespread inclination to collect all kinds of objects as well as works of art constituted a continuing attempt at reintegrating contentment with tangible, concrete 'things,' after decades of deprivation (under Spanish rule) and frustrated

longing for security and the good life" (Muensterberger 1994, p. 209).

When Venetian-style glasses became more affordable for Dutch buyers around the middle of the 17th century, they were used as luxury household goods. On Leiden's Rapenburg, these objects are mentioned in several probate inventories. A 1659 inventory of a canal house at Rapenburg 61 included "1 deel Veneetsche glasen" (a number of Venetian glasses) (Lunsingh Scheurleer, Fock, and van Dissel 1992, p. 125), and "32 christeliene glasen van verscheyden soorten" (32 crystal glasses of different types) were listed in the 1630 inventory of Rapenburg 26 (*idem* 1989, p. 575). The 1697 inventory of another canal house, located at Rapenburg 65, describes a rare Venetian glass as "een seer oud, en ongemeen raar, met Goud doorblase Venetiaans Glas, als een beker, welkers gelijk geen, of weinig te vinden is" (one very old and very rare Venetian glass, blown with gold, in the shape of a beaker, of which there is no other example to be found). This house was owned by Karel Heidanus

196

(1636–1697), who had a collection in his "antiquity room" (*idem* 1992, p. 472).

Most of the Italian luxury items introduced in the Netherlands were implements for eating and drinking. They provided their owners with a means of displaying their status and wealth during the *noenmaal* (noon meal; the main meal of the day was eaten at lunchtime until the end of the 18th century) or at feasts.[4] Glassware used at drinking rituals was sometimes decorated with engraved texts, images, and symbols to mark special occasions. Knowing how to handle these glasses in the right manner was an important social criterion. An early 18th-century engraving (Fig. 1) offers five illustrations of various social classes holding drinking glasses (De Lairesse 1707, p. 53 and fig. opp. p. 54). The text accompanying the engraving reads: "The different manners of holding a glass: one person grasps it with the whole hand (no. 1). Another holds it, almost as awkwardly, at the base (no. 2). By contrast, no. 3 shows a queen holding a goblet with three fingertips, the fifth finger carefully raised in a refined manner. No. 4 suggests a maid of honor, but is held less gracefully. In no. 5, we see another sovereign; the glass is held, adroitly and carefully, by its foot."[5]

Desirable novelties introduced into material culture pave the way for adaptations of forms and customs, as well as new inventions. This brings about a complex acculturation process, based on the mixing of local forms and designs with new outside influences. At the same time, new eating and drinking habits result in new types of utensils. As was noted earlier, luxurious and costly Venetian glassware became very popular among the rich and powerful in northern Europe during the 17th century. Within a short time, inventive ways were found to reproduce these objects locally so that they could be sold at more reasonable prices. Initially, immigrant Italian glassmakers continued to produce Venetian glasses in their new surroundings, but they soon encountered two problems. First, the batch materials needed to make these glasses could not be imported in sufficient quantities, and so these craftsmen were forced to turn to local ingredients. Second, their Dutch customers

favored somewhat different glass forms, and this prompted a number of new styles in addition to the existing Venetian ones. However, Venetian glassmakers had previously responded to Dutch tastes by making glasses in Dutch style for export, as a 17th-century English traveler observed: "For the Dutch they have high glasses, called Flutes, a full yard long. . . . For the Italians that love to drink leisurely, they have glasses that are almost as large and flat as silverplates, and almost as uneasy to drink out of" (Lassels 1670, p. 423).

By about 1600, a large number of Southern Netherlanders had already moved, along with their penchant for a more luxurious lifestyle, to the north, where they exerted considerable influence on the eating and drinking habits of their new neighbors.[6] At that time, when the Dutch burgher could afford to drink imported red wine on a more regular basis, demand increased for colorless wineglasses in the shape of a chalice on a foot. This was, in part, an alternative to the German *Römer*, which was principally used for drinking white wine. The stem decorations of these wineglasses showcased Venetian-style craftsmanship by featuring wings, snakes, and other elaborate shapes. The famous Italian tazzas (drinking bowls with a wide cup) could also be found on Dutch tables.

Archeological material from the Northern Netherlands (Henkes 1994, pp. 200–222) and depictions in Dutch paintings and engravings of this period (Fig. 2) underscore the popularity of the tall, elegant flute. One scholar has suggested that the wearing of fashionable garments with wide ruffs, which began about 1625, may have made drinking from a tall flute (as well as eating with a fork) very sensible (Fig. 3) (Mees 1997, p. 13). Venetian-style tazzas have not been found in Dutch archeological contexts as frequently as flutes, but examples from the second half of the 16th century have been excavated in the cities of Groningen, Nijmegen, and 's-Hertogenbosch (Henkes 1994, pp. 207–208). Tazzas are often depicted in Dutch paintings and engravings.

Beer beakers based on Venetian forms were produced in the Netherlands from the second half of the 16th century. One example is the waffle beaker

FIG. 2

Peter Isselburg (1568–1630), The Prodigal Son, *after*
*Gabriel Weijer, 1613. Engraving, 21.5 cm x 30.8 cm.*
*Museum Boijmans Van Beuningen, Rotterdam*
*(L 1975/84). Flute glasses are evident on the dining*
*and serving tables. On the buffet, tall covered goblets*
*and a* Stangenglas *represent elegance and wealth.*

FIG. 3

*Cornelis van Kittensteyn (about 1600–after 1638),*
Taste, *after Dirck Hals, 1623. Engraving, 22.7 cm x
25.3 cm. Museum Boijmans Van Beuningen, Rotterdam (BdH 15142, lent by the Lucas van Leyden
Foundation).*

Fig. 4

*Pieter Claesz (1597/8–1661), Breakfast Piece (with waffle beaker), 1636. Oil on panel, 36 cm x 49 cm. Museum Boijmans Van Beuningen, Rotterdam (1122).*

Fig. 5

*Small jug for oil or perfume, colorless, excavated in Rijswijk, the Netherlands. Northern or Southern Netherlands, 1600–1650. H. 8.6 cm. Stichting Museum Rijswijk, lent by the Rijksdienst voor Oudheidkundig Bodemonderzoek (h1988/5/204). A similar jug is illustrated on the table in Fig. 6.*

Fig. 6

*Jacques de Gheyn II (1565–1629),
Vanity of a Woman, 1595 or
1596. Engraving, 27.4 cm x 18.0
cm. Museum Boijmans Van
Beuningen, Rotterdam (BdH
4723, lent by the Lucas van
Leyden Foundation).*

(Fig. 4). This glass served as an elegant alternative to the simple beer beaker made of forest glass, which was imported from Germany. The waffle beaker was the most popular form of beer glass at that time. It was decorated with a waffle pattern based on a Venetian technique. Early thick-walled beakers with a coarse waffle pattern were probably manufactured in Antwerp (Henkes 1994, p. 130).

Luxurious Venetian-style glass wares made of *cristallo*, as well as colored and *lattimo* (milky white) glass, were found in the homes of the wealthy. Among these objects were jugs for oil and vinegar, liqueurs, and perfumes (Figs. 5 and 6); dishes, bowls (sometimes on a foot), and plates for serving sweets; and collectibles such as miniature vases and baskets. Several Venetian-style glass shapes were clearly copied from northern European forms. The shapes of some drinking mugs and jugs with handles, for example, are based on stoneware beer vessels.

## Conspicuous Consumption

Despite the influence of Calvinism, which counseled a modest life, 17th-century Dutch burghers reveled in a true golden age of luxury domestic objects. A famous book of emblems, written in 1614, captured the controversial spirit of the times with this text (Fig. 7), titled "Sorght voor de koele wijn niet" (Do not worry about cool wine): "It is seemly for the newly wed to take this Symbol to heart, but first to consider the expedience, expense, and necessity of both household goods and food: but if they obtain something by saving up for it or by doing good business, there will be time enough to seek pleasure, to wit: when sufficient wealth shall have been acquired to support and allow for folly" (Visscher 1614, p. 32).[7]

As the title of this emblem suggests, the prevailing notion of the day was that luxury glassware for drinking wine was not supposed to be found in a young or humble household. The ordinary objects

depicted in the emblem form a kind of still life of modesty, in sharp contrast to contemporaneous sumptuous still lifes that illustrated a longing for luxury (see Figs. 15–18).

Dutch emblem books employed an extensive number of commonplace utensils as metaphors for the idea that "there is nothing idle or vain in things." One such volume, by the famous Dutch writer Jacob Cats, expressed the sentiment like this: "[Such utensils are] silent yet speaking images, laughable yet not without wisdom, in which morality is almost tangible, for they contain a hidden power to punish inner defects" (Cats 1627, p. 7).

During this period, it seems that luxury domestic goods were both highly desired and reviled in Dutch society. The moral dilemma of reconciling the longing for riches and the presence of strict religious standards was reflected both in art and in literature. Eating and drinking habits and utensils were constantly changing. As more types of drinks were introduced, new vessels were created for them. In addition to the *roemer*, which was principally used for imported German white wine, there were smaller, colorless wineglasses (made, for example, of *verre de fougère*) for red wine. This wine, which took on a dull brownish cast in green *roemers*, became a sparkling, bright ruby red in the crystal-clear Venetian-style goblets. Here is one of the many Dutch drinking songs, taken from a 17th-century songbook, that celebrated the drinking of wine: "O fair wine! Your crystalline appearance soothes our pain. O fair wine! You banish pain and trouble from the heart. I shall extol your noble virtue as long as I live. To you, neighbor, this toast: good health and a full flute!" (Schotel 1903, p. 53).[8]

Fig. 7

*Emblem, "Sorght voor de koele wijn niet" (Do not worry about cool wine). From Visscher 1614, p. 32. Museum Boijmans Van Beuningen, Rotterdam.*

FIG. 8

*Hendrick Goltzius (1558–1617), The Young Bacchus, 1596. Engraving,
24.8 cm x 18.3 cm. Museum Boijmans Van Beuningen, Rotterdam (134).*

Wineglasses and wine drinking were also celebrated in traditional Bacchic iconography, of which
an engraving after Hendrick Goltzius (1558–1617)
is one example (Fig. 8). In the lower right and left
corners, beneath the image of Bacchus, four popular drinking glasses are depicted: an early *roemer*
and *pasglas*, both made of forest glass (right), and
a flute and wineglass apparently made in the Venetian style (left). Another engraving, by Frans van
den Wijngaerde (1614–1679) after a painting by
Peter Paul Rubens (in the Gemäldegalerie of the
Wiener Akademie), shows an intoxicated Silenus

FIG. 9

*Frans van den Wijngaerde (1614–1679), Drunken Silenus, after Peter Paul Rubens, undated. Engraving, 32.3 cm x 42.4 cm. Museum Boijmans Van Beuningen, Rotterdam (L 1977/37, lent by the Lucas van Leyden Foundation).*

(the teacher of Bacchus) in the foreground and an amorous couple in the background (Fig. 9). Between them is an impressive assortment of 21 luxury glasses and silver drinking vessels, symbolizing riches and vanity (Theuerkauff-Liederwald 1992, pp. 22–23 and fig. 4).

The growing obsession with new and status-enhancing objects was especially apparent on festive occasions, where the use of luxury utensils distinguished one household from another. The phenomenon of "conspicuous consumption"[9] involved, among other things, the presence of expensive and fragile glassware that, once broken, could never be invisibly repaired. This evidence of clambering for social standing sparked outcries from religious leaders, who warned of the decadence associated with the pursuit of splendor. Such cautionary sentiments could be found even on the glasses themselves. One wineglass, dated 1688, was diamond-point engraved by Willem Jacobsz. van Heemskerk (1613–1692) of Leiden with an admonishment to moderation: "Maet hout staet" (Moderation maintains balance) (Fig. 10). A luxury wine bottle inscribed by the same engraver maintains that "Alle ding is zo men 't acht" (Everything possesses the value one gives to it) and "Elk dings waerdy van dat men ziet is naermen 't waerd acht, meerder niet Cristalleyn" (Everything, including crystal, has the value it merits). The use of such texts on glasses seems to have simultaneously re-

FIG. 10

*Wineglass with diamond-point engraved text "Maet hout staet" (Moderation maintains balance). Low Countries, Willem Jacobsz van Heemskerk (1613–1692), dated 1688. H. 19.5 cm. Museum Boijmans Van Beuningen, Rotterdam (103).*

minded drinkers of their desire for luxury and warned them of the danger of decadence.

This type of glassware was often a luxury gift, as on the occasion of a marriage. One example is a large glass plate (now in the collection of the Rijksmuseum, Amsterdam) that Willem van Heemskerk engraved when his son Joost married Anna Conink in 1685. This plate is inscribed "iuste & syncere" (justice and sincerity) and "Bestand'ge, noit besweken Trouw, Werkt lyvelijk- en Ziel-behouw" (Strong and uncompromising fidelity maintains body and soul). While such moralistic decorations prompted the owners of glasses to ponder the implications of "an embarrassment of riches," they also confirmed the status of the objects themselves. This dichotomy emphasizes the social importance of objects at that time. As two scholars have noted: "The objects of the household represent, at least

potentially, the endogenous being of the owner. Although one has little control over the things encountered outside the home, household objects are chosen and could be freely discarded if they produced too much conflict within the self. Thus household objects constitute an ecology of signs that reflects as well as shapes the pattern of the owner's self" (Csikszentmihalyi and Rochberg-Halton 1981, p. 17).

Interestingly, the writings on modern consumer society and its products by the French social theorist Jean Baudrillard could be applied to 17th-century Dutch society, in which the consumption and value of desirable objects rapidly formed the basis of the social order. He noted that "consumer objects structure behaviour through a sign function, creating a hedonistic morality of pure satisfaction, to project one's desires onto produced goods"

(Baudrillard 1988, pp. 12–13). According to this reasoning:

> "Needs" as such are created by the objects of consumption . . ., which quite tyrannically induce categories of persons. They undertake the policing of social meanings, and the significations they engender are controlled. Objects signify social standing, and in consumer society they replace all other means of hierarchical societal division, e.g. race, gender, class. People are no longer ranked according to those obsolete mechanisms but by the commodities they own, a universal code of recognition telling us that in our modern times, the person with the Rolex watch is higher in the hierarchy. This does not mean liberation from exploitation; on the contrary, it only acts to exacerbate the desire for discrimination. We can observe the unfolding of an always renewed obsession of hierarchy and distinction (*ibid.*, pp. 16–20).

## GLASS ON THE TABLE: SHOWCASE OF DESIRE

Many 17th-century paintings and engravings depict luxury glassware in connection with the table. Dinner table settings in both domestic and public contexts functioned as a kind of showcase for the luxuries of that time. Artists portrayed tables in private households, at historic banquets and drinking parties, and in brothels and inns. Tables were also a mainstay of the still life.

In the collection of the Museum Boijmans Van Beuningen in Rotterdam is a 1667 painting by Jacob Ochtervelt (1634–1682) called *The Oyster Meal* (Fig. 11). In it, a woman holds her wineglass in the direction of a man who is offering her oysters. Their clothes provide an impression of luxury, which is reinforced by the Oriental rug and white faience wine jug on the table. Moreover, the oysters and wine are emblematic of luxury food and drink. In the background of the painting, the vague outline of a bed can be seen. In 17th-century literature, the consumption of oysters was often described in an erotic context, and the reputation of oysters as an aphrodisiac was widely known (Lammertse 1998, pp. 123–125).

The title of another famous painting, Jan Steen's *Easy Come, Easy Go* of 1661 (Fig. 12), derives from a well-known proverb of the time. The painting shows a young woman offering a man a glass of wine while an old woman prepares oysters. Again there is an Oriental rug on the table, and a huge salt dish on a silver pedestal appears in the middle of the table. The title of the painting is also to be found on the mantel, which is surmounted by a statuette of Fortune. One of her feet is atop a die, emphasizing the unpredictability of fate: good luck and wealth may come easily, but they can also disappear as quickly as they materialized. This theme is accented by the two men in the back room, who are playing *verkeerbord* (trick track), a popular board game. The old Dutch word *verkeren* means "change" or "reversal of fortune." These symbolic portrayals serve as a stark reminder that the luck and wealth of the man at the table—who is now enjoying wine from a fragile Venetian-style glass, women, and oysters—could change at any moment.

The conflict between homeliness and worldliness in the 17th century was captured in a pair of paintings by Gabriel Metsu (1629–1667). The first, *Woman with a Glass and Tankard* (Fig. 13), portrays its subject pouring wine and smoking tobacco, while the second, titled *Woman Peeling Apples in a Kitchen* (Fig. 14), is a simple genre scene. The woman in the first painting seems to tip her drinking glass, which she has just filled with wine from a white faience jug, in the direction of her apple-peeling counterpart, as if to toast her. The luxurious Oriental rug on the table contrasts sharply with the plain cloth that covers the table in the first painting. These works seem to illustrate two entirely different ways of life: one reflecting domesticity and modesty, and the other characterized by

Fig. 11

*Jacob Ochtervelt (1634–1682), The Oyster Meal, 1667. Oil on panel, 43 cm
x 33.5 cm. Museum Boijmans Van Beuningen, Rotterdam (1618).*

Fig. 12

*Jan Havicksz Steen (1626–1679), Easy Come, Easy Go, 1661. Oil on canvas, 79 cm x 104 cm. Museum Boijmans Van Beuningen, Rotterdam (2527).*

FIG. 13
*Gabriel Metsu (1629–1667),* Woman with a Glass and Tankard, *undated.*
*Oil on panel, 28 cm x 26 cm. Musée du Louvre, Paris.*

Fig. 14

*Gabriel Metsu (1629–1667),* Woman Peeling Apples in a Kitchen, *undated.*
*Oil on panel, 28 cm x 26 cm. Musée du Louvre, Paris.*

pleasure and abundance (Franits 1993, pp. 90–91, figs. 70 and 71). Most of the objects depicted in the first painting (rug, imported faience, tobacco, and glassware) are exotic imported goods.

Dutch still-life paintings from the mid-17th century depict a great variety of glassware. Venetian-style glassware figures prominently in sumptuous surroundings, where it is usually found on a table. In many such paintings, this glassware is accompanied by a stock assortment of luxury items: Oriental carpets, Chinese porcelain, Italian faience, exotic fruits, and expensive silverware, meats, and

seafood. The glasses are often filled with red wine. In 1707, these still lifes were called *Vanitassen* (Vanities): "There is another kind of still life that is by no means inferior, and it could introduce a beneficial and no less attractive change. It represents all kinds of exquisite objects such as gold, silver, crystal and other glassware, pearls, precious gems and mother-of-pearl, and it is commonly known as Vanitas. The illustrious Kalf, who has left us many delightful and outstanding examples, excelled in the genre and deserves the highest praise of all" (De Lairesse 1707, p. 266).[10]

The author expressed the intriguing opinion that the beauty and virtue of this type of still life derived solely from the selection of the most exquisite, contemporaneous, fashionable, and beautiful luxury objects: "It is unlikely that wealthy people who possess everything in abundance would gain any pleasure from old-fashioned objects such

FIG. 15
*Jan Davidsz de Heem (1606–1683/4),* Sumptuous Still Life with Ham, Lobster, and Fruit, *1652 or 1653. Oil on canvas, 75 cm x 105 cm. Museum Boijmans Van Beuningen, Rotterdam (1289).*

FIG. 16
*Abraham van Beyeren (1620–1690), Sumptuous Still Life, 1654. Oil on
canvas, 126 cm x 106 cm. Museum Boijmans Van Beuningen, Rotterdam
(St. 90, lent by the Lucas van Leyden Foundation).*

as mirrors, silver and golden bowls, ewers, trays, and other valuables, and would wish to show off with them, for they could have it all even finer and more exquisite. . . . We also observe that no objects depicted in still lifes should be represented smaller than life-size" (De Lairesse 1707, pp. 260–261).[11] Perhaps this form of painting can be connected with the "showcase" in the drawing room of the home: the buffet, where the owner's luxurious possessions—and thus his or her social standing—were on display (Grimm 1984, p. 299).

Some examples of still-life paintings containing Venetian-style glassware and other expensive objects are the work of Jan Davidsz de Heem (1606–1683/4; Fig. 15), Abraham van Beyeren (1620–1690; Fig. 16), and Willem Kalf (1619–1693; Figs.

17 and 18). The first of these artists is considered to be the creator of the so-called *pronkstilleven* (sumptuous still life), a relatively large painting that depicted costly items such as glassware and food in abundance. These pictures of surplus wealth strike a balance between ethics and aesthetics, morals and style, vanity and visual pleasure. In the 17th century, Dutch society was in the curious position of having acquired immense national wealth, but with few cultural traditions that permitted its expenditure. The ancient discourses on riches interpreted wealth through categories of morality (Bryson 1990, p. 99). "The *vanitas* is possibly deliberately built on the paradox that the conflict between world-rejection and worldly ensnarement is in fact its governing principle" (*ibid.*, p. 117).

Undoubtedly inspired by De Heem, Van Beyeren produced a number of luxurious still lifes in the mid-1650s. He repeatedly used the same set of objects, but he arranged them in various ways. The silver flagon, elaborate Venetian-style glass, and gilded chalice, for example, were costly luxuries created by master craftsmen, while the fruit, whether fresh or candied (as in the porcelain bowl), was certainly not commonly found in Dutch households. In addition to delighting the eye, these objects seem to have had a symbolic function related to the observations made above. The roses, which are shown in full bloom, will soon fade and die. The watch, which marks the passage of time, could likewise represent transience. The figure of Fortune, which decorates the beaker, might serve as another reminder to the viewer that worldly riches are easily lost.

Kalf's sumptuous still lifes are notable for their arrangement of small groups of exquisite objects. *Still Life with a Ming Bowl* (Fig. 17) shows a Chinese Wan Li bowl, an extremely precious object at that time. It most likely came to the Netherlands via the East India Company. In the painting, the bowl contains costly exotic fruits, such as oranges and lemons. One of the two glasses depicted is an elaborate goblet with a crackled surface. Both the foot and the bowl are decorated with ornate lion masks. This object may have been made in Venice during the second half of the 16th century, but it could

have been a slightly later vessel in the Venetian style that was produced in Antwerp or Liège.[12] The other glass, a flute, is probably a 17th-century Dutch product, as are the silver platter and the knife with a handle of polished semiprecious stone. Although Kalf was born in Rotterdam, he lived in Amsterdam from about 1653 until his death. This still life probably dates from the beginning of the artist's Amsterdam period (Lammertse 1998, pp. 90–91, cat. no. 21).

Was the sumptuous still life perhaps meant to cause the viewer to resist the temptations of material pleasure? As the writer of Ecclesiastes stated, everything is bound to just a short moment of existence: "Vanity of vanities! All is vanity" (1:2). It is one thing to encounter that sentiment in Scripture. However, to see that same thought expressed in a work of art is quite a different matter (Bryson 1990, pp. 115–116). In Calvin's commentary on the Book of Isaiah, luxury in households is a primary target, especially as it is found in merchants' houses in the form of pictures on the walls: "For it too often happens that riches bring self-indulgence, and superfluity of pleasure produces flabbiness as we can see in wealthy regions and cities where there are merchants. Now those who sail to distant places are no longer content with home comforts but bring back with them unknown luxuries. Therefore because wealth is generally the mother of extravagance, the prophet mentions here expensive household furnishings, by which he means the Jews brought God's judgment by the lavish way they decorated their houses" (Calvijn 1900, p. 48, Isa. 2:12–16).

Glancing through many such images, including those that are mentioned in this essay,[13] one is struck by the fact that, in almost every case, the iconographic context in which Venetian-style glassware is found is somehow related to the subject of

FIG. 17
*Willem Kalf (1619–1693), Still Life with a Ming Bowl, about 1653–1660. Oil on canvas, 62 cm x 56 cm. Museum Boijmans Van Beuningen, Rotterdam (2503).*

FIG. 18
*Willem Kalf (1619–1693), Still Life with Ewer, Vessels, and Pomegranate, undated. Oil on
canvas, 103.5 cm x 81.3 cm. The J. Paul Getty Museum, Los Angeles (54.PA.1).*

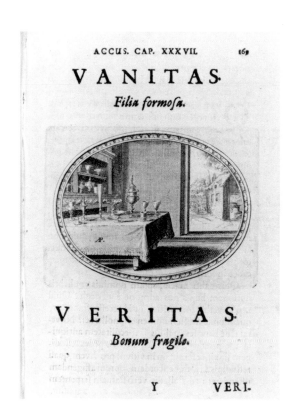

vanity and the mockery of extravagance (Figs. 19–23). Other iconographical contexts include historic banquets (Fig. 24) and domestic table scenes (Figs. 25 and 26).

What are we looking at? Does what we observe in paintings and engravings display a kind of 17th-century reality? Does it show us the way people used this type of glassware? The depicted glassware and all the other material objects found in visual sources are presented in a realistic way. They seem to refer to real objects and to real people's behavior. The visual compositions present a complex man-made world, a kind of utopia, a re-created mixture of reality and illusion. Subject and object interact to create meaning. Seeing is believing. Reality and illusion are both part of our nonlogical, subjective, and romantic world—and of the desires it produces.

FIG. 19

*Theodoor van Merlen (about 1600–1659), Veritas bonum fragile (Vanity is a charming daughter. Truth is a fragile good). Engraving in Anton de Bourgogne,* Mundi Lapis Lydius, *1639. Museum Boijmans Van Beuningen, Rotterdam.*

FIG. 20

*Jan van de Velde II (1593–1641), Vanitas (Vanity), undated. Engraving, 19.3 cm x 15.0 cm. Museum Boijmans Van Beuningen, Rotterdam (FK 115). The text beneath the engraving reads, "In weelden sijn wy dickwils geseten, de Doot veel naerder dan wy weeten" (Oft have we lived in luxury, but Death is much closer than we know).*

VANITAS. * YDELHEYT. *

Cur aurum, eõmmas, et opes, cælatáque vasa
Os Fentas, in quæ Mors habet Imperium?
Vana hæc: tu vana es: qua quæris et omnia vana.
Vanis gaudenti Mors gravis et misera est.

Gout, Gesteenten, Rycdom, en all'v cõstelycke vaeten
Wanneer de Doot coemt aen, wat sullen sy v baeten?
Tis al ydel: oby syt ydel, dat ydel is soeckt oby snel.
Die YDELHEYT bemint valt swaer de Doot bitterfel.

IACOBVS DE GEYN INVENTOR. HONDIVS EXC

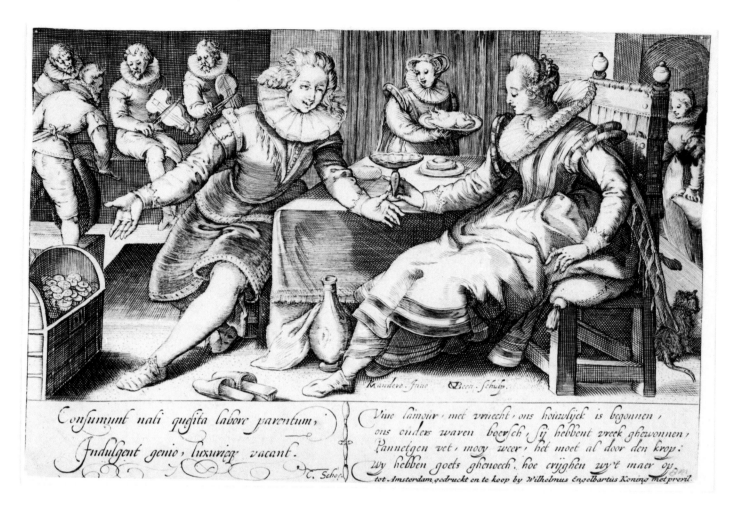

**FIG. 21**

*Jacques de Gheyn II (1565–1629), Vanity and Death,*
*about 1610. Engraving, 22.5 cm x 17.6 cm. Museum*
*Boijmans Van Beuningen, Rotterdam (L 1978/49,*
*lent by the Lucas van Leyden Foundation). The text*
*beneath the engraving reads: "Gout, Gesteenten, Ryc-*
*dom, en all' u Costlycke vaeten, Wanneer de Doot*
*comt aen, wat sullen sy y baeten? T'is al ydel: ghy*
*syt ydel. Dat ydel is soeckt ghy snel. Die Ydelheyt*
*bemint valt swaer de Doot bitterfel" (Gold, precious*
*stones, wealth, and all your costly vessels—what avail*
*they when Death approaches? It is all vanity; you are*
*vain. What you pursue is vain. He who loves vanity*
*will find Death bitter).*

**FIG. 22**

*Gilles van Breen (1560–1602), The Extravagant*
*Couple, after Karel van Mander, undated. Engraving,*
*14.0 cm x 20.7 cm. Museum Boijmans Van Beuningen,*
*Rotterdam (BdH 25835, lent by the Lucas van Leyden*
*Foundation). The text beneath the engraving reads,*
*"Vive L'amour, met vruecht, ons houwlijck is begon-*
*nen, ons ouders waren boersch, Sij hebbent vreek*
*ghewonnen, Pannetgen vet, mooy weer, het moet al*
*door den krop; Wy hebben goets ghenoech, hoe crij-*
*ghen wy 't maer op" (Long live love! With happiness*
*our marriage began. Our parents were peasants. They*
*overcame hardship, a pot of grease, fine weather—*
*it all goes down the gullet. We have earthly goods*
*aplenty, more than we can eat).*

FIG. 23

*Pieter van der Borcht (1545–1608), Monkeys as People, from the "Playing Monkeys" series, undated. Etching, 20.5 cm x 29.0 cm. Museum Boijmans Van Beuningen, Rotterdam (BdH 9847–9850, lent by the Lucas van Leyden Foundation).*

FIG. 24

*Pierre Philippe (about 1635–1664), Banquet in the Mauritshuis for Charles II, after J. Toorenvliet, 1660. Engraving, 39.9 cm x 48.6 cm. Museum Boijmans Van Beuningen, Rotterdam (BdH 12741, lent by the Lucas van Leyden Foundation).*

FIG. 25

*Nicolaes de Bruyn (1565–1656),* House of Joy, *undated. Engraving, 30.5 cm x 38.4 cm. Museum Boijmans Van Beuningen, Rotterdam (L 1977/38).*

FIG. 26

*Schelte Adamsz. Bolswert (1586–1659),* Interior, *undated. Engraving, 35.0 cm x 44.5 cm. Museum Boijmans Van Beuningen, Rotterdam (H 294).*

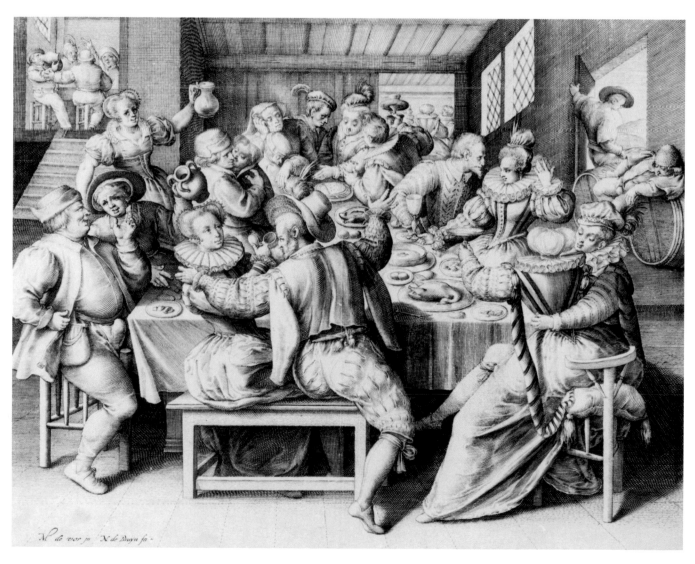

## SUPERSTITION

Investigating the connection between luxury glassware, social relations, conspicuous consumption, iconography, and the phenomenon of superstition might make for another intriguing study. One 17th-century Dutch superstition maintained that the breaking of a drinking glass announced someone's death (Schotel 1903, p. 412). In Italy, however, glasses were deliberately broken at weddings and on other occasions as a symbol of happiness.

The story was also told that Venetian glasses changed color when they were filled with a poisonous liquid. Some people believed, however, that the best Venetian drinking glasses would shatter instantly when they came in contact with a drop of poison. The first of these notions may have derived from a story concerning Saint John the Evangelist portrayed in engravings by such artists as Jean Baptist Barbé (1578–1649; Fig. 27) and Jacques Callot (1592–1635; Fig. 28). Here the evangelist is shown holding a poisoned glass chalice in Venetian style. The snake in the glass represents the poisoned liquid. The engravings relate the legend of how the priest of the temple of Diana in Ephesus gave John a poisoned cup to drink from as a test of the power of his faith. Two condemned men had already drunk from the cup and died. John not only survived unharmed, but he also restored the other two men to life. Since the Middle Ages, the emblem of the chalice had been construed by the faithful as a representation of Christianity. The two snakes on a French goblet that is dated to the 16th century make reference to the miracle of the bronze serpent (Num. 21:6–9) (see pp. 166–167, **1**). The crucifix that is also depicted on the goblet may refer to the power of the Cross as a prophylactic sign against poison. In the "Life of Saint Benedict" cycle of frescoes at the Monastery of Monte Oliveto Maggiore near Siena, Benedict breaks a glass of poisoned wine by making the sign of the Cross.

A silver-mounted goblet with Antwerp marks, now in the collection of the Rijksmuseum in Amsterdam, is fitted inside its lid with a holder for such a prophylactic device. The unicorn's horn (actually part of a narwhal horn) would have been submerged in the liquid, thus protecting the drinker (Ritsema van Eck and Zijlstra-Zweens 1993, v. 1, p. 23, no. 8).[14] The same superstitious powers ap-

**FIG. 27**

*Jean Baptist Barbé (1578–1649), Saint John, after Th. van Loon, undated. Engraving, 13.0 cm x 95.0 cm. Museum Boijmans Van Beuningen, Rotterdam (BdH 22971, lent by the Lucas van Leyden Foundation).*

Fig. **28**
*Jacques Callot (1592–1635),*
Saint John, *1631. Etching, 13.8
cm x 87.0 cm. Museum Boijmans
Van Beuningen, Rotterdam
(DN 2591/123).*

ply to other materials, such as porcelain, terra sigillata, coral, and the serpent's tongue.[15]

The appearance of the snake as a symbol, in this instance standing for Satan, is to be found in the stems and applied decorations of Venetian and Venetian-style glasses. Such a decoration may have received its form and meaning from the combination of earlier Islamic glass styles/ornamentation and Christian symbolism. Snakes or dragons adorning the stems of wineglasses may have warned of the danger of drinking too much alcohol, which is, in effect, a kind of poison. As time passed, the symbolism may have lost its meaning, while the shape was retained as a symbol of Venetian-style glassmaking virtuosity (Gianolla and Junck 1997, p. 13).

## Conclusion

We are fortunate to have a rich legacy of 17th-century Dutch paintings and engravings in which domestic life is depicted in all its material and iconographic aspects. These works provide us with an abundant source of information on various aspects of the design, function, and meaning of both everyday and luxury domestic objects, which filled the homes of Dutch burghers. By interpreting this visual resource, in combination with contemporaneous historical and archeological information, we are able to reconstruct the outer and inner (social) order of material culture as part of Dutch domestic life of that period. This effort helps us to understand how luxury goods such as Venetian-style glassware were received and valued in the Netherlands during the 1600s. It seems that this type of glassware was socially "trapped." It was a highly desirable and conspicuous commodity, but it was surrounded by prevailing cultural notions of modesty and the Christian belief that "all is vanity." Despite the ongoing influence of Calvinism and the outcries of Dutch moralists who counseled a life of restraint, 17th-century Dutch burghers reveled more and more in a true golden age of luxury domestic objects. Paintings and engravings of that time prominently portray these grand objects. It is significant, however, that in almost every case in which Venetian-style glassware is featured in such works of art, the iconographic context is related to the subject of vanity and a mockery of extravagance.

It appears that the Dutch burghers themselves were not embarrassed by riches, and they spent considerable sums to renovate and decorate their homes, which were sometimes likened to castles, jewels, and the finest suits of clothes. As a rich merchant in one 17th-century play expressed it, "What my home needs, I hurry myself to buy" (Schotel 1903, p. 2). Simon Schama confirms this outlook: "For all the pungency of the polemics against world-

liness and luxury, there seems no reason to assume that the 'core' groups of Dutch society, from the patriciate at the top to skilled artisans and tradesmen at the bottom, showed any special propensity to avoid consumption in favor of savings and investment" (Schama 1988, p. 298). The paintings and prints thus seem to encapsulate the dilemma, confronting both the desire for modesty and the longing for luxury.

Every culture seems to project its traditional and contemporary belief systems onto those things, introduced from outside, that are construed as innovative, desirable, and "exotic," thus creating a meaningful combination of the "old" and the "new" (Van Dongen 1995, p. 13). The form, function, and meaning of objects are therefore in a constant and dynamic process of change. Assessing the place of luxury in society is part of that process, acting as a barometer of the transition from the classical and medieval worldview to that of the modern era (Berry 1994, p. xii). If we look around us today and contemplate the social role of modern luxury glassware, we will note that it appears to have retained its place as a desirable luxury product. One interesting example is contained in the following report, which was published in *The Times* of London on December 31, 1987:

> A Lake District Hotel is offering weekend breaks costing nearly £1,000 a day. Guests paying £1,995 each will be served grouse, venison, fillet steak, lobster, caviar, truffles and pâté de foie gras. Miss Carolyn Graves, a director of the hotel, said, "The big-spending break is for people who work so hard that holidays are a rarity and have to be crammed full of a year's worth of pleasure." Those include return helicopter travel from up to 200 miles, a self-drive or chauffeur driven Rolls-Royce, the hotel's luxury suite with its spa bath and sunbathing tower, a case of champagne per person, the pick of the

cellar, a personal chef to cook whatever takes the guests' fancy, and two sheepskin coats and personalized crystal decanter and glasses as souvenirs.

Since this report appears in the commercial context of contemporary advertising, we can assume that it was intended to be a selling point. Labeling a consumer good or service as a "luxury" is also to make a claim about its desirability (Berry 1994, p. 3). The glassware in this extravagant setting is marked as a luxury object, one both to be desired and to convey status, and associated with expensiveness and rarity. In a similar way, the 17th-century "Venetian glasses" mentioned in the poem at the beginning of this chapter are considered to be objects of luxury in a moral atmosphere of conspicuous consumption. The poet concludes that the shopper Jorden was "sensible" when he decided to buy only "four wooden spoons and six plates for the table." How to be both rich and modest at the same time was a challenge that helped to shape 17th-century Dutch beliefs and practices.

# Façon de Venise Glass in the Netherlands

## Reino Liefkes

### ECONOMIC AND POLITICAL BACKGROUND

The Netherlands played a crucial role in the early proliferation of glassmaking *à la façon de Venise*. The industry developed rapidly as economic power and trade dominance shifted from Italy to the north. By 1500, Antwerp had surpassed Bruges as the premier northern port and the main link with the Mediterranean (Braudel 1987–1988; Zijlstra-Zweens 1993, p. 14). Although the city grew quickly during the first two decades of the 16th century, its rate of expansion was even more explosive between 1540 and 1565. By the end of that period, its population had increased to about 100,000, making it one of Europe's largest and wealthiest cities (Martens and Peeters 2001).

Politically, the situation was less stable. Charles V, who had ruled as Holy Roman emperor since 1519, was succeeded by his son, Philip II, in 1555. Philip imposed heavy taxes and left the Netherlands in charge of his representative, Margaret of

*Detail from* The Conspiracy of the Batavians under Claudius Civilis, *by Rembrandt van Rijn (Object 3c).*

Austria. He settled in Spain, where he became a zealous prosecutor of Protestant heretics. A widespread rebellion against his oppressive rule culminated in the iconoclasm of 1566. This was followed, one year later, by a Spanish invasion that triggered an 80-year war between the Netherlands and Spain. The northern provinces embraced Protestantism and declared their independence in 1581, but the southern provinces remained under Spanish rule. Antwerp, which virtually straddled the dividing line between the northern and southern provinces, was plundered twice. When the city finally succumbed to the Spanish invaders in 1585, its harbor was blockaded and many of its merchants, scholars, artists, and artisans moved northward, principally to Amsterdam.

The independence of the newly formed Dutch Republic of United Provinces ushered in a true golden age, a period of unprecedented wealth, power, and cultural development. These provinces benefited enormously from the influx of talent from the south, and the closure of the Antwerp harbor permitted the northern ports of Middelburg and Amsterdam to expand without competition.

Amsterdam, which enjoyed a near monopoly of the Mediterranean trade, further expanded its horizons with the establishment of the Dutch East and West India Companies in 1602 and 1621 respectively (Laan 1991; Royen 1991). Following the opening of its Exchange Bank in 1609, Amsterdam reigned as the world's undisputed trade leader for almost a century. The economic position of the once dominant Venetian republic declined dramatically after 1620, and it never recovered.

## GLASS IN THE VENETIAN MANNER

As the Netherlands advanced socially and economically, there was a rising demand for imported luxury goods. At the same time, however, efforts were made to encourage local production. By 1513, three Italian potters had settled in Antwerp as "galeyerspotbackers," makers of tin-glazed earthenware in the Italian style, which had previously been imported from Venice (Dumortier 1999; Wilson 1999). The Venetians had monopolized the production of luxury *cristallo*, but here, too, there was a growing desire in the Netherlands to become more self-sufficient. From the earliest evidence we have about the establishment of a glasshouse for the making of *cristallo*, authorities in Antwerp were eager to support such a venture. A city bill of 1537 shows that Lucas van Helmont received a subsidy of 63 pounds, three shillings, and three "deniers" to build a furnace because he had introduced the craft of blowing "crystalline" glass in Antwerp (Denissen 1985, p. 9). Similarly, in 1542, an Italian named Cornachini received financial support to start producing Venetian mirrors, with the proviso that he would train and employ local youths in his business.

In 1549, Jean de Lame, a merchant from Cremona living in Antwerp, was granted the exclusive right to produce "voires de cristal à la mode et façon que l'on les labeure en la cyté de Venise" (Denissen 1985, pp. 9–10).[1] This is the earliest known use of the term *façon de Venise*. A few years later, this patent was assigned to the Venetian Jacopo di Francesco, and in 1558, it was acquired by Jacopo

FIG. 1

*Covered vase, colorless, blown, ice glass technique. Low Countries, late 16th century. OH. 20.9 cm, D. 10.8 cm. The Corning Museum of Glass, Corning, New York (79.3.187, gift of The Ruth Bryan Strauss Memorial Foundation). Formerly in the collections of Jerome Strauss (S995) and R. W. M. Walker.*

**FIG. 2**

*Drinking tazza with ice glass knop, colorless with grayish tinge, opaque turquoise, gold foil, blown, mold-blown, tooled, applied. Italy or Low Countries, last quarter of the 16th century. H. 15.3 cm, D. 16.3 cm. The Corning Museum of Glass, Corning, New York (2000.3.12). Formerly in a private collection.*

Pasquetti of Brescia. Pasquetti succeeded in establishing both the glasshouse and Antwerp's position as the main center of glassmaking in the Venetian style outside Italy. In 1609, while researching his famous glassmaking treatise *L'arte vetraria* (1612), the Florentine priest Antonio Neri visited Antwerp. There he saw the production of the finest *calcedonio*, which had previously been one of the Venetian glassmakers' most closely guarded secrets (Theuerkauff-Liederwald 1994, p. 31).

The support and protection that Pasquetti received from Antwerp's authorities in building his successful glasshouse set the tone for many similar ventures. In 1561, he was granted a monopoly for the manufacture of Venetian-style glasses in the Netherlands. He received financial assistance with rent and general expenses, and he was exempt from paying taxes on the wine and beer that were

intended for consumption by glassblowers at his factory. Pasquetti even managed to obtain a monopoly on the sale of *cristallo* in the Netherlands. This monopoly was enforced at least twice in 1571, when barrels of Venetian-style glass from independent Liège were confiscated.

Following Pasquetti's death in 1574, his glasshouse and patent were inherited by two of his nephews. From 1586 until his death in 1595, Ambrosio Mongardo managed the factory with great success. Its operation then passed to his wife, Sara Vinckx. She proceeded to expand the facility by adding two pots and two glory holes in the furnace, which allowed her to employ two more glassmakers (Denissen 1985, p. 14).[2] In 1598, Sara married another Italian glassmaker, Filippo Gridolphi. Although the financial support she received from the city of Antwerp was gradually reduced, she di-

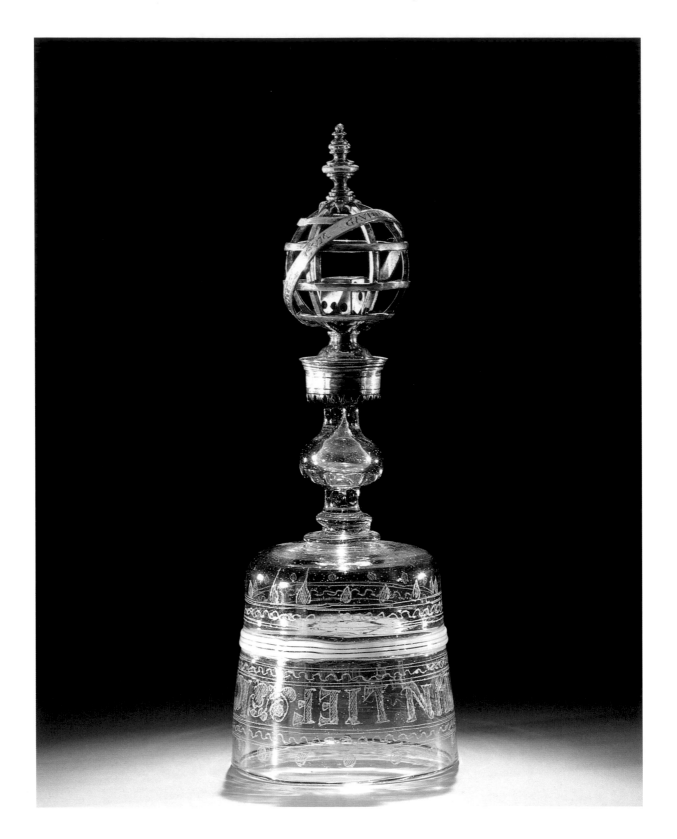

**Fig. 3**

*Dice glass, colorless, opaque white, blown, diamond-point engraved. Low Countries (glass), Northern Netherlands (decoration), about 1580–1590. H. 17 cm, D. 5.2 cm. Rijksmuseum, Amsterdam (R.B.K. 1995-4). Formerly in the collections of A. J. Guépin and Joost R. Ritman.*

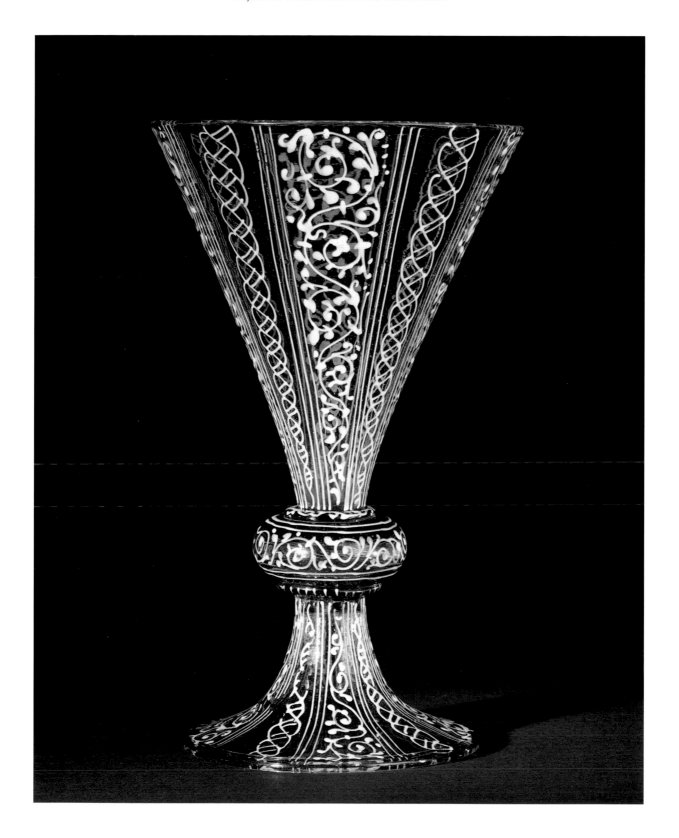

FIG. 4

*Goblet, colorless with grayish tinge, blown, enameled. Low Countries,
late 16th–early 17th century. H. 17.6 cm, D. (top) 10.4 cm. The Corning
Museum of Glass, Corning, New York (68.3.51, gift of Jerome Strauss).
Formerly in the Strauss Collection (S1711).*

Fig. 5

*Goblet, colorless with yellowish tinge, blown, pattern-molded, applied, tooled. Probably façon de Venise (Low Countries?), 17th century. H. 17.8 cm. The Corning Museum of Glass, Corning, New York (58.3.200).*

rected the glasshouse through its most prosperous period.

The situation changed with the onset of the Spanish–Dutch conflict and the division between the northern and southern provinces. The border was closed to trading, and the northern provinces no longer regarded themselves as bound by monopolies granted by their former rulers. On Jan-

uary 24, 1581, the magistrate of Middelburg granted Govaert van der Haghe, a native of Antwerp, a two-year privilege to produce and sell glass in the "Antwerp manner" (Hudig 1923, p. 23, n. 66). The fact that this glass was characterized as "Antwerp" rather than "Venetian" in style illustrates the dominance that Antwerp's glass producers enjoyed at that time. Van der Haghe was also granted a yearly subsidy of 100 guilders and freedom from taxes as well as from excise and guard duties. Later in 1581, Mongardo and his associate, Pierre de Pedralis, appealed to the magistrate in Antwerp, complaining that the Middelburg glasshouse was producing glass in Venetian style and thus infringing on the privilege that had been granted to their predecessor, Pasquetti. Mongardo lodged another complaint in 1592, emphasizing that his workers were being lured to Middelburg and London, "where they are given all freedom they could want for" (Hudig 1923, pp. 22–24, nn. 64, 66, and 68; Denissen 1985, p. 13, n. 29). His protests, which were repeated in 1597, 1598, and 1599, were ignored in Middelburg, from where Van der Haghe's glasshouse effectively controlled the Northern Netherlandish market. When the furnace at Middelburg was temporarily out of order in 1594, two Amsterdam merchants sought permission to import glass from Antwerp until Van der Haghe's factory was back in business (Hudig 1923, p. 24, n. 73; Roever 1991, p. 160; Baart 1998, p. 28).[3]

In 1597, Van der Haghe was allowed to expand his booming enterprise, receiving both a second piece of land and a renewal of his contract (Hudig 1923, p. 24, nn. 70 and 72).[4] The "Staaten" of Zeeland had already granted the glassmaker a patent, making him the only person in the province to "practice the art and trade of the blowing of glass." Van der Haghe had also received a promise from the provincial authorities to close the borders to the importation of glass from Antwerp. The city of Antwerp, in turn, received a monopoly in 1611 to produce and market its own glassware, and to sell imported Venetian glass, throughout the Southern Netherlands (*ibid.*, p. 16).[5]

FIG. 6

*Goblet or champagne, colorless with dark gray tinge, blown. Low Countries, 17th century. H. 14 cm. The Corning Museum of Glass, Corning, New York (58.3.184).*

Merchants from Amsterdam acquired the Middelburg glasshouse in 1606, and they were granted the exclusive right to market its products (Hudig 1923, pp. 25–26). However, the magistrates in Amsterdam were eager to establish a glassworks within their own city. In 1597, they concluded lengthy negotiations with the Venetian glassmaker Antonio Obizzo (or Obisy), whose construction of a factory provoked renewed protests from Sara Vinckx, owner of the Antwerp glasshouse (*ibid.*, p. 31; Roever 1991, pp. 162–163; Baart 1998, pp. 27–28).[6] Obizzo's factory was short-lived, however. In 1601, his monopoly was assumed by Jan Hendrickz Soop, who started a new glasshouse, with several furnaces and workshops, at a different site in Amsterdam (Pontanus 1614, p. 273; quoted by Hudig 1923, p. 34, n. 119, and Roever 1991, p. 157). His venture, which produced drinking glasses and trade beads, was much more successful. But he,

too, lost his monopoly when the city permitted a merchant from Antwerp, Abraham van Tongerloo, to build his own glasshouse in 1613.

Local governments supported the glass industry primarily for economic reasons. A thriving business resulted in increased wealth and eliminated expensive imports. In Amsterdam, where an influx of immigrants had resulted in a high rate of unemployment, the magistrate was particularly eager to introduce labor-intensive workplaces (Roever 1991, pp. 162–163). In drafting his contract with the city council in 1613, Van Tongerloo agreed that "besides his regular personnel," he would "permanently employ 50 men of over 16 years old, who would be allocated to him by the mayor" at a specified rate (Hudig 1923, p. 39).

The documentary evidence also suggests that support for glassmakers was motivated by local pride. When Antonio Obizzo arrived in Amsterdam

FIG. 7

*Mug, colorless, blown, ice glass technique. Low Countries, mid-17th century. H. 15.7 cm, D. (max.) 11.2 cm, W. (max.) 14.4 cm. The Corning Museum of Glass, Corning, New York (79.3.439, bequest of Jerome Strauss). Formerly in the Strauss Collection (S2623).*

in 1597 to introduce the "blowing and firing of crystalline glasses," the city provided a site for his factory and granted him various benefits. In return, it demanded that "he should aim with great zeal for perfection" and that, apart from his own profit, he should promote "the glory of the town" (Hudig 1923, pp. 29–30).[7] The city's pride in its glass industry was undoubtedly bolstered in 1608, when the United East Indian Trading Company selected gifts for the Japanese emperor. In addition to a length of black cloth, for which Amsterdam was famous, the company purchased 50 pieces of glass that had almost certainly been made in Soop's glasshouse (*ibid.*, pp. 34–35, n. 121; Baart 1998, p. 31, n. 22).[8]

Given this interest in civic pride, it is not surprising that official "histories" or descriptions of Amsterdam compare locally produced glass favorably with Venetian products. An example can be found in Johannes Isacius Pontanus's 1611 account of the city's architecture. "The glasshouse opposite Cloveniersdoelen," he wrote, "cannot be ignored. It has several furnaces and workshops, where artists make continuously very beautiful 'crystalline glasses' in countless and more varied shapes with such wonderful and excellent skill, so that they are in no way less than the formerly most famous examples from Venice. Artists daily invent new decorations and shapes" (Pontanus 1614; quoted by Hudig 1923, p. 34, n. 119). Such comparisons went well beyond glass. Throughout the 17th century, the Dutch delighted in stressing the superiority of their glorious new city to the old Venetian republic that in many ways had provided the model for Amsterdam's mercantile development. Constantijn Huygens, writing in 1624, called Amsterdam "Venice twice over" because it featured streets as well as canals (Bakker 1991, quotation on p. 19).

The Amsterdam magistrate seems to have taken a particular interest in ensuring that glasshouses added to the beauty as well as the productivity of his city (Hudig 1923, p. 33, nn. 115 and 116).[9] Van Tongerloo's plans for his factory included an impressive facade that was probably designed by the prestigious Amsterdam architect Hendrik de Keyser (*ibid.*, pp. 38–39 and n. 130).[10] Much later, when opinions changed, the authorities were compelled to observe that "great damage and disfigurement of the city" had been caused by the many sugar refineries, soap works, breweries, and glasshouses constructed at important sites. In 1652, they decreed that any new such establishments should be located at the far eastern or western end of the city (*ibid.*, p. 46).

## MARKET AND TRADE

The availability of glass in the Netherlands gradually increased in the late 16th and 17th centuries. Luxury glass, which had previously been a costly import from Venice, was now also made in Antwerp, Middelburg, and Amsterdam. Glass drinking vessels became more and more popular (Baart 1998, p. 26, n. 2).

The Antwerp glasshouse of Pasquetti and his successors had encountered little local competition until the Middelburg factory was founded. Initially, Middelburg was the only supplier of luxury glass in the Northern Netherlands, and its products were sold chiefly in Amsterdam. As has already been noted, the glasshouse had been owned since 1606 by three Amsterdam merchants, who had the exclusive right to market its products (Hudig 1923, pp. 25–26).[11] By that time, Amsterdam had its own glassworks, and the glass trade continued to be centered there throughout the 17th century (*ibid.*, p. 88).[12] During the second half of the century, however, there was a trend toward decentralization. The number of local glasshouses increased dramatically, and many seemed to have worked mainly for a local market. For example, Nicolaas Jaquet, who became director of a Rotterdam glassworks in 1681, was required by the terms of a contract renewal in May 1693 to produce "daily good crystal, crystalline, and other drinking glasses in sufficient amounts to supply the shops in town" (*ibid.*, pp. 61–62, n. 236).[13]

As the quantities of glass increased, prices declined and designs became simpler. Research is lacking on the relative availability of glass for the various social classes, but we do have some evidence from Amsterdam (Baart, Krook, and Lagerweij 1984, p. 35, n. 5; Baart 1998, p. 27),[14] where archeological inventories from two households dating from 1610 to 1625 have been compared with those of two homes from the period 1675–1700. In both instances, finds from the site of a wealthy home situated on one of the canals were compared with those from a poorer home located on a side street. Remarkably, the difference between the finds lies solely in the quantity of glasses owned, not in their quality. In the earlier period, the numbers of glasses were 24 and one respectively, while the counts were 27 and six respectively in the later period. The excavation reports also indicate a dramatic decrease in the use of *Waldglas* during the 17th century. This may perhaps be explained by the fact that local production was confined almost entirely to colorless luxury glasses.

Around 1635, Guy Libon, who had come from Liège, attempted to make coarse drinking glasses in Amsterdam with the assistance of some Altarist glassmakers. One of his partners, Jacques Casteleyn, told the city's managers how he had "introduced at great expense the production of all sorts of bottles, 'Helbronsche' (of Heilbronn type) *roemers*, and other coarse glass—which was previously imported from France, Germany, Lotharingen, Hessen, and other countries." He went on to complain that "glass traders have dumped the markets," which had prevented him from selling his inventory, and he requested either tax relief or the imposition of a tax on all imports of coarse glassware (Hudig 1923, pp. 42–43).[15] His plea was probably ignored, and the glasshouse did not survive long. It must have been almost impossible to compete with the forest glassworks of central Europe, whose products continued to be imported into the Netherlands in considerable quantities.[16] They could make glass inexpensively, and their trade was extremely lucrative (Baart, Krook, and Lagerweij 1984, pp. 41 and 44, nn. 10 and 11).[17]

The importation of fine colorless glass continued alongside the local production. In 1607, Filippo Gridolphi, owner of the Antwerp glasshouse, managed to obtain a monopoly on Venetian glass imported into the Southern Netherlands (El-Dekmak-Denissen 1988, p. 18), and this monopoly was renewed in 1611. Glasses made in Antwerp and in Venice were purchased for a banquet held in the Lille town hall in 1620 (Hudig 1923, p. 10, n. 3: "tant d'Anvers que de Venyse . . ."). A glassmaker named Miotti, from Brussels, stated in 1623 that yearly imports of "cristals fins de Venise" accounted for 80,000 guilders and that he could supply similar glasses at two-thirds that cost (*ibid.*, p. 11, n. 6). In 1648, the importing of Venetian glass was banned in the Southern Netherlands (*ibid.*, n. 7).[18]

Glass was both imported and exported in Amsterdam, the trade center of the Northern Netherlands. But even when the successful Amsterdam glasshouse at the Rozengracht was in full production (between October 1, 1667, and September 30, 1668), the value of imported glass far exceeded that of glass exports (Hudig 1923, pp. 56–57). Apart from window glass from Normandy, the value of imported glass from the "Oostlandt" (probably *Waldglas* from the Ostsee area) amounted to 22,140 guilders, while exports were valued at 5,678 guilders. In addition, mirrors and glasses imported from various sources amounted to 9,568 guilders, while exports totaled 4,611 guilders. The export figures probably represent the trade in luxury

FIG. 8

*Goblet, colorless with grayish green tinge, blown, diamond-point engraved, inscribed "DSM DRINK AND BE SOBER 1663." Southern Netherlands, second half of the 17th century. H. 15.4 cm, D. (rim) 6.9 cm. The Corning Museum of Glass, Corning, New York (73.2.25).*

FIG. 9

*Serpent-stem goblet, colorless, white, red, blue, blown, applied, tooled, diamond-point engraved. Probably Southern Netherlands, second half of the 17th century, dated 1684. H. 16.0 cm. The Corning Museum of Glass, Corning, New York (70.3.5). Engraved, on bowl, "A Monsieur Gerard Bernsaw, Marchand a Eluefeld . 1684 :le 12 .xbre" (For Mister Gerard Bernsaw, merchant from Elverfeld . 1684 :the 12th of December), and on foot, "Monsieur Clauberg cet fait la des Reun. a la Mierde(?) le 12 xbre '84" (Mister Clauberg did this at the reunion in Mierde on the 12th of December '84).*

glasses. Imports of colorless luxury glasses continued throughout most of the 17th century, but relatively few of them seem to have come from Venice (*ibid.*, p. 11, n. 9).[19]

Liège was one of Amsterdam's main suppliers of such glass, and the competition must have affected the local glasshouse severely. In 1650, glass from Liège was embargoed in the Northern Netherlands in an attempt to protect the local industry (Hudig 1923, p. 67). Since 1648, Maastricht had been jointly governed by the bishop of Liège and the Dutch "Staten Generaal" (parliament). A glasshouse started there in 1645 by Guy Libon and staffed with glassmakers from Liège was of great interest to the Bonhommes of Liège, who must have seen it as a back-door route into the Dutch market. In 1651, one year after the borders had been closed, Henri Bonhomme purchased the glasshouse for the enormous sum of 20,000 guilders (*ibid.*, pp. 66–67). Six years later, he established in Den Bosch (Bois-le-Duc) what was to become the Northern Netherlands' longest-lived glasshouse (*ibid.*, pp. 69–70). For a while, this factory seems to have operated as a branch of the Liège glassworks, but following a major split in the Bonhomme family in 1670, they became competitors. We know that, by 1690, the glasshouses in Liège and Den Bosch sold most of their glass in Amsterdam, where they maintained a warehouse for this purpose.

Protective measures were usually introduced to assist a newly established glasshouse or as the result of changing political conditions. Such a measure was instituted in 1657 on behalf of the fledgling glasshouse in Den Bosch. It stipulated that "foreign glasses" could be sold in Maastricht only on regular market days (Hudig 1923, p. 69). Middelburg, as we have seen, closed its borders to Antwerp glass soon after the northern and southern provinces were divided. In 1676, the new owners of the Rozengracht glasshouse applied for a patent, "as is usage in Flanders, Brabant, Liège, Cologne, etc.," for the production of glass and beads in Amsterdam and its environs (*ibid.*, pp. 55–56).[20]

Obviously, such protective measures were highly desirable for the entrepreneurs as a means of eliminating competition, but glassmaking was an inherently precarious industry. In Antwerp, as well as in Middelburg and Amsterdam, the initial investments in glasshouses were considerable, especially since their advanced technology and skilled workers often had to be recruited from abroad. Even when such an enterprise was up and running, it remained extremely expensive to operate. Glasshouses required unusually large quantities of raw materials and fuel. A small but particularly well documented glassworks in Gouda provides an indication of the costs involved. It was in production only between 1696 and 1698, during which time it spent 43 percent of its budget on raw materials, 33 percent on personnel, and 24 percent on fuel (Klein 1982, p. 42).[21] Although the well-developed infrastructure of the northern provinces ensured the availability of fuel and raw materials at competitive prices, the huge quantities required for the operation of a glasshouse imposed a heavy financial burden on its owners.[22]

**Fig. 10**

*Calligraphic wineglass, colorless with grayish tinge, blown, diamond-point engraved. Low Countries, about 1650–1700. H. 12.8 cm, D. (rim) 7.4 cm, (foot) 7.8 cm. The Corning Museum of Glass, Corning, New York (79.3.306, gift of Jerome Strauss). Formerly in the Strauss Collection (S1384).*

As has been noted, Dutch municipal governments were usually eager to support the development of glassworks by providing appropriate locations and buildings, capital investments, tax relief, and other financial assistance.[23] Many such ventures were launched throughout the Northern Netherlands during the 17th century. From 1666 to 1696 alone, no fewer than 19 glasshouses were constructed north of the Rhine, Waal, and Meuse Rivers (Klein 1982, p. 31).[24] Although these factories were often quite successful, they were usually short-lived. Many of them remained in business only a few years, and even the most prosperous ones managed to survive no more than a couple of decades.

This failure of the glass industry to establish itself more firmly seems incongruous with the positive business climate and buoyant market within the wealthy Dutch republic.[25] Ironically, it seems that the willingness of local governments to provide generous investments and other benefits may have been a contributing factor, as is evident from the countless complaints from glasshouse owners and their pleas to fend off competition (Klein 1982, p. 43; among the many examples in Hudig 1923, see pp. 22–24, 34, 36, 42, and 43). Companies came and went very quickly, depending on the level of support that they—or their competitors—received. Newly established enterprises obtained such generous assistance that they almost invariably destroyed their more established competitors, often capitalizing on protective measures to lure workers who had been trained elsewhere at great expense (Hudig 1923, p. 40, n. 132).[26]

## THE GLASSHOUSES

*Façon de Venise* glasshouses in the Netherlands were located in towns and cities rather than in rural areas. Since fuel and raw materials had to be imported (Hudig 1923, p. 75, n. 325),[27] a convenient connection with major waterways was essential. The building of a glassworks was a natural part of the explosive growth of many towns. In the north, confiscated church property often provided an ideal location for a glass factory. The chapel or covered courtyard afforded the lofty space required for the furnace, with additional room for the storage of fuel, raw materials, and pots. There was even enough room left over to furnish living quarters for the factory's manager (*ibid.*, pp. 29–30). Wood, which was piled up under the roof just outside the glasshouse (*ibid.*, p. 29), was the most commonly used fuel in the Netherlands throughout the 17th century. However, peat was also employed, probably to keep the furnaces fired during intervals when no glass was being blown (Klein 1982, pp. 40–41). In 1627, coal became the fuel of choice in the large glasshouse of Jean Bonhomme and Guy Libon at Liège,

which is situated amid large coal fields. Libon introduced coal in the Netherlands at his Amsterdam glasshouse about 1640 (Hudig 1923, pp. 21 and 42–43). However, because taxes on coal were high, it was not generally adopted until the end of the century (*ibid.*, pp. 74–75).[28]

Maintaining a shop on the glasshouse site was probably a common practice. This was certainly the case in Antwerp and in Amsterdam's principal glasshouses (Denissen 1985, pp. 13–14).[29] In 1664, many glasses were displayed on the shelves in the shop at the Rozengracht glassworks in Amsterdam (Zesen 1664; quoted by Hudig 1923, pp. 51–52). Glasshouses were popular tourist attractions, and they were "visited by many strangers who, amazed

FIG. 11
*Jacob van Loo (1614–1670), Interior of a Glasshouse in Amsterdam, about 1658. Oil on canvas, H. 163 cm, W. 215 cm. Statens Museum for Kunst, Copenhagen.*

by the many sorts of glass for sale, sometimes had something special blown as a souvenir" (Hudig 1923, p. 52). Factories at Nijmegen and elsewhere installed alms boxes in which visitors could deposit donations (Fokkens 1662, pp. 305–306; quoted by Hudig 1923, pp. 52–53).

Fortuitously, two 17th-century impressions of glassworks interiors have survived. Both of them are from Amsterdam. *Interior of a Glasshouse in Amsterdam*, painted by Jacob van Loo (1614–1670) about 1658, probably shows a workshop at the Rozengracht glasshouse (Fig. 11) (Baart 1998, p. 32, fig. 23). In the center of the painting, a man and a boy are mixing ingredients, while a man with Mediterranean features, who could well be the manager, looks on at the right. On the far left, a

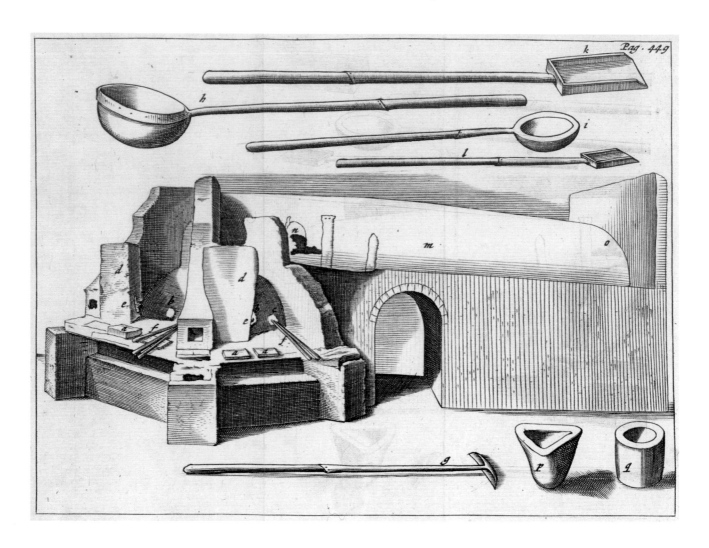

**FIG. 12**

*Antonio Neri (1576–1614), "Instrumenta et Fornax Vitraria apud Amstelodamenses" (tools and glass furnace in Amsterdam), De Arte Vitraria, 1669.*

well-dressed young man is cutting multicolored glass tubes into sections for the production of beads. Just behind him are three metal holders with which such sections were held in the furnace so that their sharp edges could be heated, smoothed, and rounded. Additional workers and the mouth of a furnace can be seen in the background.

The second illustration appears in the 1668–1669 Latin edition of Antonio Neri's *L'arte vetraria*, which was published in Amsterdam. It provides a detailed depiction of a glass furnace in that city, and it is probably the furnace that was installed in

1663 at Rozengracht (Fig. 12).[30] The depicted structure incorporates an innovative, tunnel-shaped annealing furnace, or lehr (Charleston 1978, pp. 17–18).[31] Detailed captions explain the functions of the various parts of the furnace, as well as those of the illustrated tools. Included are a triangular pot or crucible "as used in Amsterdam" and a round one "as used in Haarlem" (*ibid.*). The illustrated furnace is identical to the one depicted in the frontispiece of the same edition, which shows the interior of a glasshouse. It is therefore likely that this is an interior view of the same Rozengracht glasshouse (Hudig 1923, pp. 47–48),[32] which was very much at the forefront of technological developments. Another innovation, which is recorded for the first time in this engraving, is the glassmaker's chair, which afforded considerably more room for the shaping and tooling of the glass (Charleston 1962).

## The Glassmakers

Sixteenth- and 17th-century *façon de Venise* glasshouses were truly international workplaces. Glassmakers from various countries came and went, bringing not only their specialized skills but also their own languages and cultural backgrounds. Initially, most of the masters were Muranese who had been recruited directly from Murano or from nearby glasshouses (Hudig 1923, pp. 34–35; Klein 1982, pp. 35–36).[33] During the 17th century, there was an increase in the number of glassmakers from Liège and especially from Altare. Unlike their counterparts from Murano, Altarists were encouraged by their glassblowers' guild to practice their skills abroad, but this often meant that the consuls of Altare had to be paid as well (Hudig 1923, pp. 41–42). For this reason, it was more expensive to hire Altarists than Muranese glassmakers. After 1685, there was also an influx of French Huguenot glassworkers (Klein 1982, p. 36).[34] Germans were employed in Dutch glass factories throughout the 17th century, while English glassmakers began to work there in the mid-1600s.

Communication cannot always have been easy in this multicultural environment. Contracts were usually drawn up in French, but some glassmakers were illiterate (Klein 1982, p. 39). Louijs Mijot, for example, drew a goblet instead of signing his name (Fig. 13). Emotions often escalated, a condition that was probably exacerbated by the huge quantities of beer that were consumed by glassworkers to combat their prolonged exposure to the heat of the furnaces (Hudig 1923, p. 43).[35] Jealousies and arguments surfaced in many glasshouses, and these occasionally resulted in violence. In Haarlem, for example, an angry glassmaker once smashed four teeth from a colleague's mouth with a red-hot blowpipe (Klein 1982, p. 39; Hudig 1923, p. 53). Foreign glassworkers, who likely enjoyed a higher reputation in their native countries, found it hard to adapt to life in the cold, Protestant north. Such workers were the subject of complaints in Gouda, where it was said that they indulged themselves in excessive spending and other pleasures (Klein 1982, p. 39).

The most important position in Dutch glasshouses was that of workshop manager or *facteur*. During the 1560s and 1570s, Ambrosio Mongardo had worked under Jacopo Pasquetti in Antwerp as "principaele facteur ende toesiendere" (principal *facteur* and supervisor) (Denissen 1985, p. 13). The term *consoir* must have had a similar meaning. Nicolaas Jaquet was in charge of the glasshouse on the Spaarne in Haarlem. In 1681, as "consoir" or "conseur," he supervised the composition of the batch and the upkeep of the furnaces and pots (Hudig 1923, p. 77, n. 341).[36] He lived at the glassworks, where he tended the furnaces both day and night. Jaquet was also responsible for the stoking of the furnaces, maintaining the supply of raw materials, and paying the workers their wages (*ibid.*,

Fig. 13

*Signature of Amsterdam glassmaker Louijs Mijot in the form of a funnel-shaped goblet, 1666. Gemeentearchief, Amsterdam.*

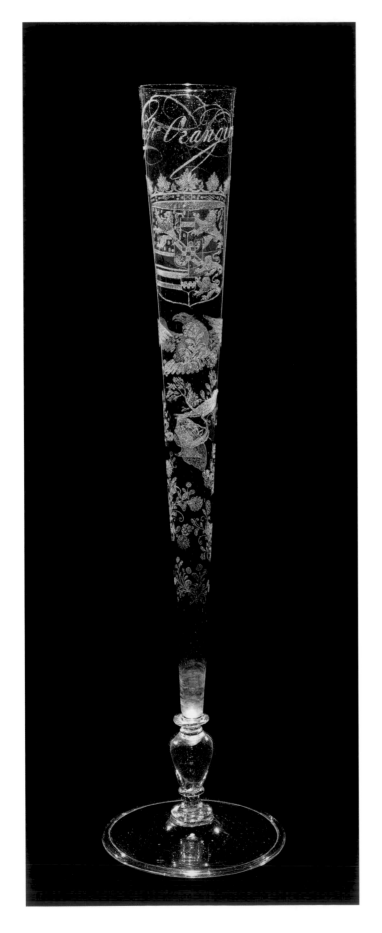

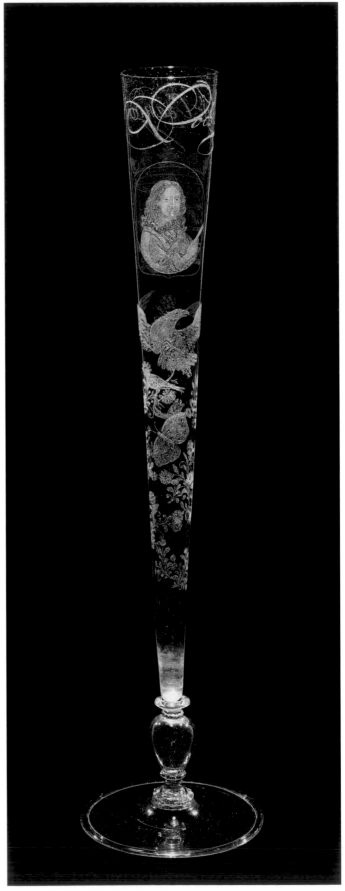

pp. 77–78, nn. 342 and 343).[37] Although the precise responsibilities of the *consoir* varied from place to place, he was always the glasshouse's technical manager. This position was usually held by Italians, although Frenchmen may have attained it later in the 17th century. The *consoir* was the employee with the greatest technical knowledge, and he was compensated accordingly (Klein 1982, pp. 37–38).[38]

Likewise, most of the master glassblowers were of Italian or French origin, and they were often lured away from other glasshouses. There were usually six such workers in each glasshouse, corresponding to the number of glory holes at the furnace (Denissen 1985, pp. 13–14).[39] Supporting the masters were one or two assistants, as well as apprentices and, sometimes, porters who placed the finished products in the annealer (*ibid.*).[40] Some glasshouses had a more detailed division of labor. The Rotterdam glassworks superintended by Jaquet in the 1680s employed a *vorblaser*, who blew the glass before the master worked it (Hudig 1923, p. 61).[41] A stoker constantly tended the furnace in order to maintain the high temperatures required for glassmaking (*ibid.*, pp. 71–72).[42] In addition to these specialists, glasshouses employed large numbers of untrained men, women, and children for all sorts of tasks.[43]

FIG. 14

*Flute with the royal arms of the Netherlands and portrait of William III, colorless, blown, diamond-point engraved. Low Countries, about 1670. H. 45.3 cm, D. (rim) 5.7 cm. The Corning Museum of Glass, Corning, New York (79.3.252, bequest of Jerome Strauss). Formerly in the collections of Victor Schick and Mr. Strauss (S332).*

FIG. 15

*Wineglass with elaborate coiled "serpent" stem, transparent light green, blown, applied. Probably Low Countries, late 17th century. H. 18.1 cm. The Corning Museum of Glass, Corning, New York (79.3.444, gift of The Ruth Bryan Strauss Memorial Foundation). Formerly in the collection of Jerome Strauss (S364).*

## CONDITIONS AND PAY

Although there is not enough documentary evidence to provide a clear picture about the wages paid to skilled glassmakers, the existing figures afford some interesting insights into working conditions and production at Dutch glass factories. Glassmakers were paid a piece-wage that was usually based on the 100 to 110 wine or beer glasses produced daily by one master and his helpers (Klein 1982, p. 39).[44] Sometimes the number of beer glasses made in a day exceeded that of wine-glasses because the former were easier and faster to make. It was probably not uncommon for a master to pay his assistants out of his own salary, as was the case with the 23-year-old master François Colnet from Liège, who worked at Amsterdam's Rozengracht glasshouse in 1675 (Hudig 1923, p. 55).[45]

Glassmakers' contracts occasionally listed specific payments for special kinds of work. At the Rozengracht factory, an Italian master, Nicolas Stua, was hired in 1667 to blow "coppen met serpenten"

(serpent glasses) for a wage of two *rijksdaalders* (two and a half guilders) per 20 with covers, and half that sum for 20 without covers. He received the same rate for 20 fine goblets with lids. Stua's contract also stated that he would earn one *rijksdaalder* for special pieces produced during a six-

FIG. 16

*Calligraphic beaker, colorless, blown, applied, diamond-point engraved. Low Countries (glass), Northern Netherlands, Leiden (decoration), engraved by Willem Jacobsz. van Heemskerk (signed), dated 1679. H. 10.2 cm, D. 10 cm. Rijksmuseum, Amsterdam (N.M. 4012). Formerly in the collection of Jonkheer J. E. van Heemskerck van Beest, The Hague.*

FIG. 17

*Beaker with birds and flowers, colorless with grayish tinge, blown, diamond-point engraved. Northern Netherlands, dated 1680. H. 7.8 cm, D. 10 cm. The Corning Museum of Glass, Corning, New York (51.3.218). Formerly in the Spitzner (Dresden) and Frederic Neuburg (Leitmaritz, 80) Collections.*

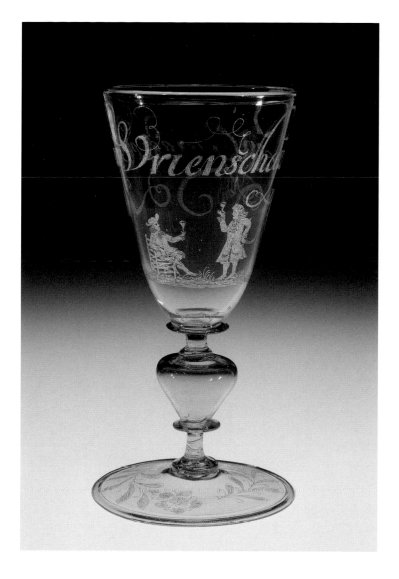

**Fig. 18**

*Goblet, colorless with grayish tinge, blown, diamond-point engraved. Northern Netherlands, in the manner of Willem Mooleyser, about 1680–1690. H. 19.8 cm. The Corning Museum of Glass, Corning, New York (58.3.175).*

hour period (Hudig 1923, p. 54). It can thus be assumed that Stua could make about 20 serpent glasses with lids or 40 without lids per day. Other glassmakers at Rozengracht spent 12 hours daily producing wine-*roemers* and three hours making beer glasses (*ibid.*, pp. 53–54, n. 176).[46]

Work at the glass furnace continued day and night in six-hour shifts (Denissen 1985, pp. 13–14).[47] There was often a period during the winter months when the fire was extinguished, furnace repairs were made, and stocks of fuel and raw materials were replenished. Beginning about 1670, it was customary to pay the workers a standard weekly sum during this time—a measure almost certainly designed to prevent them from looking for employment elsewhere (Klein 1982, p. 39, n. 47).[48]

In addition to their salaries, glassmakers sometimes received such provisions as a lamp, table and bed linens, shirts, laundry, and even a servant (Hudig 1923, pp. 41–42).[49]

Throughout the late 16th and 17th centuries, the labor market was extremely tight because *façon de Venise* glasshouses were being constructed in many parts of Europe, and the mobility of glassmakers was correspondingly high (Hudig 1923, p. 27, n. 87; Charleston 1984, p. 64; Zijlstra-Zweens 1993, p. 14).[50] Local governments invested substantial sums in new glassmaking ventures, which attracted some of the best foreign craftsmen (Hudig 1923, p. 38). Although glassmakers were often required to display samples of their work before they were hired, the art of glassmaking in the Venetian manner was still to a large extent shrouded in mystery, and city magistrates usually had to take on faith a prospective worker's inflated descriptions of his own abilities. This condition left the new industry open to fraud and other abuses. Some glassmakers vanished almost overnight with substantial outstanding debts. The most notorious case in the Netherlands concerned the French refugee Matthieu Simony de Tournay in Zutphen. He left a series of letters that give an exceptionally detailed account of what was involved in setting up a large-scale glasshouse from scratch.[51]

Simony claimed that he could make the best French window glass, the finest drinking glasses, and a huge array of colored glasses, imitation gems, and beads. In September 1689, after ordering from

Amsterdam a long black wig, he set out for Liège, Namur, and Aachen, where he treated glassmakers to dinner or lunch, clinched deals, and purchased a furnace design, 120 blowpipes, and many other tools and materials—all at the expense of investors and the Zutphen magistrate. Beginning his operation with the simultaneous construction of seven furnaces, Simony also planned a separate fritting furnace, a mill, and a cutting workshop for the decoration of his colored glass. By the beginning of 1691, everything was ready except the large furnace for window glass, but at that point the Zutphen magistrate began to run out of patience, complaining that he and his investors had still not seen a single example of Simony's glassmaking

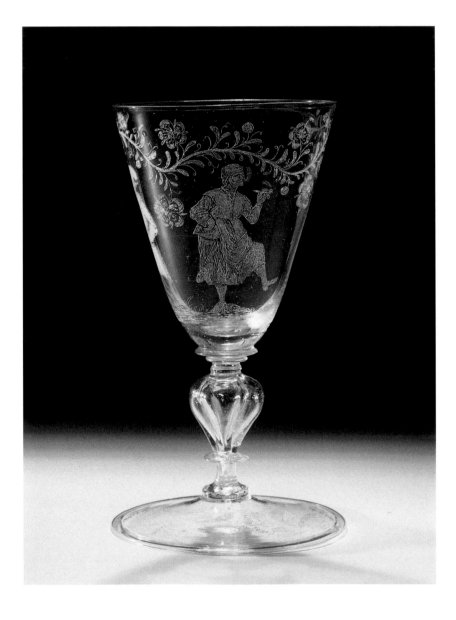

Fig. 19

*Wineglass depicting dancing peasants, colorless, blown, diamond-point engraved. Northern Netherlands, engraved by Willem Mooleyser, Rotterdam (signed), dated 1685. H. 16.4 cm, D. 9 cm. Rijksmuseum, Amsterdam (K.O.G. 149).*

**FIG. 20**
*Calligraphic bottle, colorless with greenish tinge, blown, engraved. Low Countries or Germany (bottle), Northern Netherlands, Warmond, Bastiaan Boers (engraving, signed), dated April 20, 1697. H. (without stopper) 25.4 cm, D. (max., body) 16.5 cm. The Corning Museum of Glass, Corning, New York (55.3.54).*

skills. The magistrate had received a letter from another refugee who claimed that Simony had a criminal record and that he had never worked as a glassmaker in France at all! Later that year, Simony disappeared, leaving behind huge debts and a glasshouse that probably never produced a single piece of glass under his direction. In the following year, however, the elector of Brandenburg placed Simony in charge of his Potsdam glasshouse, where he succeeded the famous Johann Kunckel. Two years later, Simony left that post under similar circumstances, subsequently turning up both in Nuremberg and in Halle.

## CONCLUSION

Simony's notorious career reflects both the mobility of the glassworkers and the sometimes uncritical desire of factory owners to hire the best of them. As the demand for glass *à la façon de Venise* expanded, new glasshouses were established, and their owners competed with one another for the finest available skills. Antwerp led the way. "Crystalline" glass came into production there in 1537, and Venetian-style mirrors followed in 1542. The term *façon de Venise* first appears in an Antwerp document of 1549. Later, factories sprang up in other parts of the Netherlands: at Middelburg in 1581, for example, and in Amsterdam in 1597. Although most of the earliest *façon de Venise* glassmakers came from Murano, in the 17th century the glass industry attracted workers from such distant locations as Altare, Germany, England, and France. Their products supplied not only the local market but also foreign markets in both the Old World and the New.

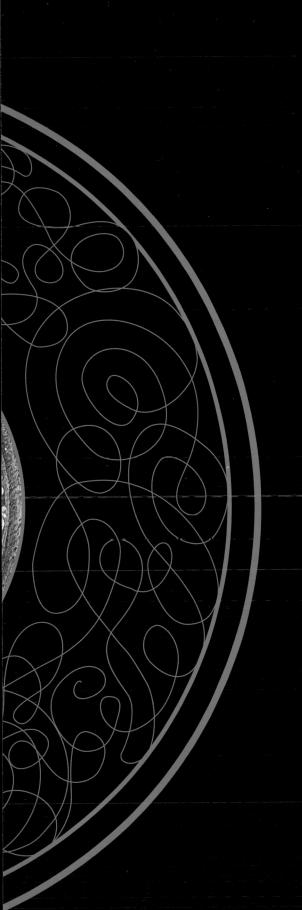

*Façon de Venise* Glass in the Netherlands

# *Objects*

Jutta-Annette Page

# 1

## Armorial Tazza

*H. 15.2 cm, D. (rim) 15.3 cm, (disk) 9.5 cm*

PROBABLY SOUTHERN NETHERLANDS, 16TH CENTURY. THE BRITISH MUSEUM, LONDON (S.390, BEQUEST OF FELIX SLADE, ESQ., F.S.A.). FORMERLY IN THE COLLECTIONS OF RALPH BERNAL (BEFORE 1855) AND MR. SLADE.

COLORLESS. BLOWN, MOLD-BLOWN, APPLIED, GILDED, ENAMELED.

1A

The tazza, which has a shallow bowl and a gilded rim, is decorated with an enameled armorial device on a colorless disk that is applied to the bottom of the bowl (**1a**). The lozenge-shaped shield consists of the following coat of arms: "quarterly 1 and 4, *Vert a lion rampant or*; 2 and 3, *Gules three fleurs-de-lis argent, impaling Azure three chevrons or*" (Tait 1979, pp. 38 and 40, no. 32).

A mold-blown lion-mask stem and a hollow ribbed knop are applied with a merese to the bottom of the bowl. The stem is connected with a merese to the shallow foot, which has a gilded edge.

COMMENT: The arms were identified by J. K. von Schroeder as those of Jac-

queline Happaert (d. 1589), daughter of Jean van Royen, seigneur of Paddeschoot, and his second wife. Jacqueline married Gilles Happaert (d. 1594), *échevin* (alderman) of Antwerp, in 1559 (Theuerkauff-Liederwald 1994, p. 250; the arms are also mentioned in Tait 1991, p. 162).

The construction of the lion-mask stem on **1** appears to be the same as that on tazzas in The Corning Museum of Glass (58.3.180) (*CMG Guide* 2001, p. 69) and the Kunstsammlungen der Veste Coburg (HA 516) (Theuerkauff-Liederwald 1994, pp. 248–250, no. 226). Theuerkauff-Liederwald (*ibid.*, p. 250) noted that the complicated technique employed in the making of the Veste Coburg

tazza indicated a Venetian provenance, but she also stated that the impure glass and the less than elegant construction point to a workshop outside Venice.

Some of the glasses that are decorated with a lion and a cartouche appear to be Spanish (Maggi 1977, p. 17). A circle of 16 five-petaled flowers similar to those on the underside of the bowl of **1** appears on the base of a glass bucket in The British Museum (S.535) (Tait 1979, p. 132, no. 227).

BIBLIOGRAPHY: *Bernal Collection* 1857, p. 286, no. 2732; *Slade Collection* 1871, p. 75; Tait 1979, pp. 38–40, and ill. p. 39; *idem* 1991, pp. 161–163.

## 2

*Roundel with Portrait
of Margaret of Austria*

D. (roundel) 8.2 cm,
(with frame) 14.4 cm

PROBABLY SOUTHERN NETHERLANDS,
POSSIBLY UTRECHT OR ANTWERP,
ABOUT 1563–1570. THE CORNING
MUSEUM OF GLASS, CORNING, NEW
YORK (81.3.43).

COLORLESS. BLOWN, ENAMELED,
GILDED, FUSED.

The roundel is slightly concave and composed of two colorless disks of thinly blown glass that are fused together. The bottom disk, which has a slightly undulating and fire-polished edge, is decorated on the front. A circular border of foliate scrollwork between solid lines is engraved in gold foil near the edge. The bust-length portrait, facing right, was painted with enamel, which extends over the gilding in a few areas. The painted modeling of the portrait was achieved with carefully hatched lines.

The subject of the portrait wears a dress of black cloth with a high collar and white ruff, and a double string of pearls around her neck. A short, diaphanous white veil with a painted silver edge is held with a band of red, blue, and white jewels in her hair. A few ornamental gold buttons decorate the sleeves and bodice of her dress. The inscription "MARGARITA AB AVSTRIA D P" was added in ground gold paint. The gold jewels are highlighted with white enamel.

After the decoration was completed, the disk was carefully reheated until the colors fused to the surface. Then, it was fused to a second layer of colorless glass, encasing the decoration. Numerous blisters, formed in the process of joining the two pieces of glass, are located in the painted area of the portrait. There is a small pontil mark on the reverse, framed by a larger circle that is ground.

The frame consists of turned wood (probably oak), with deep moldings on the front. The back is flat and ridged to hold the roundel. Fragments of paper adhere to the wood, and a rusted fragment of an iron nail or screw is embedded on one side. The front surface is stained black-brown.

COMMENT: The two circular marks on the back of the glass roundel can be explained by its manufacturing process. The smaller circle is a pontil mark that remained from the production of the base-disk. The gilded and fully painted roundel was reheated, then picked up from the front with a large molten bubble of glass, which encased the decoration. Numerous small bubbles and large blisters were trapped between the two layers of glass, probably due to an overheating of the glass disk and the enamel during the precarious fusing process. (A similar problem occurred in the making of the British Museum's tazza [**1a**]; a large crack appeared at the center of the enameled and gilded coat of arms, and the piece was re-fused.)

The bubble was then tooled into the bowl of a tazza. A stem was probably attached with a perfectly circular merese, leaving a slight bulge in the center of the concave disk. Finally, the bubble encasing the disk was cracked off and tooled to form the bowl of a vessel.

The current portrait disk is most likely a fragment from a tazzalike vessel similar to the armorial tazza in The British Museum (**1**). When this object was broken, the portrait was preserved as a roundel by removing the remnants of the merese with wheel cutting and engraving, leaving a large circular scar on the back of the portrait disk. The roughly ground edge shows that the top layer is thicker than the base-disk. A technically related but less sophisticated example is another tazza in The

2A

*Antonis Mor (about 1516–about 1576), portrait of Margaret of Austria, after 1572(?). Oil on oak panel, H. 44 cm, W. 34.5 cm. Kunsthistorisches Museum, Vienna (GG 768).*

British Museum (MLA 54, 3-2, 4). It has an applied manganese purple disk with gold-leaf decoration sandwiched between the disk and the base of the bowl (Tait 1991, pp. 161–163, no. 205).

The portrait derives from an oil painting of Duchess Margaret of Austria by Antonis Mor (about 1516–about 1576) in the Kunsthistorisches Museum, Vienna (GG 768), formerly at Ambras Castle (B33.783) (2a). Mor painted his middle-aged patron at her court in Mechelen about 1563 (Loga 1907, p. 120, fig. 16). A similar portrait by the same artist is in the Bode Museum, Berlin (*ibid.*, pl. XXIV). The duchess appears to have had a strangely shiny

skin. In the Berlin painting, Mor dealt with that issue and made his subject appear more approachable.

Margaret of Austria (1522–1586) became known as Margaret of Parma when she became duchess of Parma in 1550. She was named regent of the Netherlands in 1559, a position from which she resigned in 1567. In 1580, she was again entrusted with the civil administration of the country, but she was finally relieved of her duties in 1583.

In 1554, Mor had painted a portrait of Mary Tudor, showing the queen in French dress on her wedding day. He produced several copies of this portrait

on small wooden boards as gifts for the Knights of the Golden Fleece and Cardinal Granvelle. One of these roundels is in the Kunsthistorisches Museum, Vienna. A glass copy of a wooden roundel was noted in the Bethnal Green Museum, London, in 1907 (Loga 1907, p. 105, fig. 8). It is now lost, so it is unclear whether the object is similar to the Margaret of Austria roundel or reverse-painted or a stained glass window.[52]

BIBLIOGRAPHY: *The Corning Museum of Glass Annual Report 1981*, 1982, p. 4; "Recent Important Acquisitions," *JGS*, v. 24, 1982, p. 83, no. 21.

# 3

## Tazza and Case

*H. 5.2 cm, D. (rim) 16.6 cm*

SOUTHERN NETHERLANDS (GLASS), NORTHERN NETHERLANDS (CASE), 1573, 1586, 1591, AND 1597. RIJKSMUSEUM, AMSTERDAM (N.G. 372A, B). FORMERLY IN THE COLLECTION OF JONKHEER G. R. GERLACIUS VAN SWINDEREN, HAVANA, BY DESCENT FROM THE BLOYS VAN TRESLONG FAMILY.

COLORLESS WITH GRAYISH TINGE. BLOWN, APPLIED, ENGRAVED.

3A

The tazza consists of a shallow bowl with a fire-polished rim and an applied pedestal foot with a folded edge. Six names and mottoes were diamond-point engraved on the bowl by different hands:

(1) Below a sketchy crown, the letter "H," the year "1573," and the letters "WSMV"; below this, the motto "Dein viandt nummer acht te licht / Dein vrundt teueell vertrauwet nicht" (Do not underestimate your foe / or trust your friend too much) and the name "Jo D V Renes" (for Johannes Dominus van Reness).

(2) Below a sketchy crown, an "A," the year "1586," the motto "ungne ie serviraeij" (only one shall I serve), and the name "Jehan d'Egmont."

(3 and 4) The year "1591," the motto "sans estre ghys" (being not a "Gueux" or beggar, i.e., one of the rebels against the Spanish tyranny in the Netherlands), and the names "Droge" and "morogan."

(5) Below a crown, the letters "AE," the year "1573," the motto "Emulus . Accendit . Virtute" (An ambitious man shines with virtue), and the name "G.

D. B. D. Treslong" (Guillaume de Bloys de Treslong).

(6) Below a crown, the year "1523+," the motto "Sans Aultre" (Without any other), and the name "R. D. Bailleul" (Robert de Belle Bailloeul).

The original wooden case (**3a**) is covered with leather on the outside and lined with red cloth on the inside. The coat of arms of Chantillon is painted on the bottom. The case is fastened with a modern silk ribbon.

COMMENT: The names on the tazza are those of six eminent leaders of the revolt of the young Dutch republic against the Spanish. The tazza is thought to be that depicted in Rembrandt van Rijn's painting *The Conspiracy of the Batavians under Claudius Civilis* (**3b**). This painting is Rembrandt's largest work. It is the first in a series of paintings portraying the revolt of the Batavians, the early inhabitants of the Netherlands, against the Romans, as recorded by Tacitus (*Histories* 4.13–37). The scene is a banquet attended by Claudius Civilis, chieftain of the Batavians, and his aristocratic leaders,

3B

*Rembrandt van Rijn (1606–1669),* The
Conspiracy of the Batavians under
Claudius Civilis, *1661–1662. Oil on
canvas, H. 196 cm, W. 309 cm. Nationalmuseum, Stockholm.*

who swear an oath to rise united
against their Roman oppressors. They
are crowded around a long table covered by a white cloth, with a Venetian-
style footed wineglass on the far right.

The work, commissioned in 1661
by the burgomasters of Amsterdam,
was intended for the public gallery of
the new town hall. The choice of Rembrandt for the commission was controversial, however, and his painting remained on view only from August 1662
until the end of that year. He was never
paid for the painting.

The town hall decoration was designed to commemorate the Dutch
struggle for freedom. Under their
chieftain Gaius Julius Civilis (known
as Claudius Civilis in Germany), who
had been a Roman army officer for
many years, the Batavians revolted
against Roman rule in A.D. 69. The
burgomasters had chosen this subject

to commemorate the beginning of the
Eighty Years' War against Spanish op-
pression, which had ended successfully
in 1648.

Fokkens (1662) describes the scene
as follows: "Civilis made them all swear
an oath, scorning those who displayed
weakness. Then a large golden goblet
filled with wine was passed around,
and all of them promised to follow him
wherever he would lead them. . . . And
this is shown in the first painting, painted by Rembrandt." It has been argued,
however, that the goblet, depicted in
an earlier sketch, was replaced by the
glass drinking tazza (**3**) (Citroen 1998).

BIBLIOGRAPHY: Ritsema van Eck
1995, pp. 17–18, no. 1; Citroen 1998.

## 4

### Wafel *Beaker*

*H. 16.0–16.5 cm, D. (rim) 10.8 cm, (base) 7.7 cm*

PROBABLY SOUTHERN NETHERLANDS, ANTWERP, LATE 16TH CENTURY. THE CORNING MUSEUM OF GLASS, CORNING, NEW YORK (56.3.93). FORMERLY IN THE EIGEL COLLECTION, COLOGNE (8).

COLORLESS. BLOWN, MOLD-BLOWN, APPLIED, ENAMELED.

This beaker has a straight-sided body that increases in diameter toward the slightly flaring rim. A thick ribbon of colorless glass was trailed spirally around the bubble from bottom to top. The beginning of the trail is still visible under the base. The bubble was then further inflated in a vertically ribbed mold that cut across the trail, resulting in a pattern of soft-edged (cushion-shaped) square facets. A thick trail of colorless glass was wound around the edge of the base, overlapping at the ends, and notched to form vertical ribs. A band of gold foil was applied below the rim, and a small square of gold foil decorates each facet of the wall. The vertical depressions are emphasized by rows of small dots of white enamel, and a single larger white dot was placed in the depression above and below each facet. A row of enameled white dots also highlights the rim. The base is pushed in to form a shallow kick, and it has a rough pontil mark.

The glass has a few bubbles and impurities. There are wear marks under the base, especially below the applied foot-ring.

COMMENT: Such elaborately decorated *wafel* beakers are rare. A fragmentary beaker, found at Delft, is dated on archeological grounds to the second half of the 16th century (*Spechtergläser* 1986, p. 15, no. 2, and p. 108, no. 45; Henkes 1994, p. 134, no. 30.5).

BIBLIOGRAPHY: *Nachlässe* 1956, lot 648, pl. 46; *CMG Guide* 1958, p. 56, no. 58; *CMG Guide* 1965, p. 56, no. 64; Tait 1967, p. 105, no. 32, fig. 29; *CMG Guide* 1974, p. 56, no. 64; Strasser 1979, p. 22, fig. 7; Charleston 1980, pp. 106–107, pl. 45; *Treasures from The Corning Museum of Glass* 1992, p. 53, no. 41; Tsuchiya 2002, p. 77.

# 5

## *Windmill Beaker*

### *OH. 20.3 cm, D. (bowl) 12.6 cm*

PROBABLY LOW COUNTRIES, ANTWERP OR
AMSTERDAM, ABOUT 1630–1669. THE
CORNING MUSEUM OF GLASS, CORNING,
NEW YORK (79.3.360, GIFT OF THE RUTH
BRYAN STRAUSS MEMORIAL FOUNDATION).
FORMERLY IN THE COLLECTIONS OF H. A.
STEENGRACHT, DUIVENVOORDE; WILLIAM
RANDOLPH HEARST, SAN SIMEON, CALI-
FORNIA; AND JEROME STRAUSS (S427).

COLORLESS WITH BROWNISH GRAY TINGE.
BLOWN, PATTERN-MOLDED; SILVER MOUNTS.

This beaker is composed of a ribbed,
funnel-shaped bowl that is mounted
into a mechanical silver windmill. The
glass is capped at the base with a cylindrical silver mount, fitted with a row of
chased prongs, and engraved with lines
representing masonry. It is surmounted
by the box-shaped and gabled building
of the windmill. The structure, which
is resting on a base of three scrolls with
a central support rod, is scratch-engraved with a pattern of offset vertical
stripes. A ladder made of silver wire extends, with a slight curve, from an open
door, which is cut into the bottom of
the windmill, toward the glass bowl. A

wire railing is attached to the right side
of the ladder, while a piece of silver
tubing follows its shape downward on
the left. One end of the tube is soldered
into a hole at the building's base, while
the other, enforced with a wire ring, remains open. A second wire ring attaches
the tube to the center of the ladder for
stability.

Two male figures, cast of silver,
appear on the ladder. One ascends,
carrying a sack, while the other faces
forward, with his right arm raised,
possibly holding a goblet. A third figure stands at the open door. The four
spinning arms of the windmill are en-

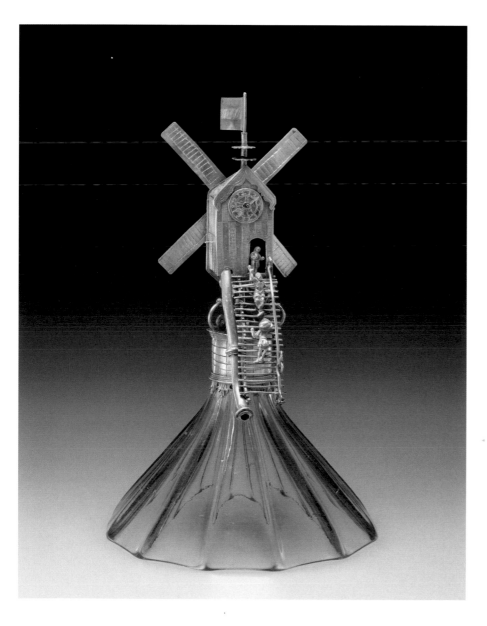

graved with a lattice pattern and connected to an arrow-shaped pointer on the opposite side, rotating in the center of a disk with the engraved numbers 1 through 12. A fourth human figure leans out of a second-story window. A flag at the top of the windmill house rotates in a tube that is decorated with two silver disks with scalloped rims. The moving flag, the arms of the windmill, and the pointer are interconnected on the inside of the windmill building. A circular silver disk on the inside of the glass bowl is engraved with an unidentified coat of arms.

COMMENT: Windmill beakers were used for drinking games. By blowing into the tube, the player set the mechanical arms spinning, and he or she was required to empty the glass before they stopped. The drinker who failed to do this had to empty the number of additional glasses indicated by the pointer.

These glasses are usually not marked, whereas parallels made entirely of silver show goldsmiths' marks. Most of these were made in the Netherlands and engraved with mottoes, names, and monograms. The Rijksmuseum in Amsterdam houses five windmill beakers in silver (Klar 1961, pp. 54–55, figs. 1–6). The oldest silver beaker is datable to about 1550 on the basis of the marks of the goldsmith Cornelys Florys, who was active in Leuwarden, and the most recent known metal beaker, dated 1713, was donated by Pieter Craay to the millers' guild in Rotterdam (*ibid.*, pp. 55–58, fig. 6). An example in the Museum Boijmans Van Beuningen, Rotterdam, bears the hallmarks of the Amsterdam silversmith Gerrit Valck (**5a**).

The oldest windmill glass appears to be a tall, diamond-point engraved flute in the Rijksmuseum, Amsterdam, with the coats of arms of Maurice of Orange and Bergen op Zoom (Klar 1961, p. 55). It is inscribed "1595" on the glass and "1585" on the mill. A similar flute with the crowned arms of the Seven United Provinces (Ritsema van Eck 1995, p. 24, no. 6, and color pl. p. 258) and two shorter examples, one with a trumpet-shaped bowl and the other with a bowl in the shape of a bell (Ritsema van Eck and Zijlstra-Zweens 1993, pp. 64–65, nos. 80 and 81) are also in the Amsterdam museum. There is another windmill glass, with the inscription "CONCORDE EN VNITE," in the Victoria and Albert Museum, London (C.416-1936) (Buckley, W. 1926, pp. 67–68, no. 54, and pl. 54; *idem* 1939, p. 268, no. 362, and pl. 118; Chambon 1955, p. 314, no. 39, pl. XI; Klar 1961, p. 57, fig. 8). A potash glass flute engraved with the monogram of Augustus the Strong (r. 1697–1704, 1709–1733), dated 1720, is in the Kunstgewerbemuseum, Berlin (Klar 1961, p. 52, fig. 1; *Ars vitraria* 1965, p. 166, no. 64).

It is not clear whether this type of vessel originated in the Netherlands or in Germany, since metal windmill beakers are known from that country as well. Most of these were made by goldsmiths in Nuremberg and Augsburg.

Wineglasses with a similar mold-blown bowl are rather common, and they elude a firm attribution (*Lehman Collection* 1993, p. 122, no. 43, and Theuerkauff-Liederwald 1994, p. 325,

5A

*Windmill beaker, silver. Low Countries, Amsterdam, Gerrit Valck, 1645. H. 19.5 cm. Museum Boijmans Van Beuningen, Rotterdam (MBZ 12, bequest of J. P. van der Schilden).*

5B

*Goblet with gilded silver whistle in the form of a dragon, colorless, blown, tooled. Low Countries, possibly Amsterdam or Antwerp, about 1630. OH. 20.5 cm, D. (rim) 9.4 cm. The Corning Museum of Glass, Corning, New York (51.3.280). Formerly in the collection of Frederic Neuburg.*

no. 318 indicate a northern European provenance and a dating from the late 16th century to the first half of the 17th century. However, the majority of glass windmill beakers originated in the Netherlands, and the Corning glass has therefore also been attributed to that country (*Lehman Collection* 1993, p. 122, fig. 43.2.).

A variation on the windmill beakers is glasses mounted with a paddle wheel, often atop a mythical beast (**5b**). By blowing into the air tube, actually a whistle, the player set the paddle wheel spinning above. A bell was often attached below to sound a successful ending to the drinking game. An inscription on a silver beaker of this type from Nuremberg that is dated 1575 indicates that such a vessel also served as a welcome glass (Klar 1961, p. 59, fig. 10). Another paddle wheel glass, formerly in the Spitzer Collection and now in the Museum für Kunst und Gewerbe, Hamburg, is mounted with a ribbed glass bowl similar to that of the Corning windmill beaker. It was dated by the museum to about 1600 and attributed to Germany ("Recent Important Acquisitions," *JGS*, v. 2, 1960, p. 142, fig. 20).

BIBLIOGRAPHY: *Antiquités* 1913, no. 920; *Glass Drinking Vessels* 1955, pp. 58–59, no. 152; *Lehman Collection* 1993, p. 122, fig. 43.2.

## 6

### *Flute Glass*

*H. 34.2 cm, D. (rim) 11.4 cm*

LOW COUNTRIES (GLASS), NORTHERN NETHERLANDS (ENGRAVING), DIAMOND-POINT ENGRAVED BY MASTER "CfM," ABOUT 1660. RIJKSMUSEUM, AMSTERDAM (N.M. 8040).

COLORLESS. BLOWN.

This vessel has a high funnel-shaped bowl, a hollow baluster stem with two mereses, and a low foot with a folded foot-ring. The bowl is engraved with a portrait of William III (1650–1702) as a child, wearing a dress and a hat with rosettes and an ostrich feather. In his right hand, he holds a staff of command, and a sprig and an orange are shown in his left hand. On the reverse of the vessel, William's crowned coat of arms is encircled by the Garter and the motto "HONI SOYT QUI MAL Y PENSE" (Evil to him who evil thinks) above a felled tree and a view of The Hague. Beneath this is a continuous band with festoons of oranges and tassels. Above and to the left of the portrait is the monogram "CfM."

COMMENT: The portrait is based on an engraving by A. Siwertsma. The leafless felled tree symbolizes the assassination of William of Orange in 1584. The sprigs sprouting from the trunk represent his successors, his two young sons Maurice and Frederick Henry. The Master "CfM" has not been identified. His dated works range from 1644 to 1663 (Smit 1994, p. 92; Ritsema van Eck 1995, p. 470). An identical flute was sold at Sotheby's in London in 1995 (*Ritman Collection* 1995, pp. 43–44, lot 49).

BIBLIOGRAPHY: Ritsema van Eck 1995, p. 54, no. 26. See also a glass dated 1657 in *Guépin Collection* 1989, lot 38.

## 7

*Goblet*

H. 15.5 cm, D. (rim) 8.8 cm,
(foot) 9.2 cm

NORTHERN NETHERLANDS, PROBABLY
WILLEM MOOLEYSER (ABOUT 1640–
1700), ABOUT 1680–1700. THE CORNING
MUSEUM OF GLASS, CORNING, NEW YORK
(79.3.239, BEQUEST OF JEROME STRAUSS).
FORMERLY IN THE STRAUSS (S2197) AND
STAAL (AMSTERDAM) COLLECTIONS.

COLORLESS WITH GREENISH GRAY
TINGE. BLOWN, TOOLED, DIAMOND-
POINT ENGRAVED.

The funnel-shaped bowl with a
rounded base is set on a hollow inverted baluster knop flanked by mereses
and a plain section above a wide, folded conical foot. The diamond-point
engraved bowl shows a pregnant
woman holding a wineglass and the
calligraphic inscription "Hansie in de
Kelder" (Little Hans in the cellar).

COMMENT: Such goblets, which were
also made in silver, were used to toast
the birth of a male child. This example
is diamond-point engraved in the style
of Willem Mooleyser, who lived and
worked in Rotterdam. An almost iden-

tical but slightly larger goblet was formerly in the Ritman Collection (*Ritman
Collection* 1995, p. 52, lot 57). Another
example, with a more elongated baluster, is in the Rijksmuseum, Amsterdam
(Ritsema van Eck 1995, p. 73, no. 42,
which attributes the glass firmly to
Mooleyser). A third glass, formerly in
the collection of K. H. Heine, is now in
the Badisches Landesmuseum Karlsruhe (*Heine Collection* 1977, no. 101).
Here, an expectant mother holding a
flower is engraved above a floral spray
with a bird.

## 8

### *Beaker on Bun Feet* (Molglas)

H. 16.1 cm

NORTHERN NETHERLANDS, ENGRAVED BY WILLEM MOOLEYSER (SIGNED), DATED 1685. THE CORNING MUSEUM OF GLASS, CORNING, NEW YORK (79.3.301, BEQUEST OF JEROME STRAUSS). FORMERLY IN THE COLLECTIONS OF FREDERIC NEUBURG AND JEROME STRAUSS (S1359).

COLORLESS WITH GRAYISH TINGE. BLOWN, DIAMOND-POINT ENGRAVED.

This cylindrical beaker has a fire-polished rim. The base has a shallow kick with a small circular pontil mark, and the edge has a trailed and flattened base-ring. Three applied circular and flattened pads serve as feet. The upper half of the beaker is diamond-point engraved with an undulating garland of flowers and foliage. The lower half of the glass is engraved with figural decoration: a dancing pair of peasants, facing each other; a man, facing left, seated in a chair, drinking from a bottle that he holds in his right hand, and holding a pipe in his left hand; and a dancing man, facing left, with sprigs in his hat, a glass in his right hand, and his left hand resting on his hip. The undulating ground with grass and other vegetation below the figures indicates an outdoor setting. Near the base, below the dancing couple, the glass is signed "W. Mooleyser 1685."

The glass has numerous small bubbles.

COMMENT: The figural decoration is probably based on engravings by Pieter Nolpe (Dozy 1897, nos. 218 and 220). The continuous undulating garland of flowers and the dancing man resemble those found on a wineglass in the Rijksmuseum, Amsterdam (K.O.G. 149), that was also engraved by Mooleyser (signed) in 1685 (Ritsema van Eck 1995, p. 66, no. 35). A similar beaker with figural decoration after engravings by Nolpe (a vine scroll beneath leaves and grapes) but without the bun feet is also in the collection of the Rijksmuseum (N.M. 4869) (*ibid.*, p. 70, no. 37).

A beaker identical to **8**, with a vine scroll similar to that on the Rijksmuseum's beaker, a dancing couple, and two dancing male figures, also signed "1685," is in the Victoria and Albert Museum, London (Buckley, W. 1926, p. 72, pl. 62B; Honey 1946, fig. 58C).

BIBLIOGRAPHY: *Glass Drinking Vessels* 1955, p. 58, no. 151; Gelder 1958, p. 58; "Important Acquisitions from the Strauss Collection," *JGS*, v. 22, 1980, p. 107, no. 24; Sutton 1986, p. 103; *Hikari no shouchu* 1992, p. 28, no. 43.

# 9

## Commemorative Dish

*H. 3.0 cm, D. 32.3 cm*

LOW COUNTRIES (DISH), NORTHERN NETHERLANDS, LEIDEN, WILLEM JACOBSZ. VAN HEEMSKERK (ENGRAVING), 1685. RIJKSMUSEUM, AMSTERDAM (N.M. 764). FORMERLY IN THE COLLECTION OF THE ENGRAVER, BY DESCENT.

COLORLESS. BLOWN, DIAMOND-POINT ENGRAVED.

**9A**

*Engraved portrait of Willem van Heemskerk. Low Countries, printed by A. Blooteling (1640–1690), after a painting by Frans van Mieris (1635–1681), 1687. H. 28.2 cm, W. 23.2 cm. Collection of Eric M. Wunsch.*

This shallow dish with a wide rim is finished with a small fold. The rim is engraved with the calligraphic inscription "Bestand'ge noit-besweken Trouw, Werkt lyvelijk—en ziel-behouw" (Steadfast faithfulness that does not waver is a soul and body saver). The bowl features a tondo with the mirror monogram "I V H A C" (for Joost van Heemskerk and Anna Conink) beneath a crown and above the inscription "IUSTE & SYNCERE" (Just and sincere).

COMMENT: The dish commemorates the marriage of M. Joost van Heemskerk, son of Willem van Heemskerk, and Anna Conink.

Willem van Heemskerk (1613–1692), was a syndic (agent) of the Drapers' Guild of the Lakenhal in Leiden. He was painted by the Leiden painter Frans van Mieris the Elder (1635–1681) in 1674. The print (**9a**) was executed by Abraham Blooteling (1640–1690), an Amsterdam engraver, draftsman, and print seller who became best known for his development of the mezzotint method of engraving.

The portrait is set in a frame that is inscribed "*WELHEM DJE WEL WJL*" (William who is willing) above, "Æts 74" (Age 74) in the upper left corner, and "Ao 1687" (Anno 1687) in the upper right corner. Below the inscription is the following poem:

Terwyl gy Vreemdeling deef stomme Print
   bekykt,
Die u den Omtrek toomt van HEEMSKERKS
   broose wesen;
Soo weet dat dit heel wel, een nogtaans
   mirist gelykt;
Wiens Hand en Geest, op Glas en blank
   papier te lesen,
Doorlugter blyken geest, der ware Wesen-
   theid
Van WELHEM, die door beids zal leven
   als hy Scheid.
   Geertruid Gordon de Graew

The poem is translated as follows:

While you, stranger, look at this mute print
Which shows you the circumference of
   Heemskerk's fragile being,
Know well, therefore, that this looks like
   an image
Whose hand and mind can be read on
   glass and paper;
Clear seems the mind of the real being,
Of Welhem (Willem), who will live through
   both as he parts.

The painting is inscribed "F. van Mieris pinx" (painted by F. van Mieris) at the lower left, and "A. Blooteling fecit" (made by A[braham] Blooteling) at the lower right.

BIBLIOGRAPHY: Ritsema van Eck 1995, p. 106, no. 87.

# Venetian and *Façon de Venise*
# Glass in England

*Hugh Willmott*

## THE HISTORICAL AND ARCHEOLOGICAL BACKGROUND

England was no stranger to high-quality glass table wares before the 16th century. By the 13th century, tall stemmed goblets were being imported from Venice and from many other European centers, and the use of fine soda glass beakers, bowls, and jugs increased in the following century. At the same time, there was a flourishing domestic industry for the production of lower-quality potash vessels, including flasks, urinals, and drinking vessels. However, the use of glass tableware was largely restricted to the upper classes of English society.

By the second half of the 15th century, the numbers of high-quality drinking vessels had greatly diminished. Domestically produced potash glass

*Detail of a Renaissance English table setting in the Victoria and Albert Museum, London (Fig. 17).*

vessels were still in circulation, but imports of fine soda glass seem to have become less popular. It is uncertain whether this reflected a reduced desire for glass or a reduction in its availability. Whatever the explanation, by the beginning of the 16th century, the use of glass in England was at its lowest point in 300 years. During the 1500s, however, this situation would be reversed, both by the importation of high-quality Venetian and *façon de Venise* wares and by the establishment of a successful native industry. So dramatic was this reversal that, by the middle of the 17th century, more glass was being used in England than ever before.

The rise of the English industry could not have occurred without a genuine and growing desire for high-quality glass wares. This trend was observed in 1587 by the Tudor chronicler William Harrison, who noted: "It is a world to see in these our days, wherein gold and silver most aboundeth, how that our gentility, as loathing those metals (because of the plenty), do now generally choose rather the Venice glasses, both for our wine and beer. . . . Such is the nature of man generally that it most coveteth things difficult to be attained . . ." (Harrison 1968, p. 128). Glass had become fashionable among the elite. It was a novel item that could be used to express new tastes. In addition, it was viewed as an exclusive product that was harder to acquire than more traditional metal wares.

The rising popularity of glass in 16th-century England can readily be seen from the finds of glass at archeological sites. Since the early 1970s, the excavation and study of Venetian and *façon de Venise* glass have been increasing. Although intact vessels from museum and art-historical collections are important in researching the evolution and development of glass styles, archeologically derived fragments can provide additional information about dating and use.

Recent excavations at 16th-century castles, palaces, and manor houses have revealed key assemblages of imported glass. Among such sites are the royal palace of Nonsuch, built by Henry VIII, and the moated manors at Acton Court, near Bristol, and Wood Hall in Linton, West Yorkshire. (The finds from these sites have not been published.) Many other 16th-century sites have produced smaller quantities of vessels of similar importance. By the 17th century, high-quality glass wares were being used in middle-class households and in urban centers across England. Large groups of such objects, often from dumps, have been found in many towns.

In considering Venetian and *façon de Venise* glass in England, as well as elsewhere, one of the key questions concerns its provenance. Although some styles can be said to reflect the traditions of one region more than another, such distinctions are often far from certain. This is surely true of the English glass industry. Based on their distribution and the concentration of findspots, some products can be described as "English" *façon de Venise*, but the provenance of other wares is unclear. However, the glass found in England includes some of the finest made anywhere in Europe, and it underscores the nation's strong desire for glass as a table ware.

## FAÇON DE VENISE IMPORTS IN ENGLAND, 1500–1640

From the beginning of the 16th century, the importation of glass into England increased. There was as yet no established industry for the making of fine wares, and any desire for them had to be satisfied by foreign producers. Consequently, during the first half of that century, glassware was a luxury that only the wealthy could afford. At that time, Venice appears to have been almost the sole source for the glass found in England. However, by the second half of the 1500s, the flourishing industries of the Low Countries provided a closer and presumably cheaper source of *façon de Venise* glassware, often in patterns that imitated those from Venice.

It is often hard to evaluate the scale of English glass imports, since records of that time were more concerned with the value than the numbers and identification of imported goods. However, two types of sources give an impression of the nature and origin of these imports. The first is books of rates, which were used by customs officials to levy the appropriate duties on goods. Unfortunately, these books tend to be very unclear in their descriptions of the vessels that passed through English ports. They refer, for example, to glasses of "Venice making" but do not itemize the specific types. Moreover, they do not indicate the quantity of vessels that entered the country. The second type of source is port books, which document the arrival of ships, as well as where they came from and the goods they carried. Again, these records are frustratingly imprecise, often referring only to "a case of glass." A further problem is that, although these books report the locations from which the ships had sailed, they do not indicate if their cargo originated there as well.

During the first half of the 17th century, large quantities of *façon de Venise* glass were imported into England. Almost all of this glass seems to have been made in the Low Countries, and especially in the vicinity of Antwerp. This may have resulted from the close political and economic connections between England and the Netherlands at that time. Products that can be identified as Venetian are few and far between.

The most distinctive early 16th-century Venetian products found in England are drinking vessels with filigree decoration. This innovative technique involved covering the surface of the vessel with decorative canes of opaque white glass at an early stage of the production process. The simplest form, *vetro a fili*, involved a single cane of opaque white glass that invariably had a colorless glass core cased in a colorless cane. *Vetro a retorti*, a more complex variation, was made by twisting opaque white and colorless canes together in a helical pattern. Although there are examples of *vetro a fili* and *retorti* glasses in colors other than opaque white, they are rare in England. Although the entire vessel could be covered, each parison was decorated separately so that there was no filigree ornamentation either on the mereses that held the vessel together or on the parts that were added later, such as prunts.

During this period, two goblet shapes were predominant. The first (**1**) was made from three separate parisons: the base in the form of a narrow pedestal, a round knop, and a tall, trumpet-shaped bowl. Some examples are undecorated, but most have one or both types of filigree ornamentation. The second goblet shape (Fig. 1) is more uniform. It features a separately blown pedestal base, a round knop on the stem, and a bowl that is broader and more spherical. This form of goblet is almost always decorated with fine vertical threads (*fili*) on the base and stem, and with bands of horizontal *retorti* on the bowl. Neither of these goblet shapes is common in England, where they have been ex-

**FIG. 1**

*Fragment of goblet, colorless, blown,* vetro a fili *and* retorti *decoration. Venice, early to mid-16th century. H. 12.5 cm. Found at Canons Ashby, near Daventry, Northamptonshire.*

cavated only at affluent sites. Examples of both forms were found at the manor on the site of the priory of Canons Ashby, near Daventry in Northamptonshire, which was the private residence of Sir John Cope between 1538 and 1558. The most complete example is illustrated in Taylor 1974, p. 63.

A variation on the goblet form found in England is the tazza, which has a similar base and stem but a bowl that is much broader than it is tall. The bowl was either vertically sided and dish-shaped (Fig. 2) or, more commonly, very shallow and turned up slightly at the rim (Fig. 3). Tazzas of the early 16th century were usually decorated with various combinations of filigree, although they could also be plain or decorated with simple trails. Perhaps the largest group of tazzas found in England to date came from the moated manor at Acton Court, near Bristol (Courtney, in press). Six examples were recovered there, four with filigree decoration and two with horizontal trails. The Acton Court tazzas are part of a much larger group of glasses that may have been purchased in 1535 be-

273

FIG. 2

*Tazza, colorless, white, blown, filigree decoration. Venice, perhaps Low Countries, mid-16th century. H. 13.8 cm, D. (rim) 27.0 cm. The Corning Museum of Glass, Corning, New York (64.3.6).*

FIG. 3

*Tazza, colorless, blown, vetro a fili and retorti decoration. Venice, perhaps Low Countries, late 16th century. H. 9.4 cm, D. 17.7 cm. The British Museum, London (S.674).*

fore a visit by Henry VIII. The date of the deposit and its connection to the king's visit are discussed in Vince and Bell 1992.

The use of *vetro a filigrana* was not restricted to goblets. Beakers with this form of decoration have also been recovered in England. However, the forms of these objects suggest that most of them originated in the Low Countries, rather than in Venice,

during the late 16th and early 17th centuries. Although many variations exist, there are two basic forms of beakers. The first is squat or shaped like a tumbler (Fig. 4), with a height that rarely exceeds its breadth. Beakers of this kind were often decorated with spiral *vetro a fili* in either opaque white or blue, and a horizontal trail was sometimes added to the edge of the rim. Squat beakers were a com-

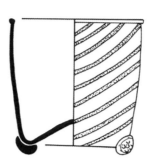

FIG. 4

*Beaker, colorless, opaque white, transparent blue, blown, mold-blown, filigree decoration. Low Countries, possibly Amsterdam, early 17th century. H. 7.6 cm, D. (rim) 8 cm. Afdeling Monument-enzorg en Archeologie, Alkmaar, the Netherlands (86DST).*

monly used *façon de Venise* form throughout the 17th century. They were certainly produced in the Low Countries during the first half of that century, and some were made as late as the 1670s in Venice. The examples made in the Low Countries are characterized by the application of three raspberry-prunted feet and an occasional prunt impressed on the side.

The second filigree form of beaker is large and cylindrical, with an everted rim (Fig. 5). It was often undecorated. Cylindrical beakers were popular in England throughout the first half of the 17th century, although filigree examples probably date from the late 16th to early 17th centuries. Some examples have thick opaque white horizontal and vertical trails, but more commonly they are decorated with marvered spiral bands of white *vetro a fili*. Excavations at Exeter have produced fragments of both types of cylindrical filigree beakers (Charleston 1984b), and their presence in other provincial towns suggests that they were an early form of high-quality glassware preferred by the middle class. Other urban finds include those published from Hull (Henderson and Jackson 1993), Lambeth (Hinton 1988), and Norwich (Haslam 1993).

Filigree was not the only decorative technique employed in the making of glass vessels that were imported into England. Other elaborate fashions can be seen, particularly in beakers that originated

FIG. 5

*Beaker, colorless, opaque white, blown, filigree decoration. Low Countries, late 16th–early 17th century. H. 18.6 cm. Museum Boijmans Van Beuningen, Rotterdam (574).*

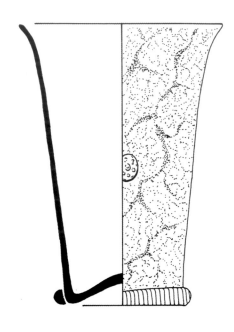

**FIG. 6**

*Beaker, transparent light gray, blown, ice glass technique, stamped, applied, tooled, gilded. Low Countries, early to mid-17th century. OH. 22.4 cm, D. (rim) 13.3 cm. The Corning Museum of Glass, Corning, New York (98.3.60).*

in the Low Countries. The style most frequently found in England is the cylindrical beaker with a *wafel* or checkered spiral trail design (**2**). A thick spiral trail was applied to the parison, which was blown in a vertically ribbed optic mold. Then the vessel was further formed. Although glassmakers in the Low Countries also used this technique on goblet bowls and on other vessels, its appearance in England is restricted to beakers. *Wafel*-decorated beakers are among the most common *façon de Venise* vessels imported into England during the late 16th and early 17th centuries. These glasses inspired domestically produced imitations in green potash glass, but they tend to have much finer trails. (For example, English potash versions of the *wafel* beaker have been found in the waste at the production site at Rosedale in North Yorkshire; Charleston 1972.) Some *wafel*-decorated beakers, such as two examples from Norwich (Haslam 1993), are further embellished with enameled dots

between the trails, but this variation is considerably rarer (see p. 260, **4**).

Another type of decoration found on *façon de Venise* imports in England is crackling on the surface of a vessel, which is known as ice glass. This was achieved by dipping the parison into water, causing the formation of stress cracks. When the vessel was further inflated and formed, these cracks were expanded to produce the characteristic rough surface. This technique, which was developed in Venice during the mid-16th century, had become a staple in the repertoire of glassmakers in the Low Countries by the start of the following century. Venetian ice glass vessels have occasionally been found in England, such as a goblet from Acton Court (Courtney, in press), although later Low Countries forms such as cylindrical beakers are more common (Fig. 6). However, ice glass vessels were never as popular in England as they were on the Continent.

FIG. 7

*Jug, colorless, opaque white, blown,* vetro a fili *decoration; silver-gilt mounts bearing the hallmarks of London, 1545–1548. Possibly England, London, dated 1548. H. 15 cm. The British Museum, London, Franks Collection (AF3133).*

Not all of the *façon de Venise* glass imported into England was highly decorated. Undecorated examples of many of the vessel forms already described have been found, and these help to emphasize the quality of the glass. Indeed, the clarity of the glass was one of its most attractive properties, as Michel de Montaigne underscored in 1588 when he wrote: "I too incline towards glasses of a particular shape . . . and I dislike all metals compared with clear transparent materials. Let my eyes too taste it to the full" (Montaigne 1991, p. 1231).

Likewise, drinking vessels were not the only glass imports to enter England during the 16th and 17th centuries. Other vessels, such as jugs (Fig. 7) and flasks, have been excavated at Acton Court (Courtney, in press), Nonsuch Palace, and elsewhere. These are rare examples, however. More commonly found are bowls or standing dishes (Fig. 8) with pedestal bases and broad, deep bodies. These are usually undecorated, although some examples have optic-blown ribs.

FIG. 8

*Pedestal bowl, colorless with grayish tinge, blown, mold-blown, applied. Probably Venice, late 16th–mid-17th century. H. 5.5 cm, D. (rim) 13.3 cm, (base) 13.0 cm. Kunstsammlungen der Veste Coburg (HA 290).*

## THE EARLY ENGLISH INDUSTRY, 1570–1595

Discussion of the early English glassmaking industry has largely centered in two areas. The first is the establishment of glass furnaces and the securing of patents and monopolies, first by Jean Carré in 1567 and then by his successor, Jacopo (Jacob) Verzelini, between 1572 and 1595. Researchers have documented an increase in the use of glass in England during the 16th century. It appears that both an increase in the importation of vessels and the revival of domestic production were stimulated by the arrival of immigrant glassworkers (Thorpe 1961; Charleston 1984a; Godfrey 1975). The earliest reference to these craftsmen dates from 1549, when eight Muranese are said to have established a furnace in London (Powell 1923, pp. 27–29). However, this venture seems to have failed. Within two years, all but one of these glassmakers had returned to Venice. It would be another 18 years before a more successful attempt would be made to found a factory for the making of fine glass in London.

Jean Carré, a native of Arras, appears to have spent most of his career as a glassworker in Antwerp. In 1567, he arrived in London, where he obtained a license to make Venetian-style glasses. Within a year, he had gained a patent, in conjunction with the Flemish merchant Anthony Becku, to be England's sole producer of window glass. At that time, Carré established a furnace at Crutched Friars, near the Tower of London, for the manufacture of *façon de Venise* drinking glasses. Documentary evidence suggests that the workers employed at his glasshouse were of Flemish origin, but in 1570 the Venetians Quiobyn Littery and Jacopo Verzelini were brought from Antwerp.

When Carré died in 1572, Verzelini took control of the glassworks. He was an experienced glassmaker, having worked in Antwerp for two decades. Within two years, he had secured a 21-year monopoly on the production of *façon de Venise* drinking glasses in England, which also prevented the importation of similar vessels from abroad. Verzelini, who seems to have managed the monopoly successfully for its duration, became a naturalized citizen of England and a well-known figure in the mercantile community. In 1594, Sir Hugh Platt offered the following recommendation of Verzelini's services: "For want of Glasses with broade skirts . . . I doe thinke there are inough to bee had if you can bee so gracious with master Iacob of the glashouse" (Platt 1979, bk. 1, p. 3). Verzelini's control of the English market for fine glassware finally ended when his monopoly expired in 1595 (Fig. 9).

The second, and more relevant, area of scholarly discussion concerning early English glass in Venetian style has been the attribution of historical glasses to the period of Verzelini. This has been accomplished on a rather less than scientific basis. In 1929, it was suggested that a group of five glasses may have been produced by Verzelini, and this group has now been expanded to include 12 vessels (Buckley, W. 1929; Charleston 1984a, p. 55). The support for this attribution has been the diamond-point engraved decoration that appears on all but one of these vessels. Diamond-point engraving involved the scoring of the glass surface with scratched lines to build up patterns of scrollwork, foliage, and even figures. It was probably first developed in Venice, where Vincenzo d'Angelo applied for a patent for the technique in 1549, although it was rapidly adopted at other glassmaking centers.

A rather circular argument has developed concerning the so-called Verzelini glasses, however. Only one engraver can be identified as having worked in England during that period. In 1583, the Frenchman Anthony de Lysle was described as a "graver in puter [pewter] and glasse," and it has therefore been assumed that he was responsible for the identified Verzelini glasses (Charleston 1984a, p. 58). Yet there is absolutely no documentary evidence that he worked either for Verzelini or on this group of glasses. The attribution is therefore questionable at best. If it cannot be demonstrated that de Lysle undertook this work, the attribution of these glasses to Verzelini becomes problematical. This is not to say that none of the so-called Verzelini glasses could have been made in London, but that making the attribution solely on the basis of the engraving is insufficient. In fact, the vast majority of Verzelini's output between the years 1572 and 1595 would not have been decorated. Curiously, only one undecorated vessel, the "Vickers Glass" in the Royal Library at Windsor (*ibid.*, p. 59), has ever been historically linked to Verzelini's workshop.

While it is frequently asserted that the Verzelini glasses are similar in their style of engraving, in fact a variety of decorative styles and motifs can be identified. In general, these styles vary with the shapes of the vessels. With the help of recently excavated engraved glasses, it is possible to make tentative suggestions as to the origin of these vessels.

The most elaborate of these glasses are decorated on the upper portion with hunting scenes, consisting of hounds chasing stags and unicorns against a wooded background. Below the hunting scenes are panels containing initialed cartouches, foliage, and dates. Three of the glasses traditionally attributed to Verzelini fall into this category. The first (**3**) is an incomplete goblet. Its stem and foot were lost long ago, and they have been replaced with soft wood and metal. Two complete and nearly identical examples (in the Fitzwilliam Museum in Cambridge [Fig. 10] and the Victoria and Albert Museum in London [Fig. 11]) show that the original stem was probably a large spherical ribbed knop attached to a flared base with engraved gadroons. All three glasses have tall U-shaped bowls and are engraved with dates between 1577 and 1581. Fragments of two similar examples were found during excavations at Southampton (Charleston 1975, pp. 221–222). They, too, appear to have been decorated with a unicorn and hounds, and one fragment retains enough of a date to indicate that it was engraved in the 1580s.

FIG. 9

*Rubbing of memorial brass plaques for Jacopo Verzelini and his wife, mounted in the northwest wall of the Church of Saint Mary the Virgin, Downe, Kent, England.*

The English provenance of these vessels is far from certain. As far as the engraving is concerned, only one has an epigraphic connection with England. The glass is engraved with the names "John,"

FIG. 10

*Goblet, colorless with grayish tinge, blown, mold-blown, applied, engraved. England, London, probably Broad Street glasshouse of Jacopo Verzelini, dated 1578. H. 21.6 cm. Fitzwilliam Museum, University of Cambridge (C.4.1967, gift of the friends of the Fitzwilliam Museum). Formerly in the collection of Commander Sir Hugh Dawson.*

FIG. 11
*Goblet with arms of Queen Elizabeth I, colorless, blown, mold-blown, applied, engraved.*
*England, London, probably Broad Street glasshouse of Jacopo Verzelini, dated 1581.*
*H. 21 cm. Victoria and Albert Museum, London (C.523-1936).*

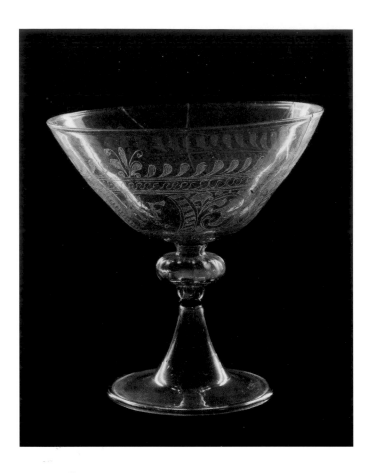

FIG. 12

*Goblet, colorless, blown, mold-blown, applied, engraved.
England, London, probably Broad Street glasshouse of
Jacopo Verzelini, dated 1580. H. 13 cm. Victoria
and Albert Museum, London (C.522-1936).*

ern France than in England (Penna 1998, p. 13, no. 89; for a large group of undecorated vessels of similar form that were found at Montbéliard, see Goetz 1990, esp. p. 200, fig. 4). One of these vessels is in the Musée de Cluny in Paris. Its bowl is also decorated with a hunting scene that encloses a cartouche containing three fleurs-de-lis, the royal emblem of France. The second vessel of this type (Fig. 12), which is made of colorless soda glass, is decorated with a band of engraved petals and scrollwork above three cartouches containing the initials "AF" (repeated twice) and the date "1580." Between the cartouches are panels with a foliage design (Charleston 1984a, pl. 12d).

The last engraved vessel that broadly fits this group is an engraved and gilded tazza excavated at Minster House, London (**4**). Its stem was formed from a ribbed, stretched ovaloid knop, which is gilded, and it has a broad, shallow bowl. The inside of the bowl is engraved with running hounds and a stag. This vessel differs in shape from the other hunting goblets, and it is hard to determine precisely where it was made. It bears no engraved names or dates, and the form of its stem is unusual for an English vessel.

The remainder of the engraved goblets that are traditionally attributed to Verzelini have several characteristics that are much more typically English. The form of their bowls and stems is similar to that of vessels that have been frequently excavated in England, and they are engraved with English mottoes. The first of these goblets (Fig. 13) has a broad, tapered bowl and a small round ribbed knop. The bowl is decorated with two horizontal bands of opaque white trails and engraved with the motto "IN:GOD:IS:AL:MI:TRVST," the initials "GS," and the date "1586." A similarly shaped goblet (Fig. 14) with a small inverted baluster stem is engraved just below the rim with "GOD.SAVE.QUYNE.ELIZ-ABETH," the initials "RP" and "MP," and the date "1586." The rest of the bowl is decorated with fine trails that overlie optic-blown vertical ribbing. Another goblet with an inverted baluster stem and a broad, tapered bowl is in the Birmingham Museum and Art Gallery (**5**). It is engraved with "TO.HIS.BROTHER.RICHARD.GRENHAL," heraldic devic-

"Jone," and "Dier," as well as the royal arms of Elizabeth I (see Fig. 11). However, this does not necessarily mean that the vessel was made and engraved in England. It could just as easily have been a special commission from abroad. Moreover, the style of the large ribbed knops on the stems and the tall U-shaped bowls are very rare among English archeological finds, and such vessels excavated without decoration would not normally be assumed to have been produced domestically.

Two additional goblets attributed to Verzelini are also of dubious English origin. Both of them have tall and narrow pedestal bases, elaborate stems formed from large spherical ribbed knops, and low and shallow everted bowls. This well-recognized form is more commonly found in north-es, and the date "1584." The final goblet with a motto (**6**) differs in form, but it has many of the other characteristics shared by these glasses, such as a broad, tapered bowl. This vessel's lion-mask stem was mold-blown, and its foot was repaired in the early 17th century. The bowl is engraved with the motto "IN.GOD.IS.AL.MI.TRVST" beneath a scrolled crest. Below the motto are panels of foliage, the initials "KY," and the date "1583."

The forms of these four goblets are recognizably English, and they have archeological parallels. Fragments of the rim of a tapered goblet bowl recovered at Wood Hall in Linton, West Yorkshire,

have an engraved foliage pattern above a thick trail similar to that found on the "Quyne Elizabeth" vessel. Likewise, fragments forming the complete profile of a goblet bowl, found at a Bloomfield Street site in London, are decorated with foliage panels and a scrolled crest above and below that resemble the ornamentation on the "KY" glass. The lead repair to the foot of the "KY" goblet is identical to those on a group of objects that are known to have been restored during the early 17th century in southeastern England (see Willmott 2001). If these glasses are indeed English, they must have been produced at Verzelini's glasshouse.

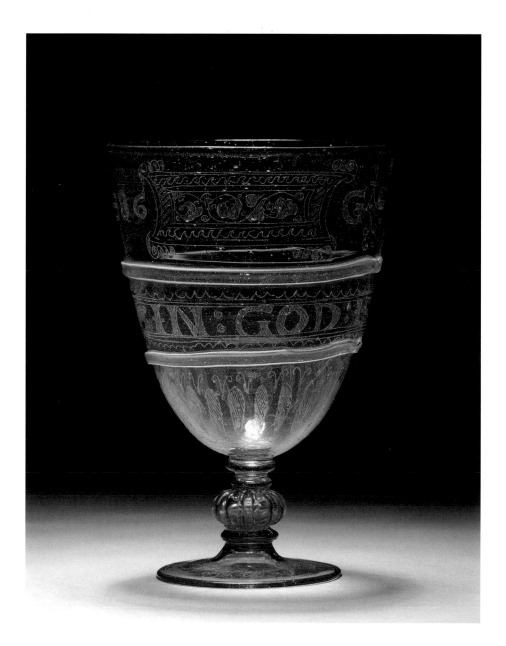

FIG. 13

*Goblet, colorless, blown, mold-blown, applied, gilded, diamond-point engraved. England, London, probably Broad Street glasshouse of Jacopo Verzelini, dated 1586. H. 13 cm, D. (rim) 8.6 cm. The British Museum, London (1895, 6-3, 17, gift of Sir A. W. Franks).*

**FIG. 14**

*Goblet, colorless, blown, trailed. England, London, probably Broad Street glasshouse of Jacopo Verzelini, dated 1586. H. 16.5 cm. Victoria and Albert Museum, London (C.226-1983).*

Another vessel that is often associated with the early English industry is the Wenyfrid Geares goblet (Fig. 15). It has a "ladder" stem that was blown in a two-piece mold, and it is also decorated with diamond-shaped bosses. The bowl features complex gilding, and its elements include the arms of the Vintners' Company and the City of London, the name "WENYFRID GEARES," the motto of the Order of the Garter, and the date "1590." It has been assumed that this glass was decorated by Anthony de Lysle, who is known to have been penalized by the Company of Pewterers in 1582–1583 for the unauthorized gilding of pewter (Charleston 1984a, p. 58). Although this attribution is uncertain, the vessel has several features that are indicative of English manufacture. The ladder stem is virtually unique to English glass, and it later became one of the clichés of the 17th-century industry under Sir Robert Mansell (see below). The broad and slightly tapered bowl can be seen on other undecorated glasses excavated in England. Finally, the epigraphic evidence of English names, heraldic devices, and mottoes gilded on the bowl would offer additional support for an English origin.

**FIG. 15**

*The Wenyfrid Geares goblet, colorless, blown, gilded. England, London, probably Broad Street glasshouse of Jacopo Verzelini, about 1590. H. 18.4 cm. The Fine Arts Museums of San Francisco, the Franz W. and Sylvia Sichel Collection (1988.15.58).*

# The Height of the English Industry, 1595–1640

Despite the wealth of historical documentation and the identification of some glasses that can be connected to the time of Verzelini, the archeological evidence suggests that the impact of this industry on the English population as a whole was relatively minor. The use of high-quality glassware in the late 16th century was still largely restricted to the upper classes, and although it is hard to quantify, the total output appears to have been quite small. However, with the next generation of glassmakers, products became cheaper and more accessible, particularly to middle-class customers. It is possible to identify English styles of *façon de Venise* glass that date to the first half of the 17th century.

In 1592, the Englishman Sir Jerome Bowes was granted a patent for the manufacture of glass that was to become effective when Verzelini's monopoly expired in 1595. This patent, initially issued for 12 years, was later extended for an additional 21 years. As soon as it became effective, Bowes financed the foundation of a furnace at Black Friars in London, which was probably staffed by Verzelini's workmen and managed by William Robson. Bowes, a retired courtier, seems to have played only a limited role in the operation of his glassworks. However, his monopoly suffered serious setbacks, not least with Edward Salter's establishment of a rival glasshouse at Winchester House in Southwark in 1608. This enterprise circumvented Bowes's patent, which pertained only to Venetian-style drinking glasses, by producing cruets, trenchers, salts, and tall-sided beakers.

But it was not the construction of rival furnaces that caused the greatest upheaval in the glass industry during the first decades of the 17th century. There were also growing concerns over the destruction of woodlands by both the iron and glass industries, which were using large quantities of wood as fuel. This resulted in a period of uncertainty for the glass monopolies until 1615, when all previous patents were suppressed by the Crown and the use of wood as a fuel was outlawed. This situation had clearly been anticipated, for as early as 1611, a company headed by Edward Zouch secured a patent to produce fine glass drinking vessels at furnaces that had been successfully modified to use coal. Zouch's company was quickly bought out by one of its directors, Sir Robert Mansell, who established a new furnace at Broad Street in London for the production of high-quality glasses.

By 1616, there was an apparent scarcity of vessel glass, particularly that made with the cheaper potash glass. This situation was probably prompted by the forced closure of the old wood-burning furnaces. In response, Mansell opened new furnaces at Wollaton in 1616 and Kimmeridge in 1617. The latter seems to have experimented with oil shale as a fuel. During the following year, Mansell succeeded in closing down all competition from forest glass makers, so that he effectively dominated the entire market. He then proceeded to establish additional furnaces at St. Catherine's in London and at Newcastle. Over the next two decades, he secured his monopoly of the English market. In 1623, his patent was reissued. Seven years later, he gained a royal decree banning the importation of all foreign vessels. The patent was renewed again in 1635, and it included Ireland as well.

The glass products of Bowes and Mansell can be clearly identified archeologically, and many of these styles were popular for nearly 50 years. Perhaps the most common and readily identified is the goblet with a cigar stem (Fig. 16). The stem of this vessel was made in the shape of a tall inverted

Fig. 16
*Goblet with cigar stem, colorless with grayish tinge, blown, applied. Possibly England, first half of the 17th century. H. 14.5 cm, D. (bowl) 12.1 cm. The Corning Museum of Glass, Corning, New York (70.3.8).*

baluster, the base was low and flaring, and the bowl was usually tall and tapered. This form was almost exclusively English, and it probably copied silver fashions of the period (Figs. 17 and 18) (Charleston 1984a, p. 68). It is also possible to identify parallels in pewter (Michaelis 1955, pl. 34).

Another type of drinking glass that was popular at this time was the goblet with a squat inverted baluster stem (Fig. 19). Although some 16th-cen-

**Fig. 17**

*Renaissance English table setting showing Verzelini goblet and silver-gilt goblet with cigar stem. Victoria and Albert Museum, London.*

**Fig. 18**

*Cup with cigar stem, silver-gilt, chased, embossed. London hallmark, 1616–1617. H. 16.7 cm. Victoria and Albert Museum, London (M20-1934).*

tury examples have been found, most of those excavated in England date to the first half of the 17th century. Both the inverted baluster and the cigar stemmed goblets appear to have been made using a type of glass that was of lower quality than that employed in the manufacture of Venetian or *façon de Venise* glass in other European centers. These vessels often have a slight green or brown tint, which was probably the result of using a mixed alkali, rather than a pure soda, flux in the batch. These two goblet styles are often excavated together, sometimes in large numbers. Fifty-five examples came from a single deposit at Gracechurch Street in London (Willmott 2000b). The English origin of these forms is confirmed by the presence of half-finished wasters of both cigar and inverted baluster stems in excavated material associated with Mansell's Broad Street furnace. (A full description and a chemical analysis of the glass waste from this furnace is found in Shepherd unpub.)

Bowes and Mansell also produced a goblet that featured a stem with mold-blown decoration. It was formed by blowing a small parison into a two-piece mold, which impressed the design on the glass. When it was removed from the mold, the bowl and

**FIG. 19**

*Fragment of goblet with inverted baluster stem, colorless with greenish-grayish tinge, blown, applied. England, early 17th century. H. 22.3 cm, D. (rim) 8.3 cm, (base) 8.8 cm. Found at Watling Street, London. Museum of London (24727).*

FIG. 20

*Schematic drawing of lion-mask stem.*

foot were added. This decorative style was initially developed in Venice during the mid-16th century, but it was rapidly adopted by other European glasshouses. Although two of the previously discussed 16th-century engraved goblets have stems of this type, it was during the early 17th century that these vessels became relatively common in England.

The mold-blown stem that has been most frequently excavated is the lion mask (Fig. 20). It is decorated on two sides with the face of a lion shown frontally, with swags between and over the seams, and gadrooning above and below. Lion-mask stems are surprisingly conservative in appearance, and those produced in Italy, Bohemia, France, the Low Countries, and England are virtually identical in form. However, it is possible to distinguish the examples made in England by carefully comparing mold forms, the quality of the glass, and the distribution of the stems. About 70 percent of the lion-mask stems found in London are demonstrably of English manufacture, and they appear to have been produced from a very small number of molds (Willmott 2000a). On occasion, lion masks were gilded, but the gilding rarely survives in archeological contexts.

Although glasses with lion-mask stems were mass-produced, they seem to have been cherished items that were retained even when they had been broken (Fig. 21). A recently identified group of 21 lion-mask and cigar stems were repaired during the first half of the 17th century (Willmott 2001). All of these repairs were made with strips or sheets of fused lead that were laid over the break to hold the two pieces together. Two of the previously discussed engraved goblets have also been repaired. The foot of one of these vessels was replaced with wood at an uncertain date, while the other goblet

FIG. 21

*Three fragments of goblets with repaired lion-mask stems, colorless, blown, applied. Probably England, early to mid-17th century (glass and repair). H. (center) 8.8 cm. Found at Bloomfield Street, London. Museum of London (A28019).*

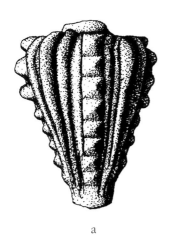

a     b

**FIG. 22**
*Schematic drawings of ladder stems*
*with teardrops (a) and scrollwork (b).*

a     b

**FIG. 23**
*Schematic drawings of ladder stems*
*with rosettes (a) and fleur-de-lis (b).*

was repaired in a manner identical to that of the group of 17th-century examples. The purpose of these repairs is less certain. They were made using a very soft material that would not have withstood repeated use, and they are often disfiguring.

The only other type of mold-blown stem found on goblets from England is the so-called ladder stem. Its name is derived from a series of bosses that are arranged vertically in a rung or ladder pattern. Because they have been found in a number of English locations but rarely on the Continent, it has long been suggested that these stems were exclusively English products (Thorpe 1961, pp. 128–129; Charleston 1984a, p. 69). This has now been confirmed by the discovery of a half-formed example in the Broad Street furnace waste. Several varieties of this stem can be identified, the earliest and simplest of which is found on the gilded Geares glass of 1590 (Charleston 1984a, pl. 14a; see also Fig. 15). This vessel is decorated with a vertical arrangement of bosses interspersed with simple elongated teardrops. Variations made during the first half of the 17th century are more complex. One has bosses alternating with oval panels of scrollwork, with a zone of gadrooning at the top (Fig. 22). Another is similar in form, but it has a raised fleur-de-lis instead of the panels of scrollwork (Fig. 23). A third variation, which is found

on occasion, has a raised rosette design in place of the scrollwork or fleur-de-lis.

Another popular drinking vessel produced by the Bowes and Mansell glasshouses was the beaker. Beginning in the second half of the 16th century, potash beakers of poor quality were made in the forest glasshouses of England. They were usually tall, slightly convex-sided vessels with pedestal bases or simple cylindrical forms. Neither of these shapes was influenced by *façon de Venise* wares. During the first half of the 17th century, English glassmakers created beakers of higher quality, often drawing on styles from elsewhere in Europe. One such form is the tall, fluted beaker, which was made from two separate parisons (Fig. 24). From the first parison, a low pedestal base was shaped, while the second parison was used to fashion the body and vertical rim of the vessel. The body was also decorated with prominent vertical opaque white trails on the lower half, and with one or more bands of horizontal opaque white and blue trails. The English fluted beaker was clearly inspired by the similar Dutch *pijp* or *pasglas* and the German *Stangenglas*, although it is distinctly different in both form and distribution. Like many of its English goblet counterparts, this beaker is made of slightly tinted mixed-alkali glass, but it is one of the few domestic forms that are decorated with colored trails.

FIG. 24

*Fluted beaker fragment, colorless with greenish tinge, blown, applied. England, early to mid-17th century. H. 17.5 cm, D. (base) 9.0 cm. Found at Gracechurch Street, London. Museum of London (15586).*

Other beaker types also seem to have been influenced by Continental parallels. The presence in England of cylindrical beakers with everted rims and filigree or *wafel* decoration, made in the Low Countries, has already been noted. However, during the first half of the 17th century, vessels similar in form but different in decoration were also produced. Although their tinted mixed-alkali glass was not quite comparable in quality to that found in other *façon de Venise* centers, they were just as competently executed. These beakers were sometimes undecorated, but they more often featured optic-blown vertical ribbing overlaid with fine colorless spiral trails (Fig. 25). This form of beaker was especially popular in London, where it was found in considerable numbers at the Gracechurch Street site (Willmott 2000b).

A more problematical category of glass in 17th-century England consists of goblets with compound stems made from twisted and colored canes, which are often referred to as serpent stems. Such vessels are well known in art-historical and museum collections, but they are considerably rarer archeologically. The stem was formed from one or more rods that were gently heated at the furnace and manipulated into contorted designs. When the stem had cooled sufficiently to retain its shape, a flared base and bowl were added. As would be ex-

pected from the very nature of this process, such stems are highly variable and hard to classify. However, three broad styles dating from the first half of the 17th century have been found in England.

The first and most zoomorphic of these styles is the so-called winged serpent or dragon stem (Figs. 26 and 27). It was formed from a single ribbed rod

FIG. 25

*Beaker, colorless with grayish tinge, blown, applied, trailed. England, early to mid-17th century. H. 9.5 cm, D. (rim) 6.8 cm, (base) 4.5 cm. Found in London. Museum of London (5148).*

**Fig. 26**

*Fragment of goblet with winged serpent stem, colorless, blown, applied, pincered. England or Low Countries, first half of the 17th century. H. 9.4 cm, D. (base) 7.4 cm. Found at Gracechurch Street, London. Museum of London (98.1/100).*

**Fig. 27**

*Fragment of goblet with winged serpent stem, colorless, blown, applied. England or Low Countries, first half of the 17th century. H. 7.5 cm. Found in London. Museum of London (5209).*

of colorless glass, which was folded into a loop near the base and horizontally coiled tightly above that point. The upper part of the rod terminated in an applied blue prunt that was manipulated into the shape of a head, and two blue wings were attached to the side of the stem. The winged serpent stem is quite rare in England, although examples have been found at Plymouth and several other urban sites (Charleston 1986, p. 46, no. 45).

More commonly found in England are coiled serpent stems (Figs. 28 and 29). This slightly less complex form was also made from a single ribbed rod of colorless glass that was manipulated into

an open loop. However, the horizontal coils above the loop were piled in a looser, wavy design. Wings and head were not added to the stem, although a blue glass claw was sometimes applied to one side.

**Fig. 28**

*Fragment of goblet with coiled serpent stem, colorless, blown, applied. England or Low Countries, first half of the 17th century. H. 10.0 cm. Found at Gracechurch Street, London. Museum of London (98.1/94).*

**Fig. 29**

*Flute with coiled serpent stem, colorless, blown, applied. Low Countries, first half of the 17th century. H. 29 cm. Museum Boijmans Van Beuningen, Rotterdam (8, gift of Dr. E. Rijckevorsel).*

These stems are widely distributed, with examples having been found as far north as Newcastle (Ellison 1979, p. 171, no. 57), and they have been excavated in considerable numbers. For example, 11 specimens were found in the Gracechurch Street deposit alone (Willmott 2000b).

The final variation of this type is the scrolled serpent stem (Fig. 30). It was formed from a single oval loop of a ribbed rod with two opposed columns of glass fashioned from a trail manipulated into the shape of a vertical scroll. The upper part of the stem was decorated with applied ornaments that were also attached to the bowl. Although this type of stem is rarely found in England, some examples are known to have originated in the Low Countries, such as a complete glass with a fluted bowl in the Rijksmuseum, Amsterdam (Ritsema van Eck and Zijlstra-Zweens 1993, p. 51, no. 60).

An entirely different form of goblet with a compound stem features a colored twist stem (Fig. 31). It is formed, not from a ribbed rod, but from a complex cane of colored rods (colorless glass cased with red, white, blue, or yellow glass). This cane is twisted into a loop or spiral shape and decorated

FIG. 30

*Flute with scrolled serpent stem, colorless with yellowish tinge, blown, applied, tooled. Probably the Netherlands, first half of the 17th century. H. 20.5 cm, D. (base) 7.5 cm. Rijksmuseum, Amsterdam (N.M. 10754-16, bequest of A. J. Enschedé).*

FIG. 31

*Drawing of goblet fragment with colored twist stem, colorless, red, opaque white, blue, blown, applied, pincered. Low Countries or Venice, mid-17th century. H. 5.5 cm. Findspot unknown, but probably London. Museum of London (16940).*

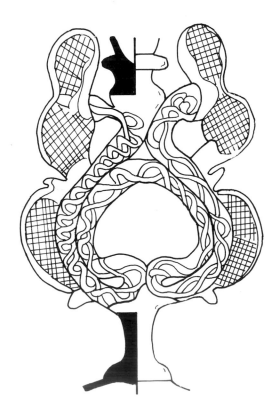

with applied wings that are often impressed with a mesh design. Although this form was well known on the Continent by the mid-17th century, it is rarely found in England.

It is normally assumed that the manufacture of goblets with compound stems originated in Venice at the end of the 16th century, and that they quickly spread to glasshouses north of the Alps by the early 17th century (Tait 1991, pp. 174–175). Some scholars believe that they were also made in England, noting that, in 1635, Mansell referred to some of his glasses as being of "extraordinary fashions" (Charleston 1984a, p. 67). However, it is very hard to identify vessels found archeologically in England with the known centers of production. Some, such as those with colored twist stems, are so rare that they were probably produced in Venice or possibly in Antwerp. Judging from their patterns of distribution, it is likely that goblets with compound stems formed from ribbed tubes originated in northern Europe. The winged serpent or dragon stem was almost certainly produced in the Low Countries, but it is difficult to suggest a provenance for the other variations. Given the relative frequency and wide distribution of the coiled serpent stem in England, it is likely that at least some were made there. While the scrolled stem was made of a slightly green tinted glass similar to that used in many other products of the Mansell era, very few examples have been found in England. Their presence in contexts in the Low Countries might suggest that they originated there.

As far as dating is concerned, while all of the examples from archeological sites in England are fairly securely dated to the first half of the 17th century, this is not the case for complete pieces. It is now well known that many 17th-century designs were reproduced in the 19th century, most notably by the Venetian Antonio Salviati (Charleston 1984a, p. 217). These reproductions and less scrupulous modern fakes make the study of goblets with compound stems especially challenging.

## THE COLLAPSE AND REVIVAL OF THE ENGLISH INDUSTRY, 1640–1680

By 1640, although the English glass industry was in its strongest position under Mansell's leadership, it nearly disintegrated. There were three reasons for this threat to its existence. First, the latest revision of Mansell's monopoly resulted in much higher rents to the Crown, and this led to higher retail prices. Second, in 1640, the Scots invaded northern England, curtailing production at Newcastle and, more important, cutting off the supply of coal for Mansell's furnaces in London. The third and final blow came with the onset of civil war in 1642, when Parliament abolished all patents relating to the glass industry.

During the next 20 years, no *façon de Venise* glass was produced in England, and excavations of imported wares from that period are extremely rare. The apparent cessation in the manufacture and use of glass tableware after the war has been heretofore attributed to the Puritans' dislike for glass. One scholar has stated that "many people regarded fine crystal as a relic of royalty" (Thorpe 1961, p. 135), while another has suggested that, during the interregnum, "the demand for luxury glass was presumably not so great" (Charleston 1984a, p. 97). However, there is no evidence to support these contentions, or the further assumption that people "confused wine glasses with drunkenness" (Thorpe 1961, p. 135).

The real reason for the lack of production during the interregnum was the economic collapse of the glassmaking industry. The mid-17th century in Europe was marked by depression in many industrial markets. It was certainly a time of stagnation in French glass production, which also marked the beginning of a well-recognized decline in the tradition of Venetian manufactures (Godfrey 1975,

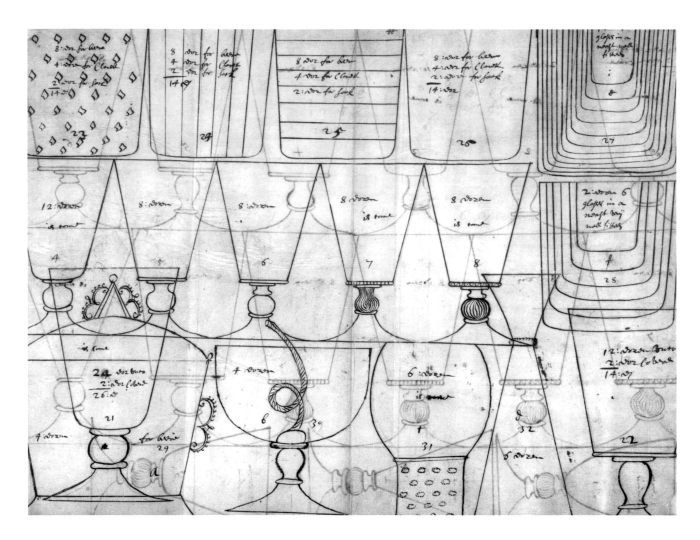

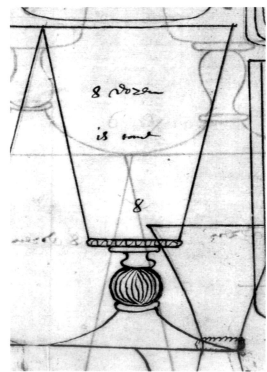

FIG. 32

*Illustrated letter of John Greene, depicting tumblers
for beer, wine, and sack (top row), and a variety of
goblets with knopped stems (bottom row). London,
1667–1672. British Library, Sloane 857, fol. 17.*

p. 134). In England, as has already been noted, this decline was signaled by the cancellation of Mansell's
patents and the disruption of supplies of raw materials
and traditional markets. The Puritan ethic and the
Commonwealth government do not appear to have affected access to, and demand for, glass. The assumption that drinking violated the Puritan ethic has been
disputed by modern historians. Cromwell has been
quoted as saying that he thought it utterly absurd "to
keep wine out of the country lest men should be drunk"
(Hill 1970, p. 198). Indeed, mass production of the
wine bottle originated during this period, and it is evi-

dent that glass was still being imported in sufficient quantities to merit taxation (Buckley, F. 1914, p. 18).

With the restoration of the monarchy in 1660, there were fresh attempts to establish a native industry for the manufacture of fine glassware. During the 1660s and early 1670s, the duke of Buckingham and his associates founded glasshouses at Charterhouse Yard, Greenwich, and Vauxhall, and they were granted a 14-year license and patent to make crystal and mirror glass. Despite these efforts, the native production of glass is not likely to have been sizable at that time, and it is virtually impossible to identify archeologically any products associated with the industry.

A further insight on the importation of glass into England at that time is the remarkable survival of eight letters written by John Greene to the Venetian Allesio Morelli between 1667 and 1672. Greene was a member of the Company of Glass Sellers,

which was established by royal charter in 1664. Its aim was to maintain a tight control over the manufacture and sale of goods, and to preserve high standards in the quality of the glass employed in both domestically produced and imported tableware.

Greene and Michael Measey were partners in a retail business located in the Poultry in London. The correspondence between Greene and Morelli was extensively illustrated, with more than 400 scaled depictions of the vessels required (Figs. 32 and 33). These letters, which have never been thoroughly published (although some are reproduced in Hartshorne 1968, pp. 440–449), demonstrate the wide range and quantities of vessels imported into England, and they are a unique source of information on this subject. While many of the vessels illustrated in the letters have yet to be found archeologically in England, significant deposits from Nottingham and Guildford have contained tumblers and goblets similar to these designs (Alvey 1973; Fryer and Shelley 1997).

Certainly any English production and importation of *façon de Venise* glass during the 1660s and 1670s would not have survived long. George Ravenscroft's development of a new glass containing as much as 30-percent lead oxide resulted in widespread changes in the industry (Charleston 1968; *idem* 1984a). Initially, the production of this glass was monopolized by English glassmakers. In addition, because of the physical and refractive properties of lead glass, unique English styles of glassware were manufactured. By the beginning of the 18th century, *façon d'Anglais* had come to dominate much of the northern European glass industry.

FIG. 33

*Wineglass of the Greene/Morelli type, colorless, blown, applied, tooled, gilded. The Netherlands, first half of the 17th century. H. 15.3 cm, D. (rim) 9 cm. Found in Delft. Collection of Harold Henkes, Rotterdam, the Netherlands (H 915).*

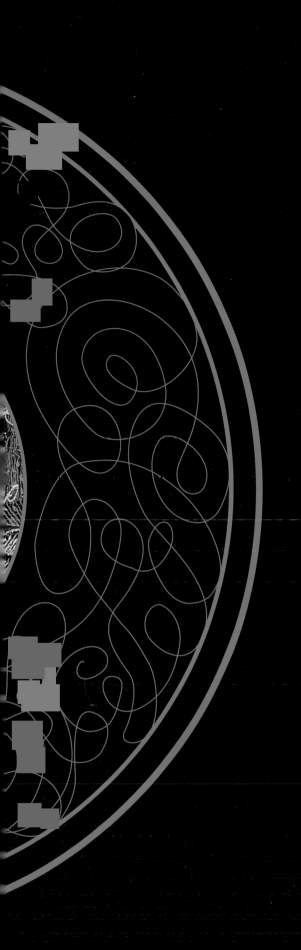

Venetian and *Façon de Venise* Glass
in England

*Objects*

## 1

*Goblet*

*H. 19.2 cm*

VENICE, MID-16TH CENTURY. THE BRITISH MUSEUM, LONDON (S.642, BEQUEST OF FELIX SLADE, ESQ., F.S.A., 1868). FORMERLY IN THE SLADE COLLECTION.

COLORLESS WITH GRAYISH TINGE. BLOWN, MOLD-BLOWN, TOOLED, FILIGREE DECORATION.

This goblet has a trumpet-shaped bowl with applied vertical stripes of filigree canes consisting of a band of five opaque white canes twisted around a thin white cane. The bowl was mold-blown into a fluted form, with eight lobes forming a pronounced scalloped rim. Toward the base, the bowl was tooled to a point, narrowing and straightening the twisted canes. The stem consists of a filigree knop that is decorated with the same cane pattern that appears on the bowl. The knop is situated between two colorless collars, which are applied below to a trumpet-shaped foot with filigree decoration and a folded edge.

COMMENT: A similar fragmentary goblet of this type was found at Liverpool Street, London, in 1871 (Museum of London, 16678, H. 12.0 cm, D. [base] 8.0 cm).

BIBLIOGRAPHY: *Slade Collection* 1871, p. 114; Tait 1979, p. 72, no. 100.

## 2

*The Culross* Wafel *Beaker*

*H. 9.5 cm, D. (rim) 6.8 cm, (base) 4.8 cm*

PROBABLY SOUTHERN NETHERLANDS, LATE 16TH CENTURY. THE BRITISH MUSEUM, LONDON (1958, 5-3, 1).

COLORLESS WITH GRAYISH TINGE. BLOWN, APPLIED.

The sides of this beaker are cylindrical, and the rim is everted. The base, which is pushed in on the underside, is decorated with a plain applied base-ring. The decoration consists of a *wafel* pattern, in which a thick ribbon of colorless glass was trailed spirally around the bubble from bottom to top. The beginning of the trail is still visible under the base of the beaker. The bubble was then further inflated in a vertically ribbed mold that cut across the trail, resulting in a pattern of soft-edged (cushion-shaped) square facets. A thick trail of colorless glass was wound around the edge of the base, overlapping at the ends.

COMMENT: This beaker is said to have been found walled up in Culross, Fifeshire, Scotland. In the 16th and 17th centuries, Culross was a thriving community that traded with other Forth ports and the Low Countries. A similar but fragmented beaker, which was found in Rotterdam, is dated to the first half of the 17th century (Henkes 1994, p. 134, no. 30.4).

BIBLIOGRAPHY: Tait 1967, p. 95, fig. 2; *idem* 1991, p. 154, fig. 196 (part of group).

## 3

*Goblet*

*H. 18.9–20.5 cm, D. (bowl, rim)*
*10.25–10.5 cm*

ENGLAND, LONDON, TRADITIONALLY
ATTRIBUTED TO BROAD STREET GLASSHOUSE
OF JACOPO VERZELINI, DATED 1577. THE
CORNING MUSEUM OF GLASS, CORNING,
NEW YORK (50.2.1); ACQUIRED FROM
STEUBEN GLASS INC. FORMERLY IN THE
COLLECTION OF HENRY BROWN, TRING,
ENGLAND.

COLORLESS WITH SMOKY TINGE. BLOWN,
APPLIED, DIAMOND-POINT ENGRAVED.

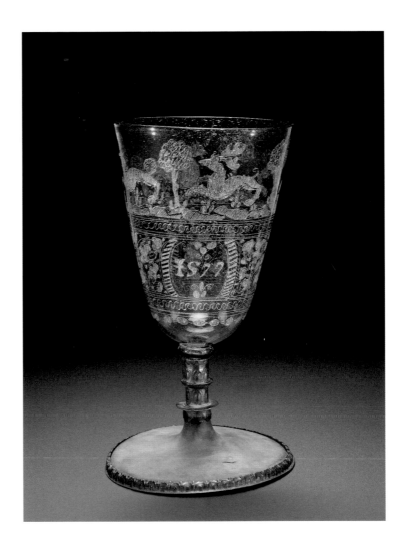

The deep conical bowl is rounded
at the base, to which a small, hollow
knop is applied. Part of the stem and
the entire foot are missing; they have
been replaced by a silver stem with
two waferlike knops and a flaring, flat
wooden foot with a silver rim. The
silver is decorated with variations of
an egg-and-dart motif. The bowl of the
goblet is diamond-point engraved in
three zones. The top zone depicts a
hunting scene, with one hound pur-
suing a unicorn and another chasing
a stag, all separated by trees. The middle zone, divided by a stylized twisted
band between engraved lines, is engraved on opposite sides with cartouches separated by foliage panels. One cartouche contains the date "1577," while
the other features the initials "RB" intertwined with "IB." The lower zone contains a horizontal band of engraved
roundels.

The glass has numerous minute
bubbles.

COMMENT: The monograms probably
indicate that this object is a marriage or
betrothal goblet. The top band, foliage
panels, and borders are similar to those
on the John Dier goblet (Bles 1925,
p. 59, pl. 12). The silverwork, which
resembles silver moldings found on
Elizabethan tigerware jugs, indicates a
replacement that is roughly contemporary with the glass. The stem and foot
are similar to those found on wooden
drinking vessels of comparable date.

BIBLIOGRAPHY: Fisher 1947; *Old English Glass* 1947; Elville 1951, p. 158, pl.
90; Buechner 1955, p. 137.

## 4

### *Tazza*

*H. 11.0 cm, D. (rim) 14.0 cm, (base) 8.2 cm*

ENGLAND, LONDON, POSSIBLY BROAD STREET GLASSHOUSE OF JACOPO VERZELINI, LATE 16TH CENTURY. MUSEUM OF LONDON (ER208).

COLORLESS. BLOWN, DIAMOND-POINT ENGRAVED, GILDED.

The base of this object is low and flaring, with an edge that is folded under. The stem is an inverted baluster with a round knop on its upper portion. It is attached with a prominent merese to a low and shallow bowl. The bowl is decorated on the interior with a scene showing a stag and hounds running between trees and foliage. At the center of the bowl is engraved, radiating gadrooning. The stem is decorated with applied gilding, and the base is engraved with roundels.

BIBLIOGRAPHY: Willmott 2002, cover illustration.

## 5

### *The Grenhal Glass*

*H. 16 cm*

ENGLAND, LONDON, PROBABLY BROAD STREET GLASSHOUSE OF JACOPO VERZELINI, ENGRAVED "TO.HIS.BROTHER.RICHARD. GRENHAL," DATED 1584. BIRMINGHAM MUSEUM AND ART GALLERY (1979M5).

COLORLESS. BLOWN, APPLIED, DIAMOND-POINT ENGRAVED.

This goblet has a round funnel bowl and a short hollow stem consisting of a ribbed, inverted baluster between short stem sections and mereses. The applied flat foot has a folded foot-ring. The bowl is diamond-point engraved with two large and two small cartouches. The larger panels are framed by curved double lines, and the smaller panels have strapwork frames superimposed on an arabesque ground. The large cartouches contain an eagle perched on an infant in swaddling clothes; an eagle's leg has been erased. The small ovals enclose the initials "RG" with a lover's knot and the date "1584." Above this is the inscription

naming Richard Grenhal. The upper side of the foot is engraved with a band of floral scrolls.

COMMENT: Richard Grenhal may have been a member of the Greenhall family of Ribchester, near Blackburn in Lancashire (Charleston 1984a, p. 57).

BIBLIOGRAPHY: *English and Continental Glass* 1978, lot 113; Charleston 1984a, p. 57 and pl. 13b.

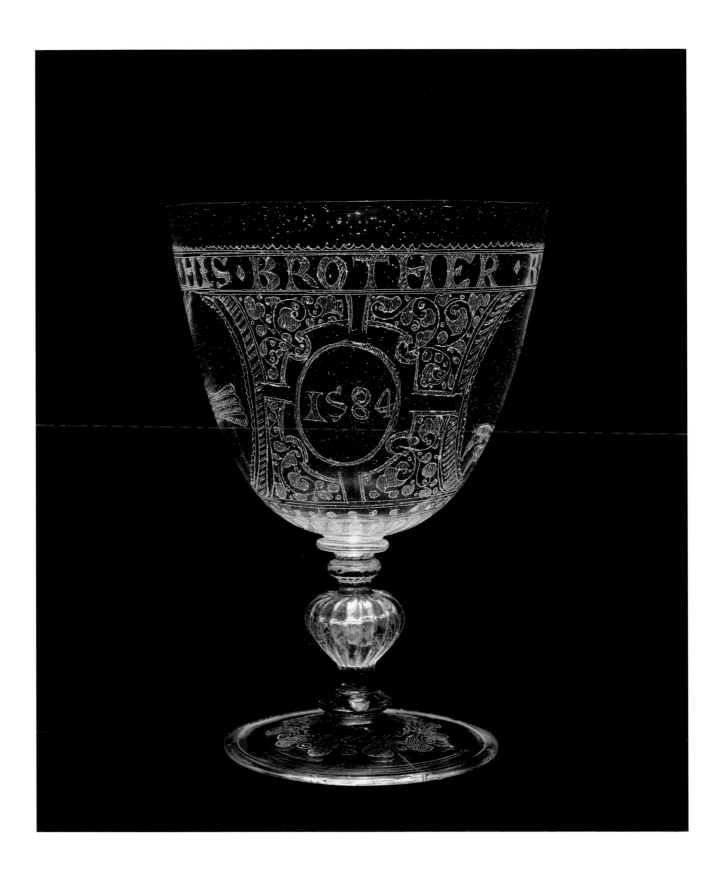

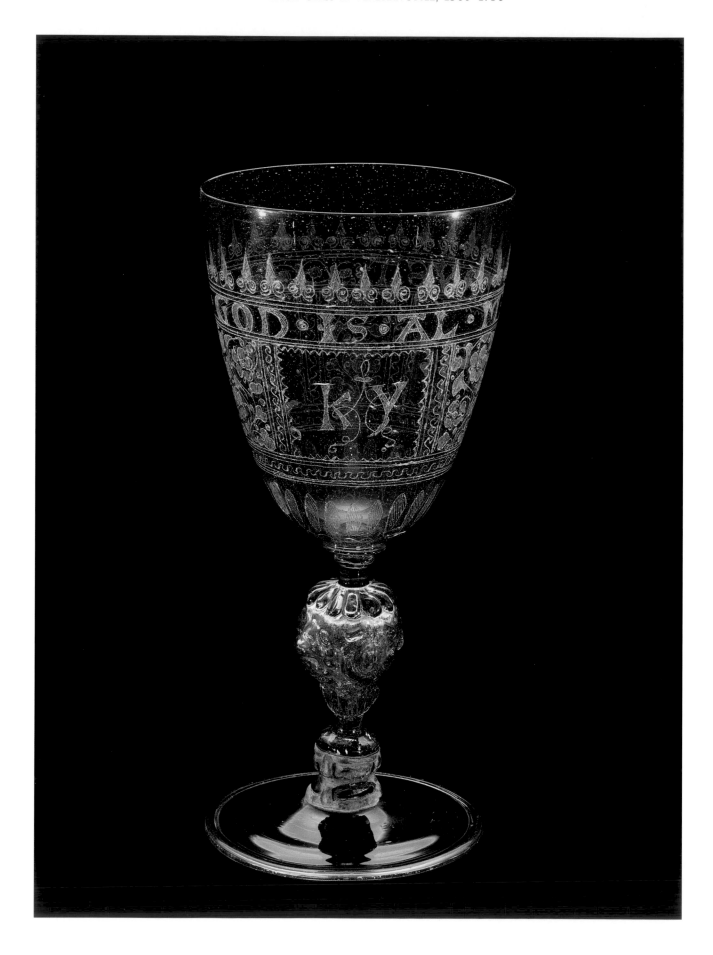

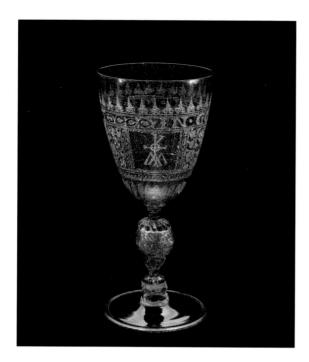
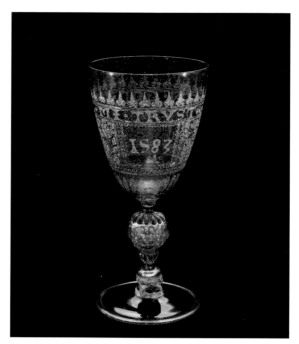

# 6

## Goblet
*OH. 21.0 cm, D. 10.4 cm*

ENGLAND, LONDON, PROBABLY BROAD
STREET GLASSHOUSE OF JACOPO VERZELINI,
DATED 1583. THE CORNING MUSEUM OF
GLASS, CORNING, NEW YORK (63.2.8);
ACQUIRED FROM CECIL DAVIS, LONDON.
FORMERLY IN THE COLLECTION OF HAMIL-
TON CLEMENTS, ESQ., SURBITON, SURREY

COLORLESS WITH GRAYISH TINGE. BLOWN,
MOLD-BLOWN, DIAMOND-POINT ENGRAVED,
GILDED; METAL.

This goblet has a large ovoid bowl,
which is joined at the base to the stem
with a thin merese. The stem consists of
a tiny ball knop above a short, straight
section followed by a gilded lion-mask
stem blown in a two-part mold. It shows
two lion masks separated by shields,
with rounded ribs on top and ribbing
at the base. This hollow part of the
stem is connected with a disk to a short
stem and a jagged, flaring section (presumably the remains of the original
foot), which is encircled by a lead or
pewter strap, followed by another metal band, a rounded disk, a third metal
band, and a circular replacement foot
with a folded rim. Beneath the base is
a rough pontil mark.

The bowl of the goblet is decorated
with a series of diamond-point engraved motifs. Near the rim is a band
of arrowheads with pairs of spirals
at their bases, below which is a band
with the inscription "IN.GOD.IS.AL.MI.
TRVST" between triple lines. The wide
zone below it is divided into six panels.
Three panels are filled with stylized
floral and foliate sprays and bordered
with rigaree bands, which alternate with
three cartouches framed with scallops.
One is engraved with the initials "KY"

tied with love knots; the second has a
merchant's mark incorporating a cross,
the letters "O" and "M," and a geomet-
rical device related to the letter "K";
in the third is the date "1583" with a
fleur-de-lis below. The remaining zone
at the base of the bowl has a rigaree-
engraved border, followed by a band of
hatched ovals and a scalloped band.

There are several short cracks in the
bowl. The original foot is missing and
repaired with a foot from another goblet of comparable date.

COMMENT: "IN.GOD.IS.AL.MI.
TRVST" is the motto of the Pewterers'
Company. The inscription also appears
on the goblet dated 1586 (see Fig. 13).

BIBLIOGRAPHY: Francis, G. R. 1926,
pl. I; pl. LXXIII, A1; and pl. LXXIV, A2;
Buckley, W. 1929, pl. 9; Thorpe 1929,
v. 1, pp. 80–83, and v. 2, pl. 1, no. 2;
*idem* 1935, pp. 150 and 154–157; Davis
1963, fig. 4; "Recent Important Acquisitions," *JGS*, v. 6, 1964, p. 165, no. 43;
Lazarus 1969, fig. 1; Charleston 1980,
pp. 94–95, pl. 39; *Hikari no shouchu*
1992, p. 22, no. 32; *CMG Guide* 2001,
p. 70.

# Endnotes

## Introduction
*Jutta-Annette Page*
(pp. 3–19)

1.  *De plantis epitome utilissima, Petri Andreae Matthioli, senensis, medici excellentissimi . . .* , Frankfurt a. Main: [Sigmund Feyerabend], 1586.
2.  Clarke 1974, pp. 23–24, citing Levi 1895, p. 28.
3.  See a goblet enameled with Adam and Eve after late 15th-century woodcuts from the Bible (Dreier 1989, pp. 38–42, no. 9).
4.  Medici Archive, Florence, v. 1176, insert 2, fol. 14.
5.  The glass shown in the painting is most closely paralleled by a glass with a hunchback that is now in the collection of The British Museum, London (MLA WB 58). A plate by Jules Labarte, illustrating objects from the Debruge-Dumenil Collection, shows grotesque Renaissance glasses that were still extant in 1847.
6.  Archivio di Stato di Firenze, Mediceo del Principato, 4949, fol. 810.
7.  Medici Archive, Florence, v. 280, fol. 57.
8.  Nesbitt 1878, p. 90, citing Vincente Cervio, *Il trinciante*, Venice, 1593.
9.  A set of portrait roundels of Becuccio and his wife, formerly inserted into the predella, is now in The Art Institute of Chicago (1964.1097a, b).
10. Medici Archive, Florence, v. 1171, insert 4, fol. 166.
11. *Ibid.*, v. 2942, unpaged.
12. *Ibid.*, v. 2951, fol. unpaged (unaddressed letter of August 14, 1618).
13. *Ibid.*, v. 2955, insert 10, fol. unpaged.

## Venetian Glass in Austria
*Jutta-Annette Page*
(pp. 20–83)

1.  Ferdinand was a member of a princely house, and Philippine Welser was a woman of lesser birth, even though she came from one of the wealthiest families in Germany, which supported the Hapsburg court financially. Therefore, she could not accede to his rank, and her children could not succeed to their father's hereditary dignities and entailed property.
2.  During the rule of Maximilian I (1493–1519), trade between Venice and Germany came to a complete halt for a number of years.
3.  The frieze relates to the so-called *Mahlbriefe*. These mottoes, proverbs, and sayings are quite common decorations on the interior walls of private buildings in Tyrol and southern Germany (Bücking 1968, p. 159).
4.  This beaker (H. 13 cm), which was formerly in the collection of Adalbert Figdor, is now in the Österreichisches Museum für Angewandte Kunst in Vienna (F 143/1935).
5.  Wine was mixed as two or three parts wine to one part water. In addition, meals were limited to a small breakfast with white bread and wine, followed by a full meal at 3 or 4 p.m., as was customary in Venice (Bücking 1968, p. 153). Widespread consumption of wine

earned for the Germans a reputation as boozers, and German writers of the 16th century criticized them for it (Adamson 1995, p. 20). By the mid-16th century, wine had ceased to be a drink for the wealthy in the German states.
6.  Landesmuseum Zurich (LM 80205). This beaker also bears a coat of arms and the dedication "Christoph Oeri 1632." The original diamond-point decoration had several reserved cartouches, as well as large, vertically oriented rectangular medallions, on which the coat of arms and the inscription were later added. The decoration includes the eagle of the Holy Roman Empire, the coat of arms of the Oeri family, and, below it, the year "1632." On the opposing sides are numerous engraved names, the arms of the Fussli family, and the name "David Fussli," *Stubenmeister* and (from 1637) guild master.
7.  Museum Carolino Augusteum, Salzburg (K 3038/49).
8.  The Höchstetters had far-reaching trade connections (Simonsfeld 1887, v. 1, p. 118), and in the early 16th century, they operated the third-largest merchant house in Augsburg, after the houses owned by the Fugger and Welser families. They maintained close business relations with the Fugger house.
9.  A reverse-painted glass panel, now lost, showed a portrait of Ferdinand and Philippine facing each other, conventional imagery depicting a loving couple. A similar double portrait of this couple, on parchment, was made by Heinrich Martin Hoffmann about 1575. For a tin plate portraying an embracing couple, see *Rudolf II and Prague* 1997, p. 689, no. V.224.
10. The chair is in the Kunsthistorisches Museum, Ambras Collection. See Habsburg 1997, p. 102, fig. 126.
11. The Ambras guest book, 1570s, is also in the Kunsthistorisches Museum.
12. This goblet, which came from the monastery of Saint Peter, Salzburg, is in the collection of Vienna's Museum für Angewandte Kunst (GI 662/1869).
13. In the inventory of Duke Ernst's estate, drawn up in 1561, numerous glass vessels, referred to as "finedisch," are included among the contents of the silver vault. Some of these objects probably came from Hall, although the clerk who provided the list, judging strictly from the appearance of the glasses, noted that all of them were of Venetian manufacture.
14. Rückert (1982, pp. 80–81) attributes the armorial plate (no. 130) and the ewer (no. 131), as well as another ewer made for Duke Wilhelm IV or Ludwig X of Bavaria (no. 132), to Dax. See also Hess and Husband 1997, p. 146, n. 9.
15. On November 27, 1598, Emperor Rudolf II confirmed the status of nobility for Dr. Chrysostomos Höchstetter (Heimer 1959, p. 53).
16. Johann Frederick I's title of elector had been removed by Charles V and awarded to his cousin Maurice of Saxony after he fought for the Protestants and lost the battle at Muhlberg, which ended the Schmalkaldic War. For five years, Johann Friedrich and Philip of Hesse had to follow the emperor in his entourage as prisoners.
17. Heimer (1959, p. 24) refers to Johann Frederick as the imprisoned elector, who was exiled in Augsburg in 1547 and returned to Saxony in 1552, following a petition that was supported by Cranach. Lucas Cranach the Elder, a Roman Catholic, worked for patrons of different confessions. See Tacke 1992.
18. In November 1565, Francesco I de' Medici had visited Vienna and Innsbruck on the occasion of his marriage to Giovanna d'Austria. In Vienna, he had been greeted by Archduke Ferdinand, and his host

at the Hofburg in Innsbruck was Emperor Maximilian II (r. 1564–1576). Francesco's personal entourage included the condottiere Paolo Giordano Orsini (Archivio di Stato di Firenze, Mediceo del Principato, 5923, fol. 158).

19. McCray (1999, p. 156) misunderstood this phrase as "they had the most imagination and fantasy."

20. Thüry 1991, p. 138, fig. 49. The terminus ante quem for the finds in the cesspit is 1605. The shell is called "geschirr zu den Farben" (vessel for colors) in Gesner 1575, pp. 315 and 333. This type of gold paint, which is often referred to as "Muschelgold" or "l'or à la coquille," consists of small fragments of gold leaf that were mixed with varnish and often sold in a shell (Perrault 1992).

21. This object, which was formerly in the collection of Dr. Adalbert Figdor, is now housed in the Museum für Angewandte Kunst in Vienna (F 158/1953). In 1588, the city of Trent had its own glasshouse (Rückert 1982, p. 82, citing Archivio Storico Lombardo, 15, 1888, p. 1022).

22. I am grateful to Catherine Hess of The J. Paul Getty Museum, Los Angeles, for drawing my attention to this vessel.

## Spanish *Façon de Venise* Glass
*Ignasi Doménech*
(pp. 84–141)

1. This information is drawn from the archives in Venice and Altare, which contain the names of glassmakers who moved to the Iberian Peninsula in the mid-16th century, although no mention is made of the towns or villages in which they settled (Frothingham 1956, p. 18).

2. *Ninou* is the contraction of the Catalan *any nou*, which means "new year."

3. I am grateful to Rainer Zietz for providing this suggestion.

## Venetian and *Façon de Venise* Glass in France in the 16th and 17th Centuries
*Marie-Laure de Rochebrune*
(pp. 142–191)

1. Between 1413 and 1415, Jean de Berry acquired "a certain quantity of glasses made in Venice . . . for a total of 138 livres" (duke of Berry's accounts, A.N., KK 250, published in Guiffrey 1894, p. 215). Around 1470, glasses called "cristallins de Venize" in the records were often acquired by René d'Anjou for his mansion in Avignon and for his castle in Angers (Robin 1985, p. 258).

2. See, in particular, the painting *Still Life: The Five Senses with Flowers*, about 1638. Norton Simon Museum, Pasadena, California.

3. Glass had been imported into Great Britain as early as the 13th century (see p. 271).

4. In 1559, Catherine de Médicis asked the French ambassador in Venice to speak in defense of a certain Save, a Muranese glassworker employed in Saint-Germain-en-Laye, who wished to return to Venice without being punished by the Venetian authorities (Bondois 1936–1937, p. 51).

5. All of these documents are housed in the Archives Nationales in Paris. They are mentioned by several authors, including Garnier 1885, p. 68; Girancourt 1886, pp. 46, 47, and 50; and Rose-Villequey 1971, p. 423, n. 70.

6. Letters issued by the king on March 24, 1600, and recorded by the parliament in Paris on May 12, 1600. A.N., Registre des Ordonnances, X1a 8644, fols. 156–159. This document was kindly provided by Michèle Bimbenet-Privat.

7. Margherita Paleologo (1510–1566), wife of Frederick II of Mantua (1500–1540), had brought to the Gonzaga family the duchy of Montferrat, which she had inherited in 1533.

8. Notably in 1619, when that glasshouse's privilege was disputed by Bernard Dubuisson, of Italian origin. At that time, the glasshouse was jointly directed by Vincent de Sarode and Horace Ponte (Boutillier 1885, p. 32).

9. Jacques de Sarode is first mentioned in the registers of the parish church in Saint-Laurent on August 20, 1587, on the occasion of the baptism of his son, Jehan (*ibid.*, p. 4). The precise date of his arrival in Nevers is unknown. It was probably between 1582, when he is noted as still residing in Lyons, and 1587.

10. In this letter, Jacques de Sarode is said to have lived in Nevers for several years. State Records, Mantua, Gonzaga, folder 663, fols. 410 and 411.

11. The duchy of Lorraine lost half of its population to war and foreign occupation between 1618 and 1697.

12. Charles de Hennezel, one of the masters of the Bois-Giset glasshouse in the Nevers region, promised to supply Jérôme and Jacques de Sarode, noblemen glassmakers living in Montenotte, with glassworkers able to produce "12,000 *liens* of flat glass."

13. The inventory of Catherine de Médicis includes "deux petits vases de verre peintz de Montpellier" (two small painted glass vases from Montpellier). The nature of glass production in Montpellier is unknown (Bonnaffé 1874, p. 92, no. 323).

14. My thanks to William Gudenrath, resident adviser of The Studio of The Corning Museum of Glass, for furnishing the information on how this object was made.

15. I am grateful to Peter M. Daly, professor emeritus of German studies, McGill University, Montreal, for his insightful and constructive comments on this entry.

16. I am grateful to Keith King for sharing his observations on this object.

## Longing for Luxury: Some Social Routes of Venetian-Style Glassware in the Netherlands during the 17th Century
*Alexandra Gaba-Van Dongen*
(pp. 192–225)

1. Jorden reysde naer Amsterdam te mart,
   Met een stijve beurs en een moedich hart,
   Om alle costelyckheyt te coopen.
   Daer ginc hy alle winckels deur-loopen.
   Hy dede langhen silvere Lampetten,
   Vergulde Schroeven, goude Brasseletten,
   Groote Diamanten van veel caraten;
   Die keurde hy nauw voor deur op de straten.
   Hy proefde Ringen, of s'hem oock pasten;
   Hy sach Fluweelen, Satijnen, Damasten,
   Turcksche Tapijten, Milaensche neer-basen,
   Schoone Porceleynen, Veneetsche glasen,
   Spiegels van Ebben-hout, Brand-ysers wichtich,
   Copere Croonen, groot en opsichtich.

Hy taelde naer vermaerde Schilderyen
Vande beste meesters van d'oude tyen,
Van Lucas van Leyden, of van Mabuysen.
Naer lang geloop deur veelderley huysen,
Naer dat hy 't al deur-pluyst en beknoeyt had,
Raet wat hy cocht, die sinnelijcke Jordaen?
Vier houte lepels en ses taffel-borden.

(English translation by Peter G. Rose)

2. "Voorder onder de nieuwe wercken ende verciersel der stadt, soo en is oock geensinns voorbij te gaen Het Glashuys, recht teghen-over de Cloveniersdoelen. Dit heeft ettelicke ovens ende winckels [werk-plaatsen] in dewelcke door gheduerighen arbeydt van constenaers seer fraeye cristallijne glaesen in verscheyden ende ontallicke gedaen-ten geformeert werden, ende ghemaeckt met soo wonderlicke ende uutnemende geestichheyt dat se de Veneetsche dewelcke tot noch toe voornamelick ghepresen zijn, in aerdicheyt ende conste gheenssins en wijcken."

3. "Glas-Huys. Dit staat by 't voornoemde Doolhof op de Roose-gragt, aan 't endt / een der voornaamste en kunstighste werk-stukken / niet alleen van Amsterdam / maar van de gheheele Wereldt; van bin-nen inkomende siet men 't wonderlikst dat met hier in de Stadt magh beoogen / daer sijn twee Ovens / plach voor desen niet meer als een te sijn / en nu van 't Jaar heefter de Meester van al dit werk / of de Heer van dit Huys, noch een laten setten: hier sijn omtrent dertigh werck-lieden in 't werck; dese Ovens branden nacht en dagh en dit vuur magh niet uyt gaan; de stoffe daer 't Glas van gemaakt wort leydt in dese vuurighe Ovens in eenige potten / die met lange ysers / die van bin-nen hol zijn / daer wort uyt gehaalt; en dese stoffe heeft de gelijkke-nisse van gloeyend Lijm / en wordt geformeert en gebogen na dat men 't maaksel der Glasen begeert / vijf of ses gaten heeft elk Oven / daer de voornoemde Stoffe door wordt uytgehaalt. In dit Glas-huys worden nu allerhande Glazen gemaekt die men kan bedenken. Door desen plagh Venetien alleen de kristallijne en fijne Glasen te maken maer nu wor-dense hier alsoo goet en fijn ghemaakt als oyt Venetien gedaan heeft / so dat nu hedensdaags daer van Amsterdam soo wel als vergelegen plaatsen beroemt is / want dit Glashuys heeft nu konstige werk vasen / die niet anders doen als sulck kristalijn Glas maken: waarlik een wonderbaerlik toestel / dat voor alle dink waerdigh om te zien is: men maakt hier niet alleen gemene en gewoonlijke drinkglasen / sulks als men gewoon is / maar alle cierlijke en uytnemende vreemt maaksel / als fluyten / Schalen / overdekte kostelijke koppen / na de maniere der goude overdekte kelcken / kostelijke kroesen / kleyne en aardige drink-kroesjes / heel witte en andere met blaauwe / en andere gekleurde ran-den / ook heel nette Wijnglasen / kopjes en ander oud en nieuw werck / ja oock datmen noyt gesien heeft: want de wercklieden maken het al soo 't de Heeren en Juffrouwen konnen bedenken; hier gaat men door groote Pakhuysen die vol Glasen van allerley maaksel en kunstigh fat-soen by duysenden leggen; ook in de Winkkel gaatmen langs de kassen daer men allerley fijn en kristalijn Glas in groten overvloet siet leggen; dit werk moet nacht en dag voort gaan / door dien 't vuur altijdt moet branden; aen Turf en Hout is alle week wel in dit Huys van doen voor 150. of 160. guldens 'daer by so veel werk-lieden en anders / dat Jaar-lijks een over groote kosten beloopt."

4. This information was provided by Margriet de Roever, Gemeen-tearchief, Amsterdam.

5. "Wyst de verschillende manierlykheid in het aanvatten van een glas aan: de een grypt het met de volle hand, No. 1. En den ander vat het met weinig meer manierlyheid onder aan. No. 2 In tegendeel ziet men No. 3 als een Vorstin, een kelk met de toppunten haarer drie vingers houden, terwyl zy de pink voorzichtig op een aangename wyze van het glas ligt. Wederom ziet gy No. 4 een Staatsjuffer verbeeldende, doch niet zo bevallig aanvatten. Een Vorst wederom No. 5. vat het zelve,

behendig en voorzichtig onder aan de voet." This book is in the col-lection of the Museum Boijmans Van Beuningen, Rotterdam.

6. See note 4.

7. "De jonge luyden, die nieulijcx gehuwet zijn, past dese Sinnepop ter herten te nemen, die eerst voor al behooren te dencken om den nootruftighen uytloop ende behoeftigheydt; soo van huysraet als van spyse: maer als zy wat koevereren met sparen of deur goede neeringhe, dan komen zy tijds ghenoegh om haer lust te soecken, te weten, als de rijckdom soo veel gegroeyt is, datse dwaesheydt en draghen kan."

8. "Groot-Hoorns-, Enkhuiser-, Alkmaarder- en Purmerender Liede-boek."

O schoone wyn! Uw kristalyn
Gezigt verligt ons alderhande smart.
O schoone wyn! Gij dryft de pyn
En zwarigheit van 't hert.
Uw edele deugd bemin ik bovenal
Soo lang ik leven sal.
Avous Buurman, dit geld u dan,
Dat 's uw gesondheyd met een volle fluit.

9. This term was coined by Thorstein Veblen in 1899 (Veblen 1994, p. 52).

10. "Daar is noch een andere soort van Stilleven, die van de ge-ringste niet is, en by de voorgaande een welstandige en niet min cier-lycke veranderinge zoude geeven. Het is die welke in allerhande koste-lykheden bestaat, als goud, zilver, kristalle en andere glazen, paerlen, edelgesteentens en paerlemoer, gemeenlyk Vanitassen genaamd. De vermaarde Kalf, die veele heerlycke en uitmuntende voorbeelden daar van heeft nagelaaten, heeft in deze zeer uitgemunt, en boven allen den hoogsten lof verdiend."

11. "Het is ook niet waarschijnlijk, dat lieden van vermogen, die alles rykelyk bezitten, eenig vermaak zouden scheppen in ouwerwetse goederen van spiegels, zilvere en goude potten, kannen, schenkborden, en andere kostelykheden meer, en met de zelve willen pronken, daar zy alles schoonder en cierlycker konnen hebben. . . . Wij stellen ook vast, dat geene voorwerpen, in de Stillevens te pas gebragt, minder dan le-vensgroot mogen verbeeld worden."

12. The Victoria and Albert Museum in London has a similar glass, illustrated in Wilkinson 1968, p. 86, fig. 41.

13. These images are part of the *Boijmans Van Beuningen Documen-tation System of Pre-industrial Utensils* © 1989, which contains alpha-betically arranged references to all of the implements depicted in prints and paintings in the museum's collection.

14. The French surgeon Ambroise Paré (1517–1590) noted that one pound of "corne di licorne" (unicorn's horn) cost 1,536 écus, com-pared with one pound of gold, which cost 148 écus (Lewin 1920, p. 44).

15. See Collard 2000. The term "terra sigillata" probably refers to "terra lemnia," which was used in powdered form as an astringent and for other medical applications.

## Façon de Venise Glass in the Netherlands
*Reino Liefkes*
(pp. 226–269)

1. In April 1537, Jacob Stuer and Bernard Swerts, who operated a "crystalline" glasshouse, sent a letter to Maria of Austria, governess of the country, and to the city magistrate. They sought permission to prac-tice their craft under imperial protection for 20 years, as well as a glass-

making monopoly in the Netherlands. It is not known whether their request was granted.

2. In 1598, Vinckx asked for permission to enlarge the furnace with two "potz ou places à besoigner." Two personnel lists dating from the time when the factory was under her direction show an increase in the number of master glassmakers from six to eight.

3. The plea was issued in December 1594 by the merchants Henric Hudde and Reynier Pauw because three crates of crystalline glasses, made in Antwerp following the collapse of the furnace in Middelburg, had been embargoed.

4. Van der Haghe also received a one-year license, a complimentary escort for his first six ships laden with raw materials, a salary increase to 250 guilders (three-fifths of which was paid by the province, and the remainder by the city), a two-year loan of 200 guilders, and assurance from the magistrate that his workforce would not be lured away to other glass factories.

5. This monopoly may have forced glasshouses in Liège, Mézières, and Cologne to go out of business temporarily.

6. In 1589, Obizzo had been sentenced *in absentia* to four years on the galleys for breaking his contract in Murano.

7. Only then would the magistrate be inclined to prevent competition. Zijlstra-Zweens (1993) suggests that the traditional rivalry between Holland and Zeeland may have played a role in this arrangement.

8. It is likely that the glass came from Soop's glasshouse because his financial backer, Jan Jansz Carel, was one of the trading company's main shareholders. A list shows that the glass pieces were of nine different types, and it provides values for all of them. The total cost of the glass was about 17 guilders, while the cloth was valued at 90 guilders. The glass included ice glass and filigree beakers, "French goblets," small bowls, "porcelains fatsoen," and round blue bottles.

9. Soop described his own factory as a "really beautiful house and a glasshouse, which was not just for living and business, but also enhanced the city." Its facade was decorated with a stone showing glassblowers and a furnace.

10. Van Tongerloo was granted a sizable, interest-free loan on the condition that his building would be completed according to the plans prescribed by the city.

11. In 1606, Miotti, the master glassblower at the factory, had to declare that the Amsterdam merchants owned the glasshouse. They paid 600 guilders for its purchase, as well as additional sums for raw materials (such as soda and wood) and tools. Miotti had to promise to sell the goods mentioned in the contract only to the Amsterdam merchants.

12. In 1696, negotiations for building a large glasshouse took place in Amsterdam. Zutphen was chosen as the location for the new factory because of its proximity to Amsterdam and Rotterdam, as well as the local availability of wood.

13. Schadee (1989, pp. 19–20) gives more details but no source. By the end of the 17th century, there were many more glasshouses working for local markets.

14. Both of these sources report the numbers of drinking glasses in some 16th-century Dutch inventories.

15. This plea is undated, but it must have been written before 1642. *Waldglas* was produced in the Northern Netherlands, but probably only in small quantities. Schadee (1989, pp. 18–19) states that, in 1614, an attempt was made to start production of "house or window glass" in Rotterdam, but this probably did not include vessels. However, Klein (1982, p. 33) assumes that vessels were included.

16. Theuerkauff-Liederwald (1994, p. 123) provides the numbers of *roemers* ordered from Amsterdam. In 1685, the Laubacher Hütte received an order from Amsterdam for 20,000 "Heilbronner Römer" and 10,000 "Schenkrömer." For more information on trade with the Netherlands, see Krimm 1984, pp. 170–175. Until 1684, the Spessart glass-

house was the main supplier of the Amsterdam merchant (*Grosskaufman*) Tönies Jacobs, who bought "tausend glass" in Cologne annually. In 1687, the Spessart glasshouse attempted to become the second supplier of Fabri, another Amsterdam merchant, in case the Laubacher Hütte could not deliver its orders to him.

17. In the 16th century, the retail price of imported glass from Germany was about 15 times its production cost. Crystalline glasses could be three to 14 times as expensive as green *roemers*.

18. De Raedt and others 1997, p. 369, states, on the basis of archeological evidence, that the importation of glass from Venice seems to have ceased in the 17th century.

19. Since the closing of the Antwerp harbors in 1609, the trade with Venice had shifted to the Northern Netherlands, but imports of Venetian glass seem to have been limited to beads and mirrors very soon thereafter. Glass and potash were among the wares listed as having been exported to Venice!

20. The owners claimed that they could export glass to England, Moscow, and the Orient.

21. These figures may have been somewhat different in other glasshouses, depending on transportation costs and other factors.

22. Denissen (1985, p. 15) states that, in 1629, the furnace at the Antwerp glasshouse was shut down in order to sell the existing stock and to save on the heavy costs of wood used in its operation. Klein (1982, p. 40) mentions that, because of a lack of wood, Soop's Amsterdam glasshouse had to cease production for four months in 1618. Soop even resorted to burning masts to provide wood for a time.

23. The first glasshouses in Antwerp, Middelburg, and Amsterdam illustrate perfectly this level of support. As has been noted, the Middelburg magistrate granted Govaert van der Haghe considerable assistance in setting up his glasshouse in 1581, and in 1586 the glassmaker was also granted citizenship. When Van der Haghe expanded his business in 1597, he received additional favorable terms, which are detailed in note 4.

24. By 1698, all but a few of these glasshouses had been liquidated, often at great loss.

25. Klein (1982, p. 43) notes the reasons for this failure, which contrasts both with the development of other industries in the Netherlands and with the progress of the glass industry elsewhere.

26. Both master glassmakers and other skilled workers were likely to be lured away by rival glasshouses. When Abraham van Tongerloo began to compete with Jan Hendrickz Soop in Amsterdam about 1613, the latter complained that his rival had taken his masters and journeymen. In this way, Soop's complaint maintained, Van Tongerloo had acquired glassmakers without any effort and at Soop's expense, and had proceeded to sell his wares below the market price.

27. In 1666, the Haarlem glasshouse imported 20 tons of sand from Jüllich in Germany.

28. Coal was used as early as 1666 to fuel the glasshouse at Haarlem, which was operated by the Englishman John Billingham. He was hired to produce mirrors as well as drinking glasses.

29. Mongardo's new glasshouse in Antwerp was equipped with a shop. A shop assistant appears on the personnel lists that date from the period when his widow, Sara Vinckx, directed the factory. Hudig (1923, p. 29, n. 102) states that the August 22, 1597, agreement between the glassmaker Antonio Obizzo and the mayor and treasurer of Amsterdam stipulated that the city would pay for the construction of a shop at the glassworks.

30. This engraving, which appears on page 449, bears the caption "Instrumenta Et Fornax Vitraria apud Amstelodamenses." There are two versions of the Amsterdam Latin edition. One has the date 1668 on the frontispiece, and the other is dated 1669.

31. The tunnel lehr is first described in Merret's 1662 English translation of Neri. It is shown and described in the 1668–1669 engraving:

"The annealing furnace (m) with its entrance opening (n) and its exit side (o)."

32. Roever (1991, p. 165) illustrates this frontispiece from a 1668 edition. P. Francis (2000, p. 48 and fig. 3) suggests that the frontispiece illustrates a glasshouse in Nijmegen, on the basis of its architectural details. This is purely speculative, however. The furnace is clearly identical to the one in Amsterdam that is illustrated elsewhere in the volume.

33. The second glasshouse in Amsterdam, which was founded in 1601 and managed by Soop, employed both glassmakers from Antwerp and many Italians who had secretly been brought in from Venice at a cost of Dfl. 5,000. Hudig (1923, p. 27) also reports that Miotti, who ran the Middelburg glasshouse in the early 17th century, was lured away to London in 1619. However, just four years later, he founded new businesses in Brussels and Namur.

34. The glassmaker Louis Gaillard, from the Dauphiné, worked in Zwolle and Gouda. He stated that he had left his country because of the "cruelty of the king of France."

35. In an undated plea to the Amsterdam government (before 1642), Jacques Casteleyn complained about "the tax on beer, which is used in great quantities because of the heat of the furnace. . . ." In many other instances, tax-free beer was supplied to glasshouses as part of a benefits package.

36. This is the same Nicolaas Jaquet who, later that year, directed the Rotterdam glasshouse. In a Liège contract of 1651, the job of *consoir* is fully described in French.

37. The *consoir*'s responsibilities were outlined by two Haarlem masters in 1681. They maintained that a *consoir* should always have 18 to 20 spare crucibles ready in order to respond to unforeseen circumstances.

38. Louis Gaillard, who was the technical manager of a small Gouda glasshouse in 1698, received—in addition to free rent, heating, and lighting—the enormous sum of Dfl. 500 per year. His piece-wages could add another Dfl. 20 weekly. A century earlier, Antonio Obizzo had earned a yearly salary of Dfl. 50 in Amsterdam. In late 16th- and early 17th-century Middelburg, annual salaries varied between Dfl. 150 and 300.

39. Sara Vinckx's personnel lists show that she employed six Italian masters. She later expanded her furnace to include two more work openings, which allowed her to employ an additional two masters. See p. 229 and n. 2.

40. Sara Vinckx's personnel lists provide an indication of the numbers of employees at her Antwerp glasshouse. The first list includes six master glassmakers, five "dienaars" (assistants), four "knechten" (apprentices), four porters, one "facteur," and a shop assistant. The second list includes two additional masters and another assistant.

41. Nicolaas Jaquet had moved to Rotterdam from Haarlem in 1681. The *vorblaser* and the two masters had special contracts. The most detailed division of duties is recorded for the window glass factory that Matthieu Simony de Tournay constructed in Zutphen. In 1690, Simony employed fellow Huguenot glassmakers for the specialized functions of *cueilleur*, who gathered glass from the pot and inflated it; *bossier*, who further inflated the glass; *ouvreur*, who opened up the glass and spread it out; and *tiseur*, who melted the glass and tended the fire.

42. An account of 1670 mentions "the furnace, the bellows and everything that belonged to it." The bellows may have been used by the stoker, but the only other recorded use of bellows was for lampworking, as described by Neri (Hudig 1923, p. 49). Hudig (*ibid.*, p. 42) also reports that Guy Libon hired a French stoker for his Amsterdam glasshouse in 1640.

43. Hudig (1923) notes several instances. In his April 26, 1613, contract with the mayor and treasurer of Amsterdam, Abraham van Tongerloo agreed that he would, "besides his regular personnel, permanently employ 50 men of over 16 years old, who would be allocat-

ed to him by the mayor. Their salary would be 5 *stuyvers* (*rappen*) per day for the first four months and six *stuyvers* after that, on the condition that damage through breakage of glass and mirrors would be at Van Tongerloo's risk" (p. 39). Soop claimed that he could employ more than 80 families (p. 35, n. 122). In Middelburg, Miotti employed 60 girls, boys, and widows (p. 26).

44. In 1640, the piece-wage for 100 wine or beer glasses was 22 *stuyvers*. Thirty years later, this had increased to 45–50 *stuyvers* for 100 wineglasses, and to 35 or 40 *stuyvers* for 100 or 110 beer glasses. At Gouda in 1697, the pay for 180–220 beer glasses was the same as that for 120 wineglasses. Hudig (1923, pp. 41–42) states that the Altarists Castellano and Marino were employed by Guy Libon in Amsterdam in 1639 to make "verres de cristalles de toutte fasson." They earned "diex pistolles despagne," for which they had to deliver 110 glasses a day.

45. For 120 beer glasses, Colnet received the relatively low sum of Dfl. 1.10, from which he was still obligated to pay his own journeymen and apprentice.

46. These were the requirements for François Colnet in 1675. Louys Myot, who worked at the same glasshouse in 1666, had an identical arrangement, but he was paid Dfl. 3.15 for the same amount of glasses.

47. This was the case at the Antwerp glasshouse during the management of Sara Vinckx.

48. These payments ranged from Dfl. 3 to Dfl. 8 per week, depending on the workers' skills. At Gouda in 1697, the workers received Dfl. 2–6 per week when the furnaces were not in operation. Hudig (1923, p. 61) states that, in Rotterdam, when the furnace was out of use from December 1683 to March 1684, the workers complained that the manager Nicolaas Jaquet paid his masters only 10 *stuyvers* and two loaves of bread per week (with a small additional sum for clothes), while less qualified personnel were simply fired.

49. The Altarists Castellano and Marino, who worked for Guy Libon in Amsterdam, were offered such additional benefits in 1639–1640.

50. Glassmakers did not always have to look for new opportunities because they were sometimes recruited by specialized agents. In 1619, James Howell, agent of Sir Robert Mansell in London, wrote from Middelburg: "Sigr Anthonio Miotti who was master of a crystall-glasse-furnace here a long time, and as I have it by good intelligence, he is one of the ablest, and most knowing men, for the guidance of a Glasswork in Christendom; Therefore according to my instructions, I send him over and hope to have done Sir Robert good service thereby." Hudig (1923, p. 69) states that Jean Tilman d'Heur, who worked for Bonhomme in Den Bosch, undertook a "study trip" to France and Italy in 1662 to recruit new glassblowers.

51. Hudig (1923, pp. 86–96) devotes a lot of attention to this case, using these letters in the Zutphen archives.

52. I am grateful to William Gudenrath and Stephen P. Koob of The Corning Museum of Glass for sharing their technical observations with me, and to Lorne Campbell of the National Gallery, London, for offering his thoughts on the painting.

# Bibliography

Most works are cited by author(s) and date (e.g., Henkes 1994). When the same author(s) published more than one work in a single year, the works are distinguished by lowercase letters immediately after the date (e.g., Rochebrune 2002a, 2002b). When two or more authors have the same surname, they are identified by the initial letters of their given names (e.g., Buckley, F. 1914; Buckley, W. 1929). Exhibition catalogs are cited by name and date (e.g., *Archéologie du Grand Louvre* 2001). Catalogs (including sale catalogs) of well-known private collections are cited by owner's name and date (e.g., *Lehman Collection* 1993). Entries beginning with a cardinal or ordinal number, expressed either as a numeral or spelled out, will be found after the alphabetical entries, arranged numerically.

The following abbreviations are used in the bibliography and in the text:

## A. Names of Publications

| | |
|---|---|
| AnnAIHV | *Annales de l'Association Internationale pour l'Histoire du Verre* |
| JGS | *Journal of Glass Studies* |
| PMA | *Post-Medieval Archaeology* |

## B. Other

| | |
|---|---|
| bk. | book |
| chap. | chapter |
| comp. | compiler |
| doc. | document |
| ed. | edited by, editor, edition |
| fig. | figure |
| fol. | folio |
| ill., ills. | illustration, illustrations |
| n., nn. | note, notes |
| n.d. | no date |
| no., nos. | number, numbers |
| n.s. | new series |
| opp. | opposite |
| p., pp. | page, pages |
| pl. | plate |
| pt. | part |
| repr. | reprint |
| rev. | revised |
| ser. | series |
| trans. | translated by, translator |
| unpub. | unpublished |
| v., vv. | volume, volumes |

*A travers le verre* 1989
*A travers le verre: Du Moyen Age à la Renaissance*, ed. Danièle Foy and Geneviève Sennequier, Rouen: Musée Départemental des Antiquités, 1989.

Adamson 1995
Melitta Weiss Adamson, "'Unus teutonicus plus bibit quam duo latini': Food and Drink in Late Medieval Germany," *Medium Aevum Quotidianum*, v. 33, 1995, pp. 8–20.

Ainaud de Lasarte [1952]
Juan Ainaud de Lasarte, *Ceramica y vidrio*, Madrid: Editorial Plus-Ultra, [1952].

*Allgemeines Künstler-Lexikon* 1995
*Allgemeines Künstler-Lexikon: Die Bildenden Künstler aller Zeiten und Völker*, v. 11, Munich and Leipzig: Saur, 1995, p. 373.

Almela y Vives 1954
F. Almela y Vives, *La antigua industria del vidrio en Valencia*, Valencia: Revista Feriario, 1954.

Alvey 1973
Robert Alvey, "A Cesspit Excavation at 26–28 High Pavement, Nottingham," *Transactions of the Thoroton Society*, v. 77, 1973, pp. 53–72.

*Antiquités* 1913
*Catalogue des antiquités et objets d'art* (collection of Baron Henri Steengracht van Duivenvoorde), sale catalog, Amsterdam: Frederik Muller & Cie, May 6–9, 1913.

*Applewhaite-Abbott Collection* 1953
*Catalogue of the Well-Known Collection of Coloured Glass and French Paperweights Formed by the Late Mrs. Applewhaite-Abbott*, pt. 4, sale catalog, London: Sotheby's, June 15, 1953.

*Archéologie de la ville Orléans* 1987
*Archéologie de la ville Orléans*, v. 3, *Revue Archéologique du Loiret*, no. 13, Neuville-aux-Bois, France: Fédération Archéologique du Loiret, 1987.

*Archéologie du Grand Louvre* 2001
*Archéologie du Grand Louvre: Le Quartier du Louvre au XVII<sup>e</sup> siècle*, Paris: Réunion des Musées Nationaux, 2001.

Archives n.d.
Archives Nationales, Minutier Central des Notaires, Paris, France.

Arnould 1990
Maurice-A. Arnould, "De pot-de-vin," in *Van Rank tot Drank*, Brussels: Didier Hatier, 1990, pp. 264–265.

*Ars vitraria* 1965
*Ars vitraria: 3000 Jahre Glas*, Berlin: Staatliche Museen zu Berlin, Kunstgewerbemuseum, 1965.

Baart 1998
Jan M. Baart, "De Amsterdamse glashuizen en hun productie," in Hubert Vreeken, *Glas in het Amsterdams Historisch Museum en Museum Willet Holthuysen*, Amsterdam: Amsterdams Historisch Museum, and Zwolle: Waanders Uitgevers, 1998, pp. 26–35.

Baart, Krook, and Lagerweij 1984
J. M. Baart, W. Krook, and A. C. Lagerweij, "Der Gebrauch von Glas in Amsterdam im 17. Jahrhundert," in Klaus Grimm, *Glück und Glas*, Munich: Verlag Kunst & Antiquitäten, 1984, pp. 34–47.

Backmann 1997
Sibylle Backmann, "Kunstagenten oder Kaufleute? Die Firma Ott im Kunsthandel (1550–1650)," in *Colloquia Augustana*, v. 5, *Kunst und ihre Auftraggeber im 16. Jahrhundert Venedig und Augsburg im Vergleich*, ed. Klaus Bergdoldt and Jochen Brüning, Berlin: Akademie, 1997, pp. 175–197.

Bakker 1991
Boudewijn Bakker, "Amsterdam en Venetië: Twee steden verbeeld," in *Amsterdam: Venetië van het Noorden*, ed. Margriet de Roever, 's-Gravenhage: Gary Schwartz, and Amsterdam: Gemeente-Archief, 1991, pp. 10–27.

Barovier Mentasti 1982
Rosa Barovier Mentasti, *Il vetro veneziano: Dal Medioevo al Novecento*, Milan: Electa, 1982.

Barrelet 1953
James Barrelet, *La Verrerie en France de l'époque gallo-romaine à nos jours*, Paris: Larousse, 1953.

Barrelet 1957
James Barrelet, "Le Verre à boire en France au XVIIIᵉ siècle," *Cahiers de la Céramique et des Arts du Feu*, no. 7, Summer 1957, pp. 100–117.

Barrelet 1964
James Barrelet, "Porcelaines de verre en France: Des secrets de Bernard Perrot aux recherches scientifiques de Réaumur," *Cahiers de la Céramique du Verre*, v. 36, 1964, pp. 254–286.

Barrera 1990
Jorge Barrera, "Le Verre à boire des fouilles de la Cour Napoléon du Louvre (Paris)," *AnnAIHV*, v. 11, Bâle, 1988 (Amsterdam, 1990), pp. 347–364.

Bassegoda y Amigó 1925
Bonaventura Bassegoda y Amigó, *Santa Maria del Mar: Monografia històrico artistica del temple*, Barcelona, 1925.

Baudrillard 1988
Jean Baudrillard, "The System of Objects," trans. Jacques Mourrain, in *Jean Baudrillard: Selected Writings*, ed. Mark Poster, Palo Alto, California: Stanford University Press, 1988, pp. 10–29.

Bauer 1980
Margrit Bauer, *Europäisches und Aussereuropäisches Glas*, Frankfurt am Main: C. and M. Pfoh Stiftung and Museum für Kunsthandwerk, 1980.

Bellanger 1988
Jacqueline Bellanger, *Verre d'usage et de prestige: France, 1500–1800*, Paris: Editions de l'Amateur, 1988.

Bénard and Dragesco 1989
Jacques Bénard and Bernard Dragesco, *Bernard Perrot et les Verreries Royales du Duché d'Orléans, 1662–1754*, Orléans: Edition des Amis du Musée d'Orléans, 1989.

Bencard 2000
Mogens Bencard, *Rosenborg Studier*, Copenhagen: De Danske Kongers Kronologiske Samling, 2000.

*Bernal Collection* 1857
Henry George Bohn, *A Guide to the Knowledge of Pottery, Porcelain, and Other Objects of Vertu. Comprising an Illustrated Catalogue of the Bernal Collection . . .* , London: the author, 1857.

Berry 1994
Christopher Berry, *The Idea of Luxury: A Conceptual and Historical Investigation*, Cambridge: Cambridge University Press, 1994.

Bie 1634
Jacques de Bie, *La France métallique contenant les actions célèbres tant publiques que privées des rois et des reines*, Paris: Jean Camusat, 1634.

Biringuccio 1990
Vannoccio Biringuccio, *The Pirotechnia of Vannoccio Biringuccio: The Classic Sixteenth-Century Treatise on Metals and Metallurgy*, trans. and ed. Cyril Stanley Smith and Maria Teach Gnudi, New York: Dover Publications Inc., 1990.

Bles 1925
Joseph Bles, *Rare English Glasses of the XVII and XVIII Centuries*, Boston: Houghton Mifflin, 1925.

Bondois 1936–1937
Paul-M. Bondois, "Le Développement de l'industrie verrière dans la région parisienne de 1515 à 1665," *Revue d'Histoire Economique et Sociale* (Paris), no. 1, 1936–1937, pp. 49–72.

Bonnaffé 1874
Edmond Bonnaffé, *Inventaire des meubles de Catherine de Médicis en 1589*, Paris: A. Aubry, 1874.

Böttiger 1909
John Böttiger, *Philipp Hainhofer und der Kunstschrank Gustav Adolfs in Uppsala*, trans. Ernst A. Meyer, Stockholm: Verlag der Lithografischen Anstalt des Generalstabs, v. 1, 1909.

Boutillier 1885
François (Abbé) Boutillier, *La Verrerie et les gentilshommes verriers de Nevers*, Nevers: Imp. Fay, G. Vallière, 1885.

Braudel 1987–1988
Fernand Braudel, *Beschaving, economie en kapitalisme (15de–18de eeuw)*, 3 vv., Amsterdam: Contact, 1987–1988.

Braun 1932
J. Braun, *Das christliche Altargerät in seinem Sein und in seiner Entwicklung*, Munich: M. Hueber, 1932.

Broc de Segange 1863
Louis du Broc de Segange, *Les Faïenciers et les émailleurs de Nevers*, Nevers: Société Nivernaise, 1863.

Browne 1672
Thomas Browne, *Pseudodoxia epidemica*, 6th ed., London: printed by J. R. for N. Ekins, 1672.

Bryson 1990
Norman Bryson, *Looking at the Overlooked: Four Essays on Still Life Painting*, London: Reaktion Books Ltd., 1990.

Bücking 1968
Jürgen Bücking, *Kultur und Gesellschaft in Tirol um 1600, des Hippolytus Guarinonius Grewel der Verwüstung menschlichen Geschlechts (1610) als kulturgeschichtliche Quelle des frühen 17. Jahrhunderts*, Lübeck and Hamburg: Matthiesen Verlag, 1968.

Buckley, F. 1914
Francis Buckley, *The Glass Trade in England in the Seventeenth Century*, London: Stevens & Sons, 1914.

Buckley, W. 1926
Wilfred Buckley, *European Glass: A Brief Outline of the History of Glass Making*, London: Ernest Benn, 1926.

Buckley, W. 1929
Wilfred Buckley, *Diamond Engraved Glasses of the Sixteenth Century, with Particular Reference to Five Attributed to Giacomo Verzelini*, London: Ernest Benn Ltd., 1929.

Buckley, W. 1939
Wilfred Buckley, *The Art of Glass*, London: Phaidon Press, and New York: Oxford University Press, 1939.

Buechner 1955
Thomas S. Buechner, "Art in Glass," *Art News Annual*, v. 24, 1955, pp. 134–150+.

Bulard 1935
Marcel Bulard, *Le Scorpion: Symbole du peuple juif dans l'art religieux des XIVᵉ, XVᵉ, XVIᵉ siècles*, no. 6 of *Annales de l'Est, Faculté de Lettres de Nancy, Mémoires*, Paris: E. de Boccard, 1935.

Burke 1992
Peter Burke, "The Uses of Italy," in *The Renaissance in National Context*, ed. Roy Porter and Mikulas Teich, Cambridge: Cambridge University Press, 1992, pp. 6–20.

Cabart 1990
Hubert Cabart, "Metz, Espace Serpenoise: Verrerie des XIV–XVIIᵉᵐᵉˢ siècles," in *Verrerie de l'Est de la France, XIIIᵉ–XVIIIᵉ siècles*, Dijon: Revue Archéologique de l'Est et du Centre-Est, 1990, pp. 223–232.

*Cabinets of Arts and Curiosities* 1995
*Cabinets of Arts and Curiosities: Five Centuries of Arts and Crafts Collecting*, Prague: Uměleckoprůmyslové Muzeum, 1995.

Calvijn 1900
Joh. Calvijn, *Uitleging op de Profetieën van de Profeten Jesaja en Jeremia*, ed. L. W. van Deventer and E. C. Gravemeijer, Utrecht: A. H. ten Bokkel Hvinink, 1900.

Capmany i de Montpalau 1779–1792
Antonio de Capmany i de Montpalau, *Memorias históricas sobre la marina, comercio y artes de la antigua ciudad de Barcelona*, Madrid: A. de Sancha, 1779–1792.

Carboni 1998
Stefano Carboni, "Gregorio's Tale; or, Of Enamelled Glass Production in Venice," in *Gilded and Enamelled Glass from the Middle East*, ed. Rachel Ward, London: British Museum Press, 1998, pp. 101–106.

Carreras 1998
Jordi Carreras, "Servidora catalane de vidre esmaltat," *Barcelona Metròpolis Mediterrània*, no. 43, Barcelona: Barcelona Municipal Council, September–October 1998, pp. 58–59.

Carreras 2001
Jordi Carreras, "Els vidres catalans *à la façon de Venise* del Museu de les Arts Decoratives de Barcelona (segles XVI–XVII)," in *I Jornades hispàniques d'història del vidre, Actes*, v. 1, ed. Teresa Carreras Rossell, Barcelona: Museu d'Arqueologia de Catalunya, 2001, pp. 143–153.

Carreras and Doménech 1994
Jordi Carreras and Ignasi Doménech, "El vidre de taula a Catalunya a l'època del Gòtic," *Del Rebost a la taula: Cocina y alimentación en la Barcelona gòtica*, Barcelona: Electa, 1994, pp. 71–76.

Carreras and Doménech 2000
Jordi Carreras and Ignasi Doménech, "El vidre sumptuari a la Corona d'Aragó entre els segles XV i XVI," *Sucre & Borja: La canyamel dels Ducs*, Gandia: Centre d'Estudis Alfons el Vell, 2000, pp. 421–426.

Carreras and Doménech 2003
Teresa Carreras and Ignasi Doménech, *Museu Cau Ferrat: La collecció de vidre*, Sitges: Consorci del Patrimoni de Sitges, 2003.

Cats 1627
Jacob Cats, "Proteus, ofte, Minne- beelden verandert," in *Sinne Minnebeelden*, Rotterdam: Bij Pictor van Walsberge, 1627, p. 7.

Chambon 1955
Raymond Chambon, *L'Histoire de la verrerie en Belgique*, Brussels: Librairie Encyclopédique, 1955.

Chambon 1961
Raymond Chambon, "La Verrerie dans le Brabant Wallon au début de la Renaissance," *JGS*, v. 3, 1961, pp. 39–49.

Charleston 1962
Robert J. Charleston, "Some Tools of the Glassmaker in Medieval and Renaissance Times, with Special Reference to the Glassmaker's Chair," *Glass Technology*, v. 3, no. 3, June 1962, pp. 107–111.

Charleston 1968
R. J. Charleston, "George Ravenscroft: New Light on the Development of His 'Christalline Glasses,'" *JGS*, v. 10, 1968, pp. 156–167.

Charleston 1972
Robert Charleston, "The Vessel Glass from Rosedale and Hutton," in David Crossley and Alan Aberg, "Sixteenth Century Glassmaking in Yorkshire: Excavations at the Furnaces of Hutton and Rosedale, North Riding, 1968–71," *PMA*, v. 6, 1972, pp. 128–150.

Charleston 1975
Robert Charleston, "The Glass," in Colin Platt and Richard Coleman-Smith, *Excavations in Medieval Southampton*, v. 2, *The Finds*, Leicester: Leicester University Press, 1975, pp. 204–226.

Charleston 1978
Robert J. Charleston, "Glass Furnaces through the Ages," *JGS*, v. 20, 1978, pp. 9–33.

Charleston 1980
Robert J. Charleston, *Masterpieces of Glass: A World History from The Corning Museum of Glass*, New York: Harry N. Abrams Inc., 1980.

Charleston 1984a
Robert J. Charleston, *English Glass and the Glass Used in England, circa 400–1940*, London: George Allen and Unwin, 1984.

Charleston 1984b
Robert Charleston, "The Glass," in John P. Allan, *Medieval and Post-Medieval Finds from Exeter, 1971–80*, Exeter Archaeological Reports, no. 3, Exeter: Exeter City Council, 1984, pp. 258–278.

Charleston 1986
Robert J. Charleston, "Glass from Plymouth," in *Plymouth Excavations. The Medieval Waterfront: Woolster Street, Castle Street*, ed. Cynthia Gaskell Brown, Plymouth, England: Plymouth City Museum and Art Gallery, 1986, pp. 36–52.

Charleston 1990
Robert J. Charleston, with contributions by David B. Whitehouse and Susanne K. Frantz, *Masterpieces of Glass: A World History from The Corning Museum of Glass*, expanded ed., New York: Harry N. Abrams Inc., 1990.

Charleston and Archer 1977
Robert J. Charleston and Michael Archer, *Glass and Stained Glass*, The James A. De Rothschild Collection at Waddesdon Manor, Fribourg: National Trust, Office du Livre, 1977.

Ciappi and others 1995
S. [Silvia] Ciappi and others, *Il vetro in Toscana: Strutture, prodotti, immagini, secc. XIII–XX*, Poggibonsi, Italy: Lalli, 1995.

Citroen 1998
Karel Citroen, "Rembrandt's Claudius Civilis: A Detail Disclosed," *Art Bulletin of Nationalmuseum Stockholm*, v. 5, 1998, pp. 73–76.

Clarke 1974
Timothy H. Clarke, "*Lattimo*—A Group of Venetian Glass Enameled on an Opaque-White Ground," *JGS*, v. 16, 1974, pp. 22–56.

*CMG Guide* 1958
T. S. Buechner and others, *Glass from The Corning Museum of Glass: A Guide to the Collections*, Corning, New York: the museum, 1958.

*CMG Guide* 1965
R. H. Brill and others, *Glass from The Corning Museum of Glass: A Guide to the Collections*, Corning, New York: the museum, 1965.

*CMG Guide* 1974
R. H. Brill and others, *Glass from The Corning Museum of Glass: A Guide to the Collections*, Corning, New York: the museum, 1974.

*CMG Guide* 2001
*The Corning Museum of Glass: A Guide to the Collections*, Corning, New York: the museum, 2001.

Collard 2000
Franck Collard, "Le Banquet fatal: La Table et le poison dans l'occident medieval," in *Actes du Colloque de Rouen*, vv. 23–25, Paris: Presses Universitaires de France, 2000, pp. 338–340.

Cordey 1930
Jean Cordey, "L'Inventaire après décès d'Anne d'Autriche et le mobilier du Louvre," *Bulletin de la Société de l'Histoire de l'Art Français*, 1930, pp. 228–275.

Courtney, in press
Paul Courtney, "Vessel Glass," in Robert Bell and Kirsty Rodwell, *Acton Court: The Evolution of an Early Tudor Courtier House*, London: English Heritage, in press.

Crépin-Leblond 1995
Thierry Crépin-Leblond, "Services en verre," in *Le Dressoir du Prince: Services d'apparat à la Renaissance*, Ecouen: Musée National de la Renaissance and Réunion des Musées Nationaux, 1995, pp. 85–94.

Csikszentmihalyi and Rochberg-Halton 1981
M. Csikszentmihalyi and E. Rochberg-Halton, *The Meaning of Things: Domestic Symbols and the Self*, Cambridge: Cambridge University Press, 1981.

Dacosta Kaufmann 1994
Thomas Dacosta Kaufmann, "From Treasury to Museum: The Collections of the Austrian Habsburgs," in *The Culture of Collecting*, ed. John Elsner and Roger Cardinal, Cambridge, Massachusetts: Harvard University Press, 1994, pp. 137–154.

Daléchamps 1586–1587
Jacques Daléchamps, *Historia Generalis Plantarum*, Lyons: Guillaume Rouillé, 1586–1587.

Daly 2000
Peter M. Daly, "Sixteenth-Century Emblems and Imprese as Indicators of Cultural Change," in *Interpretation and Allegory: Antiquity to the Modern Period*, Leiden and Boston: Brill, 2000, pp. 383–420.

Dant 1999
Tim Dant, *Material Culture in the Social World: Values, Activities, Lifestyles*, Buckingham, England: Open University Press, 1999.

Davis 1963
Frank Davis, "Talking About Sale-rooms, John Drawings and Ravenscroft Glass," *Country Life*, v. 134, no. 3462, July 11, 1963, pp. 88–89.

Davis 1972
Frank Davis, *Continental Glass*, New York: Praeger, 1972.

De Lairesse 1707
Gerard de Lairesse, *Groot Schilderboek*, Amsterdam: Willem de Coup and Petrus Schenk, 1707.

De Raedt and others 1997
Ine De Raedt and others, "Composition of 15th- to 17th-Century Glass Vessels Excavated in Antwerp, Belgium," in *Material Culture in Medieval Europe. Papers of the Medieval Europe Brugge 1997 Conference*, Zellik, Belgium: Instituut voor het Archeologisch Patrimonium, 1997, pp. 361–374.

Denissen 1985
Sabine Denissen, "Overzicht van de glasblazersfamilies te Antwerpen tijdens de 16de en de 17de eeuw," *Bulletin van de Antwerpse Vereniging voor Bodem- en Grotonderzoek*, no. 5, 1985, pp. 9–19.

Dexel 1983
Thomas Dexel, *Gebrauchsglas: Gläser des Alltags vom Spätmittelalter bis zum beginnenden 20. Jahrhundert*, Munich: Klinkhardt & Biermann, 1983.

Doering 1901
Oscar Doering, *Des Augsburger Patriciers Philipp Hainhofer Reisen nach Innsbruck und Dresden*, Vienna: Carl Graeser & Co., 1901.

Doménech 1997
Ignasi Doménech, *L'Art en transparència, v. 2, Una exposició de vidre antic, segles XVI–XVIII*, Barcelona: Sala d'Art Artur Ramón, 1997.

Doménech 1999
Ignasi Doménech, "El vidrio," in *Las artes decorativas en España*, Summa Artis, v. 45, pt. 1, Madrid: Espasa Calpe, 1999, pp. 489–540.

Doménech 2001
Ignasi Doménech, *L'art en transparència, v. 3, El vidrio y la pasión por coleccionarlo*, Barcelona: Sala d'Art Artur Ramón, 2001, pp. 9–13.

Dozy 1897
Charles Marius Dozy, "Pieter Nolpe: 1613/14–1652/53," *Oud Holland*, 1897, pp. 220–244.

Dreier 1989
Franz-Adrian Dreier, *Venezianische Gläser und "Façon de Venise"*, Berlin: D. Reimer, 1989.

Dreier 1994
Franz-Adrian Dreier, "Zur Frage der sog. 'Raimondi-Schalen.' Ein Beitrag zur Hinterglasmalerei des 16. Jahrhunderts," *Jahrbuch der Berliner Museen*, v. 36, 1994, pp. 141–163.

Dugast-Matifeux 1861
C. Dugast-Matifeux, "Les Gentilshommes Verriers de Mouchamps en Bas-Poitou, 1399," *Annales de la Société Académique de Nantes*, v. 32, 1861.

Dumortier 1999
Claire Dumortier, "Maiolica Production in Antwerp: The Documentary Evidence," in *Maiolica in the North: The Archaeology of Tin-Glazed Earthenware in North-West Europe, c. 1500–1600*, ed. David Gaimster, British Museum Occasional Papers, no. 122, London: the museum, 1999, pp. 107–111.

Egg 1962
Erich Egg, *Die Glashütten zu Hall und Innsbruck im 16. Jahrhundert*, Tiroler Wirtschaftsstudien. Schriftenreihe der Jubiläumsstiftung der Kammer der gewerblichen Wirtschaft für Tirol, v. 15, Innsbruck: Universitätsverlag Wagner, 1962.

El-Dekmak-Denissen 1988
Sabine El-Dekmak-Denissen, "Glas te Antwerpen in de 16de en de 17de eeuw," *Bulletin van de Antwerpse Vereniging voor Bodem- en Grotonderzoek*, no. 2, 1988, pp. 15–34.

Ellison 1979
Margaret Ellison, "The Glass," in "The Excavation of a 17th Century Pit at the Black Gate, Newcastle-upon-Tyne, 1975," *PMA*, v. 13, 1979, pp. 167–174.

Elville 1951
E. M. Elville, *English TableGlass*, London: Country Life, 1951.

*English and Continental Glass* 1978
*Important English and Continental Glass*, sale catalog, London: Christie's, October 3, 1978.

*English and Continental Glass* 1995
*English and Continental Glass and Paperweights*, sale catalog, London: Christie's, February 15, 1995.

Ennès 1982
Pierre Ennès, *La Verrerie ancienne*, Rennes: Ouest France, 1982.

Ennès 1997
Pierre Ennès, "Nouvelles acquisitions: Bouteille aux armes de Catherine de Médicis," *Revue du Louvre*, v. 47, nos. 5 and 6, December 1997, p. 112.

Esch 2002
Arnold Esch, "Nürnberg und Rom. Nürnbergische und andere deutsche Waren in den römischen Zollregistern der Frührenaissance," *Anzeiger des Germanischen Nationalmuseums Nürnberg*, 2002, pp. 128–139.

*European Glass* 1938
*Catalogue of a Fine Collection of Rare Gothic, Early Renaissance, and Later European Glass*, sale catalog, London: Sotheby & Co., Nov. 10, 1938.

*Exhibition of Early German Art* 1906
*Exhibition of Early German Art*, London: printed for the Burlington Fine Arts Club, 1906.

Fillon 1864
Bernard Fillon, *L'Art de terre chez les Poitevins, suivi d'une étude sur l'ancienneté de la fabrication du verre en Poitou*, Niort: L. Clouzot, 1864.

Fisher 1947
Mary Fisher, "The Earliest English Drinking Glass," *American Collector*, v. 16, no. 3, April 1947, p. 5.

Fleury, Brut, and Velde 2002
Michel Fleury, Catherine Brut, and Bruce Velde, "13th-Century Drinking Glasses from the Cour Carrée, Louvre," *JGS*, v. 44, 2002, pp. 95–110.

Fock 1992
C. Willemijn Fock, "Kunst en rariteiten in het Hollandse interieur," in *De Wereld binnen handbereik: Nederlandse kunst- en rariteitenver-

*zamelingen, 1585–1735* (catalog of exhibition at Amsterdam Historical Museum), Zwolle: Waanders Uitgevers, 1992, pp. 70–91.

Fokkens 1663
Melchior Fokkens, *Beschrijvinge der wijdt-vermaarde koop-stadt Amstelredam*, Amsterdam: [Abraham and Jan de Wees], 1663.

Folch i Torres [1926]
Joaquín Folch i Torres, *El tresor artistic de Catalunya: Els antics vidres Catalans esmaltats*, Barcelona: Editorial Poliglota, [1926].

*Four Approaches to Glass* 2001
*Four Approaches to Glass: Asian and Western Masterpieces Chosen for Their Techniques*, Tokyo: Suntory Museum of Art, 2001.

Foy, Averous, and Bourrel 1983
Danièle Foy, Jean-Claude Averous, and Bernard Bourrel, "Peyremoutou: Une verrerie du XVIIᵉ siècle dans la Montagne Noire (Tarn)," *Archéologie du Midi Médiéval*, v. 1, 1983, pp. 93–102.

Francis, G. R. 1926
Grant R. Francis, *Old English Drinking Glasses: Their Chronology and Sequence*, London: H. Jenkins Ltd., 1926.

Francis, P. 2000
Peter Francis, "The Development of Lead Glass: The European Connection," *Apollo*, v. 151, no. 456, February 2000, pp. 47–53.

Franits 1993
Wayne E. Franits, *Paragons of Virtue: Women and Domesticity in Seventeenth-Century Dutch Art*, Cambridge: Cambridge University Press, 1993.

*Franks Collection* 1912
O. M. Dalton, *The Franks Bequest. Catalogue of the Finger Rings: Early Christian, Byzantine . . . Bequeathed by Sir Augustus Wollaston Franks*, London: The British Museum, 1912.

Frémy 1909
Elphège Frémy, *Histoire de la manufacture royale des glaces de France au XVIIᵉ et au XVIIIᵉ siècle*, Paris: Librairie Plon-Nourrit, 1909.

Friedrich 1885
C. Friedrich, *Augustin Hirschvogel als Töpfer*, Nuremberg: Druck der Koenigl. bayr. Hofbuchdruckerei von Bieling-Dietz, 1885.

Frothingham 1941
Alice Wilson Frothingham, *Hispanic Glass, with Examples in the Collection of The Hispanic Society of America*, New York: the society, 1941.

Frothingham 1956
Alice Wilson Frothingham, *Barcelona Glass in Venetian Style*, New York: The Hispanic Society of America, 1956.

Frothingham 1963
Alice Wilson Frothingham, *Spanish Glass*, London: Faber and Faber, 1963.

Fryer and Shelley 1997
Kevin Fryer and Andrea Shelley, "Excavation of a Pit at 16 Tunsgate, Guildford Surrey, 1991," *PMA*, v. 31, 1997, pp. 139–230.

García Mercadal 1952
J. García Mercadal, *Viajes de extranjeros por España y Portugal*, v. 2, Madrid: Aguilar, 1952.

Garnier 1885
Edouard Garnier, "Les Gentilshommes Verriers," *Revue des Arts Décoratifs*, nos. 2–4, September/October 1885, pp. 65–70 and 97–105.

Gasparetto 1958
Astone Gasparetto, *Il vetro di Murano dalle origini e oggi*, Venice: N. Pozza, 1958.

Gasparetto 1975
Astone Gasparetto, "The Relations between Venice and Bohemia in the Field of Glassmaking at the Beginning of the Eighteenth Century," *Glass Review*, v. 30, no. 1, 1975, pp. 6–10.

Gavet Collection 1897
*Catalogue des objets d'arts . . . composant la collection de M. Emile Gavet*, Paris: Galerie Georges Petit, 1897.

Gaynor 1991
Suzanne Gaynor, "French Enameled Glass of the Renaissance," *JGS*, v. 33, 1991, pp. 42–81.

Gaynor 1994
Suzanne Gaynor, "More French Enameled Glass of the Renaissance," *JGS*, v. 36, 1994, pp. 130–133.

Geiselberger 2002
Siegmar Geiselberger, "'Gegossenes' oder 'gepresstes' Glas. Glasrelief mit dem portrait Louis XIV, von Bernardo Perrotto: Bernardo Perrotto, der judsiche Glasmacher aus Altare, das Geschlecht der Gonzaga und die Glasfiguren aus Orléans und Nevers," *Pressglas-Korrespondenz*, no. 1, 2002, pp. 37–53.

Gelder 1958
H. E. van Gelder, "De Rotterdamse glas-graveur Marinus van Gelder en Zijn tijdgenoten," *Bulletin Museum Boymans*, v. 9, no. 2, 1958, pp. 51–65.

Gerard 1633
John Gerard, *The Herball: or, Generall Historie of Plantes*, London: Adam Islip, Joice Norton, and Richard Whitakers, 1633.

Gesner 1575
K. Gesner, *Fischbuch*, Zurich, 1575 (translation of *Historiae animalium liber IV. Qui est de piscium & aquatilium animantium natura*, Zurich, 1558).

Gianolla and Junck 1997
Claudio Gianolla and Rosella Junck, *Draghi, serpenti e mostri marini nel vetro di Murano dell'800*, Venice: Junck & Gianolla, 1997.

Gil unpub.
Pere Gil, "Historia natural de Cataluña," about 1600 (manuscript from the Barcelona Episcopal Public Library, no. 115).

Giménez i Blasco 2001
Joan Giménez i Blasco, "Els Roig, un llinatge de vidriers al Mataró del segle XVII," in *I Jornades hispàniques d'història del vidre, Actes*, v. 1, ed. Teresa Carreras Rossell, Barcelona: Museu d'Arqueologia de Catalunya, 2001, pp. 179–189.

Giralt i Raventós 1957
Emili Giralt i Raventós, "El comercio maritimo de Barcelona entre 1630–1665: Hombres, técnicos y direcciones del tráfico," Ph.D. diss., Universidad de Barcelona, 1957.

Girancourt 1886
A. de Girancourt, *Nouvelle étude sur la verrerie de Rouen et la fabrication du cristal à la façon de Venise aux XVIᵉ et XVIIᵉ siècles*, Rouen: Imp. de Espérance Cagniard, 1886.

*Glas des 16. bis 19. Jahrhunderts* 1992
*Glas des 16. bis 19. Jahrhunderts. Hohlgläser aus dem Besitz des Bayerischen Nationalmuseums*, text by Rainer Rückert, Munich: Hirmer Verlag, 1992.

*Glass Drinking Vessels* 1955
[Jerome Strauss], *Glass Drinking Vessels from the Collections of Jerome Strauss and The Ruth Bryan Strauss Memorial Foundation*, Corning, New York: The Corning Museum of Glass, 1955.

*Glass of the Sultans* 2001
Stefano Carboni and David Whitehouse, with contributions by Robert H. Brill and William Gudenrath, *Glass of the Sultans*, New York: The Metropolitan Museum of Art in association with The Corning Museum of Glass, Benaki Museum, and Yale University Press, 2001.

Gobiet 1984
Ronald Gobiet, *Der Briefwechsel zwischen Philipp Hainhofer und Herzog August d. J. von Braunschweig-Lüneburg*, Munich: Deutscher Kunstverlag, 1984.

Godfrey 1975
Eleanor Godfrey, *The Development of English Glassmaking, 1560–1640*, Oxford: Clarendon Press, 1975.

Goetz 1990
Bernard Goetz, "Montbéliard—Cabaret de l'Hôtel de Ville: Verrerie du premier quart du XVII[eme] siècle," in *Verrerie de l'Est de la France, XIIIe–XVIIIe siècles: Fabrication, consommation*, Dijon: Revue Archéologique de l'Est et du Centre-Est, 1990, pp. 187–210.

Gougeon 2002
Catherine Gougeon, "La Bijouterie," in *Un temps d'exubérance: Les Arts décoratifs sous Louis XIII et Anne d'Autriche*, ed. Daniel Alcouffe and others, Paris: Réunion des Musées Nationaux, 2002, pp. 286–293.

Gozzi 1775
Gasparo Gozzi, *Del vetro: Libri quattro pubblicati in occasione de' gloriosi sponsali dell'Eccellenze Loro il signor Alvise Pisani et la nobil donna Giustiniana Pisani*, Venice: P. P. Brumoy, 1775.

Grau Monpó 2001
Antoni Grau Monpó, "L'Olleria, població cabdal en la història del vidre," in *I Jornades hispàniques d'història del vidre, Actes*, v. 1, ed. Teresa Carreras Rossell, Barcelona: Museu d'Arqueologia de Catalunya, 2001, pp. 201–211.

Graves 1960
Robert Graves, *The Greek Myths*, v. 1, London: Penguin Books, 1960.

Gréau Collection 1903
Wilhelm Froehner, *Collection Julien Gréau: Verrerie antique, émaillerie et poterie appartenant à M. John Pierpont Morgan*, Paris: Imprimerie Alsacienne Anct G. Fischbach, 1903.

Grimm 1984
Claus Grimm, "Stilleben als Quelle für Glasbesitz und Glasgebrauch," in *Glück und Glas: Zur Kulturgeschichte des Spessartsglases*, Munich: Verlag Kunst & Antiquitäten, 1984, pp. 294–309.

Gudenrath 1991
William Gudenrath, "Techniques of Glassmaking and Decoration," in *Five Thousand Years of Glass*, ed. Hugh Tait, London: British Museum Press, 1991, pp. 213–241.

Gudiol Ricart 1936
Josep [José] Gudiol Ricart, *Els vidres catalans*, Barcelona: Editorial Alpha, 1936.

Gudiol Ricart 1941
José Gudiol Ricart, *Los vidrios catalanes*, Monumenta cataloniae, v. 3, Barcelona: Editorial "Alpha," 1941.

Guépin Collection 1989
*The Guépin Collection of 17th and 18th Century Dutch Glass*, sale catalog, Amsterdam: Christie's, July 5, 1989.

Guiffrey 1894
Jules Guiffrey, *Inventaires de Jean duc de Berry (1401–1416)*, v. 1, Paris: E. Leroux, 1894.

Habsburg 1997
Géza von Habsburg, *Princely Treasures*, New York: Vendome Press, 1997.

Hall 1979
James Hall, *Dictionary of Subjects and Symbols in Art*, rev. ed., New York: Harper & Row, 1979.

Hampl 1951
Franz Hampl, "Waldviertler Glashütten," *Kulturberichte aus Niederösterreich*, v. 8, 1951, pp. 60–61.

Harrison 1968
William Harrison, *The Description of England*, ed. Georges Edelen, Ithaca, New York: Cornell University Press, 1968.

Hartshorne 1968
Albert Hartshorne, *Antique Drinking Glasses: A Pictorial History of Glass Drinking Vessels*, 2nd ed., New York: Brussel & Brussel, 1968.

Haslam 1993
Jeremy Haslam, "Glass Vessels," in *Norwich Households: Medieval and Post-Medieval Finds from Norwich Survey Excavations, 1971–78*, ed. Sue Margeson, East Anglian Archaeology Report, no. 58, Norwich: Norwich Survey/Norfolk Museums Service, Centre for East Anglian Studies, 1993, pp. 97–117.

Haynes 1948
E. Barrington Haynes, *Glass through the Ages*, Harmondsworth, England: Penguin, 1948.

Haynes 1959
E. Barrington Haynes, *Glass through the Ages*, rev. ed., Baltimore, Maryland: Penguin, 1959.

Heikamp 1986
Detlef Heikamp, *Studien zur mediceischen Glaskunst: Archivalien, Entwurfszeichnungen, Gläser und Scherben*, Florence: Leo S. Olschki for Kunsthistorisches Institut, 1986.

Heimer 1959
Heinrich Heimer, *Die Glashütte zu Hall in Tirol und die Augsburger Kaufmannsfamilie der Höchstetter*, Munich: W. & I. Salzer, 1959.

Heine Collection 1977
Sabine Baumgärtner, *Edles altes Glas: Die Sammlung Heinrich Heine im Gläserkabinett des Badischen Landesmuseums Karlsruhe*, Karlsruhe: Corona-Verlag, 1977.

Hejdová 1995
Dagmar Hejdová, "Das böhmische Glas bis zum Ende des 16. Jahrhunderts," in *Das böhmische Glas, 1700–1950*, v. 1, *Barock, Rococo, Klassizismus*, Passau: Passauer Glasmuseum, 1995, pp. 30–35.

Henderson and Jackson 1993
Julian Henderson and Susan Jackson, "Objects of Glass," in "Excavations in Hull, 1975–76," ed. David Evans, *East Riding Archaeologist*, v. 4, 1993, pp. 146–152.

Henkes 1974
H. E. Henkes, "Glasvondsten afkomstig van het kasteel te Ijsselmonde," *Hollande*, v. 6, 1974, pp. 19–32.

Henkes 1994
Harold E. Henkes, *Glas zonder glans: Vijf eeuwen gebruiksglas uit de bodem van de Lage Landen, 1300–1800/Glass without Gloss: Utility Glass from Five Centuries Excavated in the Low Countries, 1300–1800*, Rotterdam Papers 9, Rotterdam: Coördinatie Commissie van Advies inzake Archeologisch Onderzoek binnen het Ressort Rotterdam, 1994.

Héroard 1989
Jean Héroard, *Journal de Jean Héroard*, ed. Madeleine Foisil, Paris: Fayard, 1989.

Hess and Husband 1997
Catherine Hess and Timothy Husband, *European Glass in The J. Paul Getty Museum*, Los Angeles: the museum, 1997.

Hetteš 1960
Karel Hetteš, *Old Venetian Glass*, London: Spring Books, 1960.

Hetteš 1963
Karel Hetteš, "Venetian Trends in Bohemian Glassmaking in the Sixteenth and Seventeenth Centuries," *JGS*, v. 5, 1963, pp. 38–53.

Heye Collection 1957
*Sammlungen v. Blücher, Heye, Melder, Streber und anderer Kunstbesitz*, sale catalog, Cologne: Lempertz, November 21–25, 1957.

Hikari no shouchu 1992
*Hikari no shouchu: Sekai no garasu = The Glass*, Tokyo: Shueisha, 1992.

Hill 1970
Christopher Hill, *God's Englishman: Oliver Cromwell and the English Revolution*, London: Weidenfeld and Nicolson, 1970.

Hinton 1988
Peter Hinton, "Glass: Post-Medieval," in *Excavations in Southwark, 1973–76, and Lambeth, 1973–79*, ed. Peter Hinton, London: London & Middlesex Archaeological Society and Surrey Archaeological Society, Joint Publication No. 3, 1988, pp. 373–384.

Hirn 1885–1888
Joseph Hirn, *Erzherzog Ferdinand II. von Tirol, Ferdinand I*, v. 1, Innsbruck: Wagner, 1885–1888.

*Hockemeyer Collection* 1998
J. V. G. Mallet and F. A. Dreier, *The Hockemeyer Collection: Maiolica and Glass*, Bremen: H. M. Hauschild, 1998.

Hollister 1981
Paul Hollister, "'Flowers Which Clothe the Meadows in Spring': The Rebirth of Millefiori, c. 1500," *AnnAIHV*, v. 8, London and Liverpool, 1979 (Liège, 1981), pp. 221–253.

Honey 1946
W. B. Honey, *Glass: A Handbook for the Study of Glass Vessels of All Periods and Countries & a Guide to the Museum Collection*, London: Victoria and Albert Museum, 1946.

Howard 2000
Deborah Howard, *Venice & the East*, New Haven and London: Yale University Press, 2000.

Hudig 1923
Ferrand W. Hudig, *Das Glas: Mit besonderer Berucksichtigung der Sammlung im Nederlandsch Museum voor Geschiedenis en Kunst im Amsterdam*, Amsterdam: the author, 1923.

Huygens 1986
R. B. C. Huygens, ed., *Guillaume de Tyr Chronique*, Turnholti, Belgium: Brepols, 1986.

Ireland 1962
Marion P. Ireland, *Christian Symbols and Embroideries for Protestant Churches*, Glendale, California: Ireland Needlecraft, 1962.

*Islam and the Medieval West* [1975]
*Islam and the Medieval West*, comp. and ed. Stanley Ferber, [Binghamton: State University of New York at Binghamton, Center for Medieval and Early Renaissance Studies, 1975].

Jacoby 1993
David Jacoby, "Raw Materials for the Glass Industries of Venice and the Terraferma, about 1370–about 1460," *JGS*, v. 35, 1993, pp. 65–90.

Jamnitzer 1610
Christoph Jamnitzer, *Neuw Grottesssken Buch, inventirt, gradirt und verlegt durch Christoff Jamnitzer*, Nuremberg, 1610.

Jardine 1996
Lisa Jardine, *Worldly Goods: A New History of the Renaissance*, London/Basingstoke: Macmillan, 1996.

Jonkanski 1993
Dirk Jonkanski, "Oberdeutsche Baumeister in Venedig. Reiserouten und Besichtigungsprogramme," in *Venedig und Oberdeutschland in der Renaissance. Beziehungen zwischen Kunst und Wirtschaft*, ed. Bernd Roeck, Klaus Bergdolt, and Andrew John Martin, Sigmaringen: Jan Thorbecke Verlag, 1993, pp. 31–39.

Keller 1999
Christine Keller, "Glas," *Jahresbericht Musée Suisse*, v. 108, 1999, pp. 33–35.

Kerssenbrock-Krosigk 1997
Dedo von Kerssenbrock-Krosigk, "Rubinglas des ausgehenden 17. und des 18. Jahrhunderts," Ph.D. diss., Humboldt-Universität zu Berlin, 1997.

Kerssenbrock-Krosigk 2001
Dedo von Kerssenbrock-Krosigk, *Rubinglas des ausgehenden 17. und des 18. Jahrhunderts*, Mainz: Verlag Philipp von Zabern, 2001.

Kjellberg 1953
Sven T. Kjellberg, "Europeiskt Glas," *Kulteren* (Lund), 1953, pp. 54–159.

Klannte 1938
Margarette von Klannte, "Das Glas des Isergebirges," *Deutsches Archiv für Landes- und Volksforschung*, v. 2, no. 3, 1938, pp. 575–599.

Klar 1961
Martin Klar, "Ein Trinkspiel Augusts des Starken," *Forschungen und Berichte der Staatlichen Museen zu Berlin*, vv. 3 and 4, 1961, pp. 52–59.

Klein 1982
P. W. Klein, "Nederlandse glasmakerijen in de zeventiende en achttiende eeuw," *Economisch- en Sociaal-Historisch Jaarboek*, The Hague: M. Nijhoff, 1982, pp. 31–43.

Klesse and Reineking 1973
Brigitte Klesse and Gisela Reineking-Von Bock, *Glas*, 2nd rev. ed., Cologne: Kunstgewerbemuseum der Stadt Köln, 1973.

Knittler 1994
Herbert Knittler, "Die 'Glashütten zu Reichenaw,'" in *Glas aus dem Böhmerwald*, Linz: Schlossmuseum, 1994, pp. 142–147.

Komrij 1986
Gerrit Komrij, *De Nederlandse poëzie van de 17$^{de}$ en 18$^{de}$ eeuw in 1000 en enige gedichten*, Amsterdam: Bert Bakker, 1986.

Kos 1994
Mateja Kos, "The Ljubljana (Laibach) Glassworks and Its Products in the 16th Century," *JGS*, v. 36, 1994, pp. 92–97.

Kos and Šmit 2003
Mateja Kos and Ziga Šmit, "Ljubljana Glassworks: Technological Analysis of Medieval Glass," *AnnAIHV*, v. 15, New York and Corning, 2001 (Nottingham, 2003), pp. 210–212.

Krimm 1984
Stefan Krimm, "Zur Geschichte der Waldglas Produktion in Spessart," in Klaus Grimm, *Glück und Glas*, Munich: Verlag Kunst & Antiquitäten, 1984, pp. 159–179.

Krueger 1998
Ingeborg Krueger, "An Enamelled Beaker from Stralsund: A Spectacular New Find," in *Gilded and Enamelled Glass from the Middle East*, ed. Rachel Ward, London: British Museum Press, 1998, pp. 107–109.

Krueger 2002
Ingeborg Krueger, "A Second Aldrevandin Beaker and an Update on a Group of Enameled Glasses," *JGS*, v. 44, 2002, pp. 111–132.

Kybalová 1997
Jana Kybalová, "The Decorative Arts," in *Rudolf II and Prague: The Court and the City*, ed. Eliška Fučíková and others, London: Thames and Hudson, 1997, pp. 376–386.

Laan 1991
P. H. J. van der Laan, "Concurrentie in de Middellandse Zee: Amsterdam verdringt de stad van San Marco als handelsmetropool," in *Amsterdam: Venetië van het Noorden*, ed. Margriet de Roever, 's-Gravenhage: Gary Schwartz, and Amsterdam: Gemeente-Archief, 1991, pp. 28–45.

Labalme and White 1999
Patricia H. Labalme and Laura Sanguineti White, with translations by Linda Carroll, "How to (and How Not to) Get Married in Sixteenth-Century Venice (Selections from the Diaries of Marin Sanudo)," *Renaissance Quarterly*, v. 52, 1999, pp. 43–72.

*Lagonico Collection* 1991
*La Collection Lagonico, importantes céramiques d'Iznik . . .* , sale catalog, Monaco: Sotheby's, December 7, 1991.

Lammertse 1998
Friso Lammertse, *Nederlandse Genreschilderijen uit de zeventiende*

*eeuw: Eigen collectie Museum Boijmans Van Beuningen*, Rotterdam: Nai Publishers, 1998.

Larruga y Boneta 1995

E. Larruga y Boneta, *Memorias políticas y económicas sobre los frutos, fábricas, comercio y minas de España*, v. 16, Zaragoza: Gobierno de Aragón, 1995.

Lassels 1670

Richard Lassels, *The Voyage of Italy*, Paris: V. de Moutier, 1670.

Lazarus 1969

Peter Lazarus, "The Story of English Drinking Glasses. Part I: The Baluster Period, 1685–1735," *Antique Dealer and Collectors' Guide*, v. 23, no. 7, February 1969, pp. 74–78.

Le Vaillant de la Fieffe 1971

O. Le Vaillant de la Fieffe, *Les Verreries de la Normandie, les gentils-hommes & artistes verriers normands*, repr., Brionne: Le Portulan, 1971.

*Lehman Collection* 1993

Dwight P. Lanmon, with contribution by David B. Whitehouse, *The Robert Lehman Collection*, v. 11, *Glass*, New York: The Metropolitan Museum of Art in association with Princeton University Press, 1993.

Levey 1983

Santina M. Levey, *Lace: A History*, London: Victoria and Albert Museum, and Leeds: W. S. Maney, 1983.

Levi 1895

Cesare A. Levi, *L'arte del vetro in Murano nel Rinascimento, e i Berroviero*, Venice: C. Ferrari, 1895.

Lewin 1920

L. Lewin, *Die Gifte in der Weltgeschichte*, Berlin: Verlag Julius Springer, 1920.

Liefkes 1997

Reino Liefkes, ed., *Glass*, London: V&A Publications, 1997.

Loga 1907

Valerian von Loga, "Antonis Mor als Hofmaler Karls V und Philipps II," *Jahrbuch der kunsthistorischen Sammlungen des allerhöchsten Kaiserhauses*, v. 27, no. 3, 1907, pp. 91–123.

Lunsingh Scheurleer, Fock, and van Dissel 1989, 1992

T. Lunsingh Scheurleer, C. Willemijn Fock, and A. J. van Dissel, *Het Rapenburg. Geschiedenis van een Leidse gracht*, Leiden: Afdeling Geschiedenis van de Kunstnijverheid, Rijksuniversiteit Leiden, vv. IVb (1989) and VIa (1992). (Published in 6 vv., 1986–1992.)

*Macaya Collection* 1935

J. Gudiol Ricart and P. M. de Artiñano, *Vidrio: Resumen de la historia del vidrio. Catálogo de la collección Alfonso Macaya*, Barcelona: [Tipografía Casulleras], 1935.

Maggi 1977

Giovanni Maggi, *Bichierografia*, Florence: Studio per Edizione Scelte, 1977.

Mallé 1971

L. Mallé, *Museo Civico di Turino: Vetri-vetrate-giade, cristalli di rocca e pietre dure*, Turin: Museo Civico, 1971.

*Mantova e i Gonzaga di Nevers* 1999

*Mantova e i Gonzaga di Nevers = Mantoue et les Gonzague de Nevers*, Mantova: Amici di Palazzo Tè e dei Musei Mantovani, 1999.

Martens and Peeters 2001

Maximiliaan P. J. Martens and Natasja Peeters, "Antwerp Painting before Iconoclasm: Considerations on the Quantification of Taste," paper presented at XXXIII Settimana di Studi, Istituto Internazionale di Storia Economica, Prato, Italy, April–May 2001.

Martin 1993

Andrew J. Martin, "Motive für den Venedigaufenthalt oberdeutscher Maler. Von Albrecht Dürer bis Johann Carl Loth," in *Venedig und Oberdeutschland in der Renaissance. Beziehungen zwischen Kunst und Wirtschaft*, ed. Bernd Roeck, Klaus Bergdolt, and Andrew John Martin, Sigmaringen: Jan Thorbecke Verlag, 1993, pp. 22–30.

McCray 1999

W. Patrick McCray, *Glassmaking in Renaissance Venice: The Fragile Craft*, Aldershot, England: Ashgate Publishing Ltd., 1999.

Medici 1621

Giuliano de' Medici di Castellina, letter to Curzio di Lorenzo da Picchena, Florence, March 15, 1621. Archivio di Stato di Firenze, Mediceo del Principato 4949, fol. 810 (available at http://www.The Medici_Archive_Project_News_and_Notes.htm).

Mees 1997

D. C. Mees, *Kunstnijverheid, 1600–1800, en Tegels/Applied Arts, 1600–1800, and Tiles*, Rotterdam: Museum Boijmans Van Beuningen, and Amsterdam: Uitgeverij de Bataafsche Leeuw, 1997.

Mendera 2002

Marja Mendera, "Glass Production in Tuscany, 13th–16th Century: The Archaeological Evidence," in *Majolica and Glass from Italy to Antwerp and Beyond: The Transfer of Technology in the 16th–Early 17th Century*, ed. Johan Veeckman, Antwerp: City of Antwerp, 2002, pp. 263–295.

Menzhausen 1968

Joachim Menzhausen, *Das Grüne Gewölbe*, Berlin: Rembrandt, 1968.

Merrett 1662

*The Art of Glass* [by Antonio Neri] . . . *Translated into English, with Some Observations . . . by Christopher Merrett*, London: printed by A. W. for Octavian Pulleyn, 1662.

Mestre Robert 1996

Mestre Robert, *Libre de coch*, ed. Verónica Leingruber, Barcelona: Curial, 1996.

Meyer zu Capellen 2001

Jürg Meyer zu Capellen, *Raphael: A Critical Catalog of His Paintings*, v. 1, *The Beginnings in Umbria and Florence, ca. 1500–1508*, Landshut, Germany: Arcos, 2001.

Michaelis 1955

Ronald F. Michaelis, *Antique Pewter of the British Isles*, London: G. Bell & Sons, 1955.

Milanesi 1864

Gaetano Milanesi, ed., *Dell'arte del vetro per musaico: Tre trattatelli dei secoli XIV e XV*, Bologna: Press Gaetano Romagnoli, 1864.

*Mille anni di arte del vetro a Venezia* 1982

Rosa Barovier Mentasti and others, *Mille anni di arte del vetro a Venezia*, Venice: Albrizzi Editore, 1982.

Mir 1890

J. Mir, *Recuento de los bienes y alhajas de la iglesia de Lluch e inventario de los mismos*, Bolletí de la Societat Arqueològica Luliana, v. 6, Palma de Mallorca, 1890, pp. 214–215.

Molina 1902

Tirso de Molina, *El bandolero*, Barcelona: Doménech Editor, 1902.

Montaigne 1991

Michel de Montaigne, *The Complete Essays*, ed. Michael A. Screech, London: Penguin, 1991.

Muensterberger 1994

Werner Muensterberger, *Collecting: An Unruly Passion. Psychological Perspectives*, Princeton, New Jersey: Princeton University Press, 1994.

Müller 1901

Johannes Müller, "Augsburg's Warenhandel mit Venedig und Augsburger Handelspolitik im Zeitalter des dreissigjahrigen Krieges," *Archiv für Kulturgeschichte*, Cologne: Böhlau Verlag, 1901, pp. 326–337.

*Museo Poldi Pezzoli* 1983

*Museo Poldi Pezzoli: Ceramiche, vetri, mobili e arredi*, Milan: Electa Editrice, 1983.

Nachlässe 1956
Fünf westdeutsche Nachlässe und anderer deutscher und ausländischer Kunstbesitz: Gemälde des 15. bis 20. Jahrhunderts, Porzellan, Glas, Kunstgewerbe, Skulpturen, Netsuke, Möbel, Wirkteppiche, Orientteppiche, sale catalog, Cologne: Kunsthaus Math. Lempertz, November 14–17, 1956.

Neri 1612
Antonio Neri, L'arte vetraria, Florence: Giunta, 1612.

Nesbitt 1878
Alexander Nesbitt, A Descriptive Catalogue of the Glass Vessels in the South Kensington Museum. With an Introductory Notice, London: the museum, 1878.

Netzer 2000
Susanne Netzer, "Die Glassammlung des Berliner Kunstgewerbemuseums und ihre Kriegsverluste," JGS, v. 42, 2000, pp. 145–162.

Nieto Alcaide 1967
Víctor Nieto Alcaide, "'El tratado de la fábrica de vidrio' de Juan Danís y 'El modo de hacer vidrieras' de Francisco Herranz," Archivo Español de Arte, no. 159, Madrid, 1967, pp. 273–303.

Old English Glass 1947
Catalogue of the Celebrated Collection of Old English Glass and Oriental Rugs . . . First Portion, sale catalog, London: Sotheby's, February 25, 1947, lot 100.

Palumbo-Fossati 1984
Isabella Palumbo-Fossati, "L'interno della casa dell'artigiano e dell'artista nella Venezia del Cinquecento," Studi Veneziani, n.s., v. 8, 1984, pp. 109–153.

Paradin 1583
Claude Paradin, Symbola heroica, Antwerp: C. Plantini, 1583.

Pause 1996
Carl Pause, Spätmittelalterliche Glasfunde aus Venedig. Ein archäologischer Beitrag zur deutsch-venezianischen Handelsgeschichte, Bonn: Verlag Dr. Rudolf Habelt GmbH, 1996.

Pelliot 1930
Marianne Pelliot, "Verres gravés au diamant," Gazette des Beaux-Arts, ser. 6, v. 3, May 1930, pp. 302–327.

Penna 1998
Maria Penna, "Paris/Province: Etudes récentes," Bulletin de l'Association Française pour l'Archéologie de Verre, 1997–98, 1998, pp. 11–20.

Pérez Bueno 1942
Luis Pérez Bueno, Vidrios y vidrieras, Barcelona: A. Martín, 1942.

Perrault 1992
Gilles Perrault, La Dorure et polychromie sur bois, Dijon: Editions Faton, 1992.

Perrot 1958
Paul Perrot, Three Great Centuries of Venetian Glass, Corning, New York: The Corning Museum of Glass, 1958.

Phönix aus Sand und Asche 1988
Erwin Baumgartner and Ingeborg Krueger, Phönix aus Sand und Asche. Glas des Mittelalters, Munich: Klinkhardt & Biermann, 1988.

Pincus 1976
Debra Pincus, The Arco Foscari: The Building of a Triumphal Gateway in 15th-Century Venice, New York and London: Garland, 1976.

Platt 1979
Hugh Platt, The Jewell House of Art and Nature, 1594, Amsterdam: Theatrum Orbis Terrarum, 1979.

Pontanus 1614
Johannes Isacius Pontanus, Historische beschrijvinghe der seer wijt beroemde coop-stadt Amsterdam, Amsterdam: Iudocus Hondius, 1614.

Porreño 1639
B. de Porreño, Dichos y hechos del Señor Rey Don Felipe Segundo el Prudente, Potentíssimo y Glorioso Monarca de las Españas y de las Indias, Seville, 1639.

Potthof and Kossenhaschen 1933
O. D. Potthof and Georg Kossenhaschen, Kulturgeschichte der Deutschen Gaststätte, Berlin: Dr. Wilhelm Glass GmbH, 1933.

Powell 1923
Harry Powell, Glassmaking in England, Cambridge: Cambridge University Press, 1923.

Prawer 1973
Joshua Prawer, "Venezia e colonie veneziane nel regno di Gerusalemme," in Venezia e il Levante fino as secolo XV, 2 vv., ed. Agostino Pertusi, Florence: L. S. Olschki, 1973, pp. 625–656.

Primisser 1972
Alois Primisser, Die Kaiserlich-Königliche Ambraser Sammlung, Graz: Akademische Druck- und Verlagsanstalt, 1972.

Princely Magnificence 1980
Princely Magnificence: Court Jewels of the Renaissance, 1500–1630, London: Debrett's Peerage Ltd. and the Victoria and Albert Museum, 1980.

Pyhrr and Godoy 1999
Stuart W. Pyhrr and José-A. Godoy, Heroic Armor of the Italian Renaissance: Filippo Negroli and His Contemporaries, New York: The Metropolitan Museum of Art, 1999.

Rankins 1586
William Rankins, The English Ape, the Italian Imitation, the Footesteppes of Fraunce, London: imprinted by Robert Robinson, 1586.

Rigaux 1990
Dominique Rigaux, "La Cène aux écrevisses: Table et spiritualité dans les Alpes Italiennes au Quattrocento," in La Sociabilité à table, ed. M. Aurell, O. Dumoulin, and F. Thelamon, Rouen: Publications de l'Université de Rouen, no. 178, 1990, pp. 217–228.

Ritman Collection 1995
The Joseph R. Ritman Collection of 16th and 17th Century Dutch Glass, sale catalog, London: Sotheby's, November 14, 1995.

Ritsema van Eck 1995
Pieter C. Ritsema van Eck, Glass in the Rijksmuseum, v. 2, Zwolle: Waanders Uitgevers, 1995.

Ritsema van Eck and Zijlstra-Zweens 1993
Pieter C. Ritsema van Eck and Henrica M. Zijlstra-Zweens, Glass in the Rijksmuseum, v. 1, Zwolle: Waanders Uitgevers, 1993.

Robin 1985
Françoise Robin, La Cour d'Anjou Provence: La Vie artistique sous le règne de René, Paris: Picard, 1985.

Rochebrune 2000
Marie-Laure de Rochebrune, "Ceramics and Glass in Chardin's Paintings," in Chardin, London: Royal Academy of Arts, and New York: The Metropolitan Museum of Art, 2000, pp. 36–53.

Rochebrune 2002a
Marie-Laure de Rochebrune, "L'Art du verre au temps de Louis XIII," in Un temps d'exubérance: Les Arts décoratifs sous Louis XIII et Anne d'Autriche, ed. Daniel Alcouffe and others, Paris: Réunion des Musées Nationaux, 2002, pp. 368–383.

Rochebrune 2002b
Marie-Laure de Rochebrune, "La Céramique et le verre dans la peinture française au temps de Louis XIII," Dossier de l'Art (Dijon), no. 86, May 2002, pp. 30–41.

Rodriguez García 1986
Justina Rodriguez García, "El vidrio veneciano de los siglos XV al XVII y su influencia en Cataluña," Ph.D. diss., Universidad Nacional de Educación a Distancia, Madrid, 1986.

Rodriguez García 1989
Justina Rodriguez García, "Piezas de vidrio suntuario catalán en la 'Bichierografia' de Giovanni Maggi (1604)," D'Art, no. 15, 1989, pp. 181–191.

**Rodriguez García 1990**

Justina Rodriguez García, "Domenico Barovier, vetraio veneziano in Spagna (1600–1608)," *Rivista della Stazione Sperimentale del Vetro*, no. 2, 1990, pp. 129–136.

**Roever 1991**

Margriet de Roever, "Venetiaans glas uit Amsterdam: Introduktie van een luxe-industrie naar Italiaans model," in *Amsterdam: Venetië van het Noorden*, ed. Margriet de Roever, 's-Gravenhage: Gary Schwartz, and Amsterdam: Gemeente-Archief, 1991, pp. 156–173.

**Rose 1989**

Peter G. Rose, trans. and ed., *The Sensible Cook: Dutch Foodways in the Old and the New World*, Syracuse, New York: Syracuse University Press, 1989.

**Rosenberg 1928**

Marc Rosenberg, *Der Goldschmiede Merkzeichen*, 3rd ed., v. 4, *Ausland und Byzanz*, Frankfurt am Main: Frankfurter Verlags-Anstalt A.G., 1928.

*Rosenheim Collection 1923*

*Catalogue of the Works of Art . . . Collected by the Late Max Rosenheim . . . Maurice Rosenheim*, sale catalog, London: Sotheby & Co., May 10, 1923.

**Rose-Villequey 1971**

Germaine Rose-Villequey, *Verre et verriers de Lorraine au début des temps modernes*, Paris: Presses Universitaires de France, 1971.

*Rothschild Collection 2000*

*The Collection of the Late Baroness Batsheva de Rothschild*, sale catalog, London: Christie's, December 14, 2000.

**Roumegoux 1991**

Yves Roumegoux, "L'Etablissement des gentilshommes verriers italiens à Nevers à la fin du XVIᵉ siècle," in *Ateliers de verriers de l'antiquité à la période pré-industrielle*, Rouen: Association Française pour l'Archéologie du Verre, 1991, pp. 135–138.

**Rousseau 1990**

Claudia Rousseau, "The Pageant of the Muses at the Medici Wedding of 1539 and the Decoration of the Salone dei Cinquecento," in *Theatrical Spectacle and Spectacular Theater. Papers in Art History from the Pennsylvania State University*, v. 6, pt. 2, 1990, pp. 416–457.

*Roux Collection 1868*

*Catalogue des objets d'art et de haute curiosité, tableaux & pastels. Composant la précieuse collection M. Roux . . .*, sale catalog, Hôtel Drouot, February 17–20, 1868, Paris: Pillet, 1868.

**Royen 1991**

P. C. van Royen, "Naar wijder horizon: Scheepvaartbetrekkingen tussen de Lage Landen en Italië," in *Amsterdam: Venetië van het Noorden*, ed. Margriet de Roever, 's-Gravenhage: Gary Schwartz, and Amsterdam: Gemeente-Archief, 1991, pp. 104–119.

**Rückert 1982**

Rainer Rückert, *Die Glassammlung des Bayerischen Nationalmuseums München*, v. 1, Munich: Hirmer, 1982.

*Rudolf II and Prague 1997*

*Rudolf II and Prague: The Court and the City*, ed. Eliška Fučiková and others, London: Thames and Hudson, 1997.

*Sammlung . . . Lanna 1911*

*Sammlung des Freiherrn Adalbert von Lanna, Prag*, sale catalog, Berlin: Rudolph Lepke, March 21–28, 1911.

**Sánchez Cantón 1934**

F. J. Sánchez Cantón, "El primer inventario de El Pardo (1564)," *Archivo Español de arte y arqueología*, v. 10, Madrid, 1934.

**Sánchez Moreno 1997**

María José Sánchez Moreno, "La fabricación de vidrio en El Recuenco: Una indústria olvidada," *Cuadernos de etnología de Guadalajara*, no. 29, 1997, pp. 205–270.

**Sanchis Guarner 1952**

M. Sanchis Guarner, *El arte del vidro en Mallorca*, Palma de Mallorca: Panorama Balear, 1952.

**Sauzay 1882**

Alexandre Sauzay, *Notice de la verrerie et des vitraux*, Paris: C. de Mourgues Frères, 1882.

**Sauzay and Sauvageot 1861**

Alexandre Sauzay and Charles Sauvageot, *Catalogue du Musée Sauvageot*, [Paris]: Charles De Mourgues Frères, 1861.

**Scailliérez 2003**

Cécile Scailliérez, "Le 'Mensonger et l'impudique.' A propos d'un singulier portrait d'Henri IV peint dans l'entourage de Toussaint Dubreuil," *Revue du Louvre*, no. 1, 2003, pp. 37–47.

**Schadee 1989**

Nora I. Schadee, *Met rad en diamant. Gegraveerde glazen uit Rotterdamse collecties*, Rotterdam: Historisch Museum der Stad Rotterdam, 1989.

**Schama 1988**

Simon Schama, *The Embarrassment of Riches: An Interpretation of Dutch Culture in the Golden Age*, Berkeley and Los Angeles: University of California Press, 1988.

**Schlosser 1951**

Ignaz Schlosser, *Venezianische Gläser*, Vienna: Österreichische Museum für Angewandte Kunst, 1951.

**Schmidt 1912**

Robert Schmidt, *Das Glas*, Berlin and Leipzig: G. Reimer, 1912.

**Schmidt 1922**

Robert Schmidt, *Das Glas*, rev. ed., Berlin: Walter de Gruyter, 1922.

**Schmidt-Arcangeli 1997**

Catarina Schmidt-Arcangeli, "'Un tiempo aperto': Die Bellini in ihrer Bedeutung für den Fassadenentwurf der Scuola Grande di San Marco," in *Colloquia Augustana*, v. 5, *Kunst und ihre Auftraggeber im 16. Jahrhundert Venedig und Augsburg im Vergleich*, ed. Klaus Bergdoldt and Jochen Brüning, Berlin: Akademie, 1997, pp. 43–82.

**Schönherr 1900**

David von Schönherr, "Die Glashütte in Hall, 1533–1604," in *David von Schönherr's Gesammelte Schriften*, v. 1, Innsbruck: Wagner, 1900, pp. 406–422.

**Schotel 1903**

G. D. J. Schotel, *Het Oud-Hollandsch Huisgezin der Zeventiende Eeuw*, Arnhem: A. J. G. Strengholt's Uitgeversmaatschappij N.V. en Gijsbers & Van Loon, 1903.

**Schuermans 1885**

Henri Schuermans, "Lettre sur la verrerie à la façon de Venise," *Bulletin Monumental*, 1885, pp. 191–206.

*Selection IV 1974*

Hedy Backlin-Landman, with contribution by Sidney Goldstein, *Selection IV: Glass from the Museum's Collection*, Providence: Rhode Island School of Design, 1974.

**Shepherd unpub.**

John Shepherd, "The Vessel and Waste Glass, Old Broad Street," Museum of London Specialist Services Report, unpublished.

**Simons 1997**

Madelon Simons, "King Ferdinand I of Bohemia, Archduke Ferdinand II, and the Prague Court, 1527–1567," in *Rudolf II and Prague: The Court and the City*, ed. Eliška Fučiková and others, London: Thames and Hudson, 1997, pp. 80–89.

**Simonsfeld 1887**

Henry Simonsfeld, *Der Fondaco dei Tedeschi in Venedig und die deutsch-venezianischen Handelbeziehungen*, 2 vv., Stuttgart: Verlag der J. G. Gotaa'schen Buchhandlung, 1887.

*Slade Collection 1871*

Alexander Nesbitt, *Catalogue of the Collection of Glass Formed by*

*Felix Slade, Esq., F.S.A., with Notes on the History of Glassmaking,*
London: Leo Wertheimer & Co., 1871.

Smit 1984

F. G. A. M. Smit, *A Concise Catalogue of European Line-Engraved Glassware, 1570–1900,* Peterborough, England: the author, 1994.

Spallanzani 1978

Marco Spallanzani, *Le ceramiche orientali a Firenze nel Rinascimento,* Florence: Cassa di Risparmio, 1978.

*Spechtergläser* 1986

*Spechtergläser: Ausstellung im Glasmuseum Wertheim 1986,* Wertheim, the museum, 1986.

*Spitzer Collection* 1891

Frederic Spitzer, *La Collection Spitzer: Antiquité, Moyen-Age, Renaissance,* v. 3, Paris: Maison Quantin, 1891.

Šroněk 1997

Michal Šroněk, "Sculpture and Painting in Prague, 1550–1650," in *Rudolf II and Prague: The Court and the City,* ed. Eliška Fučíková and others, London: Thames and Hudson, 1997, pp. 353–375.

Starkey 1992

David Starkey, "England," in *The Renaissance in National Context,* ed. Roy Porter and Mikulas Teich, Cambridge: Cambridge University Press, 1992, pp. 146–163.

Stefaniak 1991

Regina Stefaniak, "Raphael's Santa Cecilia: A Fine and Private Vision of Virginity," *Art History,* v. 14, no. 3, 1991, pp. 345–371.

Stieda 1913

Wilhelm Stieda, "Die Glashütte Tambach," *Mitteilungen der Vereinigung für Gothaische Geschichte und Altertumsforschung,* 1915 1916, pp. 1–46.

Strasser 1979

Rudolf von Strasser, *Masterpieces of Germanic Glass, 15th–19th Centuries,* Neenah, Wisconsin: Municipal Museum Foundation, 1979.

Strasser and Spiegl 1989

Rudolf von Strasser and Walter Spiegl, *Dekoriertes Glas, Renaissance bis Biedermeier,* Munich: Klinkhardt & Biermann, 1989.

*Strasser Collection* 2002

Rudolf von Strasser and Sabine Baumgärtner, *Licht und Farbe. Dekoriertes Glas: Renaissance, Barock, Biedermeier die Sammlung Rudolf von Strasser,* Vienna: Kunsthistorisches Museum, and Milan: Skira, 2002.

Stromer 1978

Wolfgang von Stromer, "Bernardus Teotonicus und die Geschäftsbeziehungen zwischen den deutschen Ostalpen und Venedig vor Gründung des Fondaco dei Tedeschi," in *Grazer Forschungen zur Wirtschafts- und Sozialgeschichte,* v. 3, *Beiträge zur Handels- und Verkehrsgeschichte,* Graz: Selbstverlag der Lehrkanzel für Wirtschaftsund Sozialgeschichte, 1978, pp. 1–17.

Sutton 1986

Peter C. Sutton, *A Guide to Dutch Art in America,* Washington, D.C.: Netherlands-American Amity Trust, and Grand Rapids, Michigan: Eerdmans, 1986.

Syson and Thornton 2001

Luke Syson and Dora Thornton, *Objects of Virtue: Art in Renaissance Italy,* Los Angeles: J. Paul Getty Museum, 2001.

Tacke 1992

Andreas Tacke, *Der katholische Cranach,* Mainz: P. von Zabern, 1992.

Tait 1967

Hugh Tait, "Glass with Chequered Spiral-Trail Decoration: A Group Made in the Southern Netherlands in the 16th and 17th Centuries," *JGS,* v. 9, 1967, pp. 94–112.

Tait 1979

Hugh Tait, *The Golden Age of Venetian Glass,* London: British Museum Publications, 1979.

Tait 1991

Hugh Tait, ed., *Five Thousand Years of Glass,* London: British Museum Press, 1991.

Tarcsay 1998

Kinga Tarcsay, "Eine Glashütte des 17. Jahrhunderts in Reichenau im Freiwald," *Archaeologie Österreichs,* v. 9, no. 1, 1998, pp. 31–33.

Tarcsay 1999

Kinga Tarcsay, *Mittelalterliche und neuzeitliche Glasfunde aus Wien. Altfunde aus den Beständen des Historischen Museums der Stadt Wien. Beiträge zur Mittelalterarchäologie in Österreich,* v. 3, Vienna: Österreichische Gesellschaft für Mittelalterarchäologie, 1999.

Tarcsay 2001

Kinga Tarcsay, "Produktionsabfall und Halbprodukte aus Glas. Archäologische Erkenntnisse zur Glasherstellung in Ostösterreich," *Medium Aevum Quotidianum,* v. 43, 2001, pp. 125–139.

Tarcsay 2003

Kinga Tarcsay, "Die Topographia Windhagiana und die frühneuzeitliche Glasproduktion in der Herrschaft Reichenau," in *Glashütten im Gespräch. Berichte und Materialien vom 2. Internationalen Symposium zur archäologischen Erforschung mittelalterlicher und frühneuzeitlicher Glashütten Europas,* ed. Peter Steppuhn, Lübeck: Verlag Schmidt-Römhild, 2003, pp. 70–77.

Taylor 1974

Steven Taylor, "An Excavation on the Site of the Augustinian Priory, Canons Ashby, Northants," *Northamptonshire Archaeology,* v. 9, 1974, pp. 57–65.

Terlinden and Crossley 1981

A. M. Terlinden and D. W. Crossley, "Post-Medieval Glass-Making in Brabant: The Excavation of a Seventeenth-Century Furnace at Savenel, Nethen," *PMA,* v. 15, 1981, pp. 177–206.

Theuerkauff-Liederwald 1992

Anna-Elisabeth Theuerkauff-Liederwald, "Ein Stilleben mit Gläsern: Träumender Silen von Peter Paul Rubens," *Kunst und Antiquitäten,* no. 10, 1992, pp. 22–27.

Theuerkauff-Liederwald 1994

Anna-Elisabeth Theuerkauff-Liederwald, *Venezianisches Glas der Kunstsammlungen der Veste Coburg. Die Sammlung Herzog Alfreds von Sachsen-Coburg und Gotha (1844–1900). Venedig, à la façon de Venise, Spanien, Mitteleuropa,* Lingen: Luca Verlag, 1994.

Thorpe 1929

William A. Thorpe, *A History of English and Irish Glass,* 2 vv., London: Medici Society, 1929.

Thorpe 1935

William A. Thorpe, "A Historic Verzelini Glass," *Burlington Magazine,* v. 67, no. 391, October 1935, pp. 150–157.

Thorpe 1961

William A. Thorpe, *English Glass,* 3rd ed., London: Adam & Black, 1961.

Thüry 1991

Günther E. Thüry, "Austern im Salzburg des 16. Jahrhunderts," *Jahresschrift,* vv. 35/36, 1989/1990, Salzburg: Salzburger Museum Carolino Augusteum, 1991, pp. 136–142.

*Treasures from The Corning Museum of Glass* 1992

D. Whitehouse and others, *Treasures from The Corning Museum of Glass,* Tokyo: Nihon Keizai Shimbun Inc., 1992.

Treu 1981

Ursula Treu, trans. and ed., *Physiologus, Naturkunde in frühchristlicher Deutung,* Hanau: W. Dausien, 1981.

Tsuchiya 2002
Yoshio Tsuchiya, *Yōroppa amerika no antīku garasu: Shiru, kau, kataru, kanshōsuru*, Tokyo: Heibonsha, 2002.

Van Dongen 1995
Alexandra van Dongen, "The Curiosity of the World," in *One Man's Trash Is Another Man's Treasure: De metamorfose van het Europese gebruiksvoorwerp in de Nieuwe Wereld/The Metamorphosis of the European Utensil in the New World*, Rotterdam: Museum Boijmans Van Beuningen, 1995, pp. 11–25.

Vasari 1568
Giorgio Vasari, *Le vite de' piv eccellenti pittori, scultori, e architettori aretino . . .* , Florence: Appresso i Giunti, 1568.

Veblen 1994
Thorstein Veblen, *The Theory of the Leisure Class*, repr. of 1899 ed., Mineola, New York: [Dover Publications], 1994.

Velde 2000
Bruce Velde, "Les Verres façon de Venise à tiges ailées et en formes de serpents: Essai d'identification," *Bulletin de l'Association Française pour l'Archéologie du Verre*, 2000, pp. 16–17.

Venetiaans & façon de Venise glas 1991
*Venetiaans & façon de Venise glas, 1500–1700*, ed. Frides Laméris and Kitty Laméris, Lochem, the Netherlands: Uitgeversmij Antiek, 1991.

Venetian Glass 1996
*Venetian Glass = Mizu no miyako no honoo no kisekei*, Hakone, Japan: Hakone Garasu no Mori, Ukai Bijutsukan, 1996.

Vince and Bell 1992
Alan Vince and Robert Bell, "Sixteenth-Century Pottery from Acton Court, Avon," in *Everyday and Exotic Pottery from Europe. Studies in Honour of John G. Hurst*, ed. David Gaimster and Mark Redknap, Oxford: Oxbow Books, 1992, pp. 101–112.

Visscher 1614
Roemer Visscher, *Sinnepoppen*, Amsterdam: Willem Iansz, 1614.

Vreeken 1998
Hubert Vreeken, *Glas in het Amsterdam Historisch Museum en Musem Willet-Holthuysen*, Zwolle: Waanders Uitgevers, 1998.

Weiss 1974
Gustav Weiss, *Ullstein Gläserbuch–Eine Kultur- und Technikgeschichte des Glases*, Frankfurt am Main, Berlin, and Vienna: Ullstein Verlag, 1974.

Whitehouse 1972
David Whitehouse, "Chinese Porcelain in Medieval Europe," *Medieval Archaeology*, v. 16, 1972, pp. 63–78.

Whitehouse 1993
David Whitehouse, comp., *Glass: A Pocket Dictionary of Terms Commonly Used to Describe Glass and Glassmaking*, Corning, New York: The Corning Museum of Glass, 1993.

Wilkinson 1968
O. N. Wilkinson, *Old Glass*, London and Toronto: Benn, 1968.

Willmott 2000a
Hugh Willmott, "The Classification and Mould Grouping of Lion Mask Stems from London," *AnnAIHV*, v. 14, Venice and Milan, 1998 (Lochem, the Netherlands, 2000), pp. 389–395.

Willmott 2000b
Hugh Willmott, "Recent Research on the Gracechurch Street Hoard," *Glass Circle News*, no. 83, 2000, p. 6.

Willmott 2001
Hugh Willmott, "A Group of 17th-Century Glass Goblets with Restored Stems: Towards an Archaeology of Repair," *PMA*, v. 35, 2001, pp. 96–105.

Willmott 2002
Hugh Willmott, *Early Post-Medieval Vessel Glass in England, c. 1500–1670*, CBA Research Report 132, York, England: Council for British Archaeology, 2002.

Wilson 1999
Timothy Wilson, "Italian Maiolica around 1500: Some Considerations on the Background to Antwerp Maiolica," in *Maiolica in the North: The Archaeology of Tin-Glazed Earthenware in North-West Europe, c. 1500–1600*, ed. David Gaimster, British Museum Occasional Papers, no. 122, London: the museum, 1999, pp. 5–21.

Winkler 1985
Gerhard Winkler, *Humpen, Krüge, Gläser: Das schöne Biergefäss im Laufe der Jahrhunderte*, Vienna: Niederösterreichisches Landesmuseum, 1985.

Wintersteiger 1991
Robert Wintersteiger, "Die Gläser," *Jahresschrift*, vv. 35/36, 1989/1990, Salzburg: Salzburger Museum Carolino Augusteum, 1991, pp. 376–398.

Wolters 1983
Wolfgang Wolters, *Der Bilderschmuck des Dogenpalastes. Untersuchungen zur Selbstdarstellung der Republik Venedig im 16. Jahrhundert*, Wiesbaden: Steiner, 1983.

Ydema 1991
Onno Ydema, *Carpets and Their Datings in Netherlandish Paintings, 1540–1700*, Zutphen: Walburg Pers, 1991.

Zecchin 1965
Luigi Zecchin, "Sull'origine dell'arte vetraria in Altare," *Vetro e Silicati*, v. 9, no. 2 (no. 50), March–April 1965, pp. 19–22.

Zecchin 1987
Luigi Zecchin, *Vetro e vetrai di Murano: Studi sulla storia del vetro*, 3 vv., Venice: Arsenale Editrice, 1987.

Zedinek 1927
Hans Zedinek, "Wiener Glashütten des 15. und 16. Jahrhundert," *Altes Kunsthandwerk*, v. 1, no. 6, 1927, pp. 236–256.

Zedinek 1928
Hans Zedinek, "Die Glashütte zu Hall, Tirol," *Altes Kunsthandwerk*, v. 1, pt. 3, 1928, pp. 98–117.

Zeiller 1648
Martin Zeiller, *Topographia Franconiae*, Frankfurt: M. Merian, 1648.

Zeiller 1649
Martin Zeiller, *Topographia provinciarum Austriacarum, Austriae, Styriae, Carinthiae, Carniolae, Tirolis, etc.*, Frankfurt a. M.: Matthäus Merian, 1649, facsimile, Kassel: Bärenreiter-Verlag, 1963.

Zesen 1664
Filips Von Zesen, *Beschreibung der Stadt*, Amsterdam: J. Noschen, 1664.

Zijlstra-Zweens 1993
Henrica M. Zijlstra-Zweens, "Venetian Glass and Façon de Venise," in Pieter C. Ritsema van Eck and Henrica M. Zijlstra-Zweens, *Glass in the Rijksmuseum*, v. 1, Zwolle: Waanders Uitgevers, 1993, pp. 12–16.

3000 Jahre Glaskunst 1981
M. Kunz and others, *3000 Jahre Glaskunst: Von der Antike bis zum Jugendstil*, Lucerne: Kunstmuseum, 1981.

# Concordance

This concordance of glass objects that are shown, either as figures or as object entries, is arranged alphabetically by institution/collector and accession number, followed by the number of the page on which the illustration appears and the number of the figure or object entry. The numbers of object entries appear in boldface.

Afdeling Monumentenzorg en Archeologie, Alkmaar, the Netherlands
86DST: p. 275, fig. 4

Bayerisches Nationalmuseum, Munich, Germany
60/67: p. 152, fig. 9
62/55: p. 58, fig. 28
G 93: pp. 44–45, fig. 13
G 94: pp. 44–45, fig. 13
G 656: p. 46, fig. 14
GL 516: p. 47, fig. 16
GL 517: pp. 36–37, fig. 7
GL 551: p. 35, fig. 6

Birmingham Museum and Art Gallery, Birmingham, England
1979M5: pp. 304–305, **5**

The British Museum, London, England
1855, 12-1, 151: p. 49, fig. 18
1895, 6-3, 17: p. 283, fig. 13
1958, 5-3, 1: p. 301, **2**
AF3133: p. 277, fig. 7
S.390: pp. 252–253, **1**
S.491: p. 11, fig. 5
S.642: p. 300, **1**
S.671: p. 274, fig. 3
S.824: p. 153, fig. 10

The Corning Museum of Glass, Corning, New York
50.2.1: pp. 302–303, **3**
50.3.1: pp. 66–67, **2**
50.3.35: p. 102, fig. 19
51.3.118: p. v, fig. 3
51.3.218: p. 246, fig. 17
51.3.279: p. 110, fig. 28
51.3.280: p. 263, **5b**
53.3.41: p. 139, **13**
54.3.143: p. 138, **12**
55.3.54: p. 249, fig. 20
56.3.93: p. 260, **4**
56.3.193: pp. 70–71, **4**
58.3.174: p. 163, fig. 24
58.3.175: p. 247, fig. 18
58.3.180: p. iv, fig. 2
58.3.184: p. 233, fig. 6
58.3.200: p. 232, fig. 5
59.3.4: p. 140, **15**
59.3.50: p. 137, **11**

60.3.16: p. 163, fig. 24
60.3.29: p. 109, fig. 26
60.3.86: p. 120, **3**
62.3.47: p. 186, **12**
63.2.8: pp. 306–307, **6**
63.3.37: p. 87, fig. 2
64.3.6: p. 274, fig. 2
65.3.112: p. 168, **2**
66.3.58: p. 95, fig. 9
68.3.1: p. 92, fig. 4
68.3.21: pp. 74–75, **6**
68.3.51: p. 231, fig. 4
70.3.5: p. 238, fig. 9
70.3.8: p. 287, fig. 16
72.3.35: pp. 68–69, **3**
72.3.52: p. 172, **5**
73.2.25: p. 237, fig. 8
73.3.449: p. 57, fig. 27
77.3.34: pp. 180–184, **10**
79.3.187: p. 228, fig. 1
79.3.239: p. 265, **7**
79.3.252: p. 244, fig. 14
79.3.280: pp. 126–127, **7**
79.3.283: pp. 130–131, **9**
79.3.301: pp. 266–267, **8**
79.3.304: pp. 82–83, **11**
79.3.306: p. 239, fig. 10
79.3.323: p. 50, fig. 19
79.3.329: p. 79, **9**
79.3.360: pp. 261–263, **5**
79.3.439: p. 234, fig. 7
79.3.441: p. 187, **13**
79.3.444: p. 245, fig. 15
79.3.481: p. 103, fig. 22
79.3.489: p. 95, fig. 8
79.3.550: p. 163, fig. 24
79.3.600: p. 110, fig. 27
79.3.880: p. 141, **16**
79.3.1031: p. 101, fig. 18
79.3.1125: p. 108, fig. 25
81.3.43: pp. 254–256, **2**
83.3.51: p. vi, fig. 4
84.3.24: pp. ii–iii, fig. 1
97.3.30: pp. 178–179, **9**
98.3.60: p. 276, fig. 6
99.3.2: pp. 190–191, **15**
2000.3.12: p. 229, fig. 2
2001.3.56: p. 7, fig. 2
2003.3.70: pp. 128–129, **8**

The Fine Arts Museums of San Francisco, M. H. De Young Memorial Museum, San Francisco, California
1988.15.58: p. 285, fig. 15

Fitzwilliam Museum, University of Cambridge, Cambridge, England
C.4.1967: p. 280, fig. 10

Fugger Museum, Babenhausen, Germany
283-1961: pp. 80–81, **10**
291-1961: pp. 80–81, **10**

Harold Henkes, Rotterdam, the Netherlands
H 915: p. 297, fig. 33

The J. Paul Getty Museum, Los Angeles, California
84.DK.515.1-.2: p. 38, fig. 9
84.DK.519: p. 155, fig. 14
84.DK.537: p. 9, fig. 3
84.DK.545: p. 39, fig. 10
84.DK.548.1-.2: p. 34, fig. 5
84.DK.653: p. 51, fig. 20

Keith King, Paris, France
K27a: p. 185, **11**

Kunsthistorisches Museum, Vienna, Austria
KK 2788: pp. 77–78, **8**
KK 2798: p. 54, fig. 24
KK 2801: p. 54, fig. 24
KK 2852: p. 56, fig. 25
KK 2877: p. 55, fig. 24
KK 2883: p. 56, fig. 26
KK 2898: p. 56, fig. 26
KK 2905: p. 56, fig. 26
KK 2912: p. 56, fig. 26
KK 2925: p. 56, fig. 26
KK 3012: p. 52, fig. 22
KK 3015: p. 53, fig. 23
KK 3040: p. 76, **7**
KK 3295: p. 48, fig. 17
KK 3302: p. 23, fig. 2
KK 3367: p. 27, fig. 3
KK 3386: pp. 72–73, **5**

Kunstsammlungen der Veste Coburg, Coburg, Germany
HA 290: p. 277, fig. 8

The Metropolitan Museum of Art, New York, New York
1975.1.1194: pp. 144–145, fig. 4

Musée des Arts Décoratifs, Bordeaux, France
78.3.6: p. 159, fig. 19
7560: p. 158, fig. 18

Musée des Arts Décoratifs, Paris, France
2000.1.1: p. 158, fig. 17

Musée du Louvre, Paris, France
5487-17: p. 159, fig. 20
MR 2404: pp. 174–176, **7**
MRR 128: p. 157, fig. 16
OA 457-1412: pp. 176–177, **8**
OA 3111: p. 150, fig. 7
OA 11191: pp. 169–170, **3**

Musée National de la Renaissance, Ecouen, France
Ec. 282: p. 173, **6**
E.Cl. 1567: pp. 144–145, fig. 3
E.Cl. 8626: pp. 188–189, **14**

# Contributors

IGNASI DOMÉNECH is associate director of the Department of Decorative Arts at Castellana Subhastes Barcelona (259, Diputació, 08007 Barcelona, Spain). He was formerly director of the Glass Art School and head of the Department of Conservation and Restoration at the Fundació Centre del Vidre de Barcelona. Mr. Doménech received his master's degree in museology from the Universitat Autònoma Barcelona. He is the author of *Museu Cau Ferrat: La col·lecció de vidre* (with Teresa Carreras, Sitges: Consorci del Patrimoni de Sitges, 2003), *El vidrio: Tecnicas de trabajo de horno* (with P. Beceridge and E. Pascual, Barcelona: Parramón Ediciones, 2003), and "El vidrio" (in *Las artes decorativas en España*, Madrid: Espasa Calpe, 1999). He is also a former director of I Jornades Hispàniques d'Història del Vidre Barcelona. E-mail address: idomenech@hispavista.com.

ALEXANDRA GABA-VAN DONGEN is curator of collections in the Preindustrial Applied Arts Section at the Museum Boijmans Van Beuningen (Museumpark 18–20, 3015 CX Rotterdam, the Netherlands). She received her master of arts degree in art history and archeology from Leyden University. Her publications include three catalogs published by the Museum Boijmans Van Beuningen: *One Man's Trash Is Another Man's Treasure: The Metamorphosis of the European Utensil in the New World* (1995), *Utility Glass in Image and Imagination* (1994), and *Preindustrial Utensils, 1150–1800* (1991). She is a board member of the Foundation of the Dutch Utensil and the Coordination and Advice Committee of Archeological Research (Rotterdam), and a specialist adviser to the section on conservation and restoration of glass and ceramics of the Institute Collections Netherlands (Amsterdam). E-mail address: dongen@boijmans.rotterdam.nl.

REINO LIEFKES is senior curator in the Department of Sculpture, Metalwork, Ceramics, and Glass at the Victoria and Albert Museum (South Kensington, London SW7 2RL, England). From 1990 to 1992, he was curator of glass and silver at the Haags Gemeentemuseum in The Hague. Mr. Liefkes, who received his master's degree in art history from Leyden University, is the author of *Copier, Glasontwerper/Glaskunstenaar* (2nd rev. ed., Zwolle: Waanders, 2002) and the editor of *Glass* (London: V&A Publications, 1997). He is editor of the Dutch quarterly magazine *Vormen uit Vuur*, an editorial adviser to the *Journal of Glass Studies*, a member of the board of directors of The Association for the History of Glass Ltd., and a member of the Collections Committee of The Jewish Museum (London). He formerly served as president of the ICOM International Glass Committee and as treasurer of the International Association for the History of Glass. E-mail address: ceramicsandglass@vam.ac.uk.

JUTTA-ANNETTE PAGE is curator of glass and decorative arts at The Toledo Museum of Art (P.O. Box 1013, Toledo, Ohio 43697-1013) and former curator of European glass at The Corning Museum of Glass in Corning, New York. She received an M.A. in jewelry design from the Rhode Island School of Design and an M.A. in art and architectural history from Brown University. She concluded her academic training at Brown University with a Ph.D. in classical archeology, focusing on ancient gold jewelry and metalsmithing technology. Dr. Page has written several exhibition catalogs and articles, including a report on the purported 16th-century manuscript known as the Catalogue Colinet. She is also an adjunct faculty member of The Bard Graduate Center for Studies in the Decorative Arts, Design, and Culture in New York. E-mail address: jpage@toledomuseum.org.

MARIE-LAURE DE ROCHEBRUNE is curator in the Département des Objets d'Art at the Musée du Louvre (101, rue de Rivoli, 75001 Paris, France). She received her diploma from the Ecole du Patrimoine and graduated from the Sorbonne, where she studied medieval history. Her recent publications include "L'Art du verre au temps de Louis XIII" (in *Un temps d'exubérance: Les Arts décoratifs sous Louis XIII et Anne d'Autriche*, Paris: Réunion des Musées Nationaux, 2002), "La Céramique et le verre dans la peinture française au temps de Louis XIII" (in Dijon's *Dossier de l'Art*, May 2002), and "Ceramics and Glass in Chardin's Paintings" (in *Chardin*, London: Royal Academy of Arts, and New York: The Metropolitan Museum of Art, 2000). E-mail address: rochebrune@louvre.fr.

HUGH WILLMOTT is material culture consultant in the Department of Archaeology at the University of Sheffield (Northgate House, West Street, Sheffield S1 4ET, England). He received his doctor's, master's, and bachelor's degrees in archeology from the University of Durham, where he formerly served as a research associate. Dr. Willmott is the author of *A History of English Glassmaking* (Stroud: Tempus Publishing, in press) and *Early Post-Medieval Vessel Glass in England, c. 1500–1670* (York: Council for British Archaeology Research Report 132, 2002). He is a council member of The Society of Post-Medieval Archaeology; a committee member of the Finds Research Group, 700–1700 A.D.; and a member of the Institute of Field Archaeologists. E-mail address: h.willmott@sheffield.ac.uk.

# Acknowledgments

*The authors wish to thank the following individuals:*

IGNASI DOMÉNECH: Teresa Bastardes, curator, Museu de les Arts Decoratives de Barcelona; Jordi Carreras, Department of Decorative Arts, Castellana Subhastes, Barcelona; Elisenda Casanova, document technician, Consorci del Patrimoni de Sitges (Barcelona); Anna Llanes, curator, Consorci del Patrimoni de Sitges (Barcelona); Marta Montmany, director, Museu de les Arts Decoratives de Barcelona; Jutta-Annette Page, curator of glass and decorative arts, The Toledo Museum of Art.

ALEXANDRA GABA-VAN DONGEN: Harold E. Henkes, Voorst; Jutta-Annette Page, curator of glass and decorative arts, The Toledo Museum of Art; Margriet de Roever, Gemeentearchief, Amsterdam.

REINO LIEFKES: Jan Baart, Archeological Research Division, Amsterdam; Helen Clifford, independent scholar, Witney (Oxford); Janette Lefrancq, curator, Musées Royaux d'Art et d'Histoire, Brussels; Margriet de Roever, Gemeentearchief, Amsterdam; Johan Veeckman, Stad Antwerpen Afdeling Archeologie, Antwerp; Timothy Wilson, keeper of Western art, Ashmolean Museum, Oxford.

JUTTA-ANNETTE PAGE: the co-authors of this volume; Jane Arthur, head of curatorial services, Birmingham Museum and Art Gallery; Gary Baker, curator of glass and decorative arts, The Chrysler Museum of Art, Norfolk; Gail P. Bardhan, Robert H. Brill, Mary B. Chervenak, Andrew M. Fortune, William Gudenrath, Stephen P. Koob, Richard W. Price, Jacolyn S. Saunders, Jill Thomas-Clark, Nicholas L. Williams, and Violet J. Wilson, all of The Corning Museum of Glass; Jordi Carreras, Department of Decorative Arts, Castellana Subhastes, Barcelona; Günther Dankl, curator, Tiroler Landesmuseum Ferdinandeum, Innsbruck; Aileen Dawson, curator, Department of Medieval and Modern Europe, and Dora Thornton, curator of the Renaissance collections, The British Museum, London; Rudolf Distelberger, director emeritus, Kunstkammer, Kunsthistorisches Museum, Vienna; Christopher T. G. Fish, collector, Guernsey;

Markus Graf Fugger-Babenhausen, director, Fugger Museum, Babenhausen; Annemarie Jordan Gschwend, independent scholar, Zurich; Catherine Hess, associate curator of sculpture and decorative arts, The J. Paul Getty Museum, Los Angeles; Keith and Sylvie King, collectors, Paris; Michael Koch, curator, Bayerisches Nationalmuseum, Munich; Michael Kovacek, dealer, Vienna; Martha McCrory, professor, Fashion Institute of Technology, New York; Bet McLeod, assistant curator of decorative arts, Museum of Fine Arts, Boston; Brian Musselwhite, curator of decorative arts, Royal Ontario Museum, Toronto; Stuart Pyhrr, curator, Department of Arms and Armor, Lisa Pilosi, conservator, and Mark Wypyski, associate research scientist, all of the Sherman Fairchild Center for Objects Conservation, The Metropolitan Museum of Art, New York; Rainer Richter, conservator, Museum Grünes Gewölbe, Dresden; Helmut Ricke, director, Kunstmuseum Düsseldorf; Pieter Ritsema van Eck, curator emeritus, Rijksmuseum, Amsterdam; Clementine Schack von Wittenau, curator, Kunstsammlungen der Veste Coburg; Rudolf von Strasser, collector, Vienna; Aidan Weston-Lewis, senior curator, Italian and Spanish art, National Gallery of Scotland, Edinburgh; Barbara Wirth, collector, Paris; Rainer Zietz and Christopher Sheppard, dealers, London.

MARIE-LAURE DE ROCHEBRUNE: Fabienne Audebrand, researcher of historic monuments, Direction Générale des Affaires Culturelles, Orléans; Michèle Bimbenet-Privat, chief curator, Archives Nationales, Paris; Thierry Crépin-Leblond, director, Château de Blois; Alain Erlande-Brandenbourg, director, Musée National de la Renaissance, Ecouen; Mr. and Mrs. Keith King, collectors, Paris; Jean-Luc Olivié, curator, Centre du Verre, Musée des Arts Décoratifs, Paris; Barbara Wirth, collector, Paris.

HUGH WILLMOTT: Paul Courtney, independent scholar, Leicester; Hazel Forsyth, curator of early modern collections, Museum of London; Jutta-Annette Page, curator of glass and decorative arts, The Toledo Museum of Art; Jennifer Price, Department of Archaeology, University of Durham; John Shepherd, archive manager, London Archaeological Archive and Research Centre.

# Picture Credits

The Corning Museum of Glass and the authors thank the following for their kind permission to reproduce photographs: Peter Bitter of Afdeling Monumentenzorg en Archeologie, Alkmaar; Alex Barrett of akg-images; Ryan Jensen and Kristen Murray of Art Resource; Julie Clements of the Ashmolean Museum; Dr. Nina Gockerell of the Bayerisches Nationalmuseum; Iain Hamilton of the Birmingham Museums and Art Gallery; Maggie Taylor of The British Library; Sovati Smith and Tracy Ryan of The British Museum; David Corson of the Carl A. Kroch Library, Cornell University; Ignasi Doménech; Mary Haas of The Fine Arts Museums of San Francisco; Diane Hudson of the Fitzwilliam Museum; Iver Vermazen of the Gemeentearchief, Amsterdam; Jacklyn Burns of The J. Paul Getty Museum; Susan Stekel Rippley of the James Ford Bell Library, University of Minnesota; Keith King; Dr. Ilse Jung, Franz Kirchweger, Benedikt Haupt, and Christine Surtmann of the Kunsthistorisches Museum; Clementine Schack von Wittenau of the Kunstsammlungen der Veste Coburg; Deanna Cross of The Metropolitan Museum of Art; Emmanuel Magne of the Musée Crozatier, Le Puy-en-Velay; Valérie de Raignac and Bernedette de Boysson of the Musée des Arts Décoratifs, Bordeaux; Rachael Brishoual and Jean-Luc Olivié of the Musée des Arts Décoratifs, Paris; Marie-Laure de Rochebrune of the Musée du Louvre; Odile Le Conte of the Musée National de la Renaissance, Ecouen; Christine Speroni of the Musées de Strasbourg; Museo Nacional del Prado; Alexandra Gaba-Van Dongen of the Museum Boijmans Van Beuningen; Lucinda Pringle of the Museum of London; Deborah Hunter of the National Gallery of Scotland; Elizabeth Höier of the Nationalmuseum, Stockholm; Tom Lisanti of The New York Public Library; Conna Clark of the Philadelphia Museum of Art; Catherine Bossis of the Réunion des Musées Nationaux; Florence Aalbers of the Rijksmuseum; Nicola Woods of the Royal Ontario Museum; Yvonne Brandt and Rainer Richter of the Staatliche Kunstsammlungen, Dresden; Eva Marie Gertung of the Statens Museum for Kunst, Copenhagen; Eleonore Gürther and Dr. Günther Bankl of the Tiroler Landesmuseum Ferdinandeum; Nicole M. Rivette of The Toledo Museum of Art; Martin Durrant and Mary Webb of the Victoria and Albert Museum; Paul Frattaroli and Carmen Colomer of the Wallace Collection; Hugh Willmott; Barbara Wirth; and Eric M. Wunsch.

Numbers refer to pages, except where specified. All photographs are by The Corning Museum of Glass, with the exception of the following:

Afdeling Monumentenzorg en Archeologie, Alkmaar, the Netherlands: 275 (fig. 4).
Photo: akg-images: 154.

Reproduced by permission of and © copyright in this photograph reserved to the Ashmolean Museum, Oxford, England: 279.
Bayerisches Nationalmuseum, Munich, Germany: 20, 35, 36, 37 (fig. 7), 44, 45, 46 (fig. 14), 47, 58, 152.
Birmingham Museums and Art Gallery, Birmingham, England: 305.
By permission of The British Library, London, England: 296.
© The British Museum, London, England: 11, 49, 153 (fig. 10), 252, 253, 274 (fig. 3), 277 (fig. 7), 283, 300, 301.
Courtesy of the Division of Rare and Manuscript Collections, Cornell University Library, Cornell University, Ithaca, New York: 6.
The Fine Arts Museums of San Francisco, San Francisco, California, The Franz W. and Sylvia Sichel Collection: 285.
Reproduction by permission of the Syndics of the Fitzwilliam Museum, Cambridge, Cambridge, England: 280.
Fugger Museum, Babenhausen, Germany: photo by Studio Siggi Müller, 62, 80–81.
Gemeentearchief, Amsterdam, the Netherlands: 243.
Harold Henkes, Rotterdam, the Netherlands: photo by Tom Haartsen, 297.
The J. Paul Getty Museum, Los Angeles, California: 9, 34, 38, 39, 51 (fig. 20), 155, 216.
Courtesy of the James Ford Bell Library, University of Minnesota, Minneapolis, Minnesota: endpapers.
Drawing by Kim Kelley Wagner: 134–135.
Keith King, Paris, France: © Ph. Sebert, 185.
Kunsthistorisches Museum, Vienna, Austria: 22, 23, 27, 48, 52, 53, 54, 55, 56, 72, 76, 77, 256.
Kunstsammlungen der Veste Coburg, Coburg, Germany: 277 (fig. 8).
© Documentation Histoire du Louvre, Paris, France: photo by Pierre Philibert, 159 (fig. 20).
Photograph © 1995 The Metropolitan Museum of Art, New York, New York: photo by Sheldan Collins, 145 (fig. 4 and detail).
Musée Crozatier, Ville du Puy-en-Velay: 146.
Musée de l'Oeuvre Notre Dame de Strasbourg, Strasbourg, France: photo by A. Plisson, 160 (fig. 22).
Musée des Arts Décoratifs, Bordeaux, France: © photo DMB-photo by Lysiana Gauthier, 158 (fig. 18), 159 (fig. 19).
Musée des Arts Décoratifs, Paris, France: photo by Laurent-Sully Jaulmes, 158 (fig. 17).
Rights reserved © Museo Nacional del Prado, Madrid, Spain: 84, 94.
Museu de les Arts Decoratives de Barcelona, Spain: photo by Jordi Carreras with the assistance of Ignasi Doménech, 91,

# Index

HYPERBOREVS

SCRICFIN:

DEVCALIDO-NIVS OCEANVS

LAPPIA

FINMAR

SVECIA

GOTIA

SVEVICVM MARE

EVROPAE

FARRE insule

SCETLANT Insule

ORCADES Insule

HEBRIDES Insule

Brasil

Demar

OCEANVS GERMANICVS

DENE MARCK

RVGEN

FRISIA

WESTGERM

BELGIC

FRANCIA

NORMANDIE

BRETAIGNE

AQVITANICVS OCEANVS

CANTABRICVS OCEANVS

OCEANVS BRITANNICVS

SCOTIA

ANGLIA

IRLAN

BISCAIA

GALICIA

HISPANIA

NAVARRA

ARAGON

PROVENCE

DAVLPHINE

BOVRGOI

AVSTRIA

HVNGRIA

SLAVO

ISTRIA

MARE ADRIATICVM

SARDINIA

CORSICA

SICILIA

MARE

OCEANVS